The Religion of White Rage

To Dr. Charles H. Long (1926–2020)

Dr. Charles H. Long influenced how we think of and study religion more than any scholar other than those who trained us. His intellectual reach cannot be measured nor overestimated, and his imprint on this book can be clearly seen throughout its pages. We dedicate this book to his memory.

The Religion of White Rage

White Workers, Religious Fervor, and the
Myth of Black Racial Progress

Edited by
STEPHEN C. FINLEY
BIKO MANDELA GRAY
LORI LATRICE MARTIN

EDINBURGH
University Press

Edinburgh University Press is one of the leading university presses in the UK. We publish academic books and journals in our selected subject areas across the humanities and social sciences, combining cutting-edge scholarship with high editorial and production values to produce academic works of lasting importance. For more information visit our website: edinburghuniversitypress.com

© editorial matter and organization Stephen C. Finley, Biko Mandela Gray, and Lori Latrice Martin, 2020, 2022
© the chapters their several authors, 2020, 2022

First published in hardback by Edinburgh University Press 2020

Edinburgh University Press Ltd
The Tun—Holyrood Road, 12(2f) Jackson's Entry, Edinburgh EH8 8PJ

Typeset in 10/13 Giovanni by
IDSUK (DataConnection) Ltd

A CIP record for this book is available from the British Library

ISBN 978 1 4744 7370 5 (hardback)
ISBN 978 1 4744 7371 2 (paperback)
ISBN 978 1 4744 7372 9 (webready PDF)
ISBN 978 1 4744 7373 6 (epub)

The right of Stephen C. Finley, Biko Mandela Gray, and Lori Latrice Martin to be identified as the editors of this work has been asserted in accordance with the Copyright, Designs and Patents Act 1988, and the Copyright and Related Rights Regulations 2003 (SI No. 2498).

CONTENTS

Notes on the Editors and Contributors / vii
Acknowledgments / xi

INTRODUCTION / "The Souls of White Folk": Race, Affect, and Religion in the Religion of White Rage / 1
Biko Mandela Gray, Stephen C. Finley, and Lori Latrice Martin

PART ONE / White Religious Fervor, Civil Religion, and Contemporary American Politics

ONE / "Make America Great Again": Racial Pathology, White Consolidation, and Melancholia in Trump's America / 29
Stephen C. Finley

TWO / You Will Not Replace Us! An Exploration of Religio-Racial Identity in White Nationalism / 43
Darrius Hills

THREE / "I AM that I AM": The Religion of White Rage, Great Migration Detroit, and the Ford Motor Company / 58
Terri Laws and Kimberly R. Enard

FOUR / American (Un)Civil Religion, the Defense of the White Worker, and Responses to NFL Protests / 73
Lori Latrice Martin

FIVE / The Color of Belief: Black Social Christianity, White Evangelicalism, and Redbaiting the Religious Culture of the CIO in the Postwar South / 85
Elizabeth Fones-Wolf and Ken Fones-Wolf

SIX / Constitutional Whiteness: Class, Narcissism, and the
Source of White Rage / 108
Jason O. Jeffries

PART TWO / White Religious Fervor, Religious Ideology, and White Identity

SEVEN / KKK Christology: A Brief on White Class Insecurity / 125
Paul Easterling

EIGHT / Black People and White Mormon Rage: Examining Race,
Religion, and Politics in Zion / 135
Darron T. Smith, Brenda G. Harris, and Melissa Flores

NINE / Anatomizing White Rage: "Race is My Religion!" and
"White Genocide" / 149
Kate E. Temoney

TEN / Exorcising Blackness: Calling the Cops as an Affective
Performance of Gender / 166
Biko Mandela Gray

ELEVEN / White Power Barbie and Other Figures of
the Angry White Woman / 179
Danae M. Faulk

TWELVE / Weaponizing Religion: A Document Analysis of the Religious
Indoctrination of Slaves in Service of White Labor Elites / 192
E. Anthony Muhammad

THIRTEEN / The Religions of Black Resistance and White Rage:
Interpenetrative Religious Practice in the 1963 Civil Rights Struggle in
Danville, Virginia / 213
Tobin Miller Shearer

CONCLUSION / Race, Religion, and Labor Studies: The Way Forward / 227
Lori L. Martin, Stephen C. Finley, and Biko Mandela Gray

Notes / 241
Bibliography / 286
Index / 314

NOTES ON THE EDITORS AND CONTRIBUTORS

Editors

Stephen C. Finley, PhD is Associate Professor of Religious Studies and African & African American Studies and Director of the African & African American Studies Program at Louisiana State University. His primary areas of scholarship are African American religious cultures, theory and method in the study of religion, and the history of religions as informed by social theory, philosophy of race, and psychoanalysis. He is coeditor of *Esotericism in African American Religious Experience: "There Is a Mystery"...* (Brill) and author of the monograph *In and Out of This World: Material and Extraterrestrial Bodies in the Nation of Islam* (Duke University Press). His articles appear in *Black Theology: An International Journal*, the *Journal of the American Academy of Religion*, the *Western Journal of Black Studies*, the *Journal of Africana Religions*, the *International Journal of Africana Studies*, the *Journal of Academic Freedom*, and other scholarly journals and venues.

Biko Mandela Gray, PhD is Assistant Professor of Religion at Syracuse University. Working at the intersection between philosophy of religion and African American religion, his research interests are around the relationship between subjectivity, race, and religion—especially as it relates to how this relationship plays itself out in social justice movements and larger political arenas. He is working on his first monograph, tentatively called *Black Life Matter*, wherein he turns to those lost to state-sanctioned violence in order to theorize blackness and religion as critical sites for subject formation.

Lori Latrice Martin, PhD is Professor in the Department of Sociology and African and African American Studies at Louisiana State University (LSU). Dr. Martin is also LSU Faculty Athletics Representative. Her research areas are race and ethnicity, racial wealth inequality and black asset poverty, and race and sports. Dr. Martin is the author of numerous scholarly works. Her publications include *South Baton Rouge* (Arcadia Publishing), *Black Asset Poverty and the Enduring Racial Divide* (First Forum Press), *Color Struck* (Senses/Brill), *Big Box Schools: Race, Education, and the Danger of the Wal-Martization of American Public Schools* (Lexington Books), and *Introduction to Africana Studies: Lessons from W.E.B. Du Bois, E. Franklin Frazier, and the Atlanta School of Sociology* (Brill).

Contributors

Paul Easterling, PhD is a graduate of the Religious Studies Department of Rice University. He has been an Adjunct Professor of African American Studies at the University of Houston and is currently an Adjunct Professor of History and Government at Bowie State University. Currently, Dr. Easterling works as an independent scholar contributing to academic think-tanks and research databases centered on African American religious life and culture. Dr. Easterling's research interests include African American religious culture, the history of African American religion, twentieth-century African American Islam, and African American religion and popular culture.

Kimberly R. Enard, PhD, MBA, MSHA, FACHE is an Assistant Professor of Health Management and Policy in the College for Public Health and Social Justice at Saint Louis University. Her professional background encompasses more than fifteen years of management and consulting experience with large integrated health systems in areas involving business development, service line management, program planning and evaluation, quality improvement, and community engagement. In partnership with health systems and communities, her work is dedicated to addressing health inequities by designing, implementing, and evaluating strategies to improve care coordination and quality of care for safety-net populations. Dr. Enard has authored several manuscripts about safety-net populations and presented her work at local, regional, and national meetings.

Danae Faulk is a doctoral student in the Department of Religion at Syracuse University. Faulk is studying religion and the body.

Melissa Flores is a doctoral candidate at University of Utah in the Department of Education, Culture, and Society. Her research interests include racial battle fatigue and critical race theory.

Elizabeth Fones-Wolf, PhD is Professor of History at West Virginia University, where she has been the recipient of numerous awards. Her books include *Selling Free Enterprise: The Business Assault on Labor and Liberalism, 1945–60* and *Waves of Opposition: Labor and the Struggle for Democratic Radio*.

Ken Fones-Wolf, PhD holds the Stuart and Joyce Robbins Chair in History at West Virginia University. He has authored or edited seven books on labor and Appalachian history. Together in 2015, he and Elizabeth Fones-Wolf published *Struggle for the Soul of the Postwar South: White Evangelical Protestants and Operation Dixie*.

Brenda Harris, PhD is an independent scholar. Dr. Harris examines transracial adoptions and religion, among other research areas. She explores the approaches, strategies, and tactics white adoptive parents use to racially socialize their adopted black children.

Darrius Hills, PhD is Assistant Professor in Philosophy and Religious Studies at Morgan State University. His research addresses various articulations of African American religious thought, theology, womanist religious thought, philosophy of religion, American religious culture(s), and masculinity studies. Specifically, Dr. Hills draws upon womanist religious thought and literary sources as a guiding frame of reference to unpack and reconsider notions of human relationality, community, and black male identity. Most recently, Dr. Hills coauthored, with Tommy Curry, an article published in the Black Lives Matter? issue of the *Journal of Africana Religions*, titled "Cries of the Unheard: State Violence, Black Bodies, and Martin Luther King's Black Power."

Jason O. Jeffries, PhD is Assistant Professor of Religious Studies at the University of Denver. His research interests include how religion and identity formation, embodiment and African American religion, the body as a source of religious experience, and African American religion and popular culture.

Terri Laws, PhD (Religion) is Assistant Professor of African and African American Studies and Health and Human Services at the University of Michigan-Dearborn, where she teaches courses in African American religious experience and medical ethics. Her publications have appeared in the *Journal of Religion and Health* and *Pastoral Psychology*.

Edward Anthony Muhammad, PhD is a recent graduate in Qualitative Research and Evaluation Methodology at the University of Georgia. His research focuses on qualitative methodologies and critical qualitative research. His current research interests include the phenomenology of the black lived experience, philosophical hermeneutics, and qualitative investigations of the Nation of Islam. E. Anthony holds a bachelor's and a master's degree in Psychology from Southern University and the University of Baltimore, respectively.

Tobin Miller Shearer, PhD is a history professor and African American Studies Director at the University of Montana. His books include *Daily Demonstrators: The Civil Rights Movement in Mennonite Homes and Sanctuaries* and *Two Weeks Every Summer: Fresh Air Children and the Problem of Race in America*.

Darron Smith, PhD is part of the faculty in the Department of Sociology at the University of Memphis. His research and writing focuses on injustices impacting African Americans and other marginalized groups. His work includes the study and impact of race on U.S. health care, the practice of white parents adopting black and biracial children, religion, sports, politics, and other pertinent subject matters of the present time. Smith's most known work is the 2004 book *Black and Mormon*, a book-length anthology exploring black Mormons and their place in the Church of Jesus Christ of Latter-Day Saints since the 1978 priesthood revelation that lifted the ban on blacks holding priesthood in the church. His most recent book, *When Race, Religion, and Sport Collide: Black Athletes at BYU and Beyond*, explores African American male student athletes through the medium of sport in the era of the Black Lives Matter movement.

Kate E. Temoney, PhD is Assistant Professor of Religion at Montclair State University. Dr. Temoney co-chairs the Religion, Holocaust, and Genocide Unit (American Academy of Religion) and authored "'Those Who Have the Sin... Go to this Side': Genocide, Religion, and Genocide and Religion," in *The Routledge History of Genocide*, and "Religion and Genocide Nexuses: Bosnia as Case Study," in the journal *Religions*.

ACKNOWLEDGEMENTS

It takes a lot of hard work, good fortune, and a great press to produce a work such as *The Religion of White Rage*. The editors wish to thank all the contributors, who wrote fantastic chapters for this book, which is sure to make an impact on contemporary intellectual thought in the areas of religious studies, labor studies, and political thought. Likewise, we want to thank the editors at Edinburgh University Press, especially Jenny Daly and Sarah Foyle, the Edinburgh University Press Academic Press Committee and Publishing Committee, and the peer reviewers for their time, labor, and insightful feedback.

Stephen would like to thank Biko Mandela Gray and Lori Latrice Martin for believing in this project and for all of their hard work that made it a reality. They both have been sources of inspiration, intellectual insight, and friendship. The excellent quality of this book is largely due to their considerable expertise. He would also like to thank the faculty of the African and African American Studies Program at Louisiana State University, his colleagues in Religious Studies, family, and students. The Department of Religion at Rice University deserves notice here, too, since Biko, Paul Easterling, Terri Laws, Darrius Hills, Jason Jeffries, and Stephen all earned their PhDs there.

Biko would like to thank Stephen and Lori for their trust in an early-career scholar, as well as their patience and intellectual generosity in exploring these ideas. Often, scholarship feels solipsistic, but Stephen and Lori have made producing this text an incredibly productive and joyous affair. He would also like to thank his teacher, Niki Clements, for continuing to encourage him to write rigorously and passionately. And lastly, he would like to acknowledge that, without the unwavering support and everlasting love of his partner, Andrea Sawyer-Gray, he would not be possible. I love you, Andrea. And I always will.

Lori would like to thank the following individuals and organizations for their support and encouragement throughout the development of *The Religion of White Rage*: the African and African American Studies Program at Louisiana State University, Lee and Edith Burns, Derrick Martin, Jr., Emir Sykes, John and Emily Thornton, Maretta McDonald, Dominique Dillard, Mahalia Howard, Ashley Maryland, Lynette Cotto, and Ewart Forde.

INTRODUCTION

"The Souls of White Folk": Race, Affect, and Religion in the Religion of White Rage

Biko Mandela Gray, Stephen C. Finley, and Lori Latrice Martin

> Racism is a faith. It is a form of idolatry. It is an abortive search for meaning.[1]
> –George D. Kelsey, *Racism and the Christian Understanding of Man*

> "But what on earth is whiteness that one should desire it?" Then always, somehow, some way, silently but clearly, I am given to understand that whiteness is the ownership of the earth forever and ever, Amen! . . . Wave on wave, each with increasing virulence, is dashing this new religion of whiteness on the shores of our time.[2]
> –W. E. B. Du Bois, *Darkwater: Voices from within the Veil*

A Courtroom, a Lynching

The room was packed, filled with suits and professional dresses, many adorned with American flag pins. Microphones were abundant, accompanied by news cameras, all of which were focused on the desk in the middle. And then he walked in, face already flushed with anger and frustration. And his words served to match the anger he'd cultivated over the past few weeks:

> Less than two weeks ago, Dr. Ford publicly accused me of committing wrongdoing at an event more than thirty-six years ago, when we were both in high school. I denied the allegation immediately, categorically, and unequivocally . . . This confirmation process has become a national disgrace . . . [the committee has replaced] advice and consent with search and destroy. Since my nomination in July, there has been a frenzy on the left to come up with something—*anything*—to block my confirmation.[3]

For just over forty-four minutes, Brett Kavanaugh laid out a case for himself—not simply for his nomination to the Supreme Court, but also for his *personal* character; his statement was an apologetic, a defense of his goodness, his *innocence*, in the face of accusations of sexual violence. Kavanaugh, in short, was *pissed*. He was maligned, he told the committee; and it was largely the Democrats' fault. Choked up, almost screaming at times, Kavanaugh vigorously and, some might claim, violently, defended himself. And, as we know now, it worked. A few days later, Kavanaugh was confirmed to the Supreme Court, kicking and screaming his way to the highest judicial appointment in the country.

This, of course, wasn't the first time a white man had manipulated political processes to gain power. From the Watergate scandal to Willie Horton ads, white men—the sharpest embodiment of the violence, and innocence, of whiteness—have pulled racialized strings of benefit and privilege in order to gain and maintain political office. In this regard, Kavanaugh's confirmation wasn't surprising.

But Kavanaugh's performance of rage was striking. His screaming, ranting, and raving had everything to do with the myth of the hardworking American male whose success is his own and no one else's—and as such, Kavanaugh laid out an affective case for himself as the victim. He was clear that it was he, *not* Dr. Ford, who was maligned; he, *Kavanaugh*, the man whose hard work had placed him just a short distance away from sitting in one of the highest seats of power in the United States: "Senator, I was at the top of my class academically, busted my butt in school. Captain of the varsity basketball team. Got into Yale College. When I got into Yale College, got into Yale Law School. Worked my tail off."[4]

Claims such as these—claims used multiple times during Kavanaugh's statement—do not simply serve to legitimate Kavanaugh as qualified for a SCOTUS seat; they also invoke a *myth*, a religious origin story, a narrative of symbols and tropes which are central to the sociocultural and sociopolitical formation and maintenance of the United States. This myth is the story of the bootstrapper, the one who works hard in order to achieve success. Woven into Kavanaugh's affective circulation of anger and (performative) despair was a religious conviction, a conviction steeped in what historian of religions Charles H. Long might call an "ultimate orientation" toward the primacy and normativity of individual grit-turned-success.[5]

We, of course, know that Kavanaugh's claim to hard work isn't quite as straightforward as it seems; he was a prep school graduate, and such high school training provided him with the networks and connections that made such an "elite" education possible. But such is the nature of myth; it need not be true—or false—to have a real impact, to ground one's sense of orientation toward the world. Whether it is the story of Adam and Eve in the second creation account in Genesis, or the story of a hardworking person who—all on their own—creates a successful life for themselves, myths offer ways of giving a person the possibility of situating themselves within a complex and constantly changing world. In short, *myths ground being.*

Kavanaugh, however, is not alone. It is difficult not to see a connection between Kavanaugh's affectively charged mythical invocations and the president who nominated him in the first place. As Kavanaugh used rage for political advancement, so did the president. In an article for *Snopes* online magazine, Dan MacGuill "fact-checked" whether or not then-candidate Donald Trump stoked violence at his rallies and in his speech. The article, still available on the magazine's website, features a cartoon in which a fiery and caricaturized Donald Trump is surrounded by speech bubbles featuring some of his most virulent and violent claims during his rallies.[6] The "fact-checking," of course, found it "true"; Donald Trump did, indeed, say these things at his rallies, using anger and rage to amplify his message and continue to garner support. And the crowds loved it. Raucous cheering can be heard within each video, as the crowd literally falls into a frenzied and frantic appreciation of their chosen leader.[7] These crowds—largely white, and largely figured as "working class"—were also stoking the myth of the hardworking bootstrapper. Having been failed by this myth, Trump's claims to violence, situated within false promises of better lives and an America made "great again" through virulently xenophobic and anti-black policies and practices, were nothing less than the stoking of pro-white rage.

In fact, Trump's continued assault against anything that *isn't* white—his perpetual lambasting of Colin Kaepernick is just one example—articulates and continues to fan the flames of white resentment, which easily collapses into what cannot be called anything else other than white *rage*. From the expression of enraged offense to the impassioned call to violence, both Kavanaugh and Trump operate as heuristic figures who reveal and channel the white rage that shows up as white violence.

Within Kavanaugh's defense and Trump's rhetoric, then, we are confronted—or forced to wrestle—with the intertwining of three apparently disparate realities: race, affect, and religion. Kavanaugh's racial identity doesn't rise to the fore for many people, but to ignore his racial identity is tantamount to ignoring the fact that his nomination would not have been possible outside of Donald Trump's election to the presidency—an election that had everything to do with white resentment framed in terms of middle- and working-class neglect. (As we show in the conclusion to this book, the myth has little to do with *class* and everything to do with neglected categories of race, affect, and religion in labor studies).

Resentment is key here; Kavanaugh's racial identity may not have been on display, but his anger was—and it was precisely this anger that motivated and inspired his Republican colleagues to push his nomination through. Kavanaugh performed his whiteness, not through displays of anti-black sentiment (though his treatment of Senators Cory Booker and Kamala Harris did raise eyebrows, as he called Booker by his first name and continually challenged Harris's credibility), but instead by expressing an explosive rage, and a vicious circular logic forms: Kavanaugh performs whiteness as anger, but he would not have been able to be so angry if he weren't white.

This dynamic isn't simply limited to white conservatives, however. Though Dr. Ford herself did not express rage, the political discourse, her advocates did. Kavanaugh directed his rage toward Ford and the DNC, but Ford's supporters and the Democratic Party writ large directed their rage *toward* Kavanaugh. Rage worked both ways in this hearing. The logic isn't simply cyclical or circular; it's insular. Only whiteness can be mad, which means that only whiteness gets to *legitimately* express anger.

When one thinks about the gendered nature of the Kavanaugh hearings, what one sees are two distinct manifestations of white rage—both of which center white normativity and black erasure. The first trajectory might be understood as the rage that supported and supports *critiques* and criticisms of claims of sexist discrimination and sexual violence; the second trajectory might be understood as that which supports the very white men who perpetuate such violence. On the one hand, the #MeToo movement—which, despite the fact that it was started by a black woman, has found its most vocal and visible expression through white women—articulates the righteous and justified rage against explicit structural and interpersonal forms of sexual violence; on the other hand, *the majority of white women voted for Donald Trump*, which, as Kavanaugh has pointed out in his testimony, apparently stems from the discrepancy between "working one's butt off" and reaping the benefits therein. Kavanaugh was enraged not simply because his character had been maligned; he was angry because those years at Yale and on the bench were not enough simply to push him through, because the myth of hard work paying off had not taken to his own life.

These two expressions—one in which white women push for issues of sexual justice, and the other in which white women push for reaping what they understand as their entitlements to the benefits of the United States—are indeed oppositional. But they nevertheless share one critical similarity: *neither of them are interested in the lives of non-white people*. Despite the fact that black women statistically suffer sexual violence at higher rates than their counterparts, and despite the fact that #MeToo was started by Tarauna Burke, an African American woman, who has been almost wholly erased in the "me too" narratives, the movement for sexual justice and against institutional and interpersonal forms of sexist violence has consistently *centered* white women at the expense of non-white women, particularly black women. In this regard, what reigns supreme is neither sexual violence, sexual justice, nor even the benefits of hard work; what reigns supreme is *whiteness*. It is whiteness that is centered in both affective trajectories, and it is whiteness—articulated in and through rage, belief, and "hard work," which is to say, the quintessential white American religious mythology— that maintains its centrality as the focal point of and for "social justice" reform as well as the resistance to such reforms.

Whiteness is not limited to white people, though they are its most palpable expression. In this regard, whiteness extends far beyond Kavanaugh's (and, for that matter, Ford's) physical characteristics. Whiteness names itself as that which is centered, magnified, and rendered normative through various forms of public discourse. As a matter of fact—and this is the argument of this book—whiteness is precisely *a racialized, social, affective, and religious norm that allows for manifold expressions of (out)rage at the perception that such a norm would be challenged or dislodged.*

"Perception" is key here; the *actual* displacement of white normativity is questionable at best and highly doubtful at worst, as virtually all of the public institutions remain oriented around epistemological, ontological, social, and religious efforts at maintaining whiteness's significance as a norm. To make this clear, we turn to another story, a bit older but no less palpable, that religion scholar Christopher Driscoll recounts in his text *White Lies*:

> On October 13, 1938, 19-year-old W. C. Williams hung from a tree near Ruston, Louisiana . . . Williams was sought for questioning about another murder, of a white man, and the beating of the white man's mistress. After hiding out for four days, Williams finally surrendered to a small, gun-toting, emotionally charged group of young white men. Soon a brief confrontation ensued between Lincoln Parish Sheriff Bryan Thigpin . . . and *the ever-growing mob of white captors* [emphasis added].[8]

This confrontation did not end well—or at least it didn't for Williams:

> With the mob threatening to shoot Williams on the spot, Thigpin *struck a deal* with the mob for them to "walk Williams through the woods to a side road, where they promised to meet the sheriff and surrender their prisoner." Soon after the mob left with their "prisoner," Thigpin heard shots. Knowing what had happened, *the capitulating sheriff drove back into town "believing there was nothing further [he] could do"* [emphasis added].[9]

Upon further and closer consideration and examination, it is clear that Thigpin's perceived helplessness at the moment when the shots rang out names whiteness as a point of ultimate orientation. It is only in the face of something ultimate—whether we choose to call that ultimate something "God" or not—that one can feel such helplessness. This helplessness becomes religious by way of it becoming *legitimate*; it becomes what Lewis Gordon might call the enactment of "taking oneself too seriously," which means that the norms of the world no longer show themselves as mutable but instead transcendent, metaphysical. Thigpin was helpless because he mistook the fabrication of whiteness as a metaphysical *fact*.

In this regard, Thigpin's helplessness is not simply religious; it is also theodicean. This lynching case exemplifies what Lewis Gordon, drawing from Sylvia Wynter, might call a "biodicy." As Gordon claims, "Among its many consequences, race is about in one sense who lives and who dies. In another sense, its normative significance leads to a rephrasing of who is *supposed* to live and who to die [original emphasis]."[10] Thigpin's perceived helplessness, then, has everything to do with his having internalized the ultimate significance of (his and the lynch mob's) whiteness; their rage was uncontested because it could *not be* contested, because the possibility of contesting such rage would call into question the very legitimacy of the white claims to injury and offense that had occasioned such rage—and therefore such violence—in the first place.

Gordon is not alone. In fact, as early as 1973, philosopher William R. Jones raised a pointed yet continually relevant question to black theologians: could God be a white racist?[11] Jones, like Gordon, wondered aloud about the relationship between race and theodicy; theodicy is not simply the questioning of the problem of evil, but the act of justifying it. It is precisely this justification that lends itself to various schemes of legitimation and substantiation that prevent the obvious enactment of various forms of moral evil.

Turning again to Gordon, "Human beings are not omniscient and therefore cannot possibly understand the full significance of what *appears* to be evil and unjust. That familiar response boils down to the old adage, 'G-d knows.'"[12] We can hear in Thigpin's "negotiations," as well as in his feeling of helplessness, this very adage. "G-d"—which, in this case, is the white mob—knew, which means that there was nothing to be done because nothing *could have been done*. The mob was already angry; Thigpin had no choice but to respect or even revere such rage. And this helplessness operated as a form of affective legitimation that mitigated any attempt to render culpable a group of angry white people in their explicit act of moral evil.

But the reverse could also be true. Is it possible that Thigpin's perceived helplessness was also because he, too, experienced rage? If, as Sara Ahmed writes, emotions serve to form the surfaces of subjects and objects, then it is possible that Thigpin's own engagement "gave him away" in similar ways to Kavanaugh and his Republican supporters.[13] In this regard, the feeling of helplessness was not constituted by the act of violence, but instead conditioned it, exposing Thigpin's "capitulation" as already present in an inchoate form at the very moment he "negotiated" with the lynch mob.

We must remind you, reader, that our attention to the specificity of particular cases should not be understood as merely a close reading of these case studies. We turn to these studies to show a connection between white rage and the maintenance of white supremacy. Thigpin and Kavanaugh are connected through their roles as affective conductors whose enactments served to both legitimate and be legitimated by the unshakeable norm of whiteness itself. Whiteness, then, exceeds the *white people* who embody it and perform it, as it invokes affective and religious sensibilities that produce a fidelity to mythical, political, and social frameworks that can *only* be made fully available to those who *are* white. The whiteness that Kavanaugh embodied and performed, and the whiteness that Thigpin embodied and enabled, was an affective and religious reality; in those hearings, and at that lynching, *the religion of white rage* expressed itself.

White Rage as a Religious Disposition

Exploring the various affective and religious vectors of whiteness in the United States, the authors in this volume—each in their own way and through various methodological, theoretical, and disciplinary approaches—raise considerable questions, concerns, and thoughts about the inextricable and normative relationship between whiteness, affect, and religion in the United States. Drawing from religious studies, philosophy, sociology, and other approaches, the authors in this text claim that *white rage is a religious disposition*, one organized around and toward the normativity of whiteness and the benefits such whiteness conveys. What the coeditors seek to do in this introduction, then, is lay out a conceptual mapping of the three constitutive terms—religion, whiteness, and rage—that form the theoretical nucleus out of which the following essays emerge. We begin with whiteness as religious, moving toward rage, and then articulating the relationship between the two and the *white worker* as the mythological site for the articulation of the religion of white rage.

As we noted above, Charles Long defined religion as "orientation in the ultimate sense, that is, how one comes to terms with the ultimate significance of one's place in the world." Religion is about orientation, but not simply any orientation; it is about how one comes to understand oneself and one's community in relation to the manifold and dynamic world within which one finds oneself. This notion of religion is useful, in large part because it allows one to understand the relations that constitute one's movement through the world, and more specifically, those social norms that hold one's *lebenswelt* together.

It is precisely normativity that invokes religion. To be "oriented in the ultimate sense" is to already have organized one's life around a norm or series of norms whose significance cannot be overstated. By suggesting that Thigpin's capitulation, as well as Kavanaugh's enraged performance, are enactments of the normativity of whiteness is to already suggest that both of them were oriented around the idea that whiteness could not be shaken. Kavanaugh's confirmation and Thigpin's failure both speak to a theodicean framework in which the veracity of whiteness was not, would not, and could not be contested. As many of the essays in this volume will articulate, the notion of ultimate orientation grounds the very possibility of white rage's presence and legitimation. Whiteness may not be a "G-d," but it sure acts like one.

Whiteness as the Religious and the Visible

Much has been written about whiteness. Indeed, the burgeoning and increasingly growing field of critical whiteness studies has become part of the larger field of critical race theory, with a host of books and articles devoted to the critical analysis—and possible dismantling—of whiteness as a pernicious (even if unspoken) norm of knowledge, culture, politics, and religion. Such analyses move beyond the (mere) articulation of white supremacist resentment. In other words, the violence of whiteness includes, but extends beyond, xenophobic or anti-black rhetoric or physical violence. Philosopher George Yancy offers one of the better definitions of whiteness. In *What White Looks Like: African American Philosophers on the Whiteness Question*, he defines whiteness as "*a synergistic system of transversal relationships of privileges, norms, rights, modes of self-perception and the perception of others, unquestioned presumptions, deceptions, beliefs, 'truths,' behaviors, advantages, modes of comportment, and sites of power and hegemony that benefit whites individually and institutionally.*"[14] In other words, whiteness is that which interfaces with the world. It structures relations and generates power. Which means that it is more than sentiment, more than a mere construct, which is too simplistic a frame to account for its impactful and near-totalizing social ontology. The best way to understand whiteness, its endurance, and its power is as *religious*.

Whiteness is a mythical posture that colonizes individual, institutional, discursive, and affective margins, bringing them under the power of its unacknowledged center.[15] It is this "unacknowledged center" that is one of the hallmarks of whiteness for Yancy.[16] But there is more, much more. Long, a historian of religions and the preeminent theorist of religion and race, contends that this mythic *center*, the posture out of which whiteness operates often invisibly, is the epistemological and religious center of white supremacy, what he calls "western ideology."[17] Drawing largely from Mircea Eliade's seminal text in the history of religions, *The Myth of the Eternal Return, or Cosmos and History*,[18] Long contends that cultures operated out of a center historically, and for our purposes, then, whiteness is an enactment of an archaic ontology in which "the center defines the locus of reality,"[19] which is only properly understood as religious. Long explains:

> Again, the prestige of the beginnings in Eliade's thought is predicated on his conception of the center as symbolizing the beginnings ... Around the center, other dimensions of life are organized; the center gives coherence to the common life, and through the center, the common life participates in reality. The center holds together in symbolic forms, human, natural, and supernatural realities.[20]

This was a ceremonial and ritual center. The sacred was apprehended most profoundly in this ceremonial center. In the modern era (read: Western), however, the prestige of the center was transferred to the civilizational or citied center. Citied traditions, then, "express centrifugal and centripetal dynamic forces; they tend to bring power into their centers and redistribute the power from the center."[21] In other words, there tends to be an "imperialistic principle inherent in the earliest citied traditions."[22] For Long, this pattern is clear in the military, political, and economic structures of citied traditions. Social relations in such a configuration are always hierarchical as opposed to the egalitarianism of earlier archaic cultures.

This way of understanding whiteness as religious coheres nicely with what Du Bois, as early as 1910, named "The religion of whiteness."[23] In an essay called "The Souls of White Folk," Du Bois rails against Europe and America for its pillaging and raping of the world's resources and people, sanctioned particularly against the global majority of people of color.[24] Reminiscent of Long's theorizing of religion, Du Bois sees whiteness as imperialistic. It seeks to devour the world, to own its people and resources, which it views as its birthright to plunder and consume. Time and time again, in the context of the essay, Du Bois, while remaining vigilant of the fact that the religion of whiteness and its attendant violence is global in scope, affecting many different nations of people, returns to the source of white violence—anti-blackness:

> How many of us today fully realize the current theory of colonial expansion, of the relation of Europe which is white, to the world which is black and brown and yellow? Bluntly put, that theory is this: It is the duty of white Europe to divide up the darker world and administer it for Europe's good . . . The European world is using black and brown men for all the uses which men know. Slowly but surely white culture is evolving the theory that only "darkies" are born beasts of burden for white folk . . . The supporting arguments grow and twist themselves in the mouths of merchant, scientist, soldier, traveler, writer, and missionary: Darker peoples are dark in mind as well as in body; of dark, uncertain, and imperfect decent; of frailer, cheaper stuff; . . . "half-devil and half-child." Such as they are civilization must, naturally, raise them, but soberly and in limited ways. They are not simply dark white men. They are not "men" in the sense that Europeans are men.[25]

Du Bois is no doubt careful in his language, particularly in his use of the terms "dark" and "darkies," for the quintessential darkie in the white imaginary has always been the "black." In this sense, darkies were not "men"; they were not human, not people, and as such, they were not gendered. They were simply black, black bodies, data, "who raise cotton, gather rubber, fetch ivory, and dig diamonds."[26] What Du Bois argues is also consistent with Long's notion of civilization and cited traditions.

While one tends to think of "civilization" or "civilized" as a virtue, this is not the case for Du Bois and Long. Civilization, a term and symbol that signified Europe and white culture, is barbaric; it operates out of its center, which it fails to acknowledge, even through violent expansion.[27] It is a religious notion that ostensibly sets apart the white world from the rest of the world, highlighting its special and technological character in a vein similar to being "chosen."[28] Yet, civilization needs the "primitive," the other, for its existence and identity, and so it signifies on people who then become the raw material out of which it builds its world, thus justifying its activities through linguistic duplicity. Indeed, "the term 'civilization'—a term that embodies the notion of the primitive—became a part of Western languages in the eighteenth century."[29] The emergence of civilization was conterminous with appearance of whiteness, which, Du Bois rightly concludes, "is a very modern thing."[30]

What of this "great [white] religion" for Du Bois?[31] To begin with, the *sine qua non* of the religion of whiteness is *rage*, and rage gives way to various forms of violence. As the description of whiteness in "The Souls of White Folk" illustrates, Du Bois has neither time nor patience for it. None. He is especially harsh in his criticism of America, which he views as exceptionally hypocritical. America's religion of white rage is, undeniably, more egregious than that of Europe, for it claims chosenness, specialness, freedom, and equality. Its "chiefest industry" being war, it has been anything but that for African Americans, who are the central object of its rage and violence.[32] America "trains her immigrants to this despising of 'niggers' from the day of their landing, and they carry and send the news back to the submerged classes in their fatherlands."[33] Du Bois continues:

> It is curious to see America, the United States, looking on herself, first, as a sort of natural peacemaker, then as a moral protagonist in this terrible time. No nation is less fitted for this rôle. For two or more centuries America has marched proudly in the van of human hatred,—making bonfires of human flesh and laughing at them hideously, and making the insulting of millions more than a matter of dislike,—rather *a great religion*, a world war-cry: Up white, down black; to your tents O white folk and world war with black and parti-colored mongrel beasts![34]

America evinces a hypocrisy that social theorists E. Franklin Frazer and Bobby E. Wright have characterized as "pathological."[35] America criticizes the world for its absence of democracy and for human rights violations, but it treats black people with the utmost contempt and exploitation. Du Bois retorts, "But say to a people: 'The one virtue is to be white,' and the people rush to the inevitable conclusion, 'Kill the "nigger"'!"[36]

One final note about the religion of white rage and the place of the white worker in it. For Du Bois, there is no black composite of the white worker, the white laborer. Never has been, never will be. The white worker has always been part of the religion of whiteness. As such, *black-white labor relations are irreducible to class*, for the white worker would likely benefit from "the exploitation of darker peoples."[37] In addition, white workers, says Du Bois, may find their way into the ranks of "men," by which he means "humans," through electoral politics, self-assertion, and education; but not the black laborer, for whom "the whites shall rule forever and forever and everywhere."[38] Likewise, the black worker—the black world—in the present configuration of the worlds, will never benefit from their own labor to the extent of the white. They will only get the "pittance that the white world throws [them] disdainfully."[39] Thus, it is not economics that ultimately motivates white people to act violently and exploitatively; these are religious acts which are constitutive of the very notion of whiteness. Violence and rage are the ideological facts of whiteness, they issue from the very data of white supremacy, the hierarchicalizing of people and the notion that whiteness has a primary relation with and to the Divine. Du Bois is clear that "this assumption that of all the hues of God whiteness alone is inherently and obviously better than brownness or tan leads to curious acts."[40]

As such, not *all* acts are invisible, and Du Bois endeavors to lay whiteness bare. He is explicit that he sees whiteness with the incisive intuition and insight of a black clairvoyant, a conjure man, and this makes white people angry.[41] "This is not Europe gone mad; this is not aberration nor insanity; this *is* Europe; this seeming Terrible is the real soul of white culture—, stripped and visible today."[42] Though it is true that the dangers of whiteness are made visible when one uses a racial slur or when Donald Trump, the forty-fifth president of the United States, calls African and Afro-Caribbean countries "shitholes"—and there are essays in this volume devoted to unpacking and critically analyzing such explicit forms of violence—it is also true that the *source* of such explicit violence rests in the often unspoken, unthought, and uncritically adopted normativity of whiteness as an innocent—or at least neutral—and generative source of goodness.

Whiteness as the Invisible, Unthought, and Therefore, the Norm

Whiteness, then, must endeavor to remain invisible, to punish those who mark its appearance, to make its critics *the problem*. Yancy, for example, highlights the reality that "a key feature of the social ontology of whiteness is that whites attempt to avoid discussing their own social, political, economic, and cultural investments in whiteness. Many whites fail to see their complicity with the systemic workings of white supremacy."[43] This blindness to one's own complicity in whiteness is *precisely* the source of the violence of white normativity. Not to see what one is—to take on only the identity of the one who sees and not the one who is seen—is a critical characteristic of whiteness, of people who see themselves as white, of those who cannot help but utter "all lives matter" or "not all white people" in response to passionate and truthful claims about the violence of white supremacy and white normativity. Not to see oneself is to already have announced one's investiture in whiteness.

Such a lack of awareness speaks to what we might call the phenomenology of whiteness, a phrase that may have been popularized by feminist philosopher Sara Ahmed.[44] For Ahmed, the phenomenology of whiteness is organized around the fact that "whiteness is lived as a background to experience."[45] Living as "background" is precisely what is meant when we say that whiteness does not see itself. Put philosophically, the phenomenology of whiteness is precisely the lived experience of whiteness as *the condition of possibility* of and for any other modality of life, of lived engagement. To be white is to live as the condition and not the *conditioned*; it is, drawing from Husserl, to operate not as the terminus of one's perception, but to be that which perceives. It is, in other words, to be the *gaze* upon the world.

To be the gaze has significant power. Above and beyond being merely the "one who sees," a gaze is *normative*; to gaze is to *constitute* the other, to give meanings to others in such a way as to make such meanings "stick." Moreover, the responsibility for such constitution is *displaced* onto that upon which one gazes; to see a "tree" is to disallow that which has been understood as a tree to have a say. Operating as a "background to experience," whiteness affords the possibility of engaging with the world without having to take responsibility for one's own legacy in shaping that world. Whiteness names others without having to be named; it acts without having to take responsibility for its actions. Whiteness allows people to enact racist activities without acknowledging that they are racist; it conditions, as one of the chapters in this volume argues, the possibility of calling the police for the most basic of human activities—golfing, swimming, fundraising, barbecuing, and even sleeping—while maintaining one's own innocence against the charge of white supremacist violence. Disguised through legal, social, and political norms, whiteness affords the possibility of surprise and shock at the reality of racism while distancing oneself from the guilt of "actually" being racist. Whiteness is, therefore, the existential disposition of seeing without having to be seen, of looking at and therefore constituting the world without having to take responsibility for the implications of such constitution.

To embody this disposition—and whiteness is *both* embodied and discursive—certainly has its benefits. To be able to act without taking responsibility, to see and treat others without having to worry about repercussions, allows for white communities to enact violence without owning up to such violence, to "throw rocks and hide your hands," as the saying goes. But these benefits extend far beyond enacting protected forms of violence. Because whiteness operates as "an ongoing and unfinished history, which orientates bodies in specific directions, which in turn shapes what it is that bodies 'can do,'"[46] whiteness is an existential inheritance, an ontological *entitlement*, whose benefits are conferred without merit and maintained without question. To be white, then, is to be gifted the possibility of not only shaping the world, but also being entitled to whatever benefits the world offers.

That is, of course, until those not deemed as white start making and laying claim to the same benefits. Having been given the ontological entitlement to the benefits of this world, having been bestowed the metaphysical guarantee of unlimited and unfettered access to whatever one might desire, whiteness throws temper tantrums when such benefits are even deemed accessible to and by non-white others.

This "white–non-white" distinction is crucial. Inasmuch as there are, indeed, other racialized identities in the United States, the racial schema in the U.S. nevertheless still operates along a binary logic. One is either white or one isn't—which is tantamount to being (understood as) black. In Duboisian thought, all non-white others are constituted as "niggers." In other words, non-white people become "black" through a series of legal, political, social, and even religious norms that treat such communities *as if* they were black. Although such a binary can indeed be read as collapsing distinctions between what we now call "people of color," there is a very real way in which *blackness* unfortunately becomes an umbrella term for those who cannot (or can no longer) present themselves as the "background" itself. Unable to "be" normative, non-white communities collapse into the abnormality of blackness—and are therefore, for better or worse, treated as such. It is no accident, then, that immigrant Muslims or Mexicans have been referred to as "the new niggers" or as "sand niggers." Anti-blackness is the default position; it is the unthought reference to non-white, who is not black but who is the object of rage within the contemporary and temporal gaze of whiteness. One only has to do a simple internet search to see the myriad of examples of this. Associating someone with blackness, even if he or she is a European immigrant, is an apparent affront to their status; to demean their status is to "blacken" or "niggerize" them. In a recent illustration, New York governor Andrew Cuomo, referring to a derogatory term for southern Italians (note that they are degraded because of an alleged trace of black heritage), said that "nigger wops, n-word wops" is a term that some use.[47] Likewise, CNN correspondent Chris Cuomo, the governor's brother, recently said that the word "Fredo," the name of a fictional character from *The Godfather: Part II*, was like "the n-word for us."[48] Notice a pattern?

Our point here, however, is not so much about this binary as it is about the whiteness that governs such binary logics. Kavanaugh was not concerned about those who weren't white during his tirade about his own self-making; that was about *him*, and about the people like him who worked hard only to be slighted by a "liberal" politics of identity. Such a move speaks more to the frustration, anger, and outrage at no longer being able to *be* the norm. No longer entitled to the benefits that a normative status may offer, the white who lives in the face of perceived non-white—which, again, is tantamount to *black*—progress is the white who remains concerned about the loss of his or her normative identity. And the apparent dissolution of one's normative benefits lends itself to a host of affective responses, all of which are organized around anger, ire, and—yes—rage.

Whiteness as an Affective Economy of Rage

To think with rage is to already think with and about affects and their possibilities. Affect studies scholarship has often articulated affect in its Spinozan form—as the "capacity to affect and be affected," articulating not simply the relata (the entities of relation) but also the relation itself. As Melissa Gregg and Gregory Seigworth put it in *The Affect Theory Reader*:

> Affect can be understood then as a gradient of bodily capacity—a supple incrementalism of ever-modulating force-relations—that rises and falls not only along various rhythms and modalities of encounter but also through the troughs and sieves of sensation and sensibility, an incrementalism that coincides with belong to compartments of matter of virtually any and every sort.[49]

Although affects are about entities in relation, they are also about how relations are constituted. The "ever-modulating force-relations" that move "not only along various rhythms and modalities of encounter" have everything to do with the construction, maintenance, and meaning of relationality itself. In other words, affect explores the dynamics of relation, exposing and exploring the conditions of possibility of (the meaning of) our various encounters with others, human, non-human, and otherwise.

The word "relation" is key here. "Relation" should not be understood as simply interpersonal. In fact, as affect theorists such as Brian Massumi point out, affect is often articulated as pre- and transpersonal "intensities" that both govern and are governed by the movement of people, bodies, non-human animals, and environments. We bring this up because, far and above describing interpersonal and individual modes of encounter, affect can and will name how *publics* are structured.

The pre- and transpersonal nature of affect, however, should not be taken—as Massumi often does—as a dismissal of the particular. In fact, the particularity of a body's movement and expression can, will, and must raise questions about our affective possibilities. Ben Highmore expounds:

> Affect gives you away: the telltale heart; my clammy hands; the note of anger in your voice; the sparkle of glee in their eyes. You may protest your innocence, but we both know, don't we, that who you *really* are, or *what* you really are, is going to be found in the pumping of your blood, the quantity and quality of your perspiration, the breathless anticipation in your throat, the way you can't stop yourself from grinning, the glassy sheen in your eyes.[50]

Kavanaugh's tears, flushed face, and raised voice, for example, "gave him away," as someone who was enraged. Such embodiments of rage can and will be manifested *through* bodies: a Charlottesville rally gone wrong (or right, depending on one's perspective); a Women's March; a March for Our Lives. In fact, as Debra Thompson points out, much of black political and social organizing has had rage as its affective engine; rage moves the individual and social body to express itself as enraged.[51]

There is a sticking point, however: while Kavanaugh's rage was expressed in and through his particular body, it found its legitimacy in and through vocal forms of support for his performance. In a nationally televised job interview, the United States public watched a man throw a temper tantrum. However, instead of being publicly (and maybe even privately) sanctioned for his performance, Kavanaugh was offered the job *because* he threw the tantrum, ranting, raving, and crying his way to the Supreme Court of the United States. As a *Saturday Night Live* sketch parodied, the Republican leadership was excited and emboldened by Kavanaugh's performance, *not* concerned or embarrassed; and we would be mistaken to assume that their responses were limited to them.

White rage, therefore, is a publicly legitimated emotion. It might even be said, as we are saying here, that white rage is best understood as a scheme of racial legitimation. You would be wrong, dear reader, to assume that our analysis of Kavanaugh is limited, or even primarily focused upon, Kavanaugh in his particularity. Kavanaugh himself is not important in this analysis; what *is* important is the *legitimacy* of his particular performance, the various ways in which his rage was supported, justified, sanctioned, and encouraged by the United States legislative and sociopolitical institutions. The question before us, then, is a question about the affective context, the emotional horizon and landscape, out of which such legitimation is made possible.

After all, generalized rage—rage that can and will be expressed by anyone—does not always carry the professional, legal, political, and social legitimacy that Kavanaugh's did. Kavanaugh's rage was legitimated in and through the normative racial order of the United States—a racial order that is, always has been, and maybe always will be, normatively coded as *white*. As Debra Thompson points out:

> The privileges associated with whiteness constitute every facet of social and political life, including the determination of which racial groups can express what kinds of emotions in the polis. The very expression of anger in democratic politics is governed by what Arlie Russell Hothschild calls "feeling rules," that is, the social norms that establish the conceptions of entitlement,

obligation, or appropriateness that regulate emotional exchanges . . . these "feeling rules" are highly racialized, used in the service of the American racial order to sanction certain emotions as legitimate or . . . illegitimate, depending on the status of the racial group proclaiming the emotion.⁵²

Governed by a set of racialized "feeling rules," U.S. public life regulates and is regulated by the il/legitimacy of particular emotional and affective expressions and performances based upon the particularity of the *body* expressing or performing said emotion. Rage, therefore, is *racialized* within the context of the United States, gaining or losing credibility based upon who is expressing it.

Our move away from Kavanaugh and to white rage more generally is important. After all, Kavanaugh's rage is not the only performance of white rage that has gained legitimation in the U.S. public. As we noted above, white rage carries no political allegiances; it is not simply the *conservative* expression of white rage that gains legitimacy in public. If we consider, for example, the disparate responses between the Black Lives Matter movement and the #NeverAgain movement for gun control, we see the same machinations of de/legitimation operative. Multiple tweets, donations, and even massive media coverage accompanied the demonstration, all of whom laid claim to the "inspirational" nature of a group of majority white students whose primary chant was "We call BS." Again, flushed faces, watery eyes, and raised voices abounded; but, unlike the Black Lives Matter movement's marches, protests, speakouts, and direct actions, these angry young white kids were not criticized, condemned, dismissed, or even targeted by large swaths of the public. (Righteously) ranting, raving, and crying their way to the nation's capital, this group of young and largely white organizers found support, not condescension and controversy, for their rage.

Our point here is not to condemn the student-organizers. To read us in this way would be to *mis*read us, and—yet again—focus on the particular at the expense of the public dynamics that the particular announces and exposes. What we are highlighting here—as we just did with Kavanaugh—is white rage as the *legitimation* of white normativity. Our focus here is not on the Parkland students, but instead on the racial order that legitimates and is legitimated by white rage. Affectively understood, white rage—as a modality of relation—needs no political allegiance; its primary expression, goal, and sustenance is the formation and maintenance of white normativity.

Understanding white rage in affect-theoretical terms displaces necessarily the centrality of individual actors and allows for us to ask more expansive questions about *how* such rage came to be legitimated as a mode of expression and relation. Such a line of questioning entails nothing less than an interrogation of the intensity and trajectory of such affective realities. In this regard, white rage can and will find its expression in and through explicit actions of emotional expression, but, as Carol Anderson points out in *White Rage*, it can also work its way in a more diffuse fashion, operating along lines of subtle intensity that are so slight as to almost seem imperceptible.

> White rage is not about visible violence, but rather works its way through the courts, the legislatures, and a range of government bureaucracies. It wreaks havoc subtly, almost imperceptibly. Too imperceptibly, certainly, for a nation consistently drawn to the spectacular—to what it can *see*. It's not the Klan. White rage doesn't have to wear sheets, burn crosses, or take to the streets. Working in the halls of power, it can achieve its ends far more effectively, far more destructively.[53]

White rage need not emerge or manifest itself as the explicit and extremist white supremacist violence that characterized the Charlottesville attacks. In fact, if we follow Anderson's logic and historical analysis, it is precisely *from* the diffuse character of institutionalized discrimination that white rage finds its legitimacy.

In other words, white rage, as we noted before, is manifold in its trajectories, manifestations, and emphases. Though many of these will be covered in the book, for heuristic purposes it might be best to understand white rage as flowing and manifesting in (at least) two different ways. The first we might call *aggressive* white rage. This form of rage is best understood as the public and visceral expressions of consternation, ire, and outright anger that maintain white normativity (think Charlottesville, Brett Kavanaugh, the March for Our Lives, etc.). The second form of white rage might be called *diffuse* white rage, in that the very possibility of legitimation only occurs through what Sara Ahmed calls "affective economies," that is, the accumulated value of certain affects over time. This latter form, present in and through legal, social, and cultural institutions that maintain the normativity of white rage, finds little explicit expression, but—again returning to Anderson—is all the more pernicious *because* of its diffuse character.

It is important to continue to point out that we are focused on the *legitimation*, and not necessarily the acts themselves. To align the March for Our Lives with the Charlottesville rally is to suggest not that both acts were similar in content, but that they were similar in the legitimation of their content. Public consternation at Heather Heyer's tragic death might have followed Charlottesville, but the forty-fifth president himself refused to castigate the white supremacists who enacted such lethal violence.

For "a nation consistently drawn to the spectacular," the most identifiable form of white rage was the aggressive form, embodied in the mob who eventually shot, killed, and hung W. C. Williams. But this isn't the only form of rage flowing in and through this story. In fact, Sheriff Thigpin himself was an affective conductor, for it is through both the "deal" he struck with the mob, and his "capitulation" to the murder that eventually ensued, that such violence was enabled and tacitly encouraged.

Thigpin also embodied a certain form of rage, although it is far more removed—and therefore less apparent—than the rage of the mob. In this story, both aggressive and diffuse forms of white rage legitimate the normativity of whiteness through the flow and accumulation of affect. The "feeling rules" are put in place; the only thing that matters once the rules are instituted is the continued support and maintenance of such prescribed affective parameters. Whether the rage is articulated as the "progressive" attempt to pacify "white workers" or an outright refusal to condemn what was clearly an act of anti-black hatred in Charlottesville; whether it is a capitulation to a lynch mob or the lynching itself; whether it is the expression of indignation at accusations of sexual assault or the ire that erupts from such an enactment, what remains the case is that the manifold expressions of white rage both legitimate and are legitimated by a significant historical and social predilection toward the normativity of whiteness itself. The reasoning for this, as we have shown and will show throughout the text, has everything to do with religion, race, and the idea of the white worker.

The emergence of the white worker and whiteness that produced the white rage described throughout the book developed hundreds of years ago. Just as sociologist Jordanna Matlon argues that masculinity and the feminization of work emerged as a project of colonialism, we argue that the same may be said for the white worker, especially white men workers. In "Racial Capitalism and the Crisis of Black Masculinity," Matlon argues, "Reflecting the ethos of European industrialization, the colonial quest established gendered work regimes among native populations in cities predicated on wage labor; through this process, the categories of 'man' and 'worker' were collapsed."[54] Given that colonialism was a project of *racial* capitalism, it could also be argued, as we do here, that the racial hierarchy was the catalyst of colonialism and one consequence was that the categories of man and white and worker were collapsed. Wages, Matlon also argues, came to validate a man's identity of himself as a provider, which was a condition of masculinity. We extend Matlon's argument and contend that wages came to validate white men's identity as a condition of masculinity and also as a condition of American identity.

The Significance and Organization of *The Religion of White Rage*

The Religion of White Rage is the first book to theorize, describe, and quantify the relationship between *white workers* and *American religion* from a variety of disciplinary locations. We argue throughout the book that the white laborer and various modes of American religion, including—and especially—what we are calling the "religion of white rage" are always constituted in and by causal and correlative relationships, which are, first and foremost, responses to the activities or perceived meanings, desires, politics, and life-ways of African Americans.

As we reflect on the nature of contemporary times, we find ourselves continually exploring the relationship between white religious fervor, the perceived "loss" of certain kinds of economic and material privileges, and what many might perceive as African American uplift. While the contemporary context might bring this into sharp relief, our contention is that *the rise of white religious fervor is correlative to the twin notions of perceived white loss and perceived black progress*. This correlation results in an affective context of white rage, wherein white people—quintessentially categorized under the heading of "white laborers" or "white workers"—uncritically and wholeheartedly draw from often-racialized religious sensibilities to justify simultaneously white supremacy and black inferiority. From Charlottesville to the uncritical support for the current president from the evangelical community, what we see is that it is not economics but *race* and religion that stand as the primary motivating factors for the rise of both explicit and implicit forms of white supremacy and white normativity, and we understand this rise as religious in nature.

The religion of white rage is not limited to neo-Nazis or belligerent SCOTUS candidates, but also shows up in and as unintentional forms of white normativity. This is both historical and contemporary: we reflect on the current sociopolitical and religious landscape in the United States and show ways in which it is filled with contradictions, tensions, outright hypocrisy if we are to be honest, and racism. We articulate the relationship between white rage, religious fervor, "American" identity, and perceived black racial progress throughout American history. Our chief argument throughout the book is that the category of the "white laborer" and white religious fervor are more pronounced and more sharply identified in moments of perceived black uplift.

Several key concepts that have different meanings are clarified. We elaborate on how the understanding of terms like "religion" and "labor" is often fraught and possibly differs from one discipline to the next. We have already discussed the term "religion" at length in this introduction, but with regard to "laborer," we have a twofold approach: 1) "laborer" and 'worker' are metonymic terms for whiteness, speaking to the normativity of whiteness through certain claims about white entitlement to the material benefits of the country ("Joe the plumber" is a popular way of capturing the metonymic white laborer); 2) "laborer" can also be broadly conceived in more social-scientific terms as a person or group of people who often are working- or lower-middle-class people. We further make the case that the religion of white rage can be (and is) expressed when resentful white laborers take center stage not simply as the reason for political shifts, but also as the primary group to which the country should devote its attention.

Given this twofold approach, the chapters in this volume fluctuate between metonymic and class-based approaches to white workers. Some chapters will be explicit about the white worker, while others implicitly make connections between white workers and whiteness through the continued antagonism toward, fear of, and rage against non-white peoples—particularly black people. In this regard, the "white worker" flows in, through, and between the chapters as both metaphor and empirical class identifier. Both are present throughout, but—as we show in the conclusion—the "white worker" was, is, and remains a metaphor, a mythic construct that stands in for whiteness more generally.

The book chapters are organized in two sections. The first section, named "White Religious Fervor and Contemporary American Politics," explores the relationship between ultimate orientation, whiteness, white workers, and contemporary U.S. politics, ultimately showing how whiteness presents itself as a center or norm around which U.S. political and social life is organized. This organization is also a foil, however: to be organized around whiteness is to be organized *against* blackness. These essays, therefore, draw from various methodological and disciplinary formations to explore how whiteness develops itself *against* blackness.

Stephen C. Finley's chapter, "Make America Great Again," shows how white religious fervor is always a response to the perceived African American progress or desire for progress in America. Drawing from various modes of psychoanalysis, Finley makes it clear that whiteness is, at base, a psychoanalytic attachment to blackness as a religious and phobogenic object. Whiteness therefore consolidates itself around the fear of blackness—a fear that, as Finley concludes, has implications for the study of religion.

In "You Will Not Replace Us!" Darrius Hills describes how the 2017 protests and riots in Charlottesville, Virginia, yielded strong scholarly interest in the interplay between right-wing politics, racial demagoguery, and racialized violence but failed to offer an interrogation of the religious undertones that so often accompany expressions of white nationalism in contemporary

American discourses. Drawing from discourses of paranoia, Hills delineates how the white supremacists at Charlottesville expose a paranoia about their perceived victimhood in relation to non-whites, and are legitimated by a president who stands as their white spokesperson. Hills concludes by asking about the constructive responses to such paranoia, suggesting that a reconfiguration of humanity might offer resources for responding to this problem.

In "I AM That I AM," Terri Laws and Kimberly Enard argue that the religion of whiteness is held together through ideology and ritual: an ideology that worships white supremacy and periodic rituals of threatened or actual violence or rage which emerge when threatened by black presence and progress, in this instance during the Great Migration era in Detroit. Drawing from sociological and history-of-religions analysis, Laws and Enard articulate the Great Migration as imbricated in the problematic power dynamics of white supremacy. Providing a social-historical analysis of the Ford Motor Company, Laws and Enard alert us to the relationship between whiteness, rage, white supremacy, and labor within the context of the United States, showing us that the religion of white rage "still matters" to and for the material outlook of people of color—particularly African Americans.

In, "American (Un)Civil Religion, the Defense of the White Worker, and Responses to NFL Protests," Lori Latrice Martin responds to athlete activists by largely white workers. Specifically, she stresses the need to understand the linkages between three important concepts: "American civil religion," perceived black progress by white workers, and what she calls "white religious shock," or the disorientation white workers experience when they encounter challenges to the white social order, manifested in what is best described as white fervor. The linkages between white laborers, religion, and perceived black progress become more salient than in the responses to protests by players in the National Football League by President Donald Trump and the league's (and President Trump's) largely white worker fan base. Martin details how American civil religion is defined and how it functions.

In "The Color of Belief: Black Social Christianity, White Evangelicalism, and Redbaiting the Religious Culture of the CIO in the Postwar South," Elizabeth and Ken Fones-Wolf describe how white workers interpreted the problems and possibilities facing the South at the end of World War II through their largely religious culture, evangelical Protestantism. They outline how white workers typically imagined the upheaval in their worlds through the end-times theology of dispensational premillennialism. Their grim visions of the imminent struggle with the Antichrist caused them to fear and despise those most interested in transforming the South, especially the Congress of Industrial Organizations (CIO). The chapter investigates the simultaneous growth of black aspirations and white anxieties that emerged with the CIO's Operation Dixie, perhaps the most ambitious effort to transform the South prior to the civil rights movement. In particular, by exploring the conflicting doctrines of both white and black Protestant evangelicals, the authors analyze the sources of white resistance to labor's campaign to create a South that strove for economic and social justice. The failure to sanctify Operation Dixie ultimately set the stage for massive resistance and the long decline of organized labor in the United States.

In "Constitutional Whiteness," Jason Jefferies comments on the United States Constitution as a sacred document, however exclusive, which outlines the religious rights, freedoms, morals, and ethics of citizens of the United States of America. He reveals how from its foundation, the Constitution is exclusive in terms of race and racialized bodies, especially in regards to participation in political life and sociopolitical action. Because the Constitution is designed for protection and inclusion of white bodies, it establishes what Jeffries calls "white-being"—namely, the establishment of "true whiteness" as connected to property rights and ownership. White workers seek to achieve this white-being, but, unfortunately, they cannot. As such, they displace their failures onto non-white people, particularly black people. Drawing from object-relations theory, Jeffries concludes that working-class whites experience narcissistic white rage in response to black uplift, political progress, or social activism.

Part two, "White Religious Fervor, Religious Ideology, and White Identity," explores the relationship between religious ideologies—whether they be theological, affective, or institutional in nature—and white identity. Exploring everything from group identification to gender, these essays sketch how white identity forms itself in relation to the presence of blackness, as well as the invocation of certain social, cultural, political, and religious logics.

In "KKK Christology: A Brief on White Class Insecurity," Paul Easterling develops a character sketch of the KKK Christ. Arguing that the Klan is an organization of primarily working-class individuals and families, Easterling highlights concerns focused around class insecurity, but also demonstrates that this class insecurity cannot be disconnected from the historical fact that the KKK is in fact a Christian organization with a unique Christology that must be studied in order to better understand the root of its hate. The KKK makes use of Christian symbols and biblical texts, and argues that its mission is a holy charge bestowed upon it by the Christian God; as such, Easterling draws from discourses in theodicy in order to have us to consider whether or not God can be understood as solely—or even primarily—benevolent.

In "Black People and White Mormon Rage: Examining Race, Religion and Politics in Zion," Darron Smith, Brenda Harris, and Melissa Flores theorize that the apparent contradictions of injustices realized from white Mormon beliefs involve complex entanglements between the white racial frame, conservative political ideology, and white European religious thought, as they apply to people of African heritage. These socially constructed frames of race, religion, and politics influence the understandings and actions of individuals and groups sometimes to the detriment and violent harm of innocent others. This nexus of race, religion, and politics applied to contemporary race relations is readily seen within the microcosm of the LDS Church, which has a long and troubling racist history itself.

In "Anatomizing White Rage: 'Race Is My Religion!' and 'White Genocide,'" Kate E. Temoney unpacks the religious aspects of claims of efforts to wipe out the white race as an approach to analyzing the white rage shared by an increasing number of antagonistic and loosely affiliated movements of American white nationalists. Contemporary white supremacists claims that "their race is their religion," downplaying the divide between the collectively racialized theologies of pro-Christian white supremacists and non-Christian religious movements and the atheistic bend of anti-religion white nationalists, Temoney argues. Despite the irreligiosity of the latter, white nationalists are united in their defense of white privilege with devotion akin to religious zealotry in its functionality and intensity. This characterization rests on the parochial association of "religion" with a historical, cumulative tradition (e.g. Christianity). The constructs of "white" and "religion" and their elision, then, functionally allow "whiteness" to stand as a single and singular identity for negotiating the world. This creates an imagined community whose fragility and ideological heterogeneity is subsumed under the pressing imperative to collectively combat "white genocide." "Racial" and "religious" groups are protected under the 1948 Convention on the Prevention and Punishment of the Crime of Genocide. Therefore, styling whites as a race, whites as religious, or even race as a religion are tactics for legitimizing white victimhood and inviting the excesses of religious fervor as indispensable to the superseding focus on protecting whites not merely as a perceived group but as an actual group.

Gender must be an important part of any conversations about the religion of white rage. Biko Gray's chapter, "Exorcising Blackness: Calling the Cops as an Affective Performance of Gender," claims that white women solidify their normative gender identities through acts of "affective exorcism." By calling the cops on black people for various things, white women embody and reify a historical identity of white womanhood that is formed against the encroaching threat of blackness. In so doing, these white women establish themselves *as* women through the performative outrage of the presence of black people. Moreover, in so doing, they also establish themselves as *innocent*, invoking a theodicean logic that makes black people the embodiment of an evil threat when read against these women's perceived innocence.

Similarly, Danae Faulk's work addresses the religion of white rage and the importance of considering gender. Specifically, in "White Power Barbie and Other Figures of the Angry White Woman," Faulk considers the role white women play in the production of anti-black, religious fervor through an affective analysis of the rise to fame of Tomi Lahren—a cis-gendered woman who performs an aggressive, affective style normatively coded as masculine whiteness. Placing Lahren into the context of a longer U.S. religious history of angry white women who are often more vitriolic and outspoken than their white male counterparts, Faulk shows that such articulations of feminized white rage offer white women an avenue to tap into the entanglement of power and white pleasure afforded to white, masculine subjects through anti-black sentiments invoking the sacrality of white America. Lahren's performances of outrage, often couched as responses to the moral injury of perceived black success and "reverse racism," stand on the ideology of white women as protectors of the religious and moral spheres of American life. In comparing her to the public spectacles of liberal white women's rage, Faulk argues that Lahren is emblematic of a long tradition of white women across all political lines defining and negotiating their gendered experiences as white women affectively through, rather than against, white patriarchy and anti-black sentiments.

For E. Anthony Muhammad, the use of religion in the dehumanization of black bodies spans religions. In his chapter, "Weaponizing Religion: A Document Analysis of the Religious Indoctrination of Slaves in Service of White Labor Elites," Muhammad explores the product of this subjugation by engaging in a document analysis of official catechisms produced by the Protestant Episcopal church for both whites and enslaved blacks during the antebellum period. In contextualizing these documents, this study analyzes the fluctuating milieu of white religious fervor in the colonial South. Particular attention is paid to the economic and social justifications of the religious indoctrination of slaves; justifications that ensured the ascendency of the white labor class at the expense of the anxiously perceived humanization of the black enslaved. A thematic analysis of the respective catechisms elucidates the particularly pernicious way in which religious indoctrination was weaponized against the psychological functioning of the enslaved.

"The Religions of Black Resistance and White Rage: Interpenetrative Religious Practice in the 1963 Civil Rights Struggle in Danville, Virginia," by Tobin Miller Shearer, explores the violent response to the 1963 civil rights protests in Danville, Virginia. Shearer turns to this event as an opportunity for examining the interpenetrative nature of white religion in the South. By analyzing challenges to the city's white supremacist leadership structures and segregationist practices, white reactivity to the public display of black religious piety becomes evident. Shearer's chapter contends that the interpenetrative nature of black and white religion in the South in the early 1960s simultaneously undermined and strengthened white hegemony even as it fostered a religion of white rage. The prayer forms, pious injunctions, and faith-based organizing by African American activists enlivened and empowered the black community to challenge segregationists while also intensifying white backlash and weakening, at least temporarily, black resistance to Jim Crow. This particular religious expression of white rage, bolstered by formal, sanctioned civil religious prayers and dedications, helped create the conditions in which a large group of black religious activists peacefully engaged in a prayer vigil at City Hall on June 10, 1963, came under attack from firefighters, police, and deputized garbage men armed with fire hoses and night sticks. The rage of the white assailants emerged from the religious practices they shared with the black community, not those that were unfamiliar to them. Shearer challenges the existing historiography offered by scholars like Mark Chapman, David Garrow, and Charles Payne and builds on the new narratives crafted by historians like Carolyn René Dupont, Paul Harvey, and Kerry Pimblott.

Taken together, the collection of chapters allows us to map out the disciplines, methodologies, themes, and conceptual framework for understanding the significance of the emerging field of *Race, Religion, and Labor Studies*.

Part One

White Religious Fervor, Civil Religion, and Contemporary American Politics

ONE

"Make America Great Again": Racial Pathology, White Consolidation, and Melancholia in Trump's America[1]

Stephen C. Finley

The Negro is a phobogenic object, a stimulus to anxiety.[2]

–Frantz Fanon

I came into the world imbued with the will to find a meaning in things, my spirit filled with the desire to attain to the source of the world, and then I found that I was an object in the midst of other objects.[3]

–Franz Fanon

Alternatively, why does blackness suggest sexual allure in spite of the feeling that it conveys something negative?[4]

–Robert E. Hood

Something Old is New Again: "Make America Great Again" as a Call for White Consolidation and Mythic Return

Donald Trump became president of the United States in 2016, which ushered in a new era in American social relations. It was not so much that the acrimonious racial climate became palpable in a way that had never been seen; it had been. African Americans knew very well what was going on. History was replete with painful illustrations of our tenuous and contentious existence in the country—from several hundred years of enslavement to a century or more of lynching, to legally codified white racial terror and police brutality—black people remain ever-present in their awareness of how fragile civility is. But for many people it was new. Some had never seen a president so freely express racial animus and congeal such a large portion of the white populous into a fervor that could be witnessed so regularly in the news media and, more vociferously, on social media. Things appeared out of control. Yet, something was uncanny, eerily familiar, a pattern that repeated itself throughout American history: with any minute step toward racial progress or even the perception of progress comes the violent response from all sectors—actively or passively—of white communities.[5]

Donald Trump called for this white response during his campaign, concealed in the slogan "Make America Great Again."[6] America apparently heard. White America. Militias increased. White nationalist and white supremacist movements appeared from out of the shadows. The policing by white people—often by white women—of African American bodies engaging in routine and mundane aspects of their lives, who were then reported to law enforcement, or worse yet, shot at, seemed to increase. Black America heard it, too, but African Americans were suspicious. What could such a call mean except violence for us? When had America been great—during slavery? Jim Crow? The period of lynching that lasted about a century from the beginnings of Reconstruction? That ostensible American "greatness" had grave consequences for African Americans. It signaled white consolidation, a backlash. Martin Luther King, Jr. wrote in detail about this phenomenon. It appears and reappears predictably when white people rage against apparent black progress. In some of his least lauded but arguably most radical writings in his last book, *Where Do We Go from Here? Chaos or Community?*, King writes:

> Ever since the birth of our nation, white America has had a schizophrenic personality on the question of race. She has been torn between selves—a self in which she proudly professed the great principles of democracy and a self in which she sadly practiced the antithesis of democracy. This tragic duality has produced a strange indecisiveness and ambivalence toward the Negro, causing America to take a step backward simultaneously with every step forward on the question of racial justice, to be at once attracted to the Negro and repelled by him, to love him and to hate him. There has *never* been a solid, unified and determined thrust to make justice a reality for Afro-Americans. This step backward has a new name today. It is called the *"white backlash* [emphasis added]." But the white backlash is nothing new. It is the surfacing of old prejudices, hostilities, and ambivalences that have always been there.[7]

Here, King supports my contention that there is a pattern to the "backlash." In the next section, I use psychoanalysis to unpack and expose the structure and motivation for this backlash, particularly as it relates to what

King calls the simultaneous attraction and repulsion of white people toward black people that is consistent with Robert Hood's observation in the third epigraph that frames this chapter. The question that King does not answer is: Why are white people so opposed to black progress? What is the reason for their violent response, their consolidation, in which various factions—often opposed to one another politically and economically—come together in service of continued white domination? I want to emphasize that this consolidation is always a reaction to perceived black progress, even when such presumed occurrences are unquantifiable or are quantitatively false.

The Elaine Massacre is one example of white consolidation. It took place a century ago when black sharecroppers in Arkansas attempted to organize themselves to gain a greater share of the profits from their labor. The sharecroppers simply wanted just and equitable wages for their products, knowing that the white land owners were stealing most of the profits, without ever accounting honestly for what was produced and, in addition, by charging absurd amounts of money for the use of their land. The black farmers merely wanted fairness. On September 30, 1919, they met at a local church to plan their organizing efforts, which included joining a union called the Progressive Farmers and Household Union of America. White men, many of whom were law enforcement, shot up the church late that night. Some of the men in the church defended themselves, firing shots back.[8]

The Arkansas governor at the time, Charles Brough, commissioned federal soldiers to intervene, not to protect the black farmers and families, but to "kill them if they failed to surrender immediately,"[9] giving license for white people to massacre black people indiscriminately. Their attempted self-defense was framed as an insurrection. As a result, more than 200 African Americans were slaughtered, many in a mass lynching. These murders included women and children. Yet, twelve black men were charged with murder, and the black community of Elaine was terrorized and destroyed. The murder of African Americans and the destruction of their towns and communities were not uncommon. Throughout the history of the United States, there are many examples—from Tulsa (Greenwood), Oklahoma, to Rosewood, Florida.

It is important to note, in this illustration, the way that white consolidation functions: 1) Various white institutions come to bear on maintaining white domination and sanctioning white violence (almost without exception. In this case, the Supreme Court, in one of the few instances in American history, ruled that African American rights to due process were violated). This may include churches, police, the courts, journalists, etc. 2) Substantial white differences dissolve in the crucible of white violence in service of white desire and need. Rich and poor, Republican and Democrat, liberal and conservative, across genders and sexual orientations, etc., white people participate actively or passively, by non-action, therefore consent. 3) White narratives (sometimes outright lies) justify this violence by blaming black victims (resembling a collective psychoanalytic defense mechanism), by appealing to mythologies about black violence, cultural defects, and lasciviousness, and by citing or alluding to white, and ultimately religious, narratives about whiteness as the preeminent orientation. Passive narratives may also appeal to the slow nature of progress and the need to work within the "system" for change even though the system is structured in and by whiteness. 4) African Americans are disciplined in some form, through official means or by extrajudicial ones by cultural consent. 5) The cycle repeats when white people see their worldview and way of life as in jeopardy from black progress.

The religious site of white consolidation is the mythical white worker. Through the process of white consolidation, white people are represented in and by the white worker, the quintessential white subject. This chapter, as well as the volume in which it is located, maintains that these processes and the complex—whiteness—in which they exist and from which they flow are first and foremost religious. Quite obviously, of course, I am not the first to point out the religious nature of whiteness. Scholars have done so for some time now. Subsequently, in what could be read as a religious definition of whiteness, James W. Perkinson's article "The Ghost in the Global Machine: White Violence, Indigenous Resistance, and Race as Religiousness" seeks to give expression to a coherent notion of whiteness as religion and as religious. Perkinson proclaims:

> In sum, 'whiteness' thus discerned—in my own on-going attempt to name and alter the affliction damning the majority of people of pallor to a zombie-like existence of sleep-walking cooperation with their singularly rapacious neoliberal and imperial masters—is many things. It operates as a violent and violating continuum of select biological features, taken up in manipulative discursive schemas, implemented in and implementing discriminatory institutional practices, habituated in coercive cultural and sexual orientations, materialized in aggressive social architectures and urban demographics, that nonetheless remains a spiritual and political choice.[10]

Perkinson articulates what he calls a "profile" of whiteness, which includes individual decisions, economic and political factors, affective moods, and cultural, gendered, and erotic modalities that culminate and interface with the world, garnering and accumulating benefits, while enacting violence on the world.[11] In the words of W. E. B. Du Bois: "'But what on earth is whiteness that one should desire it?' Then, always, somehow, some way, silently but clearly, I am given to understand that whiteness is the ownership of the earth forever and ever, Amen!"[12] In my own words now, what is religious about the whiteness that Perkinson is describing is that it is an aggregated complex of individual and collective relations of power, corporate networks, institutions, affects, cosmologies, myths, representations, epistemes, politics, and economics that congeal in the meaning and status of the bodies of those who live, identify, and are perceived as white, which structure the world, experiences, and relations with—and to an extent *of*—others (who are not white or perceived as white), and which function as the organizing interface with the world. In short, whiteness organizes, makes sense of, and overdetermines reality.

As a consequence, Perkinson tracks this whiteness through the disciplinary method of history of religious phenomenology, since he is most concerned with "the religiousness of such a whiteness."[13] While Perkinson tracks the religion of whiteness through the history of religions, in part, because he wants to disrupt it, I utilize a Fanon-inspired psychoanalytic approach for the same purpose, that is, to mark, make visible, and reduce whiteness to its constituent elements and to expose its religious purpose. While religious, this whiteness is not a self-contained totality, though it often appears as such. On the contrary, whiteness is also a *need* and *desire* and therefore a *lack* and *absence*. Thus, I am interested in the motivation, meaning, and function of whiteness as a religious orientation.

On Whiteness, Race, and Religion: Toward and Beyond a Fanonian Psychoanalytic Interpretation

There is a structure to this phenomenon. White religious fervor is always a response to perceived African American progress or desire for progress in the United States. Hence, whiteness needs the black object, African Americans in this case, for its own existence. It is constituted and maintained through a perpetual exchange of often-binary taxonomies that valorize whiteness and deprecate blackness. As such, whiteness will always have a relation to—and be dependent upon—blackness. This is the working thesis of this chapter. For this reason, black activity that seeks its own freedom and independence is always met with a backlash, again, which I call "white consolidation," since it is much more than a violent racial backlash. To be sure, violence is always an aspect of this white consolidation, but there is something more, something religious, that I want to explore later in this chapter. Robert Hood attempts to track these matters in his book *Begrimed and Black: Christian Traditions on Blacks and Blackness*. Hood argues that the meaning of blackness in the West is attributable to the cosmologies and mythologies of Christian traditions. The thesis is only partially correct. Hood asks, "Can blackness only be defined by contrasting it to whiteness and therefore making its core meaning dependent on whiteness?"[14] In my definition and Perkinson's expression of whiteness above, it is clear that whiteness exceeds Christian traditions. My argument reverses Hood's basic question of ontology. Or rather, I shift from Hood's ontology of blackness to a metaphysics of whiteness, since I want to answer and respond to the inverse of his question. Whiteness needs blackness, not the reverse. More specifically, it requires blackness as an object.

In the psychoanalytic vocabulary of Frantz Fanon—which drew upon Freud, Lacan, Jung, Adler, and others—black bodies are "phobogenic," that is, objects constituted by white culture whose "place" must be maintained to protect whiteness from its irrational fear of contamination and loss. They are perceived and experienced as bodies that elicit fear and rage (the two often go together), in particular for white people, a dynamic that Fanon addresses in his seminal work, *Black Skin, White Masks*. I do want to be clear, however, and note the racist and colonial legacy of psychoanalysis, which, through evolutionary notions of race and culture, incorporated such ideas of the primitive as cultural and psychical defect into psychoanalysis. Freud, for instance, used the language of the "primitive" to describe psychopathology.[15] Furthermore, Fanon argued against the universality of Freud's notion of the oedipal complex, suggesting cultural variations that rendered it moot in Africana cultures.[16] And, yet, Fanon saw psychoanalysis as the preeminent means of unconcealing the psychical motivation of white racism. Indeed, Celia Brickman's *Aboriginal Populations in the Mind: Race and Primitivity in Psychoanalysis* contends that "as a critical discourse it [psychoanalysis] is eminently suited to analyze and deconstruct colonialist thought, as has been shown by its use in the exemplary works of Frantz Fanon."[17] Likewise, I want to utilize Fanon as a basis for uncovering this whiteness that needs the black phobogenic object by making two primary claims about the irrational fear that, according to Fanon, white people invest in black bodies.

First, this irrational fear *is the fear, disavowal, and concealment of what is experienced as a homoerotic incursion of the black world into the white world, in which it understands itself in the passive position*. Fanon referred to this "phobia" as "destructuration."[18] What he intends, here, is the white desire and need to maintain the distinction between "worlds," though it (the complex of whiteness) needs *the black* for its own existential articulation of its world and for its maintenance. By "destructuration," Fanon also had in mind the way that the presence of blackness, of the black object, threatens a particularly white cosmology and psychic structure that has as its center, ironically and contradictorily, a black object. It is this apparent contradiction—of desire and animus, of consumption and expurgation, and of danger and attraction—that is the *sine qua non* of the *religion of white rage*, and indeed, of classical religious theory, which I explore in the conclusion.[19]

Fanon locates the matter of black bodies as phobogenic both in the biological and the phenomenological realms. Which is to say, for me at least, the issue of white fear of blackness is about whites' own perceptions of physical black bodies and the affective responses and mythologies that are developed, which then both precede and inform appearances of the black in the imaginary and consciousness of white people. In Fanon's words:

> Let us try to determine what are the constituents of Negrophobia. This phobia is to be found on an instinctual, biological level. At the extreme, I should say that the Negro, because of his body, impedes the closing of the postural schema of the white man—at the point, naturally, at which the black man makes his entry into the phenomenal world of the white man. This is not the place in which to state the conclusions I drew from studying the influence exerted on the body by the appearance of another body. (Let us assume, for example, that four fifteen-year-old boys, all more or less athletic, are doing the high jump. One of them wins by jumping four feet ten inches. Then a fifth boy arrives and tops the mark by a half-inch. The four boys experience a destructuration.)[20]

Fanon shares further insight from Lacanian psychoanalysis in a footnote to the statement above, where he says:

> It would indeed be interesting, on the basis of Lacan's theory of the *mirror period*, to investigate the extent to which the *imago* of his fellow built up in the young white at the usual age would undergo an imaginary aggression with the appearance of the Negro. When one has grasped the mechanism described by Lacan, one can have no further doubt that the real Other for the white man is and will continue to be the black man.[21]

This reflection is based upon Lacan's psychoanalytic developmental theory of the point at which a child recognizes itself as a self (i.e., as an *I*) in a mirror.[22]

Fanon muses on the possibility—again, based upon Lacan's theory— that a projection occurs for the white as they experience the *appearance* of someone who is black due to a disturbance of white people's idealized view of themselves, their *imago*. Moreover, Fanon notes that the "real Other" for white people was and will be black people. This is an important insight that the editors of *The Religion of White Rage* indicate in the introduction to this volume. That is to say, racial animus in the United States has always been generated, not largely by immigration, but by anti-blackness in which immigrants are coded as "not-white-therefore-black." In return, immigrant groups are socialized into American racial hierarchy, which is then coded as "not-white-but-at-least-not-black." Blackness, then, is maintained at the bottom-center of American racial relations while exploitation of black bodies becomes the vehicle for social mobility.

Another feature of destructuration for Fanon is that it is experienced as *homoerotic*. Perhaps conceptualized in the androcentric configurations of the oedipal complex—or a critique of them—Fanon, in my estimation, intimates that white men envy black men. Regarding this psychoanalytic notion of destructuration, I am interested in the homoerotic implications. To be sure, these appear in sublimated configuration in *often*-coded racialized patriotic art forms, most clearly seen in nineteenth- and twentieth-century patriotic anthems, pledges, and cinema, which emphasize white masculine manhood and virtuous white womanhood; but I am most concerned with the religious implications, which I will later describe briefly.[23] These are coded in sexual and erotic terms as the black world which makes penetrations into whiteness, destabilizing the white world. At bottom, or should I say, "at its core," is *projection*. Which is to say, that which intrudes upon the white—fantasized as both violent and erotic—is the black penis. Accordingly, "the Negro is eclipsed. He is turned into a penis. He *is* a penis,"[24] "a terrifying penis."[25] And this *penis*—again, a representation of black masculine force and of the disturbance of an idealized white fantasy of the world in which it is centered—becomes the master signifier of a fear of loss of that world. Fanon maintains, for example:

> The civilized white man retains an irrational longing for unusual eras of sexual license, of orgiastic scenes, of unpunished rapes, of unrepressed incest. In one way theses fantasies respond to Freud's life instinct. Projecting his own desires onto the Negro, the white man behaves "as if" the Negro really had them.[26]

Fanon contends that the black is eclipsed in these fantasies and reduced to a racist *imago*, which is then, I argue, sublimated in contemporary white art forms. Historian of religion Charles H. Long refers to these significations, which he understands as religious, as the "second creation."[27] Long asserts:

> These terms are part and parcel of the universalizing and critical structures of the modern Western consciousness. In many respects, most of those cultures which have given rise to the religions of the oppressed were "created" for the second time by the critical categories of the West.[28]

He continues, "These people were created out of the theoretical disciplines stemming from the Enlightenment."[29]

Given such discursive violence, the object is not known and cannot be known—black people, then, are specters, which merely haunt the existence of the Western world: "The first true word about them in this 'second creation' was from a knowledge *about* them rather than a knowledge *of* them. No intimacy of language was to be found in this second creation."[30] Black people are, thus, perpetual problems of the West, especially in the United States, which *regresses* during moments of political strife and contention in which its world is cast as in jeopardy, primarily because of the threat of black people, especially of black men.

One of the most famous illustrations of this was the case of "Willie" Horton, who was a felon, who benefited from a furlough program while Michael Dukakis was governor of Massachusetts. While on furlough from a Massachusetts prison in 1974, Horton raped a white woman and robbed her fiancé. During Dukakis's bid for the American presidency against the elder George H. W. Bush in 1988, the Bush campaign ran an attack ad against Dukakis, suggesting that *this* was what could be expected if Dukakis was elected president rather than George Bush. The implications were clear: the white world needed protection from African American men, who might otherwise rob and rape white men and women, respectively. It is no wonder that—during this age of the racial politics of Donald Trump—conversations about the Willie Horton ad, which was endorsed by supporters of Bush, have found their way into contemporary American politics.[31] The ad instantiates historical racialized tropes about African American men as the impetus for white social movements and political action. The stereotypes reduce and reproduce American mythologies about black people as inhuman. Likewise, for Fanon, the black is not a person, is not human. It is an *object*. Overdetermined and supersaturated by centuries of racial mythologies, philosophies of inferiority, and irrational fear, the relationship to the black as phobogenic object is precisely the site for a psychoanalytic reading of the religion of white rage, since what it offers is a language and method in which to investigate white people's affective and religious relationship to black people in the current moment.

The second primary claim is that *whiteness is dependent on the black object and experiences anxiety and irrational fear of its loss*. This is the function and meaning of white consolidation, that is, to maintain black as object and to protect whiteness from potential transversals and presumed contamination and to ensure the centered endurance of whiteness as a complex. For this to be so, it needs the negative binary meanings that it ascribes to blackness, and whiteness does not exist outside of this relationship with blackness (and the greater world of color). Robin DiAngelo's *White Fragility: Why It's So Hard to Talk to White People about Racism* has received mixed reviews, but a strength of the book is DiAngelo's understanding of the relationship between whiteness and blackness. Consistent with my argument, DiAngelo maintains:

> Whiteness has always been predicated on blackness . . . there was no concept of race or a white race before the need to justify the enslavement of Africans. Creating a separate and inferior black race simultaneously created the "superior" white race: one concept could not exist without the other. In this sense, whites need black people; blackness is essential to the creation of white identity.[32]

In other words, whiteness has no inherent meaning. It attains its meaning through *difference* and *negation*, and as Fanon indicated, the black object will always be the "real Other" onto which these meanings are projected.[33]

Accordingly, this object-Other is phobogenic for white people, which Fanon casts—following other psychoanalysts—as a neurosis, which is linked to, in my own words, a primary narcissistic object loss, in this case, a subjective insecurity due to the absence of the mother.[34] I conceptualize "mother" here as the absence or loss of an atavistic conception of origins and belonging. In Freudian terms, then, this fixation with and need for a black object is both regressive and erotic, that is, a reversion to an earlier stage in development in which it is psychically invested and bonded.[35] Which is to say, there is a substantial investment of libidinal energy, which would accompany an object-cathexis, the resolution of which has to be realized in order to move through human development healthily. Instead, whiteness is cathected to the black object. In its inability to emancipate blackness (or itself from blackness)—because of the anxiety and irrational fear that accompanies the idea of losing its object and the meanings that it projects on it, out of which its own identity and world emerges—whiteness exists in, rather *is*, a state of *melancholia*. Freud distinguished melancholia from mourning. Mourning is healthy and conscious. For him, it was/is the ability to grieve the loss of a love object in which libido would be withdrawn from its attachments to that object, making a person available to form new attachments.[36] Melancholia (unconscious) is pathological for Freud. It prevails when one refuses to grieve, to release an object and one's investments, hence, to engage in the process of de-idealization and decathexis.[37]

I contend that whiteness is an enduring state of melancholia because it is nostalgic for an idealized past, an imperialistic and colonial age, in which it had its origins.[38] It is characterized by a fear of loss of and a simultaneous attachment to the black object. Regarding whiteness's melancholia, Anne Anlin Cheng would seem to agree. In her *The Melancholy of Race: Psychoanalysis, Assimilation, and Hidden Grief*, she claims:

> Dominant white identity in America operates melancholically—as an elaborate identificatory system based on psychical and social consumption-and-denial. This diligent system of melancholic retention appears in different guises. Both racist and white liberal discourses participate in this dynamic, albeit out of different motivations. The racists need to develop elaborate ideologies in order to accommodate their actions with official ideals, while white liberals need to keep burying the racial others in order to memorialize them.[39]

Cheng contends that those who say that they are neutral or that they do not have ideological commitments are the most melancholic of all—following Toni Morrison—because of the difficult psychical work of not-seeing. I disagree with an aspect of Cheng's contention, however. She frames her method of psychoanalysis of whiteness in terms of "racists and liberals," a distinction without a difference. Both are racist, and both are necessary for the maintenance of white domination, the current racial arrangements, and their material effects. I signal my denial of this distinction in my conception of "white consolidation," in this chapter, by the trope "active and passive" to signal the fact that the passivity of some whites, "liberals" in Cheng's language, is also necessary to uphold and reproduce the system of whiteness, which African American scholars, such as E. Franklin Frazer in the early 1920s and Bobby E. Wright in the 1980s, were also characterizing as psychopathology.[40]

Whiteness is melancholic and, therefore, pathological because of a perpetual return to its myth of beginnings and its mythicized representation—the white worker—in times of perceived crisis and loss, loss of its symbols, culture, worldview, and the benefits therein.[41] Thus, it desires to replace what it perceives as potentially lost with something new—the black object, the ultimate symbol of the colonial age of conquest and civilization. In America, this sense of beginnings is utterly and indissociably linked to the enslavement of African Americans (and the displacement of Native Americans). "Make America Great Again" is, therefore, a melancholic trope, a cry for meaning, and the mythological attempt to traverse time and space to re-enact and re-establish an exemplary model of life for white people. In the case of the black object, whiteness refuses object-relational substitution, a transitional object that might allow it to become something else, something more developed and egalitarian. Instead, it hangs onto the black object, which it drags and dirties.[42] It is tethered to it. It needs it.

The fantasy to which "Make America Great Again" points is, in fact, a myth of eternal return.[43] The call is quintessentially white and religious as the atavistic enactment of an archaic ontology, which is characterized by a platonic structure in the attempt to render the mythic and the existential consonant.[44] In Freudian terms, it is a regression to an idealized state of existence (of early childhood), a narcissism, which arrests white communal development because of its resistance—passively or actively—to racial progress.[45] Despite these insights from studies of psychoanalysis and race,[46] Fanon's psychoanalytic and phenomenological argumentation seems to dispute the contention that whiteness is dependent upon blackness for its meaning and therefore is lived and enacted as an irrational fear of loss: "For not only must the black man be black; he must be black in relation to the white man. Some critics will take it on themselves to remind us that this proposition has a converse. I say that this is false."[47] If, indeed, Fanon disputes that blackness is a necessary condition that marks whiteness and makes its emergence and maintenance possible, then I offer the preceding as an extension and critical intervention into Fanonian psychoanalysis. His argument that the black object is phobogenic, a stimulus to anxiety, would seem to imply this as a possibility if not a necessity.

Black People as the *Mysterium Tremendum et Fascinans* of the Religion of White Rage: A Conclusion

The Religion of White Rage argues that white religious fervor is a response to perceived black racial progress or desire for progress in America and simultaneously a fear of loss—loss of all kinds of social, economic, erotic, political, psychological, and material benefits that attend whiteness as an embodied and discursive reality. Though the signifier can be separated from the signified, these benefits are largely accumulated by those who identify as and, at the same time, are perceived as white. Moreover, whiteness is best understood as a religious orientation, which, in the context of the present volume, erupts and consolidates during moments of crisis when it perceives its world to be in jeopardy. We want to understand these moments as generative of the religion of white rage, producing religious fervor, revival-like activities and narratives; sometimes congealing in mass movements and appeals for a return to mythical white utopias and originary form—the white worker; and tacitly sanctioned by their very existence even when they are explicitly criticized by white people, who seek to distinguish themselves as "good" whites. Sometimes these movements institutionalize and become "mainstream" religious communities that the culture recognizes as such, and sometimes they do not.

I have argued something similar here. My chapter has contended that whiteness constructs black people as objects, which they need for their own identity and existence. This whiteness then serves as their primary religious orientation. Whenever whiteness feels threated, when it perceives the potential risk—even if this threat is not a quantitative or factual reality—that it might be decentered cosmologically and in the culture, thus relinquishing accumulation, whiteness consolidates, often across multiple indices of violence. This perceived threat, consolidation, and repetition are structural aspects of the religion of white rage. Moreover, this structure always includes a narrative retrieval that cites the need for return to a mythical space of white utopia. "Make America Great Again" is such a call to retrieve a myth of beginnings in service of its contemporary enactment in the world. In other words, this structure is one of ritual and myth. I have then interpreted these phenomena using and extending a Fanonian psychoanalysis.

My conclusions are about the nature of the black object upon which whiteness depends. First, for Fanon, the black object is experienced as an irrational fear of the homoerotic, and, second, whiteness suffers an irrational fear at the potential loss of the black object. That whiteness is ambivalent about the black object, which many writers, including Fanon, Robert Hood, Martin Luther King, Jr., and James Perkinson, noted, frames the thrust of my final observation. That is to say, the black object is regarded with attraction and repulsion, desire and disdain, hate and allure, fear and fascination, and I want to suggest that this is the same structure that appears in the classical theory of religion, namely, of Rudolph Otto.

Otto argues in his classic, *The Idea of the Holy* (1923), that religious experience is *sui generis*, that is, it is irreducible to any other category. It is a thing in and of itself. It is a state or condition that is wholly other or from something other than natural order. Because it is non-rational (neither rational nor irrational) and irreducible it cannot be defined or described. It can only be approximated through symbols or ideograms, which can only point the way to it but can never capture it. "It cannot be expressed by means of anything else, just because it is so primary and elementary a datum in our psychical life, and therefore only definable through itself."[48] The primary datum of religious consciousness is this non-rational feeling of the numinous which leads to annihilation of the self, "submerged and overwhelmed by its own nothingness in contrast to that which is supreme above all creatures."[49] One feels only one's creatureliness as the numinous is felt as an objective presence outside the self. Otto argues that this feeling of the numinous, this irreducible religious experience, has a structure, in his words: "*Mysterium Tremendum et Fascinans*," fear and fascination, awfulness/terror and attractiveness, the same psychic structure in which whiteness experiences the black object.

I conclude with this observation: whereas in Otto's schema, the numinous—the irreducible datum of the religious—is felt as an object outside of the self, which annihilates the self, we find in whiteness a metaphysical inversion of Otto in which the *Mysterium Tremendum et Fascinans* becomes the *black object*. Like the numinous, it is experienced as an objective reality external to it. In other words, whiteness needs blackness as a metaphysical—and therefore religious—*object*, along the lines of Rudolf Otto's analysis. However, instead of annihilating the subject, as is the case in Otto's analysis, whiteness uses black religious objects to produce a metaphysics where it *remains* the subject. The black object, which whiteness needs and upon which it is dependent, therefore, becomes a source, perhaps *the* source *sui generis* for the religious consciousness and religious meaning of whiteness.

TWO

You Will Not Replace Us! An Exploration of Religio-Racial Identity in White Nationalism

Darrius Hills

Vice News Tonight produced a documentary entitled "Charlottesville: Race and Terror," featuring several interviews from prominent white nationalists and spokespersons for the "Unite the Right" rally.[1] Early footage from the segment captured crowds of whites, mostly male, carrying Tiki torches and chanting the following: "Jews will not replace us!," "Blood and Soil," and "Whose streets?! Our streets!" The 2017 protests and riots in Charlottesville, Virginia, featuring the display of white nationalist fervor, which has only swelled post-election 2016, has yielded strong scholarly interest in the interplay between right-wing politics, racial demagoguery, and racialized violence. What is also striking are the deeply felt sentiments and the entrenched sense of insularity that drives white nationalist efforts to cultivate political and ideological resources toward the building of a white nation-state in America. Underscoring many of these efforts is an existential concern about the displacement of Western cultural vitality. Thomas Williams traces the white nationalist rallying cry centering on white "replacement" to French existentialist thinkers such as Renaud Camus, who, in response to demographic shifts in Europe, due to the influx of black and brown immigrants, lamented, as recently as 2012, *le grand remplacement,* or the great replacement of Europeans from their native environs.[2] The possibility of white ethnic and civilizational substitution, to restate, is an existential crisis. Given the implications of this intense racialized sense of meaning and its concomitant geography of space and place, or the constitutive frames of reference meant to order and sanction some bodies and not others in particular locales, another potential area for further thinking involves the interrogation of possible religious undertones that may underscore expressions of white nationalism in contemporary American discourses. For all intents and purposes, white nationalism, or white nationalist ideology broadly conceived, is expressed through racialist philosophies aimed at upholding the cultural, intellectual, and political superiority and enfranchisement of those of European descent. This defense is furthermore articulated through a concern for the continuation of white cultural survival, which will be discussed below.

But what is religious about white nationalism? Is "religion" a useful description at all? What is it, in the worldview of the white nationalist, that speaks to the preservation and defense of the collective racial self that may reveal categories of meaning that parallel religious fervor? I draw upon the work of Charles Long and Emile Durkheim to suggest how religiosity functions in white nationalist thought, with particular attention to the powerful mechanisms of identity formation that yield meaning and structure to mark one as part of a specialized tribe, and thus teases out how current expressions of white loss in white nationalist ideologies accentuate the intersections of religious thought and race in American culture. I argue that white nationalists, facing the realities of a shifting, globalized context that problematizes the staying power of their dominance, have recalibrated and regrouped to create a unique racial identity infused with religious significance meant to sustain itself in light of this shifting.

Replacement Woes: The Paranoid Style and the Hope of White Reclamation

For many, the 2008 presidential election was a watershed moment in American race relations. President Obama's victory seemed to represent strong crossover appeal among African American, Latinx, and white demographics. Obama seemed to symbolize that America had fulfilled its promise of a "post-racial" society: we'd moved closer toward an unhyphenated America born of post-civil rights racial politics, and we now truly embodied the belief in the "content of one's character" rather than skin color. How wrong this supposition was. In the wake of the transition toward the Obama administration, hate crimes rose significantly, rumors and conspiracies about President Obama's racial and religious biography found an eager audience among far-right, conservative demographics, and perhaps most interestingly, white Americans expressed a fading optimism about their place, space, and futurity.[3] This is the social and psychological phenomenon that characterizes the state of white feelings of loss. It is an existential crisis premised upon the strain of polemical tension: the desire for white supremacy and the perception of a fading (but not final) grasp on the reins of political, social, and economic control under white Americans.

White racial loss, to be clear, is more a sentiment than reflective of material reality. Per most sources of empirical data on wealth and health gaps along racial lines, it is quite obvious that white America, collectively speaking, is doing quite well. However, if it is true that full equality feels like oppression to the privileged, then the material and social gains of minoritized communities are no doubt a source of consternation among whites suffering nostalgic yearning for *racial status quo ante*. Following this observation, the white nationalist cries of "You will not replace us!" begin to reveal a deeper internal psychical reckoning. The sentiment of white racial loss is situated within the tailspin of *replacement woes*. In the case of their impassioned defense of Confederate markers, for example, the fears are palpable because the removal of cultural linchpins that literally map out a white "world" indicate an unsuitability of their environment that is no longer inhabitable due to the presence and intrusion of "others," who've largely overtaken white place and space. The vestiges of white culture are being hurled into "oblivion."[4] Richard Hofstadter's classic work on the "paranoid style" in American political life and psychology may provide some useful clarity and insight into the phenomenon of white nationalist replacement woes.[5]

Having roots in the McCarthyism of 1950s and continuing into the contemporary "culture warrior" posture of the evangelical religious right,[6] the paranoid style describes a psychological maladaptation in American politics that imagines that one's political interests and group are subject to regimes premised upon hostility and disenfranchisement in which there is "the existence of a vast, insidious, preternaturally effective international conspiratorial network designed to perpetrate acts of the most fiendish character"[7] against specific groups. For our present context, with specific attention to white nationalist re-emergence and its links to the political right wing, the paranoid style features an interesting mix of conspiratorial inclinations and the distrust of "others" beyond the national, regional, and ethnic borders.

When considered from a contemporary standpoint, the paranoid style is tethered to the heart of present manifestations of right-wing political presentation. The *political* paranoid holds that society as we know it is decayed, socially and culturally. Hofstadter remarks, pointing to both the feelings of loss and nostalgic hopefulness of renewal:

> The modern right wing feels dispossessed: America has been largely taken away from them and their kind, though they are determined to try to repossess it and to prevent the final destructive act of subversion. The old American virtues have already been eaten away by cosmopolitans and intellectuals; the old competitive capitalism has been gradually undermined by socialist and communist schemers; the old national security and independence have

been destroyed by treasonous plots, having as their most powerful agents not merely outsiders and foreigners but major statesmen seated at the very centers of American power.[8]

While Hofstadter used this concept to describe his particular context and the social and psychological components of the conservative politics of 1950s America, his analysis remains a reliable heuristic to understand the mindset of white nationalists of the present and uncovers the rationale underscoring their political maneuvering. In particular, there is a conspiratorial bent underscoring the paranoid style—one linked to the large-scale persecution of certain groups. In the case of the white nationalists, the conspiratorial paranoia is linked to the belief that white culture and peoplehood are targeted for eradication—whether through the "threat" of multiculturalism, or through outright violence from the inferior non-whites. In the vein of the paranoid style, white nationalist replacement woes feature added historical and political significance. The insistence that white peoplehood, values, culture, and presence not be "replaced" is a desperate revelation of the fears pertaining to white existence in a world marked by non-homogeneity and difference.

For many of these nationalists, racialized replacement is akin to social death—an eschatological fading of the late, great white race on the heels of integrationism, patriarchal decline, and the social, political, and economic advancement of non-whites. The death and decline of whiteness, imagined or real, will always be met with resistance and a traumatic confrontation with the implications of mortality. It is important to note that death in this sense is not particularly a concern with, or fear of, physical death, but rather, the death of a systematized, institutional, and cultural mainstay of whiteness as dominant and prescriptive for American life. Christopher Driscoll refers to this kind of death as the dismantling of the "white man's god complex"—or the tendency to deify and heighten whiteness in ways that are particularly destructive for non-white bodies.[9] Kelly Brown Douglas's *Stand Your Ground: Black Bodies and the Justice of God* (2015) highlights some of the consequences of the effort to safeguard cherished white space and place, which she locates squarely in gun laws that authorize and legitimate deadly force against even the assumption of encroachment by non-white others.[10] As threats to the preservation of white space and place, Trayvon Martin and even more recently, Botham Jean, were both casualties of the ontological expansion of whiteness in ways that rendered suspect the "dangerous," menacing black male body.[11]

The decline of whiteness, says the paranoid, requires revolutionary attention, and in particular, needs someone who can articulate the presumed persecutory and dehumanizing regime perpetrated against whites. Who, therefore, arises as a kind of white ethno-nationalist spokesman in these periods of great decline? It is reasonable to cite President Trump as an embodiment of many of the characteristics of the paranoid spokesman. In returning to Hofstadter, such a spokesman

> sees the fate of [civilization] in apocalyptic terms—he traffics in the birth and death of whole worlds, whole political orders, whole systems of human values. He is always manning the barricades of civilization. He constantly lives at a turning point: it is now or never in organizing resistance to conspiracy.[12]

A good example of this level of rhetoric on Trump's part is easily identifiable in both his inauguration speech, which liberally discussed the "carnage" of American culture, save his leadership, and his ongoing anti-FBI platform, citing the influence of liberal progressivism and a "deep state" conspiracy undermining his presidency.[13] It is important to recall that with the paranoid style as exemplified in a figure like Trump, the distinguishing feature is not "the absence of verifiable facts, but rather the curious leap in imagination that is always made at some critical point in the recital of events."[14] With authoritarian bluster, unburdened by either facts or nuance, Trump has been popular among white, conservative communities because of an ardent, jingoistic exhortation of American exceptionalism—an insistence upon "America First" that is both homiletical and political grandstanding, positioning the United States as the perpetual "winner" over against "losers."[15]

Replacement-as-death, as a feature of white nationalist concern, also includes an assumption of white loss that is always linked with the prospect of non-white success, access, achievement, or improvement that calls into question white male supremacy and *cultural hegemony*. The politics of progress and cultural hegemony is particularly evident in the current administration's response to the cultural and regional shifting within the immigration debate. In recent speeches, President Trump's rhetoric has fallen squarely in line with white nationalist talking points about the loss, replacement, and transformation pertaining to white, European cultural norms. During a NATO-hosted summit meeting, Trump lamented that Europe "was losing its culture," in the face of its increase in migrant communities, and suggested a similar outcome for America if the border barriers were not strengthened. According to this racial logic, a "better" society is a homogenous white society. In another speech, to Naval Academy graduates, Trump lauded America's heroic "ancestors [who] tamed a continent," leading many critics to link his comments to a genocidal drive evoking America's sordid history in its treatment of native, indigenous populations. Those ancestors referenced, to be sure, easily pass the test as the "mighty white [and male] heroes"[16] violently and victoriously creating a place for the emergence and birth of a white nation-state, or a colonial system of governance administered through the rigid demarcation of essential differences between peoples and cultures.[17] Michael Kimmel offers additional descriptions of this sense of racialized loss as a function of bewilderment responsive to a more racially and sexually egalitarian society, referring to it as white (male) "aggrieved entitlement."[18] Given the aggrieved status that now presumably characterizes the white social and racial body in America, a voice is needed to correct and right the racial and cultural wrongs.

It is this feature of President Trump's presence in American political and social life that has been most impactful upon the perceptions of race and place for non-white communities. While the paranoid style that has fueled white replacement woes seems, at the outset, devoted to a vision of hopelessness, this vision stops short of the full-out nihilism that may naturally arise from such a posture toward the world.[19] This perhaps explains why, in part, Trump has a great tendency to overstate his impact upon the restoration and renewal of this great decline of American exceptionalism. In his mind, he is the grand "deal maker" who can make all things right and save America from itself. There remains, however, the question of why and how such a person appeals to scores of working-class whites who have no cultural or class-based connection to President Trump—that is, aside from the racial category "white."

Many white Americans, even in poor and working-class sectors, see in the president a representation of their own social aspirations, which Hofstadter described as "status politics," in political decision making, and furthermore tether to him a *messianic* hope of renewal, restoration, and reclamation of white place and space in light of the presumed decline of (white) America under former President Obama. Status politics are aspirational and hierarchical in nature, indicative of the ways in which persons lodged within lower social and economic classes uphold political ideals and practices that reveal vicarious desires for advancement through an identification with the privileged classes above them—both in culture and in financial influence.[20] The interstices of white cultural complexity are also critical here, particularly when considered alongside historical studies on the different modes of "whiteness" as reflected in and demarcated by class and caste.

Keri Leigh Merritt's important work, *Masterless Men: Poor Whites and Slavery in the Antebellum South*, offers an insightful reminder that among whites there has been an evolving and complex system of white identity formation tied to equally evolving notions of class and cultural distinctiveness. Like other racial and ethnic groups, white Americans are complex—there is no universal whiteness in American culture. This is important to remember, as it prompts an awareness of both the convergence and the divergence of political, social, and economic interests among different classes of whites, and how these may impact their commitment to particular racial politics. As Merritt notes, during the antebellum period, there was often strong distrust and outright hostility between landless and non-slave-holding whites and the white slave-owning aristocracy. Poorer whites often held a strong sense of class consciousness—prompting tension with wealthier counterparts who deemed them uncouth burdens.[21] These conflicts were exacerbated through the white elites' maintenance of economic power through social control of poor whites through vagrancy laws, the prohibition of alcoholic consumption, and the stifling of interracial association between poorer whites, slaves, and free blacks.[22] Nancy Isenberg's *White Trash* provides a historical overview of the varied manifestations and (self-)perceptions of "whiteness" at the dawn of the American republic and into the present. Like Merritt, Isenberg's study also reveals the extent to which there were markers of caste and class in white communities across the American Southland and beyond, and posits this demographic as the "forgotten men"—a symbol of white struggle and hardship.[23] The forgotten-man theme is particularly relevant, especially when juxtaposed with the reality of strong representations of whites in poorer, less healthy, and economically strapped communities largely run by conservative leadership who voted for Donald Trump.[24]

Studies such as Merritt's and Isenberg's on the intersections between whiteness, labor, and class are necessary because both illustrate the deeply ingrained sources of social, racial, and perhaps existential, dissatisfaction felt by many whites from lower socioeconomic backgrounds that may prompt them to vote with their racial *bona fides* while eschewing economic and political interests.[25] If the aphorism "If you can't beat 'em, join 'em" is operative, many white Americans may see the current White House administration as the last, best hope for the reclamation of higher class and racial aspirations in light of the onslaught of miseries imagined as a result of the racial and cultural disorientation wielded by the gains of multiculturalism, integration, and the shifting terrain of religious demographical representation.

Many white Americans have looked to President Trump for a sense of hope in the midst of the racial, cultural, and economic storm.[26] Another factor to consider is why they've done so, and through what means. The rise in white nationalist activity and participation, which is also coupled with a rise in hate crimes, offers some indication behind the culture and psychology of whites who embrace of the tenets of white nationalist identity and politics, which promise a collectivized and reclaimed racial personhood. The next portion of this chapter shall offer an interpretation of white nationalist identity formation as a religious endeavor, to the degree that it offers white Americans a sense of purpose, belonging, and orientation in a "new" America that no longer reflects racial and cultural homogeneity. As illustrated through the anthropological and sociological theory of religion in the work of Emile Durkheim, the survival, renewal, and reclamation of the "white tribe" embodies a sense of ultimacy and finality—giving white nationalists the psychical and philosophical wherewithal to advance their view of the world and their values.

The Tribe is my Purpose: Totemic Religion and White Nationalist Identity

Black bodies have often functioned as the forge on which whiteness itself—white humanity, white culture, white values—is articulated and defined. Particularly, black bodies have been exploited and commodified through the institution of slavery, but have also functioned as sites of death-dealing surveillance and suspicion within the context of proximal contact with whites. Kelly Brown Douglas notes that black bodies in America are *problem bodies*, perpetually imagined as impositions upon whiteness as sacred space and cherished property. Such a discursive framing of the [lack] of humanity of African Americans and other non-white groups is reified, with deadly consequences, through firearm laws that loosen the reins on the applicability of justifiable deadly force.[27]

In a social context that reads black boys and men as more threatening, intractable, and menacing, and black girls and women with additional apprehension, "stand your ground" culture does not bode well for the African American community's wellbeing and safety.[28] Tommy Curry's new work, *The Man-Not: Race, Class, Genre, and the Dilemmas of Black Manhood*, also explores the black male body as a defective, problem body. Curry cites how the black male body is *only body*, which then becomes a proxy for the entirety of his being. The construction of black men in this manner, both in academic theories and in the racist and class-based institutional framing of American life, thought, and political arrangements, renders black men invisible and irredeemable as subjects worthy of further study as victims of violence themselves.[29]

Through the construction of white space, place, embodiment, and gender identity, there has been a long effort in America to set apart and distinguish the white collective and individual body from non-white others. The consequence of a rarefied conception of white identity is linked to what Henri Bergson referred to as a "closed society." Closed societies are social systems in which ambiguity, complexity, and "messiness" are not tolerated and deemed destructive to the formation and distinctiveness of the group or societal cohesion. Here, monolithic uniformity and rigid boundaries are the operative mechanism(s) of group life and group think.[30] Such a system features an insider/outsider paradigm—a veritable tribe meant to provide inclusion and distinction to the "in-crowd" while sanctioning, rendering suspect, and ostracizing those beyond its scope. Given the perception of disorientation, displacement, and loss of cultural vitality, the white nationalist collective has regrouped as part of the process of constructing a closed white-race society. As we will uncover in the work of Emile Durkheim, religious behavior(s) function(s) similarly.

Charles Long theorizes the nature of the religious as a uniquely human enterprise to meaningfully reconcile oneself with reality. Long understands religion as "orientation in the ultimate sense," with regard to "how one comes to terms with the ultimate significance of one's place in the world."[31] A focus on the relational and orienting features of religion is useful, as it assists in explaining and clarifying how displaced whites may find recourse in response to cultural and racial loss through the self-affirmative presumptions of white superiority in white nationalist ideology. It is worth repeating that the legibility of whiteness, or more specifically, white cultural survival, is considered on the decline in both conservative Republican and white nationalist spaces. This is at the heart of the replacement woes mentioned above. In white nationalist psychology, the decline of white cultural values, along with the numerical representation of white, European, and Anglo-Saxon persons, is virtually synonymous to a racialized bloodletting—the death of whiteness. Given this observation, it is necessary to again give some attention to a working definition of white nationalism. Damon Berry argues that white nationalism in America "is far from monolithic, but obsession with white racial survival defines and unites white nationalists more than any other issue."[32] Definitive framings of white nationalism are difficult because of the many expressions of nationalist discourses centering white and European identity—expressions that obviously expand far beyond the continental U.S. and thus embody different historical, social, and political reference points not necessarily pertinent to historical currents and trends unique to race in American culture. Acknowledging this limitation, I shall simply begin with an assessment of general characteristics reified in white nationalist discourse: *the appeal to racial protectionism/preservation as a means of safeguarding white survival.*

For instance, Michael Barkun traces and constructs the terms and tenets of the Christian Identity movement as a unique *religio-racial* organization devoted to the promotion and interests of white cultural survival. In using the term "religio-racial," which I borrow from Judith Weisenfeld,[33] I refer to the process of vesting white European identity, heritage, and cultural norms with a sense of ultimacy as a reference point in the construction of reality. In other words, white religio-racial identity formation is the expansion of white identity and cultural norms toward a category of ultimate meaning and orientation for white nationalists. Barkun notes that on these terms, whites in the Christian Identity movement subscribe to three key features: 1) white "Aryans" are the true chosen people of Israel, 2) Jews are unconnected to the Israelites, and 3) the world is nearing an apocalyptic struggle between Aryans and the Jewish conspiracy.[34] Christian Identity is anti-Semitic in its theological constructions of race and society; what also stands out in Identity religious thought is the construction of whiteness and white people as an ultimate reference point for the orientation of reality[35] *and* communal construction. White culture, norms, and embodiment, in recalling Bergson, map a closed community demarcated along the lines of race. The closed nature of white identity in the nationalist platform, with implications for the structuring of institutions, is a means of rendering distinctive the white social and physical body and promoting white racial survival in the midst of a cultural and racial shift in America that has displaced whites and white space. What is the nationalist rallying cry "Blood and soil!" but an articulation of the desire for expansion into and onto terrain, geographically and otherwise, considered endemic to white, American birthright, but now deemed zones of (un)inhabitability due to the presence of inferior others?

As noted through Long, religious sentiments and beliefs provide a sense of familiarity and belonging. The "religious" encompasses those behaviors and beliefs that are ultimately significant in their assistance to the quintessentially human endeavor to reconcile oneself with place and function over the course of life. Guided by this assessment of religion, and in shifting to Durkheim and totemic theory, I ask: What, then, are such means of orientation, familiarity, and belonging within the white nationalist religious imagination? What are some of the activities and rituals that contribute to the allaying of white nationalist fears and concerns regarding white place, space, and futurity in the face of a rapidly shifting American demographic that is increasingly brown, increasingly immigrant, and increasingly less white?[36]

Emile Durkheim's *Elementary Forms of Religious Life* (1912) maps the deeply participatory and social quality of religion and the formation of religious identity. While his original research centered on Aboriginal and tribal communal life, organization, and structure, for our purposes, it is his totemic theorization of religion that is useful for the analysis of white nationalism as a religious system and as a construction of identity. Durkheim believed that at the basis of all collective systems of belief there are "fundamental representations and ritual practices" that are elemental in human religious conviction and behavior.³⁷ The efficacy of religious collective systems of faith and/or behaviors is decided upon within the group and reinforced as useful and valuable within the context of the community, which in Durkheim's study centered on observations of aboriginal tribes and clans. The organization of tribes and clans, as Durkheim notes, was built upon democratized symbols that signaled the special nature—the distinct status—of one community over against (an)other community/ies. These symbols, the totems, are communal signifiers that "set apart" varied tribes and clans and distinguish them from other groups.

What I wish to consider is how *whiteness* may function as a totem in white nationalist identity formation. As noted from in Barkun's case study, the construction of white identity in terms of religio-racial tribalism enables the possibility of *ultimate distinction/distinctiveness* tethered to phenotypical white ancestry, culture, and heritage. In totemic religious ideology and practice, the totem is a distinctive marker that embodies a clan, tribe, or society's identity—and represents its highest aspirations, configures its social relations and networks, and unifies its ideal of communal selfhood while also reifying a distinctive identity. However, whiteness is also ontological. As totem, whiteness takes on an emblematic and symbolic quality that aids in the forging of a social world; it symbolizes the existence of a special "team"—a separate community united in and through its shared commitment to the preservation and survival of its specialized status as set apart from other teams. Individuals, says Durkheim, are joined within the totem through kinship, but of "a very special sort"—one grounded not necessarily in blood ties and family, but through a collective acceptance of the totem of the group.³⁸

In framing *whiteness* as a religious totem, the white nationalist struggle to preserve and safeguard the vestiges of white cultural, communal, and ancestral norms can be framed as a sacred and religious undertaking guided by the larger, and possibly penultimate, goal of rendering white culture and identity more legible in a world that is no longer familiar—a world in which white homogeneity cannot be taken for granted, socially or politically. The protection and survival of the symbols and culture prominent in white nationalist platforms parallels that of a religious cause marked by the fight to preserve and render familiar whiteness and white spaces, and therefore, ensure some remnant of white survival. White nationalists see themselves as the newly marginalized peoples facing sure extinction should their political aspiration(s) not be realized and should whites fail to raise their racial consciousness in a polemical manner. Jared Taylor, considered to be the figurehead of the intellectual wing of nationalist thought via his conception of "race realism" and white advocacy, believes that multiculturalism, and the uptick of acceptance for immigrants, will inevitably lead to the "oblivion" of the white race and white culture.[39] Undergirding all of these sentiments is of course the specter of white fear and the perception of white loss, which demands defense through the cultivation of white nation-state political framings over against the perception of non-white progress.

The "threat" preceding this fear of loss and decline, notably as linked to multiculturalism and integration, is posited as a direct assault upon white, Western values and culture. Even the mission and ethos that underscores many white nationalist platforms, and white supremacy groups generally, known as the "14 Words," hints at this fear of existential and cultural loss: "We must secure the existence of our race and a future for white children."[40] The 14 Words powerfully address the underlying existential concerns and themes of loss that are imagined as part of the matrix of the burdens of cosmopolitan culture and the need for barriers in the safeguarding of white futurity. Given these initial observations, white nationalism may be framed as any ideology or platform that perceives of white, European communities as under threat from non-white "others." This perception provides the justification necessary for the political, economic, and social organization and development of a white nation-state. The creation of such a white nation-state ensures the survival of white people(s) and culture over against the rising tides of multiculturalism.

To be sure, the heightened enthusiastic response of whites toward many of these features of white nationalist thought is disturbing—for any tendency among racial groups and ethnicities to promote insidious brands of separatism is unsettling for many Americans. Given the reality of the increase in white nationalist activity, activism, and enthusiasm in the current political climate,[41] scholars examining the intersections of religion and race are left with much material, culturally and socially, to interrogate in light of the role that that President Trump's rhetoric and political ideology have played as a galvanizing polemic that implicates race, religious symbolism, and the impact upon American politics and race relations. To complete this chapter, I turn to womanist religious thought, discourses developed by black women scholars of religion, as a useful conversation partner that may assist our efforts to unearth new conceptual frameworks that can challenge the divisive and "set-apart" racial logics that have gained such power and are instilled into our national consciousness. It is my view that these perspectives provide a relational impetus that is a healthy alternative to racialized estrangement in the current climate.

A Response: A Reconsideration of Humanity

White nationalist fears of replacement, while clearly linked to a paranoia regarding the arrangement of white place and space, also suggest a certain (dis)ease with the prospect of knowing and being known by "others." That is, white nationalists are driven by the logics of estrangement from neighbor—rendering non-whites unknown and unknowable in their particularized racial imagination. In the great zeal and haste to demarcate white race and space, white nationalists have become so entrenched in the preservation of their own articulation of racial identity, what Paul Gilroy refers to as "epidermal thinking,"[42] that they have also diminished the possibility of connection to neighbor. Contemporary scholars of African American religious thought and theology have established clear links between religious thinking and colonial logics resulting in the disconnect and rupture of communal ties. Willie Jennings's *The Christian Imagination: Theology and the Origins of Race* discusses the implications of this estrangement through a critique of Christian thought and the problem of its "diseased social imagination," rooted in a proclivity for fusing religious fervor with colonial empire and the displacement of African diasporic communities. Sylvester Johnson makes use of historical and post-colonial critique to map out the social, political, and economic structures that conditioned the religious traditions of the African Diaspora, noting that any serious consideration of black religion generally must be framed in relation to the "architecture of empire" in the colonial world—resulting in the stifling of the humanity of the Africans and African Americans through the construction of a white nation-state.[43] In keeping with these and other perspectives in religious studies that critique the insidious fusion of race and place as grounded in exclusionary theologies and discourses that dismantle the ties of relationality,[44] I turn to insights from M. Shawn Copeland's *Enfleshing Freedom: Body, Race, and Being* to suggest recourse from regressive outlines of white nationalist arrangements of space, place, and identity.

In commenting on the "racialized horizon" as the constructive apparatus that legitimizes the exclusionary framings of race and space in human community, Copeland cites the construction of bias as central to its scope. Engaging the process theology of Bernard Lonergan,[45] Copeland traces racialized biases to "more or less conscious and deliberate choice, in light of what we perceive as a potential threat to our well-being, to exclude further information or data from consideration in our understanding, judgment, discernment, decision, and action."[46] Bias, on this measure, is indeed exclusionary, but also prompts apprehension and fearfulness of new insights and experiences. Pertinent to our concerns with white nationalism and religious thought, this apprehension is extended toward *persons and bodies* deemed outside of the purview and communal construction of whiteness. This modality of bias retreats from the confrontation and presence of the "other"—rendering the other unknown and unknowable—an outright refusal of the moment of encounter.[47]

In response to the exclusionary logics of white supremacy and perhaps white theologies, an alternative read on black bodies and dispossessed groups that centralizes the relational and the communal as productive in identity formation may be fruitful. Citing the need for remembering the bodies and experiences of black women as the new subject of theological anthropology, and thus, sacralizing black bodies as sites of redemption and meaning, Copeland addresses the primordial foundation of identity through the notion of the *humanum*. The quest for the humanum in each of us involves the expansion of human identity toward the realm of the relational and connective, which then becomes the means of achieving solidarity. The humanum concept is a dynamic read of the nature of human selfhood, involving the "recognition of the humanity of the 'other' as human along with regard for the 'other' in her (and his) own otherness."[48]

The human, ontologically considered, is relational in orientation, movement, and purpose. To reject either this feature of our identity or the effort to heighten it, is to transgress the humanum in favor of an asymmetrical and unbalanced existence; this only exacerbates disunity and brokenness in relationships, interpersonally and within the larger web of social life. In other words, the segregationist and estrangement logics of white supremacy and white nationalism are inhuman—a complete disavowal of the relational and connective ties that locate humanity on the trajectory toward a more humane and cohesive version of itself. The biases and exclusionary logics that ground white nationalist identity formation, which I link to religio-racial totemism, are indicative of a particularly insidious form of (de)humanization—an anti-relational, anti-neighbor conception of human identity that is destructive to the degree that it kills any hope for mutuality, reciprocal exchange, and the sharing of knowledge. It is also important to point out that violation of the humanum is doubly damaging, both for white nationalists and for those deemed "other." It is damaging to the white nationalists because they are in effect deprived of full life by acting in bad faith as it relates to the structure and content of human identity as a relational social. It is damaging to "others" because precisely in and through the othering process, non-white bodies and perspectives are relegated to zones of non-being, which prompt the very kinds of violent discursive and physical regimes that render such bodies suspicious, and thus, subject to violent resistance.[49]

What is needed at this historical moment is an embrace of solidarity and connection as key to human (self-)understanding. Copeland finds recourse through the symbolic and embodied character of the Eucharist—a participatory framing of both human identity and communal ties toward the hope of reconciliation and renewal.[50] While the confessional implications of Copeland's perspective go beyond the objectives of this chapter, I single out her attention to eucharistic solidarity to point to it as a resource that religious and secular alike can draw upon as a creative medium through which to imagine and practice political, economic, and social resolutions to the community-killing logics embodied in white nationalist thinking. A critical question confronting us on these issues is how do we best draw upon our creative and connective energies to remake ourselves and our varied "worlds" as persons charged with creating more livable spaces for all—spaces that are shaped by difference and polyvocality, and that are underscored by a willingness to embrace these features with mutual respect.

THREE

"I AM that I AM": The Religion of White Rage, Great Migration Detroit, and the Ford Motor Company

Terri Laws and Kimberly R. Enard

Introduction

The term "rage" conjures an image of an instant, even unexpected or unwarranted, emotional conflagration that erupts as the violent expression of extreme anger. Much like a volcano, the conditions for eruption are ever present. Or perhaps, like "road rage," the reaction to the perceived offense is disproportionately explosive relative to the actual cause. It is a matter of when, not if, an eruption will occur, and what will be the trigger. For scholar Carol Anderson,

> The trigger for white rage, inevitably, is black advancement. It is not the mere presence of black people that is the problem; rather, it is blackness with ambition, with drive, with purpose, with aspirations, and with demands for full and equal citizenship. It is blackness that refuses to accept subjugation, to give up.[1]

Here, black presence and its perceived advancement in search of social, economic, civic, and/or political equality are the threats that trigger white rage. They disrupt the firmly held belief that whiteness is supreme; nothing is above it in status or being. "I AM" is the proxy authority God gave a reluctant Moses to reference when he would inevitably be questioned about his authority to lead the Israelites out of Egyptian bondage. In short, "I AM" is *the* aim; it requires of itself and its challengers neither explanation nor justification. "I AM" can be, but is not a reference to *a* being; it simply "is," so it can be status, personal characteristic, being, etc. It is self-defining ideology.

In this chapter, we describe the *something* to which black people refuse to give up and subjugate themselves: the religion of white rage and its idol, white racial supremacy. We argue that the religion of whiteness is held together through ideology and ritual: an ideology that worships white supremacy and periodic rituals of threatened or actual violence or rage which emerge when threatened by black presence and progress, in this instance during the Great Migration era in Detroit. Whites saw a threatening advancement in the arrival of blacks[2] from Southern states in search of freedom from race-based oppression, including physical violence, and jobs in the burgeoning auto industry. This advancement was assisted by the paternalistic "great white father of Dearborn,"[3] Henry Ford, who founded the Ford Motor Company in 1903. Using interdisciplinary references from labor economics, religious studies, public health research, and the history of black Detroit, we examine the religion of white rage in its function as a set of socioeconomic and cultural processes that nurture and legitimate eruptions of white rage for the sake of white racial superiority, specifically as expressed by the demands of white workers. This process uncovers the anxiety of white workers in the face of perceived competition from black labor. This perception emerges even when the ultimate source of the "competition" is a more powerful white man, Henry Ford. Historically, complex and dynamic forms of black religious activity in society countered white religious rage, at times in traditions inherently understood as religious, at other times cloaked in civic and political activity. In whatever form this black activity has taken, its aim has been to refuse to presume that the religion of white rage should be able to operate as though there were no other sociocultural streams in the country. An example from the Great Migration era demonstrates this argument and pattern, yet this pattern is not only historical. Just as troublesome is the way the combination of the idol of white racial supremacy and ritual expressions of white rage reveals that the religion of white rage affects the health of contemporary white and black laborers and the communities where they live.

The Religiosity of White Rage

White supremacy is the aim or end goal of the religion of white rage. As a teleological definition of religion, it allows for worship of a supreme being as well as for worship of an ideology to be the driving force for a collective or community of persons who share the same resolve for themselves and their world. They make meaning of their reality through the lens of the religious aim. These definitions provide flexibility in that which is the focus of religious thought and activity. They offer a grounding perspective of that which is central in worship, the object or aim of obeisance and deference. In Charles Long, for example, "religion is 'orientation'; that is, the means by which persons 'come to terms with the ultimate significance of their place in the world.'"[4] Paul Tillich offers a similar definition for religion: it is one's "ultimate concern."[5] Tillich is also helpful for understanding an approach to the study of religion. In one of his methods of study, culture provides fodder for religious reflection. This engagement goes both ways: culture and religion are mutually reinforcing. Religion carries ideas about culture, and culture, in its narrative and activity expressions, reflects religious imaginary—whether in opposition to cultural developments or in support of seeing culture as all that is reality. Long is also helpful in this endeavor. For him, religion is generative beyond the thoughts that it contains; it both is and generates "experience, expression, motivations, intentions, behaviors" and more.[6] Thus, when white rage is present and allowed to express itself with impunity, it can pose a threat to anyone outside its circle of followers. In short, white supremacy is religious because it is its own ultimate concern of (white) human experience. It is self-referential in the same way that the God of Israel spoke of God's authority, "I AM that I AM." Anyone with this supreme authority can generate, can be motivated by, can express white supremacy through intentions and behaviors. This leads us to *how* the religion of white rage functions within American society. First, we explain the theoretical underpinnings.

To think through *how* the orientation to a belief in white racial superiority functions, we appeal to religion that is *eminently social*, in the words of classic theorist Emile Durkheim.[7] In this vein, religion supports ideas and activities that are meaningful to the collective. The ideas and activities are represented in myths, symbols, and rituals to teach and reinforce the ideals of the "religion" as understood by members of the group or collective. They bind together members of a group whose shared thought and action provides direct and indirect benefits from the material to the emotional.[8] In Durkheim's original theory, he did not intend an orientation; he focused on a sense of identity and how knowledge gets built around supporting that identity through social agreement.[9] Later scholars have extended his work in ways that allow it to be used with the notion of religion as orientation through the concept of the sacred. That which is sacred is identified as something set apart from the common or the day-to-day relevance. Gordon Lynch, building upon Jeffrey Alexander, provides for an understanding of the sacred to fit into this collective interpretive function.[10] Sacred is subjective, determined by the collective's perspective.[11] "(Sacred) things are always identified and protected in mythic story and ritual behavior. Profane [or common] things, contaminants that they are, are always kept at a safe distance."[12]

Long acknowledges that there is a "dominant [American] mythology" that, here, should be thought of as a grounding narrative of the religion of white rage; however, he does not concede that it lives alone in the United States. African Americans, too, have their own narrative of their experience in the U.S.; like its white counterpart, it has social, economic, political, cultural, and religious aspects. Still, the dominant nature of white rage suggests that it needs to be understood for how it works as religious influence in society and within institutions.

For collective white labor, black labor that dares to seek full employment—with health benefits; black labor that seeks to defy the statistic that calculates their unemployment at twice of the rate of white unemployment—in a good economy or bad, is, in the language of Anderson, aspirational black labor, a threat to white labor's sacred right to achieve the freedoms ensconced in the nation's founding documents. Protection of this sacred right is an expression of America's mythic narrative.

For sociologist of religion Robert Bellah, the mythic narrative of America is older than the nation itself, having its genesis in its colonial period.

> In the beginning, and to some extent ever since, Americans have interpreted their history as having religious meaning. They saw themselves as being a "people" in the classical and biblical sense of the word. They hoped they were a people of God.[13]

Early settlers believed that a covenant with God pointed them toward an attitude of liberty as a matter of conversion.[14] This conversion-related pursuit was both individual and collective. There was only a need to identify who fit within the covenant; this was institutionalized through the Constitution and operationalized through the decennial census.[15] Two sets of personal characteristics were especially relevant across the six categories of individuals to be counted in the first census in 1790: whether the person was free and whether the person was white and male.[16]

Race-based slavery was the result of a determination to view black people as inferior, thereby generating racism, which has been called "America's original sin."[17] This phrase, as used by Jim Wallis, a Detroit-born, white evangelical practical theologian, is grounded in Christian teaching that sin is an "evil" in need of "a *spiritual* and moral transformation [which] must be named, exposed, and understood before it can be repented of [emphasis added]."[18] In their enslavement, Africans who were exposed to Christianity were hardly protected from a version that was without harms. Black-theology scholar Dwight Hopkins analyzed slave narratives to understand their religious experience from their perspective, not as interpreted by whites. In one story, representative of the white supremacy embedded within Christianity, a slaveholder came upon a slave he owned; he found the enslaved man praying. Inserting himself into the spiritual life of the enslaved man's petitions to his God, the slaveholder demanded to know what the man was praying about. The enslaved man answered:

> "Oh Marster, I'se just prayin' to Jesus 'cause I wants to go to Heaven when I dies." Belligerently and arrogantly, the Marster replied, "You's my Negro. I get ye to Heaven." Here we touch the heart of white Christianity and theology. The white man believed he filled the mediating and liberating role of Jesus Christ. As the anointed Jesus, the white man possessed omnipotent and salvific capabilities. For black chattel to reach God, then, whites forced African Americans to accept the status of the white race as divine mediator.[19]

The mythic narrative and the slaveholder's white supremacy–laden Christianity both served a religious purpose. "We need myths if we are to transcend the banality of material life. We need narratives if we are to make progress. . ."[20] The covenant was available only to white men, and at that, primarily well-resourced white men. They were in the group that was "a [collective] people of God."[21] Religion does many things for its adherents; among them it provides a sense of identity and group belonging, and it provides a worldview that brings meaning to reality, which may surround a central tenet within the worldview.[22] The central American identity is its earliest and most powerful: white, male, wealthy, and a property owner, and the ritualized expression of rage reasserts the mythic narrative in this idolatrous identity. In the religion of white rage, white (male) supremacy is exclusive in its functionality; one belongs, or one does not. This exclusivity, however, does not preclude the left out from seeing its benefits through some form of proxy.

For application, we turn to the role of white labor in the religion of white rage and the maintenance of the narrative supported by white supremacy. The racial identities of U.S. residents are made official through census categories. The central identity is institutionalized in the first census in 1790. The categories spoke to the purposes of the residents: for example, there were two categories for "free white males," those over sixteen and those under; being over sixteen could make a free white male eligible for militia conscription.[23] Historian Nell Painter notes:

> Unfree white persons, of whom there were many in the new union, seem to have fallen through the cracks in 1790, though the . . . mention of the qualifier "free" by inference recognizes the non-free white status of those

in servitude. Had all whites been free and whiteness meant freedom . . . no need would have existed to add "free" to "white."[24]

Clearly, unfree whites held a lesser social and economic status. Census categories changed with the needs of the government; as the number of unfree whites fell, so too did the need for the category of "free white male."[25] Yet, we suggest, while the institutionalized category faded, the cultural category did not. The striving for access to the status and benefits of the "free white male" would continue to demand equality in supremacy—as "white and male." With the characteristics of identity but not the status, white laborers are stirred by the religion of white rage to strive for a *proxy* power of white supremacy. Henry Ford's Great Migration–era introduction of black workers into his Detroit area workforce set the stage for the pursuit of proxy power from white supremacy and for the ritualized assertion of proxy power so as to attain it, grounded in the religion of white rage.

"The Great White Father of Dearborn"

Henry Ford was born into an Irish immigrant family in a rural township near Dearborn, Michigan, which borders Detroit.[26] Critical interpreters of Ford, the industrialist, have detailed his obsessive penchant for continuous improvement and order and control.[27] Ford, as a famous man of his historical era, is well known for having held anti-Semitic views, including his executive committee membership of the America First Committee.[28] Ford has not been so easily identified as an anti-black racist. He revered Tuskegee scientist George Washington Carver,[29] and by 1930, Detroit's black population and black employment in the auto industry had exploded, in no small part based on the hiring of black men at the Ford Motor Company.[30] There are various theories about Ford's willingness to hire black men, including his belief that they were less inclined than other workers to organize themselves into labor unions.[31] A multitude of reasons is possible. What cannot be overlooked is Ford's paternalistic reach into Detroit's black community. His involvement in black civic organizations and, notably, black churches, led contemporaneous black columnist Horace Cayton, Jr. to name Ford the "great white father of Dearborn,"[32] in reference to his relationship with Detroit's black elites and the inhibitive effects of these alliances on the autonomy of black workers during the volatile years of the burgeoning collective labor movement.

A confluence of events resulted in the environment that made it possible for Ford Motor Company to become the largest employer of black workers in the auto industry: the simplification of the Ford Motor Company manufacturing process, immigration policy changes that created worker shortages, and the availability of black men to be hired. Henry Ford's habit of tinkering helped him, and his company developed the Model T as a mass market car that contributed to major social and economic changes in American life. Ford is credited as the innovator who implemented the manufacturing assembly line.[33] With this improvement, Ford employees stood in one place efficiently and repetitively adding their assigned component onto a moving autobody until it could be driven off the assembly line.[34] This assembly process made it possible for lower-skilled and unskilled workers to be hired to produce Ford Motor Company cars;[35] previously cars had been built by skilled craftsmen, mostly natives or descendants from Germany and England.[36] By 1914 more than 70 percent of the Ford workforce was foreign born, increasingly from eastern and southern Europe and the Arab world.[37] The beginning of World War I[38] and new U.S. immigration policy restrictions passed in 1921 and 1924 severely limited the flow of immigrant labor. These changes created additional opportunities for previously agrarian black Southerners. The jobs pulled black people northward. Economic concerns and the constant threat of anti-black oppression and violence also pushed blacks to risk all and leave their homes.

> Black migrants to the urban North brought with them expectations of independence, economic security, and property ownership, all of which had been systematically thwarted in the post-emancipation South . . . Sharecropping, debt-peonage, and systematic violence bound many Southern blacks to the enforced dependence of landlessness and labor for landowning whites.[39]

The Ford Motor Company was not the first of the Northern automobile manufacturers to hire black men, but by 1919, Ford's company quickly became among the most prominent.[40]

One additional factor set the stage for display of the religion of white rage: black men, alongside other Ford Motor Company workers, were eligible to earn Ford's 1914 wage innovation: five dollars a day pay. Ford's famous earnings scheme was a business innovation intended to slow the 10 percent per day absenteeism that came from the boring repetitiveness built into achieving his coveted efficiency.[41] When instituted, the five dollars were divided into a wage for labor and a bit more than half for profit sharing to reach the famous earnings calculation.[42] It was unparalleled; the work day of the time was generally nine hours and the best workers might earn 32 cents an hour.[43] But the extraordinary earnings, like other Ford kindnesses, came with requirements to retain the profit-sharing portion. The Ford Motor Company's Sociological Department conducted intrusive home visits to ensure that workers and their families lived in decent housing; maintained clean homes; had savings and responsibly managed their household money; and were teetotalers.[44] These were all values that Ford believed to be important. In Detroit's black community, Ford's reach did not end at the threshold of their homes; he held sway in their institutions, including black churches.

Many industrialists worked through Detroit civic organizations, such as the National Urban League and the National Association for the Advancement of Colored People (NAACP), to act as employment agents screening prospective black laborers. But Henry Ford also developed a network of African American pastors who provided character references for congregants seeking employment at his plants.[45] Second Baptist, founded in 1836, continues as one of the oldest black congregations in the state of Michigan; it was an Underground Railroad station. It was also a "Ford church."[46] According to August Meier and Elliot Rudwick, among other issues in his plant, there were

> (frequent) . . . bloody fights within the plant between black and white workers, and among the blacks themselves, Ford personally outlined to [Rev. Robert L.] Bradby [the pastor of Second Baptist] his desire to recruit *carefully selected* Negro workmen [emphasis added]. The preacher agreed both to recommend "very high type fellows" for jobs at Ford and to help the company resolve its internal personnel problems, promising "to acquaint the colored workers with the responsibilities of employment . . . telling them that they should be 'steady workers' so as to prove the worthiness of colored industrial workers."[47]

Arguably, at least in the short term, Bradby's willingness to engage with Ford as an employment agent was beneficial to those who worshiped with his congregation; black Southern migrants quickly learned that Second Baptist was a church with a coveted connection.[48]

The affiliation between Ford and black pastors has generated scholarship that examines the impact on the independence of pastors such as Bradby as well as Ford's view of black employees. John Brueggemann, following Lloyd Bailer, notes that "Ford offered special opportunities and resources to blacks."[49] Beth Tompkins Bates critiques scholarship that interprets blacks as uncritically allied with Ford as inadequately complex.[50] Then there was the previously mentioned Horace Cayton, Jr., who was unconflicted about Ford's interests and his efforts to influence black Detroit's "upper class"; although they eventually advised against Ford's anti-union stance and supported labor organizing. However, into the early 1940s, many black leaders stood with the "great white father of Dearborn."[51]

Cayton's moniker for Ford is at once a term of spiritual as well as socioeconomic and political effect. It recalls Hopkins's interpretation (above) of white slave master theology that severely tainted the American Christianity presented to enslaved Africans, making it into a white supremacist ideology which essentially casts white men as having divine authority to control daily black life as well as their slaves' access to an afterlife. It also indicts the choices that those who interacted with Ford made on their own behalf. Identifying Ford as the "great white father of Dearborn" serves one more conspicuous function within a context in which nearly half of blacks in the auto industry were working at the Ford Motor Company, the majority of them at one site, the River Rouge plant near Dearborn: it suggests the need for a close examination of whether there was equality between "all God's children," that is, between Ford's "black children" and his "white children," and the effect of "intrafamilial relationship." Finally, Ford used his power as a white man and as an industrialist religiously, under the definitions set out by both Long and Tillich. For Ford, his orientation was to whatever was his perspective. His way should always be seen as best. His ultimate concern was his view, his way of being, and his way of doing.

Labor and economy historians understand Ford to have been not just controlling but paternalistic with impacts on his entire workforce, black, white, and immigrant. A paternalistic perspective marries the Latin roots of the term with a 1950s television title to provide a vivid picture: "father knows best"—and, in this case, "father Ford" demands his way. Brueggemann argues that Ford's paternalism maintained the status quo for each worker group.[52] Ford hired black men through black churches and civic organizations, and although black rank-and-file workers had access to the five-dollar day earnings, there were limits to their ability to climb beyond the unskilled labor in which 75 percent of them worked. Additionally, the sheer number of black men who worked at Ford suggests that black workers had fewer options for employment.[53] Ford's dominance as an employer and his and the other industrialists' paternalism came with a cost:

> Bonacich (1976:42) explains that employers' attempts to displace dominant white labor with cheaper labor, were "sometimes accompanied by efforts to gain the loyalty of black work forces, thereby forestalling the development of unions among them and maintaining the 'cheap labor' status . . . On a larger scale, employers would make overtures to black workers and community leaders, giving money and urging workers to come to the employer for aid. Leaders in the black community would, in turn, urge black workers to be a docile and loyal workforce, keeping faith with the employer."[54]

Within the frames of religion in this chapter, the divine properties powerful white men assumed for themselves through the nation's mythic narrative continued in the twentieth century in the form of socioeconomic effects. Henry Ford offered black workers eligibility for unprecedented wages but limited their opportunity for individual advancement and collective equality. This was a costly concession.

Across industrial Detroit, employers and white workers practiced various forms of whiteness as discrimination against black employment applicants and black workers. In plentiful times, white applicants, qualified or not, could be hired on sight where black applicants would be told that there were no openings.[55] As white workers began to organize into collective bargaining units, they supported practices such as seniority, knowing that their longevity would protect them from job loss during downturns in the cyclical auto industry.[56] Members of skilled trade unions were typically white; blacks were locked out of those professions that came with higher wages.[57] Whether the issue was housing or jobs, white workers balked when it appeared that black workers might gain a semblance of equality.

> When discrimination made economic sense, in terms of white workers' competitive advantage (building trades), or internal labor market decisions (auto industry), or pandering to customers' racism (retail), it was practiced widely. It often provided what David Roediger has called a 'psychological wage,' that reinforced white identity. . .[58]

White identity made white men superior, at least it did in their ideal ideology. In a religious sense, everything needed to be oriented to this ideal, including the political, legal, economic, and social policies and practices. But the ultimate power lay with a rich white man—as it had in other historical periods in the U.S. Power and identity were oriented to men like Henry Ford. It was up to less powerful men to attempt to wrest the power of whiteness from them for themselves, in reality or by proxy.

Religion and Ritualization in the Religion of White Rage

As religious orientation, white supremacy requires obeisance to the idol of white superiority, and when whiteness does not receive its due honor, its underlying rage stands ready to erupt into violence—physical or discursive—to demand, rectify, and restore the expected social-institutional pattern. The introduction of black workers into manufacturing settings during the Great Migration brought millions of African Americans out of the rural South into factories in Northern cities, spaces that were nearly exclusively occupied by white American men, European immigrants, and a few Middle Eastern immigrants. In the auto industry, "nationwide the number of black auto workers grew from .5% in 1910 to 4% in 1920 to 7% in 1930. In Detroit, however, by 1930 14% of auto workers were black,"[59] twice the national rate. This highly visible level of black presence upset the social and economic order of the day, especially after black men became eligible for a similar level of earnings. To recall Anderson, black presence was one thing, but blacks earning similar income would have looked like black advancement, which would have been a threat to the idol of white superiority and a trigger for white rage as ritualized necessity to reassert orthodoxy—the right order of white supremacy.[60]

Catherine Bell's in-depth study of ritual theory and practice provides conceptual framing for our brief look at black workers' decisions to participate (or not) in white workers' organizing activities at the Ford Motor Company. Bell argues that ritualization establishes power relationships.[61] "This [power] is not a relationship in which one social group has absolute control over another, but one that simultaneously involves both consent and resistance, misunderstanding and appropriation."[62] Its productivity or effectiveness is for a certain time and space.[63] This makes it conceptually relevant to clashes with Henry Ford, white workers, and black workers. The relatively desegregated demographics of the Rouge plant with black and white workers in close proximity provides a test case for how ritualization in the religion of white rage operates. Brueggemann suggests that establishing an employer-employee relationship in which one group of employees (whites) are in a position to be more autonomous, hence confrontational, with the employer provides the constricted necessity-opportunity for the employee group with fewer options to choose to negotiate using strategies other than direct confrontation.[64] By implication: How was the ritual of rage functioning at Ford? Who was initiating it? What was the response of consent? Of resistance?

The auto industry has cycles of prosperity and bust. The Ford Motor Company had managed to build an affordable, mass market car accessible to a wide swath of the American population, but during the Great Depression, the ability to afford even this modestly priced car greatly declined. By 1931 Ford car sales had fallen to a mere 500,000 units due to the Depression and competition from other car makers.[65] With an excess of cars they could not sell, this bust cycle was more than the normal downturn; it cost 150,000 men working at Ford in Detroit their jobs and their family's income.[66] The frustration and anger of lost earnings and joblessness began to boil over in labor-organizing efforts. Overwhelmingly, organizers were white men, and their activities sometimes erupted into demands backed by violence. Black men had a choice to make: Would their responses to these ritualized expressions counteract or unintentionally contribute to the religion of white rage?

After the federal government legalized the right of workers to organize themselves into collectives, the Ford Motor Company was the last of the major automobile manufacturers to recognize labor unions and collective bargaining.[67] The overlap of the Great Migration and the Great Depression highlights how early organizing efforts at Ford fell along racial lines. The years between 1932 and 1941 were pivotal in the birth of Detroit labor organizing at Ford. Henry Ford attempted to maintain employment and wages for workers in his company despite the severe economic downturn. When his hopes could not be sustained, Ford's ultimate concern, the phrase Tillich used to define religion, and his methodological orientation, ensconced in Long's definition of religion, came into clearer sight. Whether out of his paternalistic leanings, his drive for engineered perfection, or his ego—all contemporaneous and historical interpretations of Henry Ford, the man and industrialist—Ford willingly fostered violence, including interracial violence, to sustain his power. Ultimately, he showed his orientation to be autocratic. We briefly examine how ritualized violence reinforces the religion of white rage. In doing so, we learn that the targeted audience of the power reassertion is not always obvious as one might presume.

Three highlighted episodes at the Ford Motor Company River Rouge plant are remarkable for their varying degrees of the ritualized expression of rage in the religion of white rage: the 1932 Ford Hunger March, the 1937 Battle of the Overpass, and a final, 1941 Ford strike. The immediate effects were to signal socioeconomic reminders of the worth of white men, and the larger purpose was to protect their systemic worth as a collective. Each of these crucial episodes was a fight for which white men would share concerns, including material concerns, within the religion of white supremacy. In the larger scheme, whiteness is essentially a natural rather than aberrant state, as are the benefits that come with that status, such as sufficient employment. Threats to whiteness prompt a ritualized power-restoring response which is often violent:

> The ultimate purpose of ritualization is neither the immediate goals avowed by the community or the officiant nor the more abstract functions of social solidarity and conflict resolution: it is nothing other than the production of the ritualized agents, persons who have an instinctive knowledge of these schemes *embedded in their bodies, in their sense of reality* [emphasis added], and in their understanding of how to act in ways that both maintain and qualify the complex microrelations of power.[68]

The bodily embeddedness is whiteness; the reality is the presumption—even if subconscious—of benefit. Even with the Ford Motor Company as one of the most important employers, black men had no plan to idly stand by in worship of whiteness. In Detroit, their ideals were their sense of dignity and worth, the same culturally expressed values that led them out of the dismal socioeconomic conditions and ritualized violence and terrorism that created the exodus that was the Great Migration.

The 1932 Ford Hunger March was a demand for restored employment, free medical care at the Ford Hospital for the employed and unemployed, heating energy assistance, immediate payments to provide income to the marchers, and an array of improved working conditions and no discrimination against black workers.[69] Most of the marchers to the Ford Rouge plant were former Ford employees. Marchers were met with water hoses and bullets turned on them by Dearborn police, Henry Ford's enforcer, Harry Bennett, and men from the company's Service Department. Four white marchers were killed; fifty-nine men were injured. There was a second march to bury the dead marchers at a local cemetery. Later, when a another of the injured, a black man, died, the cemetery allowed only that he could be cremated but not buried with the other martyred marchers. Determined black workers later had the man's ashes spread over the Rouge plant by airplane.

By the 1937 Battle of the Overpass, labor organizing was legal. Organizing volunteers, including Walter Reuther, who would eventually become president of the United Auto Workers, went to the Rouge plant to distribute leaflets. Again, Ford's henchmen responded violently; they beat the organizers bloody. There were no deaths, but newspaper photographers captured the bloody scene, exposing Ford for his actual tactics, rather than his carefully crafted public image as the caring capitalist.[70] This time, both Bennett's Service Department and union organizers included black men.[71]

By the time of the 1941 strike, the Ford Motor Company had been found in violation of the National Labor Relations Act by hindering workers' right to consider forming a union.[72] As the major employer of black workers in Detroit and a benefactor to black pastors and black communities, Henry Ford attempted to trade on his beneficence when it seemed black loyalty was not as solid as it had once appeared—neither from black ministers nor from those employed in his hallmark River Rouge plant. Rev. Charles Hill had trained for pastoral leadership at Second Baptist, the most prominent of the black "Ford churches." When Hill became pastor at Hartford Avenue Baptist, he made it a safe place. While some black ministers were under threat from the Ford Motor Company of "political intimidation and economic terrorism intended to prevent [them] and their congregations from taking any kind of active interest in the UAW's efforts," Hill allowed organizers to hold fake "prayer meetings" at the Hartford.[73] Such clandestine cover helped to birth United Autoworkers Local 600. Black workers and the broader black Detroit religious and civic community leadership demonstrated a complex approach to the religion of white rage rather than an easy interpretation of concession.

Henry Ford's embrace of paternalism ultimately had to die for his company to live. Worker protests grew out of the frustrations of job cuts, work week reductions that translated to smaller paychecks, and an inadequate safety net. At his command, bullets rained down on the workers for whom he supposedly cared so much. The 1932 Ford Hunger March, the Battle of the Overpass, and the final strike were expressions of rage fought over power focused on ideals of white supremacy. In retrospect, in the context of the Great Depression, the need for bread not bullets seems a reasonable demand for charity and fairness, but it is more than that. In forming a collective, white workers might have continued to exclude black workers from their ranks. Ultimately, however, capital "L" labor, the movement, gained their power through a friendlier legislative environment, through their own willingness to demonstrate *en masse,* and by including blacks in their public ranks when it worked to their benefit.[74] But they only learned this *after* Henry Ford (and other auto makers) demonstrated his willingness to use force against them as well as to use black workers as strike breakers in lieu of striking white men. With fewer employment options, some black workers sided with Ford and the "wisdom" of black elites.[75] Eventually, black workers turned their backs on the "great white father of Dearborn" as had white working men. With the help of just enough black ministers who were willing to stand against conventional narratives, black Rouge workers realized that their freedom lay in their hands and in their own ideal of who they were.

Conclusion: Why the Religion of White Rage *Still* Matters

This chapter has focused on a historical application of the religion of white rage and its self-referent aim to sustain white supremacy. It was reinforced through the ritualized expressions of rage as physical violence, through legislative processes, and at the ballot box. Sometimes the source of the white rage came through the direct actions or on the orders of the most powerful of white men such as Henry Ford. At other times, it came from working-class white men who expressed the rage of white supremacy by demanding and accessing proxy power. Even some black working-class men sought to access the proxy power of the religion of white rage as Ford's enforcers. Through the 1930s, white workers were willing to exclude black workers until they realized that to do so was to forgo the potential of their own collective power.

The pursuit of white supremacy among white elites and white workers continues in the twenty-first century—most often discursively—but with somatic effects. Between 2013 and 2018, psychiatrist and public health researcher Jonathan Metzl interviewed residents in three states about their perspectives on issues linked to poorer health: the expansion of Medicaid that would provide access to publicly backed health insurance for working-class wage earners in Tennessee, gun control laws in Missouri, and cuts to funding for public education in Kansas. Despite their links to improved health outcomes, Metzl found that residents of each state broadly rejected these initiatives because they were government programs. He wrote: "I kept thinking that at some point, the drive for self-preservation might trump political ideology. Why would someone reject their own health care, or keep guns unlocked when their children were home?"[76] Metzl came to understand that for his interviewees, a negative racial narrative is attached to each of these measures that might otherwise gain support. Acceptance of the possibility of any good that might be associated with them was a high price to pay. Metzl opened his book with the story of Trevor, a dying 41-year-old, uninsured and no longer able to work, who was against these forms of government assistance. Implicit in his rejection, "Trevor voiced a literal willingness to die for his place in [a] hierarchy [that identified him as white], rather than participate in a system that might put him on the same plane as immigrants or racial minorities."[77] Trevor lived with, and would soon die from, his accumulated illnesses, as well as "the toxic effects of dogma."[78] Especially for workers, dogma in the religion of white rage kills.[79]

FOUR

American (Un)Civil Religion, the Defense of the White Worker, and Responses to NFL Protests

Lori Latrice Martin

Recent protests by college and professional athletes against unnatural black deaths have received a lot of attention in mainstream media, on social media platforms, and in scholarly publications but often for all the wrong reasons. Much of the attention is focused on whether sporting events are appropriate venues for addressing social justice issues, whether some forms of protest are perceived by the public as more or less deviant than other forms, and whether protestors should receive sanctions from their respective leagues and/or teams.[1] Absent from many of the discussions is a focus, first and foremost, on the black deaths that led to the protest. Also missing are in-depth thoughtful analyses on responses to the protests. Specifically, critical analyses of responses to the protests—from "Main Street" to 1600 Pennsylvania Avenue—are needed to understand the linkages between three important concepts: "American civil religion," perceived black progress by white workers, and what I call "white religious shock," or the disorientation white workers experience when they encounter challenges to the white social order, manifested in what is best described as white fervor.

I argue that nowhere are the linkages between white laborers, religion, and perceived black progress more salient than in the responses to protests by players in the National Football League by President Donald Trump and the league's (and Trump's) largely white-worker fan base. I begin with a review of how American civil religion is defined and how it functions. I explore how American civil religion and the state are co-constitutive and how football functions in the service of American civil religion to bind together seemingly disparate groups of white people at the top of a racialized social system, while simultaneously seeking to bind people of color, black people in particular, at the system's lowest level. Lastly, I introduce a typology based on the intensity of racial consciousness and the intensity of belief in American civil religion.

American (Un)Civil Religion Defined

For many centuries black and white people have contemplated what it means to be an American, who and what America values, and whether the American dream exists for all, or just for some. Responses to these all-important questions vary by race given the centrality of race in the history, present, and undoubtedly future of the nation. Conversations about race and movement forward around issues of race stall before they start for a number of reasons, not the least of which is a relatively understudied concept that was popular in the sociology of religion in the late 1960s through the mid-1970s. American civil religion was popularized by sociologist Robert Bellah, and openly criticized by many others, including acclaimed religious scholar Charles Long.

Bellah defines American civil religion as "the subordination of the nation to ethical principles that transcend it in terms which it should be judged."[2] Bellah argues that American civil religion is deserving of the same level of rigorous scholarly engagement as any other religion.[3] He makes the case that American civil religion includes the same elements of religious viewpoints shared by a majority of Americans. Rituals, beliefs, and symbols are the ways the public religion is expressed, argues Bellah. The inauguration of a new or returning U.S. president is one example, perhaps the most important ceremony in American civil religion, says Bellah. During the ceremony, the president makes a promise not only to the people of the nation but also to God. The president relays that while he must answer to the people, ultimately he is responsible to a much higher authority, Bellah writes. American civil religion not only holds the president responsible to the people and to God, but it also obligates Americans to work together and individually to carry out God's will. American civil religion grammar is careful not to define narrowly, if at all, the God to which it refers. There's "no mention of Jesus, for example, but [it is] very specific on the topic of America."[4] American civil religion is what Bellah calls a "genuine vehicle of national religious self-understanding."[5]

Bellah describes the relationship between American civil religion and America's concept of itself. Evidence may be found in the founding documents, including the U.S. Constitution and the Declaration of Independence.[6] Bellah asserts, "The words and acts of the founding fathers, especially the first few presidents shaped the form and tone of the civil religion as it has been maintained ever since."[7]

It is important to note that these documents essentially equated Americans with white people and whiteness and also marked black people as less than human and justifiably chattel property. Bellah illustrates this point in what he chooses to highlight as central themes in American civil religion—of which there are three.[8] The first theme involved the American Revolution and the issue of independence. God's will was the focus. The second theme was associated with the Civil War and involved death, sacrifice, and rebirth. The issue was slavery and the institutionalization of democracy. The third theme occurred as Bellah published his classic work. He described the problem of a responsible revolutionary world. The three themes—independence, the Civil War, and responsibility—all speak to the normativity of a white historical narrative, one in which the protagonists are white men fighting for what are read as valorous aims. As such, Bellah intentionally or unwittingly avoids talking about race, even though each of the themes was centered on critical epochs in American history where contestations over race were at their highest points. Therefore, although Bellah does not devote much attention to discussions about race, it is clear that American civil religion and whiteness are inseparable.

To Bellah's three themes, I would add a fourth and a fifth theme. The fourth theme would include the issues of patriotism renewed with the backdrop of the attacks of September 11, 2001. Jermaine McDonald made a similar observation in his article "A Fourth Time of Trial."[9] The fifth theme would address the problem of what I call "white religious shock" and is shaped by the effects of the Great Recession, the two-term tenure of a black president who many working-class white people believe was not born in the U.S., and the campaign to "Make America Great Again."

Charles Long defines religion as an "orientation in the ultimate sense, that is, how one comes to terms with the ultimate significance of one's place in the world."[10] Long went on to write, "The religion of any people is more than a structure of thought; it is experience, expression, motivation, intentions, behaviors, styles, and rhythms."[11] Long's definition goes far beyond other definitions, which view religion as merely a social institution, or from the perspective of popularly accepted denominations. Based on Long's definition, we can understand whiteness as a type of religion, as Stephen C. Finley and I argued in "The Complexity of Color and the Religion of Whiteness," in a book I coedited, *Color Struck*.[12] It is also apparent how white people could experience shock or a sense of disorientation when they perceive challenges to the image and determination of themselves and of the nation.

September 11, 2001 fundamentally changed the way Americans viewed themselves and the nation. Any sense of personal safety and national security was shattered on that day. Many Americans, white Americans in particular, literally wrapped themselves in national symbols, such as the American flag. They embraced and hero-worshiped first responders and the military, and participated in a host of rituals and ceremonies that not only honored those killed but also embraced American civil religion. A renewal of American patriotism, or allegiance to the nation, was on full display following the attacks.[13]

Economic losses resulting from the Great Recession contributed to the sense among many white workers, in particular, that their self-image and self-determination were being challenged and the self-image and self-determination of the nation too. Although black people, and other people of color, fared far worse than white workers, white workers lost homes and jobs, and saw their modest portfolios shrink. They also expressed concern about the nation's place in the world economy given the downturn and how such a change might impact how the rest of the world sees America.

The election of a black president also created a sense of white religious shock. The mere fact that one of the eligibility requirements to become president is that one is born in the United States is telling. Most thought they would never live to see the day when someone who identified racially as black would sit in the Oval Office. Throughout Barack Obama's presidential campaign and through much of his presidency, questions surrounding his place of birth—dubbed the "birther movement"—were led by people like Donald Trump. Trump's challenge of Obama's birthplace endeared him in the hearts of many white workers who appreciated Trump's affluence, power, and willingness to outwardly challenge Obama after a post-civil rights period where overt expressions of racially laden comments were frowned upon. Not only did Trump challenge Obama about his birthplace but he was also successful in compelling Obama to produce "papers" to prove his birthplace or right to be called an American, which he and others dismissed anyway. Trump's call to "Make America Great Again" appealed to white workers. It appealed to white workers despite the fact he offered no indication as to when America had been great before, what led to America's decline, and how anyone would know when greatness was restored. Nevertheless, calls to construct walls to keep out presumably brown migrants into the United States, who Trump also sought to broadly criminalize, and to ban travel from certain predominately Muslim countries, presumably as a preemptive attempt at thwarting another terrorist attack on American soil, resonated with white workers and contributed to Trump's defeat of Hillary Rodham Clinton. The idea that a black president might represent black racial progress, despite the fact that black people experienced significant losses during the Obama administration, and the popularity of the "Make America Great Again" campaign were brilliantly summarized by Long. Long wrote, "The inordinate fear that they have of minorities is an expression of the fear they have when they contemplate the possibility of seeing themselves as they really are."[14]

Four Functions of Football in American Civil Religion

American civil religion is important as a framework for understanding whiteness. It should be noted that some scholars have steered away from discussions about American civil religion, apparently including even Robert Bellah at some point, because of criticisms.[15] Hortense Spillers outlined some of the reasons for the rejection, which, she says,

> vary across a range of misgivings, from what [the scholars] would consider the distastefulness of the very idea, to definitional objections, others maintain that aspects of American Christianity express a greater number of anthropocentric notions than theocratic ones and that they manifest greater compatibility with secular morality than with biblical.[16]

Nevertheless, American civil religion is worth saving as much as Bellah's arguments hold true today.

Grace Kao and Jerome Copulsky are among the more recent scholars to find value in studying American civil religion. Kao and Copulsky analyzed the pledge of allegiance and American civil religion.[17] They also identified four perspectives through which the pledge of allegiance and civil religion can be understood to function. I draw from their work in demonstrating how professional American football can also be understood to function.

Kao and Copulsky offer a brief history of the pledge of allegiance. They focus on the pledge because they see it as the most popular and most recognizable American civil religion ceremony. They observe that millions of schoolchildren recite the pledge every day. U.S. senators begin each session with the reciting of the pledge. Civil organizations across the country also include the pledge as part of their meetings and events. The scholars also address changes to the pledge, which was written in 1892 by Baptist minister Frances Bellamy, over time. For example, they note changes in 1923, 1924, 1942, and 1954, when "under God" was added to the statement. What they don't say is that these changes also occurred as important social and demographic changes were taking place in the U.S., which many white workers may have perceived as racial progress for black people and thus a threat to their self-image and self-determination, and the image and determination of the nation.

The original pledge did not include the words "United States of America," but merely referenced allegiance to the flag and the Republic. The identity of the Republic was included in the change made in 1923. It is important to note that at the time the pledge was first written white immigrants from countries considered undesirable to whites who were already in the U.S. were beginning to arrive in great numbers. These white ethnic groups hailed from southern, central, and eastern Europe. The 1923 change to the pledge follows the passage of a discriminatory immigration act, which was intended to curtail immigration from countries in those parts of Europe. The act established a quota system limiting the number of people who could arrive from those countries, based in part upon how many people had arrived in the decades preceding the act. While communism is sometimes cited as the driving force for the inclusion of the words "under God" in 1954, the fact that the nation was dealing with a host of challenges to long-standing Jim Crow laws cannot be overlooked. The addition of the phrase followed a historic bus boycott in Baton Rouge, Louisiana, and took place in the same year as the U.S. Supreme Court decided the landmark *Brown v. Board of Education of Topeka, Kansas*, which represented years of efforts on the part of black people to ensure that they and their children had access to a quality education.

An examination of the sermon delivered by Presbyterian minister George Docherty, who along with the Knights of Columbus is credited with successfully amending the pledge, shows how narrowly defined American life was in the minds of many whites and how little consideration was given to the experience of black people in America.[18] Docherty said the spirit of America lies in the people and the military. Speaking on the birthday of Abraham Lincoln, seen by some as the Messiah of American civil religion for having saved the union, Docherty made it clear that the American way of life involves sports, capitalism, consumerism, entertainment, leisure, ethnocentrism, and white privilege and the benefits thereof. Specifically, he made mention of going to the ball game, shopping at Sears, going to amusement parks, driving on the "right" side of the road, staying in hotels, and being bored by television commercials. Docherty added that throughout American history "the providence of God was being fulfilled."[19] While the pledge refers specifically to the United States of America, Docherty made the claim in his sermon that the statement could really apply to any republic and that the phrase once uttered by Lincoln, "Under God," is the "definitive character of the American way of life."[20]

By the way, Docherty saw no problem with using "under God" as opposed to "under Jesus Christ" or some other religious figure as a way to consolidate largely white Christians from a variety of belief systems. He also addressed the fact that not all Americans, white Americans specifically, were Christian or believed in the existence of God. Docherty described the term "atheist American" as essentially oxymoronic and called atheists "spiritual parasites."[21] He said, "If he denies the Christian ethic, he falls short of the American ideal of life."[22]

Kao and Copulsky understand the importance of the pledge in American civil religion and discuss preservationist, pluralist, priestly, and prophetic functions. American civil religion for Kao and Copulsky refers to "a symbolic system that binds members of a political community to one another through shared historical narratives, myths, rituals, and some notion of transcendence."[23] The preservationist function claims that the system is necessary to maintain cultural coherence, national identity, stability, and central institutions, while the pluralist perspective functions to promote change and greater inclusion, for example, to move beyond assumptions of Christianity as normative.[24] The priestly perspective functions to affirm, celebrate, and endorse the national image and identity. Finally, the prophetic perspective function explores what the character of the nation *ought* to be.

While Kao and Copulsky make a compelling argument for the significance of the pledge of allegiance in American life and American civil religion, it could also be argued that sports, particularly football, also serve similar functions and may reach an even broader audience than those reciting the pledge in schools, in the U.S. Senate, and in civic organizations.[25] Based upon Nielsen ratings, 60 percent of the television programs that adults between the ages of eighteen and forty-nine watched in 2017 were sports programs.[26] Although viewing of NFL games declined by 9 percent from the previous year, shows like *Super Bowl LI, AFC Championship, NFL Divisional Playoffs*, and *Sunday Night Football* made up the top five most-watched television programs for 2017. Nearly fifty million people alone watched the Super Bowl on television. Football also surpassed baseball several decades ago as "America's favorite game."[27]

Michael Butterworth has published a number of scholarly works on the importance of sports in American life, including football.[28] He describes the marriage of commercial sports and the American culture of militarism. Ceremonies at professional football leagues, which are now commonplace, normalized war and endorsed the "war on terror," argues Butterworth. Moreover, he contends, "sport rhetoric is an especially persuasive vehicle for sustaining and extending the culture of militarism."[29] Butterworth describes "the rhetorical production of citizenship through sport."[30] He also outlines ways in which events like the Super Bowl connect sports, politics, and commonly held myths about America, including American exceptionalism.

Football with all its pageantry could be read under a preservationist understanding of civil religion to function for the purpose of continuing traditions, rituals, tropes, and a sense of national identity and cultural coherence. The playing of the national anthem, performances by military officials, days devoted to first responders, current military personnel, and veterans, and special tributes to the armed forces during time-outs, halftime, and commercial breaks are just a few examples. The shared experience associated with watching one's favorite team or attending a Super Bowl–themed event are part of what many people consider part of the American way of life.

Sports are often viewed as one of the few level playing fields in America. Despite years of segregation in sports and evidence of the discrimination and unequal treatment black athletes have experienced, many Americans, especially white Americans, are quite skeptical about claims that sports are anything but a playing field where people complete based largely on their physical abilities and strong work ethic. Thus, football could be understood from the pluralist perspective, and it could be argued that football is an inclusive place where there is room for fans and players of all backgrounds so long as they are supportive of the team, leading some to believe that the relationships as fans extend beyond the stadium.

Studies have shown that white men workers make up the largest segment of the football fan bases.[31] From the continuing presence of cheerleaders on the sidelines to commercials and sponsors that are clearly directed to this population, it is clear that white men workers are the target audience. It should not be lost on anyone that this is the same demographic that makes up Donald Trump's political base. Football brings this demographic together regularly and predictably to legitimate the state, its institutions, and its policies. Nationally and locally elected officials are common presences at football games. The president even hosts the winning Super Bowl team, although some have declined such efforts. Again, the presence of the military, not to mention the money that changed hands between the NFL and the Department of Defense to include salutes to the military during games, provide further evidence of football in this function.[32]

While the priestly perspective of football in civil religion functions as an endorsement of civil religion, the prophetic perspective challenges it. Protests by Colin Kaepernick, former quarterback from the NFL's San Francisco 49ers, and other players are illustrative of football in this function. In August 2016, Kaepernick refused to stand during the playing of the national anthem, which is customary, and later he decided to kneel as it played.[33] He wanted to draw attention to the killing of unarmed black men by police across the country and to draw attention to other racial injustices.[34] Just a few weeks before Kaepernick began his effort to change the conversation about race in America, especially among the largely white male worker fans, police in Baton Rouge, Louisiana, killed Alton Sterling. Shortly thereafter, police in Falcon Heights,

Minnesota, killed Philando Castile. Sterling and Castile, both fathers and black men in their thirties, joined a long and still growing list of unnatural black deaths at the hands of law enforcement officials and private citizens.

The tension between football functioning at the priestly and the prophetic perspectives is at the heart of the clash between the athlete activists and the fans, predominately white working men, who used to "love" them as long as they were in uniform and hopefully winning. The black professional American football players are soon reminded that despite all their success on the gridiron, in the end, for many of them, the NFL stands for "Negroes for Life." I use the term "Negroes" here as it reflects a common term used after the end of physical black bondage and prior to most calls for acknowledgment of the historical origin of enslaved people from Africa and throughout the Diaspora. Although comments from President Trump attempted to deflect attention away from the reason for the protests to an assessment of the method and place of the protests, his viewpoint was not novel. As the "high priest" of American civil religion, he not only has his finger on the pulse of his base but he represents the state and its national identity. What he says, for white men workers, is like hearing from directly from God. American civil religion and the state are not separate as some might suggest. I argue that American civil religion and the state are co-constitutive; each has an equal share and responsibility in creating, legitimating, and sustaining the other.

Racial Consciousness and Belief in American Civil Religion: A Matter of Intensity

As stated previously, responses to the NFL protests were not about how and where protests should rightfully take place; responses to the NFL protests were about (re)affirming American civil religion, particularly for white men workers. The intensity of the responses to the protests varied. Some fans requested refunds from cable subscribers, while others sought refunds for their tickets. Some local bars and restaurants refused to show NFL games. Some fans booed during the protest or broke out in chants of "USA" in unison. Variations in the reactions to the NFL protests point to the complexity associated with adherence to American civil religion and to one's level of racial consciousness or understanding what Carole Stewart refers to as the "lived meaning" resulting from adherence to American civil religion and the United States' destiny.[35] To that end, I created a typology including the following types: white priestly preservationists, well-meaning whites, race contrarians, and black activists. It is important to note that these types are not necessarily mutually exclusive. They are fluid and may vary by context, place, and time, for example. I also wish to provide further comments about my use of the term "racial consciousness" here. For the purposes of this book chapter, high racial consciousness refers to the extent to which black people identify with the historical struggle for social justice for that group and understand that what happens to black people as a group affects what happens to them as individuals. The opposite is true for black people with low racial consciousness. White people with low racial consciousness refuse to, or fail to, acknowledge the unearned benefits they receive based upon their race and are threatened by perceived black progress. White people with high racial consciousness have a greater awareness about the role of race in the American social structure and may acknowledge at least some of the ways in which they benefit because of their membership in the dominant race in America.

Figure 4.1 Typology of racial consciousness and belief in American civil religion

Racial Consciousness

◄──────────────────────────────────────►

Low Racial Consciousness   High Racial Consciousness

White priestly preservationist Low racial consciousness and high adherence in American civil religion White working class fearful of racial progress demonstrate intense white religious shock and white fervor under the guise of preserving their individual and national heritage	*Well-meaning whites* Low racial consciousness and low adherence in American civil religion Neoliberal white people who enjoy unearned benefits associated with whiteness and recognize shortcomings of the state, friends and neighbors but do nothing meaningful to bring challenge anti-black sentiments. Well-meaning whites are accomplices in enduring racial divide. May also include non-theists.
Race contrarians High racial consciousness and high adherence in American civil religion Racial and ethnic minorities who are relatively optimistic about ability of America to reimagine and reinvent itself to become a more just and equitable society. May include recent immigrants influenced by global myth of racism and individuals with low levels of racial fate or connection between what happens to black people affecting what happens to them.	*Black activists* High racial consciousness and low adherence in American civil religion Black people engaged in passive and active forms of resistance to expose society as it is as opposed to society as it *ought* be.

American Civil Religion

◄──────────────────────────────────────►

High Adherence to American   Low Adherence to American
Civil Religion   Civil Religion

White priestly preservationists have low racial consciousness and high adherence to American civil religion. Previous research has shown that race is indeed a significant determinant of adherence to civil religion with white people being more civil-religious than black people in America.[36] The type includes white workers fearful of racial progress who demonstrate intense white religious shock and white fervor under the guise of preserving their individual and national heritage. White workers brandishing divisive symbols, such as the Confederate flags, Tiki torches, and white nationalist apparel, are examples of white priestly preservationists and arguably are most likely to demonstrate their white rage in a variety of forms, including physical assaults on non-white groups as well as the consumption of and participation in the use of social media to harass and intimidate those critical of their beliefs, including black elected officials, black professors critical of whiteness, and other people of color.

Well-meaning whites might include neoliberal white people who enjoy unearned benefits associated with whiteness and recognize shortcomings of the state and friends and neighbors but do nothing meaningful to bring about change. They have relatively low racial consciousness and low adherence to American civil religion. Well-meaning whites are complicit in the actions of white priestly preservationists because they do not actively work to confront them and the silence of many is equivalent to cosigning on their beliefs.

Black activists have high racial consciousness and low adherence to American civil religion. Black activists include black people engaged in passive and active forms of resistance to expose society as it is as opposed to society as it ought to be. These individuals understand what W. E. B. Du Bois sought to capture in his discussion about the challenges associated with black people, who must reconcile their racial identity and their "American" identity. Du Bois described the group I call black activists as engaged in *true* patriotism.[37] Black activists are most at risk for physical and virtual affects on their bodies and their character. They understand the risks but are prepared to make the necessary sacrifices in the hope that change will come even if it is not during their lifetime.

Racial contrarians, on the other hand, have high racial consciousness and high adherence to American civil religion. This type would likely include racial and ethnic minorities who are relatively optimistic about the ability of America to reimagine and reinvent itself to become a more just and equitable society. Racial contrarians may also include recent immigrants influenced by global myths about racism and anti-black sentiments. Much like the well-meaning whites, racial contrarians do little to bend the arc more toward justice, through their unwillingness to be openly critical about the exciting racial social order, while remaining susceptible to the white rage of disenchanted white workers like the white priestly preservationists.

Conclusion

American civil religion is as old as the founding of the nation. Indeed the founding documents, myths about the conquests of people of color, romanticizing about slavery and the Civil War, and exaggerations about pioneers and "how the west was won," continue to influence Americans and American civil religion today. This is not to suggest that American civil religion as a subject of scholarly inquiry is not without its limitations, as identified earlier in the chapter, but it is certainly worthy of further interrogation. There are so many possibilities that exist for understanding the religion of white rage through the lens of American civil religion. One could explore the ways in which colleges and universities function in relationship to American civil religion. What about the criminal justice system, public school system, and other important social institutions?

Throughout this chapter I have defined American civil religion and reviewed some of the important documents and important thinkers. I draw from the work of Robert Bellah and added two important themes to cover the time period following the original publication of his oft-cited article on American civil religion. I also review the four functions of American civil religion and extended that discussion by showing how football, America's favorite pastime,[38] also functions in service to American civil religion, in ways that may reach more people than even the pledge of allegiance. A review of the context in which changes occurred to the pledge reveals the connectedness between American civil religion and race, in ways that do not appear in most of the works on American civil religion. I go as far as to argue that American civil religion and whiteness, in particular, are inseparable. I not only introduce the concept of white religious shock, but I also introduce a typology for thinking about American civil religion as complex and in relationship to another concept—racial consciousness. It is my sincere hope that this book chapter will be generative and lead to subsequent discussions and publications across disciplines about the linkages between religion as an orientation, white workers, and perceived black progress.

FIVE

The Color of Belief: Black Social Christianity, White Evangelicalism, and Redbaiting the Religious Culture of the CIO in the Postwar South

Elizabeth Fones-Wolf and Ken Fones-Wolf

On May 18, 1946, an anxious and unsettled crowd of about 250 white evangelicals gathered at Knoxville, Tennessee's Bible Baptist Tabernacle to protest the cancellation of the popular *Radio Bible Hour* by the local radio station. Bowing to pressure from advertisers, the National Association of Broadcasters, and the Federal Council of Churches of Christ in America (FCC), many radio stations had adopted a code that forbade selling airtime to commercial religious broadcasts, which could at times be inflammatory and controversial, in favor of free sustaining airtime donated to mainline ministerial associations. Contests over these decisions were both heated and widespread in the World War II-era United States.[1] What makes the meeting in Knoxville particularly interesting were the ways that speakers used the episode to stir racial advancement, organized labor, modernist religion, and communism into a dangerous brew. Rev. A. A. Haggard from nearby Maryville charged that communists had "definite plans to take over America this year" using "organized labor and Negroes" and that "all fundamentalist preachers are first on the communist death list." Haggard was followed by Rev. Clarence Garrett, who praised the Ku Klux Klan for keeping order after blacks had been "stirred up by communists preaching social equality." To Garrett, the Klan was the one group that could withstand communism, the Congress of Industrial Organizations (CIO), racial equality, and the FCC. Otherwise, religious freedom was at risk.[2]

The ease with which Haggard and Garrett linked the progress of unions, communism, and liberal Protestantism with fears of racial advancement tells us a great deal about the transforming impact of World War II. The mood of the South had changed. During the Depression, many working-class whites had embraced Franklin Roosevelt's New Deal, joined labor organizations, and prodded their churches to support collective bargaining and federal programs for social welfare. In the mines and mills of cities like Birmingham and Memphis, the cotton fields of the Mississippi Delta, and the coal fields of Appalachia, unions—many with socialist and communist leaders—challenged entrenched politics and explored interracial social movements.[3] A Social Gospel spirit arose that seemed eager to break with the Southern norms on race and class issues. The YWCA and the Fellowship of Southern Churchmen critiqued Jim Crow and anti-unionism, and the socially progressive Southern Conference for Human Welfare announced its arrival in Birmingham in November 1938 with a multiracial gathering that took on the character of a prophetic religious revival determined to tackle economic, political, and racial issues.[4] Even normally reticent groups like the Southern Baptist Convention and the Church of God made accommodations to labor unions and offered assistance to African Americans.[5]

World War II conditions gave working people, black and white, opportunities to advance their goals despite organized labor's agreement not to disrupt production to gain advantages. Greater federal government intervention and tight labor markets improved job prospects and collective bargaining for some four million new members, including 750,000 blacks.[6] As the war drew to a close, the CIO, the most progressive labor federation, sensed that the time was right for an aggressive campaign to unionize the South. The American Federation of Labor (AFL) quickly followed suit. Central to labor's ability to breach America's most anti-union citadel was a strategy that prevented Southern employers from dividing workers by race. The CIO saw signs that it had an ally in Southern churches. Jack McMichael of the Methodist Church praised unions for a "new social climate in the South" that rejected the "unhuman and unbrotherly" regime of Jim Crow, and a group of Southern Baptists began a new journal, *Christian Frontiers*, which recognized unions and African Americans as essential to the spiritual and economic basis for democracy in the South.[7]

This optimism was not to last. The horrors of war and suspicions of growing federal state power alarmed many Southerners, none more than Southern evangelical ministers. Increasingly, Southern churchgoers saw the world refracted through premillennial dispensationalism. The CIO, in this perspective, became a harbinger of the approaching endtimes for its association with the political left, an overreaching government, and modernist religion. Most abhorrent to Southerners, however, was the fact that the CIO also declared against lynching, voting restrictions, and job discrimination. In the minds of many white evangelicals, the CIO's pronouncements on racial justice were proof that they should avoid unions and follow the Bible's sanction to "not be unequally yoked together with unbelievers" (2 Corinthians 6:14).[8]

The problem with the advice propounded by white anti-union evangelicals was that black workers were not unbelievers. Indeed, African American churches in the South shared the same evangelical culture as their white counterparts, but interpreted their beliefs to bolster a Social Gospel commitment to economic and social justice.[9] In the years following World War II, as African Americans made new demands on the political and economic institutions that had denied them full citizenship, the contradictions of white evangelicalism were on full display. Rather than embrace the struggle of black Christians for equality, white evangelicals disparaged black advancement along with unions and communism as threats to their own security. This chapter examines this important episode in resurgent white evangelicalism and the consequences of its role in undermining the possibility for remaking the South and the nation.

Days of Hope

The Great Depression opened a window of opportunity for the South's white and black working-class Christians to address social and economic injustices. The poverty of landlessness and low wages brought both them closer to each other in the material conditions of their lives and provided a rationale for cooperation. In fact, among the poor, there emerged a folk Christianity that often crossed racial boundaries. As noted by religious historian John Hayes, this "hard, hard religion" used an array of cultural material—song, story, lore, and proverb—to explore such phenomena as "the value of a single small life, alienation and genuine identity, glimpsing the sacred in a disenchanted world, and fighting chaos and a nihilistic spiral of violence."[10] Popular religious beliefs about God's grace, salvation, and even the worldly presence of Satan bridged a racial divide in the South. While often dismissed as fatalistic or otherworldly, for poor blacks and whites their faith could reassure, provide hope, ease resentments, and calm fears.[11]

For some, religious belief was more than a coping mechanism. The Depression sparked the upswing of a prophetic Social Gospel movement in the South that sought to contest the power of employers, government officials, and landowners to sustain the low-wage economy of the region. One source of this flowering of social Christianity emerged from a group of young churchpeople who gathered at Monteagle, Tennessee, in 1934 to explore how they might put "the resources of their faith to work for God and man" at this crucial time. Out of that meeting came the Conference of

Younger Churchmen of the South, soon to take the name the Fellowship of Southern Churchmen. Led by an imaginative, interracial group of clergy and lay activists, the Fellowship carried a religious message into the fight for social justice. Members showed up in campaigns to organize the unemployed in Louisiana and tenant farmers and agricultural laborers in Missouri and Arkansas; in cooperative and interracial agricultural communities in Mississippi; and in labor struggles in the coal fields of Kentucky and ore mines of Alabama.[12]

An even more remarkable group of Christian-infused activists emerged from Alva W. Taylor's circle of students at the Vanderbilt School of Religion. Including such prominent leftists as Howard Kester, Don West, Ward Rodgers, and Claude Williams, this group transformed Taylor's Social Gospel philosophy into a prophetic radicalism that they carried into labor contests throughout the South over the ensuing decades. These men, and frequently their wives and sometimes their children, were participants in the Southern Tenant Farmers Union; the United Cannery, Agricultural, Packing, and Allied Workers; the Food, Tobacco, and Allied Workers; the United Mine Workers; the Mine, Mill, and Smelter Workers; and the Socialist and Communist parties.[13] They brought with them an uncompromising commitment to both the labor movement and black equality.

In the depths of the Depression, the message of social Christianity resonated among workers in unlikely places. In Birmingham, Alabama, coal and ore miners, who frequently sang in gospel quartets, broke the powerful grip of the Tennessee Coal and Iron Company and the American Cast Iron Pipe Company and built strong unions that won collective bargaining agreements. CIO activists in Memphis, Tennessee, drawing upon the "intensely religious culture of the African-American community," defied the brutal strong-arm thugs of the Edward H. Crump political machine to organize workers in the factories and warehouses of the Bluff City. Black gospel songs became union anthems at the hands of talented troubadours.[14] CIO unions in coal and steel had numerous contracts; in the tobacco and lumber industries organizers had established beachheads in North Carolina and Alabama; garment worker unions were scattered through Virginia, Tennessee, and Louisiana; the United Rubber Workers made Gadsden, Alabama a union town; and auto and packinghouse unions were in Texas, Georgia, and Alabama.[15] While hardly secure, organized labor could view the New Deal years as a time of hope for a new day.

In many cases, workers adhered to religious faith as a guiding principle in their commitment to unions. Debbie Spicer, daughter and wife of Kentucky coal miners, believed that the Lord ensured the success of the United Mine

Workers (UMW). Even when anti-union thugs dynamited the church of one preacher and union man, it was impossible to harm him, according to Spicer: "You can't destroy a child of God as long as the Lord's got something for him to do," she testified.[16] Frank Bonds believed that the miners of Docena, Alabama, "had a very strong faith" that contributed to the sense of community that brought the union to local mines.[17] Eula McGill, whose "very religious" father helped build the labor movement in Gadsden, Alabama, recalled that his faith taught that "if a person lives in this world without trying to make it a better place to live in, [then] he's not living, he's just taking up space."[18] Henry Wade, who sang in the choir at his Baptist church in Dalton, Georgia, became a lifelong Democrat and union supporter because of the New Deal's intervention in the economy on behalf of workers. He recalled the passage of the Fair Labor Standards Act as the "greatest day in my life."[19]

Black workers, however, faced barriers to their participation in the campaign to transform the South. Much New Deal legislation specifically ignored sectors of the economy where blacks were heavily concentrated. Employers and many unions continued to bar African Americans or relegate them to the dirtiest, most dangerous, and lowest-paying jobs. When the New Deal's National Industrial Recovery Act established standards for wages, Southern industries either argued for lower rates based on racial and regional differences or used the codes as a rationale to replace black workers with white ones. In many areas where black workers had earlier gained a toehold in industrial employment, they cynically claimed that NRA (the initials of the National Recovery Act, the agency responsible for administrating the New Deal's industrial codes) stood for "Negro Removal Act."[20]

Nevertheless, in places where African Americans made up such a significant portion of the workforce that unions could not ignore them, black workers brought their strong religious beliefs to union membership. To Morris Benson, a black steelworker in Birmingham, the union was "like a church," it created unity, strength, and "togetherness."[21] CIO unions that pursued interracial organizing recognized black Christianity as an asset and allowed African Americans to play a major role in building the union. The UMW, for instance, recruited Earl Brown to be an organizer because the union realized he was "a religious person" who knew "how to treat people."[22] CIO organizer Lucy Mason wrote glowingly of black workers bringing their Christianity into the union hall when given the chance. She had hopes that this "natural expression of religion" would be the means "by which prejudice and misunderstanding are replaced by appreciation and good-will."[23]

Churches responded to the social messages that their congregants took from their religious beliefs. In white churches, working people at times received encouragement from ministers who urged their congregations to link religious belief to expectations of a more just society. Even the normally conservative Southern Baptist Convention felt obliged to support social action. One rural Alabama Baptist minister resented that "the poor or landless man, wage earners and sharecroppers . . . are nothing but slaves for the big land holders."[24] Rev. Charles R. Bell of Anniston, Alabama, voted for the Socialist Party in the 1930s and supported strikers in the local mills. Revs. L. L. Gwaltney, editor of the *Alabama Baptist*, and Acker C. Miller, head of the Texas Baptist Social Service Commission, pushed the Southern Baptist Convention in 1938 to adopt a resolution recognizing "the right of labor to organize and to engage in collective bargaining to the end that labor may have a fair and living wage."[25] Some Methodist ministers were equally enthusiastic about the New Deal's possibilities. One Southern Methodist editor declared: "The Blue Eagle is now perched on my door. I have signed up for the war against the depression." Another saw the Roosevelt administration's programs "as putting into practice many ideas given by Jesus in his Parables."[26]

Other ministers adopted a decidedly more activist approach to poverty and inequality. South Carolina–born Witherspoon Dodge was an unconventional but popular Presbyterian minister in Atlanta when the Depression hit. Already an advocate for the Social Gospel in the South, Dodge believed that the "righteous and loving will of God" should be "a powerful spiritual and social dynamic." Frustrated by the timidity of mainstream churches, he left the church in 1937 to work on the staff of the Textile Workers Organizing Committee throughout the South. Once severely beaten by anti-union thugs, Dodge nevertheless began a long career helping build the labor movement and speaking out for black civil rights.[27] Likewise, Methodist minister Charles C. Webber left his work with the church to become an organizer for the Amalgamated Clothing Workers in Richmond, Virginia, eventually serving as president of the Virginia CIO.[28]

Black churches, recalling the long history of exclusion by AFL unions, were more skeptical about the New Deal and the CIO's promise. The *National Baptist Union Review*, the organ of the smaller of the two major Baptist churches, was an inveterate foe of the New Deal and unions. The National Baptist Convention, Inc. (NBC), the largest African American church, only slowly became more favorable. In 1934, Rev. L. K. Williams, president of the NBC, said of the NRA: "None of us who have taken the time to study the results as affecting our race, can fail to see that it has been detrimental to us as a group." He criticized the New Deal program for trying to pay black workers lower wages and for the NRA's tendency to replace black with white workers.[29] On unions, Williams was equally skeptical at first, but the CIO gradually won his guarded support; in 1937, he noted that while labor agitation "has been a costly experiment," black workers "should join any or all Unions that will grant [them] justice and equal rights." However, he also asserted that blacks should be prepared to form their own unions and that the church should support the right to strike but also the right to cross picket lines when unions acted to exclude workers from industrial jobs.[30]

Church women also were of mixed minds. One of the more interesting disagreements over the hope for change in the South occurred at the National Baptist Women's Convention in 1936. The president, Mrs. S. W. Layten, asserted that Republican leadership had brought the nation to its "highest peak in civilization." To her, the New Deal meant "reckless spending, heavy taxation, millions unemployed and demoralized by living on the dole." Vice-President Nannie Burroughs, after a tour of the region, disagreed: "What we saw, heard and felt on this swing into the deep South assured us that a new day is dawning in Dixie." But even Burroughs still withheld full support. "The subtle scheme of giving white people jobs and giving Negroes relief is simply making bad matters worse," she argued.[31]

Despite such reservations, black churches increasingly found hope in the CIO's new attitude toward African Americans. This hope grew from seeds planted by some of the leading black Baptists in the late nineteenth and early twentieth centuries, men and women, like Burroughs, who "espoused a social gospel in the broad sense of the category," according to religious historian Gary Dorrien.[32] In Southern communities, black ministers found it more dangerous to express such thoughts openly. In Birmingham, for instance, where black workers built a fairly strong union culture, few remember getting help from ministers. In the iron ore mines of Muscoda, Alabama, the local minister refused to take sides when the union arrived. Instead, he felt that "the devil" was in the camp due to the rising labor tensions.[33] But on occasion, particularly among those part-time ministers who also worked in the mines and mills, there was more support. Samuel Andrews, a preacher-miner in Ensley, Alabama, was a strong union man who hosted meetings in his church.[34] Organizer Lucy Mason witnessed the growing confidence that African American churchgoers had in the CIO. In April 1941, she visited meetings of predominately black unions around the Memphis area. She noted that the meetings opened with a spiritual or hymn, prayer, "quotations from the Bible, [and] references to God and Jesus." Union representatives used "religious metaphors in appealing to people" who were devoted and had "faith in CIO."[35]

Attempts to link Christianity with labor and the New Deal generated strong opposition, particularly among white fundamentalists. In fact, even among clergy with working-class congregations who at first welcomed government assistance, there were concerns about an overreaching federal government that would destroy the work ethic and the central place of the church in community welfare. Dallas's J. Frank Norris and Louisiana's Gerald L. K. Smith, two of the nation's most prominent fundamentalists who initially embraced the New Deal, soon turned against Roosevelt and kept up a steady drumbeat of dire predictions about the consequences of liberalism. They were joined by such men as the fundamentalist revivalists Joe Jeffers and William Bell Riley, who toured the South, excoriating Roosevelt as the Antichrist and New Deal programs as symbols of the coming endtimes.[36] Radio preachers, like Charles Fuller and J. Harold Smith, as well as prophetic premillennial publications, including *Prophecy Monthly*, *Sword of the Lord* and *The Fundamentalist*, spread the frightful messages.[37]

Drawing the special ire of premillennial evangelicals was the labor movement. For many, unions symbolized the dangerous drift of American society toward atheistic socialism. The association of unions with Catholics and Jews made it easier for evangelicals to attack organized labor. Gerald Winrod, for example, wrote a piece claiming that the National Recovery Act, with its support for unions, concentrated too much economic power in the hands of Jewish socialists. Such legislation, through the lens of biblical prophecy about "Beast Worship," signaled the coming apocalypse, brought on by the false prophet Roosevelt.[38] Meanwhile, J. Harold Smith coined the simple warning: "C.I.O. stands for Christ Is Out, Communism Is On."[39] When the economy slumped toward recession in 1938, evangelicals amplified a chorus that included industrialists, Republicans, Southern Democrats, and others who felt that Roosevelt, with the assistance of union leaders and communists, was steering the country toward disaster.

Anti-union evangelicals pointed to the emphasis on materialism, conflict, and left-wing politics that ran counter to their reading of the Bible. This perspective crystallized in strident labor-denouncing publications edited by the likes of Rev. E. G. "Parson Jack" Johnston and Sherman Patterson. Johnston, who built a large following at the Baptist Tabernacle in Columbus, Georgia, began a monthly titled *The Trumpet* during the Depression. This publication, which carried the subhead "Orthodox—Fundamental—Pre-Millennial—Missionary," denounced unions and the New Deal as subversive and communist-dominated. It was *The Trumpet* that introduced the biblical admonition against unions, "Be ye not unequally yoked together with unbelievers," that became a rallying cry in the postwar era.[40] Patterson began publishing his monthly, *Militant Truth*, in Chattanooga, Tennessee, in 1939. Its masthead read: "Interpreting Current Events from a Fundamental Christian and Constitutional American Viewpoint."[41] Both of these papers received generous support from conservative evangelical businessmen and employer organizations. They routinely appeared, unsolicited, in the mailboxes of workers whenever unions conducted organizing drives.

While conservative evangelicals devoted a great deal of attention to unions and the political left, African Americans largely remained outside their intense gaze. This is not to suggest that hard times broke down barriers between conservative black and white Christians in the South. Rather, it testified more to the fact that black workers were hardly reaping the benefits of the New Deal's programs. Moreover, in many cases where unions accepted black workers into their ranks, they made only token efforts to break down job discrimination or give African Americans leadership roles or an equal voice in union decisions. Reuben Davis, who eventually followed his father into work on the Louisville and Nashville Railroad, recalled that during the 1930s, the union allowed only white oilers. Blacks, who did most of the work and received most of the blame if there were problems, could not rise above the category of helper.[42] This was the case even where black workers made up a majority of the membership. Earl Brown, an Alabama coal miner, remembered that the company assigned blacks to the most dangerous jobs and denied them opportunities for advancement, even after the UMW arrived on the scene. Similarly, Leon Alexander experienced hostility from white union members into the 1940s for trying to ensure that both blacks and whites benefited equally from the union.[43] Throughout the South, despite the prominent role played by black workers in building the CIO, "black deference and white paternalism remained essential elements of the CIO scene."[44]

White evangelicals probably also counted on the political timidity of black churches. Black churches overwhelmingly rejected communism. In Norfolk, Virginia, for example, black ministers led the campaign against the influence of the Communist Party in the African American community. The National Baptist Convention had strong fundamentalist inclinations as well, particularly from its president, L. K. Williams. At the 1939 annual session of the NBC, Williams chastised African Americans who saw in communism "the only remedy for the ills of the Negro and oppressed, suffering minorities." He warned that "it offers, as well, the abolishment of the Church and the substitution of blind, cruel force for the suffering love and a personal, active, loving God."[45] The bi-monthly black newspaper *Georgia Baptist* sounded quite a bit like white evangelicals with respect to communists: "They are like termites that get into the inside of the framing of a building and destroy it before the owner realizes that anything is the matter." The only way "to meet communism is with the Gospel of the Lord Jesus Christ," the author recommended.[46]

As the 1930s came to an end, the South had experienced major changes. Southern workers, black and white, began to think more positively about the role of unions in improving their prospects for material gains and security. A more expansive federal government had protected many in their choosing to be represented by a union and now guaranteed fair labor standards. However, black and white workers placed different demands on the unions they joined. Whites wanted to improve wages and working conditions while also protecting their claims to the best industrial jobs. They preferred the exclusive craft unions of the AFL, but where labor processes negated craft exclusivity, they joined the new industrial unions of the CIO. In CIO unions, they relied on contracts with seniority provisions and other discriminatory practices to protect their privileges. Black workers, too, wanted improved wages and working conditions, but they also expected unions to force employers to treat them fairly and allow them to advance to better-paying jobs on an equal footing with whites. The unions with the best reputations for meeting the demands of African American workers were those CIO unions led by people with ties to the left, especially the Communist Party. This made it easier for an increasingly vocal conservative white evangelical movement to associate unions and communism with the growing activism of black workers.

The Promises and Perils of Wartime America

The approach of World War II provided a new burst of energy for both black workers and the CIO. From 1937 to 1939, workers found themselves under siege. For labor, a slow economy tipped the scales toward employers in their efforts to thwart unions; charges of communist domination brought congressional scrutiny and divisions within the labor movement; and courts ruled in ways that constrained labor's militance.[47] World War II improved the environment. Tightening labor markets, a growing realization that the federal government needed to play an even greater role in managing the nation's production, and an emerging popular belief that labor should be a partner in the war effort enabled unions to press for more favorable treatment in maintaining their security, securing collective bargaining rights, and participating in decisions about the economy. Because of their importance in the mass production industries that would drive the country's production miracles during the war, CIO unions had even greater clout. Indeed, during World War II the CIO would expand to nearly four million members and become a powerful force in the nation's politics and economy.[48]

For black workers, however, it was unclear how such changes would affect them. As the nation began preparing for war, African American leaders pushed to be included in government and industry plans. Historian William P. Jones described the range of black activism. In the fall of 1940, Congress passed the Selective Service Act, but the administration refused to desegregate the armed forces or remove barriers against blacks moving into the officer corps. African American activists seethed; a group called Conscientious Objectors against Jim Crow began to counsel young black men to request exemption from the draft until they were treated as full equals. Meanwhile, A. Philip Randolph, president of the Brotherhood of Sleeping Car Porters, charged that AFL unions blocked black workers from obtaining jobs in the defense industries, even where employers had agreed to hire them. By January 1941, Randolph was planning a march on Washington, DC, to protest discrimination. In February, working with the NAACP and the Urban League, he exerted enough pressure that Senator Robert Wagner called for an investigation into the discriminatory practices of defense contractors. Experiencing only lukewarm responses, in May, Randolph issued a formal call for an "all-out march" of at least 50,000 protestors to take place in Washington on July 1. Just a week before the scheduled march, President Roosevelt finally acceded to some of Randolph's demands, establishing the Fair Employment Practices Committee (FEPC) to enforce an executive order that defense contracts and training programs not discriminate on the basis of race.[49]

The rhetoric of the war preparations, crystallized in President Roosevelt's "Four Freedoms" address in January 1941, emboldened African Americans, including religious leaders. At the 1941 National Baptist Convention, Nannie Burroughs charged that the four freedoms should begin at home. "Discrimination, Jim Crowism, and segregation and unemployment, from which the Negro people suffer in normal times, have become much more acute as the country drives to war," she claimed. A year later, the new president of the NBC, Rev. David V. Jemison, warned that the morale of African Americans fighting this war was not what it had been during World War I. To the question "What do Negroes want?" he answered with a list that included eliminating legal injustice, job discrimination, lynching, unequal accommodations, and unequal educational opportunities. Jemison wanted the country "to emancipate in fact as well as in name 13 million American born citizens."[50]

Black Methodist churches in the South were similarly emboldened, but targeted labor unions as well as the government. African Methodist Episcopal bishop Noah W. Williams organized a campaign to petition President Roosevelt about discrimination. The petition asserted:

> We are protesting against our nation giving endorsement and encouragement to labor unions that do not permit our people to work because they do not belong to these unions, and do not permit us to join the unions because of race and color.[51]

William Stuart Nelson, frustrated by ongoing discrimination, wrote in the *AME Zion Quarterly Review* that the growing power of organized labor had been "inimical to the industrial advancement of Negro workers. Even in CIO unions—the much-touted harbingers of the new (liberal) unionism," upgrading of black workers in industries "has met bitter opposition of white members."[52]

Black workers, however, distinguished the imperfect CIO unions from the AFL unions. At the Firestone plant in Memphis, Tennessee, Clarence Coe and George Holloway recalled their resentment against the AFL local union, dominated by white workers. But in the heady atmosphere of wartime labor shortages, black workers became uncooperative and "would slow down work so the whites couldn't make any money." Within a year, workers demanded a new election and voted in the CIO's United Rubber Workers by a large margin.[53] The union also helped open up opportunities for black women, who had been excluded by the company before World War II. Once hired, the union provided more security in obtaining fair treatment. Irene Branch started to quit several times because she "wasn't treated right," and recalled that if it "wasn't for that union, I wouldn't have been in there."[54] But even after a victory engineered by black workers, Firestone denied black workers equal pay and job advancement.

African American miners and steelworkers in Birmingham, Alabama, experienced similar mixed messages from unions. When Colonel Stone Johnson joined a union shop at the Louisville and Nashville Railroad, he was delighted that "black or white, all labor made the same thing" for similar work. However, he recalled, "where segregation came in was on the promotion." The union, which was not open to blacks, did nothing to stop the railroad from hiring new white workers in better job categories while blacks "were still a laborer, and you would know all the work, but you didn't get the preference."[55] Luther McKinstry, a miner at Tennessee Coal and Iron, remembered, "There were white-men jobs and black-men jobs . . . But any of the jobs, like millwright helper, you could work them, but you couldn't make one-day or one-minute seniority" toward acquiring the better-paying job permanently. Ultimately, McKinstry would have to sue the company and then the union to become a crane operator.[56]

Despite ongoing discrimination, black workers largely welcomed the gains they made from being in unions. For many, as is evident from oral histories of Alabama miners and steelworkers, adherence to the union acquired a religious significance. Leon Alexander, who served as a grievance handler in the UMW during the war, gained respect from his fellow miners "because [he] used a Christian principle in dealing with" their grievances. For steelworker Morris Benson, the union was like a church.

When he faced racist coworkers he drew upon his faith; "by being a Christian, I thought [the racist coworker] just hadn't got a hold of himself, and I pitied him." But, "if God's spirit is in you" then you can overcome nastiness."[57] John Garner, a devout coal miner who interpreted much of his life through biblical passages, became a staunch UMW supporter as well as a communist. He pointed to "Second Kings" as a justification for struggling against injustices and Revelations for confidence that "there's gonna take place a new heaven and a new earth," and that the wicked will not change their ways "until they get the sword."[58] Most were less apocalyptic than Garner, but nearly all praised the improvements gained through the admittedly imperfect CIO unions even as they pushed those unions to open opportunities for African Americans and treat blacks as equals.

In a few places where black workers constituted a majority in the workplace and where communist-led unions gave them full support, African Americans met astounding, if brief, success. In Winston-Salem, North Carolina, for example, the black leadership of Local 22 of the Food, Tobacco, Agricultural, and Allied Workers forced the powerful R. J. Reynolds Company to the bargaining table. Local 22 shattered some of the discriminatory practices of the company and began the process of transforming Winston-Salem politics.[59] Similarly, the left-led Mine, Mill, and Smelter Workers in the Birmingham area, led by the indomitable Asbury Howard, not only improved the conditions for workers, black and white, in iron ore mining but also played a huge role in registering black voters in the heart of Alabama. In St. Louis, United Electrical Workers District 8 was not a majority black organization, but its leadership fought segregation during the war and became a potent voice for black political rights in the area.[60]

There were many signs that African Americans took the freedom and democracy rhetoric of the wartime Roosevelt administration to heart, epitomized by the "Double V" slogan that called for victory over fascist racial supremacy at home as well as abroad. This slogan, which first appeared in the *Pittsburgh Courier* in February 1942, was, according to historian James Sparrow, "an echo, almost certainly unintended by Roosevelt, of his pledge to wipe out 'sources of international brutality, wherever they exist.'"[61] Blacks fought against discrimination on a variety of fronts during the war, demanding equal access to public transportation and public housing, the desegregation of the armed forces, and the right to vote. One of the most intriguing episodes demonstrating a growing confidence in asserting full citizenship involved the response of soldiers in 1944 to the failure of Alabama to prosecute the white perpetrators of the rape of Recy Taylor, a black wife and mother. Taylor had summoned the courage to identify her attackers and demand that they be arrested. But when the all-white grand jury refused to indict, support for equal justice for Taylor poured in from all over the country as the case became a national issue. In Belgium, thirty-three African American soldiers put down their guns and wrote Alabama governor Chauncey Sparks that his failure to act "is a matter of grave concern to everyone believing in the principles of American democracy." The soldiers reminded Sparks that "we are engaged in a war for freedom."[62]

The campaigns for equal citizenship for African Americans elicited a backlash. AFL unions, such as the Machinists and the Boilermakers, maintained their efforts to officially bar blacks and relegate them to separate auxiliary locals for as long as possible. When they could no longer defy government directives, members tried to prevent black advancements with brutality or subterfuge. In the upper South, Baltimore shipyards and steel mills, controlled by both AFL and CIO unions, became the scenes of "hate strikes" undertaken by white workers against the promotion of African Americans into traditionally white jobs. In the deep South, Mobile, Alabama, was the scene of one of the most violent job actions in May 1943 when hundreds of white workers roamed the shipyards indiscriminately attacking blacks to drive them from the Alabama Dry Dock Company's property.[63] A month later, a flood of black and white workers into defense jobs in Beaumont, Texas, exploded into a race riot when reports of black soldiers raping white women swirled through the community. The year 1943 was particularly brutal; there were some 240 violent interracial clashes in American cities.[64]

Rumors of aggressive black behavior, some quite ridiculous, were rampant. Throughout the South, for instance, society women circulated stories of black women forming secretive "Eleanor Clubs," named after the sympathetic first lady, to force white women to work in their own kitchens by going on strike. As James T. Sparrow points out, however, such rumors became another facet of the ways that the war threatened to upend the Southern social order in the minds of whites. At the behest of liberals like Eleanor Roosevelt, the federal government was helping CIO unions, communists, and socialists "to place Negroes on a basis of equality with whites with respect to all forms of employment," according to a Virginia U.S. Employment Service memo.[65]

There was some justification that Eleanor Clubs were only the tip of the iceberg. During the war, the U.S. House of Representatives twice passed legislation eliminating the poll tax, only to be stymied by a Southern filibuster in the Senate. In 1944, the U.S. Supreme Court ruled the Democratic white primary unconstitutional in *Smith v. Allwright*. The FEPC had gradually acquired greater influence in the North, particularly with the CIO's official cooperation, and in January 1944, the House introduced legislation to establish a permanent Fair Employment Practices Commission "to police both employers and labor unions" in rooting out discrimination from the nation's workplaces.⁶⁶

Inevitably, Southern whites linked this activity to religion. One of the rumors associated with the Eleanor Clubs was that black women were organizing in their churches. In November, 1944, when the Atlanta regional FEPC director, Witherspoon Dodge, himself a former Presbyterian minister and later CIO organizer, brought news of the possibility of congressional statutory authority for a permanent FEPC, he announced it at the Mt. Olive Baptist Church during the monthly meeting of the Atlanta NAACP. Dodge predicted that not even the "heated opposition" of Georgia senator Richard B. Russell could stop the momentum.⁶⁷ Mississippi senator Theodore Bilbo singled out black Baptist minister William Holmes Borders of Atlanta for his work in petitioning Congress on behalf of a permanent FEPC. Bilbo charged that Borders was part of a "hotbed of 'Reds' . . . who believe that through the FEPC they will hasten the day of destroying the color line" and bringing about "social equality" of the races. Bilbo promised: "I will leave nothing undone this side of heaven or hell to defeat this damnable legislative scheme."⁶⁸

To segregationist Southerners, mainline white churches were no safer as bulwarks against black equality. The Southern and Northern branches of the Methodist church united in 1944 and while the new denomination segregated black Methodists into their own conference, Methodists seemed unreliable on race issues. The denomination was home to Lillian Smith, who wrote an unflinching novel about interracial romance, *Strange Fruit*, in 1944 and went on to criticize the Methodists' "enforced segregation." Methodist female leaders Dorothy Tilly and Jessie Daniel Ames were among the South's leading fighters against lynching and racial injustice.⁶⁹ In 1944, Methodist bishop Francis J. McConnell appointed Rev. Charles Webber, the former director of the Methodist Federation for Social Service, to be "chaplain to organized labor" and reassigned him to Virginia, where he helped black workers in their fight against the P. D. Gwaltney Company in Smithfield. Webber quickly earned the rancor of Southern Methodists when he worked with the CIO to abolish the poll tax and pass a fair employment practices law.⁷⁰ Such an example frightened the Southern Baptist Convention and the Presbyterian Church in the United States, still regionally confined to the South and fearful of the tendency toward unity.⁷¹

Particularly anathema to the emerging new evangelicalism was the support of national and international ecumenical associations. The World Council of Churches began planning during World War II to develop a global "human rights" position that would allow for a just and durable postwar peace. Such a peace would recognize "a worldwide 'family'—a nonterritorial, nonracial, nonpolitical Christendom," according to religion scholar John S. Nurser. The Federal Council of Churches of Christ in America (FCC) took the lead in furthering the discussion of the idea during the war, understanding that it was committing the primary ecumenical association in the United States to fighting against racial inequality, a position that African Americans with their Double V campaign understood all too well.[72] In the immediate aftermath of the war, this human rights discourse became part of the United Nations and helped infuse a "theology of brotherhood" into the progressive politics of the South through such organizations as the Fellowship of Southern Churchmen, the Southern Conference for Human Welfare, and the Commission on Interracial Cooperation.[73] Nothing drove home the dread of such ecumenical beliefs among Southern white supremacists better than the appointment of the clergyman Dr. Benjamin Mays, president of Morehouse College, to be a board member of the FCC and a delegate to the World Council of Churches meeting in Amsterdam in 1948. The growing commitment of the FCC to fight racial inequality led to disaffiliations in the South and attacks on Federal Council spokespersons who tried to work in the region.[74]

Postwar Evangelicalism

The end of the war brought with it a flurry of violence and lynchings in the South as whites anticipated an upheaval in the social order. The Double V campaign and the international focus on human rights, which included the treatment of minorities in the United States, sparked a desperate reaction on the part of defenders of white supremacy. The Southern Conference for Human Welfare (SCHW) identified eighteen victims of lynchings in the South and this did not include the hundreds of victims of police and mob brutality in "racial disorders" in places such as Columbia, Tennessee, and Athens, Alabama. Many of the targets of these racial attacks were active or former servicemen, just recently returned to a nation unsure of its political and economic stability.[75]

In fact, African Americans were asserting their rights as citizens and registering to vote in record numbers, with some promising developments. The SCHW touted "hopeful cracks in the political fences of southern reactionaries" in New Orleans and Atlanta in 1946. "Negro votes" played an important role in the victories of Helen Douglas Mankin in Georgia's Fifth Congressional District and deLesseps Morrison as the new mayor of New Orleans. The SCHW praised the alliance of blacks, church groups, organized labor, veterans, and women's groups, which led to "a heavy turnout at the polls."[76] The impact of such mobilizations was noticeable: Rev. William

Holmes Borders, a prominent black preacher in Atlanta, recalled asking the mayor for black police and being told "without the slightest blinking of an eye, that we'd get black police about as soon as we'd get deacons in the [white] First Baptist Church." After Mankin's victory, the mayor replied to the same request: "How many do you want?"[77]

White supremacists, as evidenced by the violence noted above, were less cowed. Groups that attached themselves to religion, like the Christian Americans, began mobilizing as early as 1943 to attack both labor unions and African American attempts to break the plantation mentality of the low-wage, Jim Crow South. The Houston-based organization, funded by corporate executives such as Texas oil millionaire John Henry Kirby, wrote anti-labor legislation and lobbied for its passage in Texas, Arkansas, Mississippi, Georgia, and Tennessee, successfully promoting a right-to-work law in Arkansas. Even before the end of the war, the Christian Americans were linking unions with black advancement. One quote taken from the group warned: "From now on white women and white men will be forced into organizations with black African apes whom they will have to call 'brother' or lose their jobs."[78]

The Christian Americans were not the only group using religion to mask their objectives. The Ku Klux Klan also enjoyed a resurgence in the immediate postwar years. In October 1945, the Klan held a "fiery cross" ceremony near Atlanta after which "letters from throughout the country ... poured into the office of Dr. Samuel Green, grand dragon of Georgia." Atlanta's police chief from 1947 to 1972 remembered that "at one time most of the members of the police department were members of the Ku Klux Klan" and that they relished opportunities to keep blacks in their place.[79] Other states witnessed similar Klan revivals and religious leaders worried that "its queer, perverted ideology has somehow, in the minds of the uninformed, gotten mixed up with Christianity." Similarly, members of the liberal Fellowship of Southern Churchmen pleaded with the Southern Baptist Convention to denounce "certain Fascist-minded crusaders" like Gerald L. K. Smith, who "prostitutes Christianity" to promote his journal, *The Cross and the Flag*.[80]

Some of the religious opposition to both unions and black civil rights came from the surging holiness, pentecostal, and fundamentalist churches that associated with modernism, the growing power of the state, communism, and unbiblical trends interpreted through a premillennial lens. Reading the events of the day through the prism of the endtimes, Gerald Winrod's magazine, *The Defender*, charged: "The CIO, dominated by the Communistic Party has tried to create RACIAL DISCORD" to further its objectives of communist world dominance. *The Pentecostal Evangel* asserted that religion was barred from unions and that the "one big sin of our times" was "the rejection of Christ by employer and employee alike." Of the United Auto Workers strike in the winter of 1945-6, the paper claimed: "The Bible speaks of such conditions existing in the last days. Read the fifth chapter of James."[81]

For other premillennialists, the future of America as God's chosen land relied on developing a Christian free enterprise. John R. Rice's *Sword of the Lord* carried a front-page article written by Rev. Carl McIntire arguing that "the scriptures establish capitalism and free enterprise, and are against communism and socialism," which he equated with the modernists in the FCC. Alarmed that liberal Protestantism appeared to favor a more activist state and emphasized progress in humanitarian enterprises, McIntire scoured the Bible for justifications of private enterprise, property, and the profit motive. He warned his followers of the modernist-communist threat to American liberties that would undermine political, economic, and religious freedoms. These freedoms had rallied the nation and allowed it "to come forth from the battlefields victorious."[82]

Ironically, Southerners opposed to the economic and racial equality fostered by the FCC received an unexpected boost from the founding of a new ecumenical body, the National Association of Evangelicals (NAE), in 1942. Created as an anti-modernist counterweight to the FCC, the NAE under its leader Harold Ockenga believed that the war demonstrated that the only path to durable peace and "the rescue of western civilization" was through a "revival of evangelical Christianity," not secular-sounding pronouncements about human rights.[83] The NAE decried the "modernist regimentation" of government rules during the war that had been supported by the FCC. Christian free enterprise was the antidote to modernism and liberalism.[84]

The NAE cultivated a close relationship with the National Association of Manufacturers and effortlessly linked labor struggles with the efforts of African Americans to obtain their full citizenship. The organization bitterly denounced strikes and opposed a permanent Fair Employment Practices Act as "class legislation" that would "encourage rule by minorities," create social friction, imperil the freedom of Protestant organizations, and "give political bureaucracy another instrument of terror."[85] The NAE also worried that during the war blacks developed "an increasing attitude of resistance to efforts of unthinking whites to 'keep them in their place.' Organizations for race rights and advancement have stimulated this attitude."[86]

There was urgency in the NAE's efforts because the CIO had announced its plan to begin a massive union organizing campaign throughout the South, one that aimed to transform both labor relations and the political climate that had been so detrimental to liberal measures in the U.S. Congress. While Van Bittner, the director of the CIO's Southern Organizing

Campaign, promised to focus on union membership and winning collective bargaining rights, nearly everyone realized that success would require bringing African American workers into the fold and destroying the barriers to voting that kept reactionary politicians in control of the region. While the CIO tried to walk a tightrope between its stated goals and the broader aspirations that motivated blacks and their progressive allies, the specter of a truly radical upheaval of Southern norms facilitated conservatives who strove to characterize the campaign as a communist-led conspiracy.[87]

Conservative businessmen contributed heavily to the creeds of Christian free enterprise as an antidote to communism, modernism, and the destruction of the Southern way of life, which included white supremacy. In the Southwest, oilmen such as Sid Richardson, "Tex" Thornton, and H. L. Hunt plowed huge postwar profits into conservative seminaries and Bible colleges; entrepreneurs Jesse H. Jones, J. Howard Pew, and Robert G. LeTourneau bankrolled conservative religious colleges; and the NAE counted upon its numerous Christian Business Men's Committees to sponsor religious revivals and the Youth for Christ rallies that brought a young Billy Graham to national attention.[88]

The clearest articulations of the connections between anti-union businessmen, Christian-proclaiming reactionaries, and anxiety about the class and racial turmoil threatening the South were found in the little newspapers edited by "Parson Jack" Johnston and Sherman Patterson. Printed at various places in the South and often changing name, their four- or eight-page papers railed against Jews, Catholics, and blacks who gained support from the CIO; against the misinformed racial theories of the Methodist Church; and against opponents of fundamentalism. In league with textile firms and the Southern States Industrial Council, Patterson's *Militant Truth* showed up mysteriously in the mailboxes of workers whenever a union organizing drive came to town. It pointed out the biblical command to not be "yoked with unbelievers" (2 Corinthians 6:14) and then emphasized the atheistic and heretical beliefs of CIO leaders who were Catholic, Jewish, or even worse, godless communists. When union activists claimed religious sanction, Patterson replied: "Even as the devil himself quotes Scripture, so do the satanic hordes of socialism, communism, modernism and materialism stop at nothing in their efforts of deception, to undermine and destroy all that God-fearing, home-loving patriotic Americans hold dear."[89]

In an ironic twist, it was the association of unions with black workers, many of whom had strong evangelical Protestant beliefs, which convinced many white anti-union evangelicals that unions were communistic. Vernon W. Patterson, president of the National Laymen's Evangelistic Association, claimed that the recent spate of racial incidents in the South had been caused by Northern radicals intent upon promoting "indiscriminate intermingling of the races" and disrupting a situation where the races lived together "in friendliness and harmony with few disturbances to mar the relationship." Followers of the teachings of Karl Marx, Patterson charged, helped by "race legislation," such as anti-poll tax, anti-lynching, and fair employment practices bills, fomented race hatred and racial strife, aided by the misguided "Social Gospel" of labor unions and the FCC.[90]

These papers managed to tap the anxieties facing both employers and workers with respect to race. For employers, Sherman Patterson and Johnston opposed unions that sought to include blacks, thereby destroying a critical source of low-wage labor in the South, and give a religious patina to the charges that interracial unionism was an atheistic communist plot. For workers, the papers emphasized that following such leaders not only was religious heresy, but also threatened the advantages of whiteness that they enjoyed, including job preferences and the availability of African American women for cheap domestic labor. Furthermore, the promise of additional economic development and manufacturing jobs in the region would diminish if companies could not expect to pay lower wages than in the North.[91]

Fears of labor and racial assertiveness resonated for many Southern evangelicals in the postwar era because opponents couched their consequences in the framework of the endtimes. For many Southern whites, premillennial dispensationalism seemed to capture their feelings about where the world was headed in the wake of a horrid world war and the signs that global conflict was not done. The CIO union campaign promised to hasten the reign of the Antichrist, according to the *Pentecostal Evangel*. The paper pointed to the CIO's participation in the World Federation of Trade Unions, which was "one of the factors that is preparing the way for One World, eventually to be headed by the Antichrist." Similarly, it interpreted union programs to provide benefits only for paid-up members through Revelation 13:17; "No man might buy or sell, save he that had the mark, or the name of the beast, or the number of his name."[92] Alarmed evangelicals made it clear that supporters of unions and the programs they backed would try to sanctify those programs with a moralistic religion. In particular, they cited the FCC as purveyors of a false Christianity that placed man-made reforms above the church's duty to guarantee individual salvation and freedom of worship. John Rice's *Sword of the Lord* warned that "Christians must not fellowship with or support Modernists" who were "under an awful curse from God and from Christ."[93]

Especially dangerous in the postwar environment, according to many evangelicals, was legislation for fair employment practices. Glenwood Blackmore, writing in *United Evangelical Action*, criticized religious leaders who supported FEPC bills as naïve: "They allow their interest in the amelioration of the American Negro to blind them to the far more important considerations in this political plot to destroy fundamental American liberties." Such legislation was communist-inspired and ignored the fact that "the Negro in America is farther advanced materially and spiritually than the Negro anywhere else in the world," Blackmore asserted; there was "no doubt in my [Blackmore's] mind that God intended the races to be separate." Rather than rely on the "spirit of Christ in the lives of individuals," a permanent FEPC "would give political bureaucracy another instrument of terrorism" and "imperil the freedom and integrity of Protestant organizations."[94]

Evangelical concerns about the CIO's campaign to rouse the social justice sentiments of the Southern working class filtered into mainline denominations. Methodists in the South objected to the appointment of Charles Webber as "Minister to Labor" by a Northern bishop. Webber had been elected as president of the Virginia CIO and director of its Political Action Committee. He also angered the local Methodist bishop by organizing black workers and organizing opposition to the re-election of Senator Harry F. Byrd, who was anti-labor and anti-civil rights.[95] Likewise, the *Wesleyan Christian Advocate* of Macon, Georgia, cautioned against labor leaders "who with marvelous cunning try in every possible way to stir up discord and strife among our people." The editor coupled union activism with an attack on Jim Crow: if it were abolished, "the culture of the South would be destroyed; the morals of our people would degenerate beyond description."[96]

The Southern-based Presbyterian Church in the United States, which had thus far avoided the unification that had so tested Methodists, singled out Northern ministers, often sent by the FCC to speak for the CIO, for special animosity. Numerous complaints about James Myers and Cameron Hall, both Presbyterian ministers active in the Federal Council, reached church officials, one claiming that Myers was "an unadulterated CIO organizer parading in the guise of a Presbyterian minister."[97] Southern Presbyterians expressed fears that the CIO would bring federal government intervention into regional race relations. Rev. J. E. Flow, believing that the CIO's Southern Organizing Campaign was promoting racial demands, replied: "If we have to choose between segregation of the races and race riots, we prefer segregation of the races, or even 'Jim Crowism.'"[98]

The largest religious body of white Southerners, the Southern Baptist Convention, sought to remain officially neutral on labor-management relations, but the denomination dreaded communist influence in the CIO's campaign. Moreover, the Baptists had many noted fundamentalists among their clergy who hoped to push the church against liberalism and a more active, intrusive state. Thus the CIO was unlikely to win friends among Baptists when they favored laws relating to wages, hours, fair employment practices, or even elimination of the poll tax. In Richmond, Virginia, the Baptist weekly the *Religious Herald* angrily objected to the CIO's pamphlet "The Church and the CIO Must Cooperate," which sought to win support from churches for its Southern Organizing Campaign. The editor challenged the notion that the CIO would bring "a more abundant life" to all men with its program and asserted that the only thing a church *must* do is "to preach the Gospel of Christ to men everywhere."[99]

The premillennial and evangelical messages of these churches helped turn Southern white workers against the overtures of the CIO. The entreaties of religious bodies against being yoked with non-believers, together with the claims that communists (read non-believers) were behind any unions that would attempt to include African Americans, proved to be a convincing argument for many Southern white evangelicals against joining CIO unions.[100] The tragedy of this argument is that it ignored the reality that black and white workers frequently shared the same evangelical beliefs. It is tempting to conclude that many white workers so easily accepted the contentions made by advocates of a Christian free-enterprise ideology because they were fearful of losing the advantages of white supremacy. Certainly, proponents of that ideology made every effort to link union success with the advancement of black workers.

At the same time, in the decade before *Brown v. Board of Education*, the lynching of Emmett Till, and the Montgomery bus boycott, the evangelical injunction against being yoked with non-believers did not become for most Southerners a religion of white rage. There were acts of rage against African Americans, at times perpetrated by groups like the Christian Americans and the Ku Klux Klan that sought to cloak their actions under a perverted religious doctrine. However, church groups and publications, even those that worried that unions would undermine Jim Crow, denounced the Klan and the Christian Americans. The *Wesleyan Christian Advocate*, for example, reconsidered its opposition to federal intervention in civil rights abuses after the brutal lynching of four African Americans in Monroe, Georgia.[101] The *Religious Herald* of Richmond proudly pointed to a Southern Baptist conference proclamation that "the use of the sacred symbol of the Christian faith by the hooded promoters of race hatred and bigotry is a presumptuous sacrilege and a menace to the progress of worldwide evangelism to the Christian cause."[102] In *United Evangelical Action*, Gilbert James denounced racism in all its forms and even advocated for a fair employment practices law, asserting that the "Bible knows all mankind only as children of Adam and no color or so-called racial distinctions are made in the Scriptures."[103] These publications were hardly friends of unions or black equality, but they tended to blame racial unrest on the interventions of unions, communists, and outsiders rather than focus on the real aspirations of working-class blacks for full citizenship.

Nevertheless, the upheavals in Southern society caused by depression, war, and postwar anxieties set the stage for a dramatic struggle over the "theology of segregationism" rooted in the language of miscegenation during the decade after the *Brown* decision. The premillennialism of most Southern evangelicals, which had been nourished by the calamities and conflicts of the two decades that preceded the classic phase of the civil rights movement, gave a fire to what historian Jane Dailey asserts was "a religious conflict over orthodoxy between two strongly held Christian traditions."[104] Opponents of black demands for equality could still blame communists, liberals, and Northerners, but the actions of masses of African Americans in the South truly elicited a religion of white rage.

SIX

Constitutional Whiteness: Class, Narcissism, and the Source of White Rage

Jason O. Jeffries

"We the people of the United States," the opening words in the Preamble to the Constitution, are as powerful as "Let there be light," because of their creative properties. Much like the words scribed in Genesis 1:3, "We the people" marks the beginning point of creation. By the pronouncement of both of these phrases, the old has become new. Formlessness took shape, and nature became tamed. These words literally created new worlds. More importantly, "we the people," and the words that follow in both the Preamble and the Constitution, shed light on many of the beliefs, rituals, and symbols of the civil religion of the United States.

At first glance, the Constitution signifies that the nation was created as an inclusive one and would be attentive to the rights and desires of its people. This phrase sets the tone for what will be believed by Americans from the ratification of the Constitution until this day. This is part of the reason that the sacred text, cultural symbols, and principles represented by the Constitution can evoke visceral responses from "people" at certain ritualized moments. Take for example, how many of the athletes that represent the United States, in the Olympic Games, often shed tears at medal ceremonies when they see the flag raised and the hear the national anthem play. The emotion is present because they represent "the people" and themselves.

Although the words "we the people" invoke community and unity, from its foundation, the Constitution is exclusive in terms of race and gender, especially concerning the participation of citizens in political life and sociopolitical action. Exclusivity, here, not only represents the existence of geospatial boundaries for social interaction, but also alludes to the walling off or protection of white property and white bodies from invasion, incursion, or intrusion by non-whites. Many who consider themselves white reveal their need to defend and protect these boundaries every time social progress is seen as subordinating idealistic white interests. Because the Constitution is designed for the protection and inclusion of particular white bodies, whites often experience black uplift, political progress, or social activism, as an embodied invasion of physical and spatial boundaries. Their religious commitment to the Constitution as a sacred document and the experience of black uplift as a type of invasion causes white laborers to respond to perceived black progress and uplift viscerally and physically, by any means, in order to maintain the boundaries of their ideals, social space, economic environment, and bodies. From its foundation, the Constitution is exclusive in terms of race and class. Ultimately, white working-class people are casualties of the constitutional codex.

In this chapter, I contend that the Constitution not only establishes the birth of a nation, but it also establishes a particular type of whiteness that exceeds the intentional thoughts and actions of the average white American. Despite the realities of American capitalism and white success, these ideals live in the subconscious of white citizens, especially white males. Failure to achieve this white-being is akin to a narcissistic disorder and is the cause for racist and violent responses to black progress. In the first section of the chapter, I will outline the ways in which the Founding Fathers, the Constitutional Conventions and ratification of the Constitution established white-being, a race classification that accounts for class distinctions among early European settlers in the New World. I will demonstrate that the Constitution is an exclusive document, writing to protect particular social and political issues, especially wealthy, European colonists. Since the Constitution is a document that protects the interests of this particular class group, I argue that the Constitution establishes white-being. In the second section, I describe how white-being, created by the Constitution and its writers, results in white rage toward black and brown progress in the United States. White-being is a form of primary narcissism that cannot be maintained by the average working-class white. As a result, it leads to many variations of narcissistic rage.

Erasing Class Assumptions

Despite the religious fervor and the unshakable belief in these American ideas, the Constitution has always been an exclusive document in terms of race, gender, and class. It was formed by wealthy, white, aristocrats who intended to protect their own interests. They embraced the document without critical reflection on what is actually present in the United States. It is clear that the Constitution excluded people of African descent in its definition of "citizen," but there were more groups of people excluded from the inalienable rights written throughout the pages of the document. In addition to the exclusion of black people, white women and indigenous populations were prevented from enjoying particular rights, such as land ownership and voting. The Constitution was never intended to protect the interests of black people (free or bondspersons), white women, Native Americans, or any other group of non-white people. Enslaved Africans, regardless of gender designation, enjoyed none of the freedoms and rights outlined in the original or mythical Constitution, the written Constitution along with the traditions, beliefs, and additional rights ascribed to it.[1] White women were not afforded the right to vote. A white woman's ability to enjoy certain freedoms depended heavily on her marital relationship with a white man. Native Americans were considered part of nature and were removed from the land they possessed by force, signifying they had no civil rights that white immigrants had to respect.[2]

However, a closer examination of the sacred document and the events surrounding its development, especially in regards to class, will reveal that it did not extend these rights even to all white men. The Constitution also excluded poor white men. Many of the rights and privileges in the Constitution were reserved for property owners. This is a distinction of class. During the penning of the Constitution, there were debates about whether those who did not own property should enjoy the right to vote or participate in the polis.[3]

Many of the ideas and principles that Americans hold dear are attributed to the Constitution. Many of the large concepts believed to be part of the Constitution are not even mentioned at all. Eric Black argues that many people assume these concepts are part of the Constitution, but they were never mentioned in the original document when it was ratified in 1776.[4] They were added by amendments to the Bill of Rights, but have been extended back to the founding of the United States. He points out that many of these ideals have the power of law only because we believe they are part of the Constitution.[5] They are actually part of what he labels the mythic Constitution. The mythic Constitution is the interpretations and traditions believed to be part of the Constitution, but really included in the Bill of Rights and also more than 200 years of U.S. Supreme Court interpretations. If this is the case, we should examine the actual contents of the Constitution. Through such an examination, we will see that the Constitution is a document that establishes particular rights to wealthy, white men.

Ideas such as free speech, freedom of religion, a free press, and the right to a fair trial were not included in the original document; however, many believe these rights historically extend to the founding of the nation. The original document was ratified in 1787 by ten states without a Bill of Rights for the citizens.[6] The initial concern of the writers of the Constitution was not the rights of the citizens.

The Constitution also, in some ways, excluded poor white men. Those white men who did not own property could not vote or participate in the polis. The civilian and religious rights outlined in the Constitution were reserved for European settlers who had obtained a certain level of wealth which allowed them to live a life of leisure and possess personal property. Because of the religious belief in the perceived right given to whites in the name of the Constitution, many white, working-class citizens ignore the reality that it is a document that never really extended rights to them. Instead of facing this reality, many white, working-class people together become disenchanted with their own progress in comparison to the ever-increasing perceived progress of African Americans and other minorities in the United States. The weight of their failure as white, privileged citizens, is placed on the backs of non-whites, especially African Americans, and is expressed in the form of violence and hostility toward people of color. Criticism of the Constitution and its underlying, classed code(x) is ignored and white working-class people fail to evaluate the ways in which the Constitution contributes to their failure to achieve the American dream.

The Founding Fathers, who were wealthy aristocrats, were concerned about forging a strong central government out of the thirteen territories that had the power to regulate commerce, settle interstate disputes through the judicial system, and pay off the bonds that many of them held as a result of financing the Revolutionary War. The Constitution was written to insure the rights and secure the interests of the Founding Fathers themselves and people in their social and economic class. The most important right that the Constitution establishes for white, male citizens is the right to own property. The United States of America, at its core, was a British empire expansion project. Many of the explorers who came to the New World came with the hopes of building wealth.

By the time of the American Revolution, there was tremendous economic disparity within the developing American society, between white laborers and those who participated in the polis. The top 10 percent of the wealth holders controlled 50 percent of the nation's wealth. Although the wealth gap may seem stunning in this early stage in the life of the nation, it was acceptable in comparison to the wealth disparity in European nations.[7] Another reason this wealth gap was acceptable to early citizens of the colonies was in part due to the presence of both Native Americans and slaves, who, although present, were not considered part of the society.[8] This is significant to the mindset of the white men who were considered lower class because they would see themselves in comparison to both indigenous and slave communities in terms of wealth accumulation. Regardless of how poor they were in light of the Founders and the wealthy aristocrats, they would never be as poor as enslaved African people or as indigenous communities who did not yet practice the concept of personal property ownership.

Because the initial concerns of the Founding Fathers were to protect their own interests when they penned the Constitution, it is fair to say that the document was not made in the interests of all European immigrants, or early colonists. Regardless of the narratives of American exceptionalism and themes that borrow from Exodus and situate America as the new Promised Land that give colonial immigrants the opportunity to succeed and build wealth regardless of their social status in Europe, America is a country that, from its very foundation, already inherently fostered a class divide among its immigrant population. This class divide, along with the concerns of the Founders, created white-being. I define white-being as *the standards and actions colonial immigrants and their descendants must follow in order to be considered truly white, and enjoy all of the benefits that whiteness offers, especially life, liberty, and the pursuit of happiness.* White-being accounts for class and understands whiteness as a social construct that resides in the subconscious of white people, especially white males. Although whiteness, in a more traditional understanding, is widely based on the color of the skin, there is an element of whiteness that we misunderstand when we only focus on it in this way.

Understanding whiteness on the basis of skin color dismisses the creation of whiteness in the context of both colonialization and immigration, especially in the United States. This approach also takes lightly the history of how particular European ethnic groups within the United States have become "white" over the course of decades and centuries. As Hebert Gans argues, there is an economic component to race that leaves African Americans remaining at the bottom of the economic scale in the United States because they can never be granted white status. Although many European ethnic groups have immigrated to the United States, Irish, Italian and Jewish people were not considered white, because of some of their physical features and social stereotypes.

In the context of the United States, race and class are closely related. Gans argues that ideas of race and class have marked black bodies and laboring bodies since before the formation of the United States. According to Gans, during the settlement of the New World, white Anglo-Saxon Christians were the holders of cultural and political power. They assumed that European whiteness marked the top of the class hierarchy. In contrast, the body features of blacks (skin color, head size, size of nose, etc.) had been established as the markers of the lowest class at the bottom of the class hierarchy as evidenced by their involvement in slavery.[9] Gans, in his argument, focuses on the phenomenon that continues to leave African Americans at the bottom of economic development today. Although slavery was ended in 1863, African American descendants of slavery still struggle to achieve the American dream. In post-slavery times, immigrants from various countries have come to America and have surpassed African Americans economically. Gans partially attributes the success of certain ethnic groups to their ability to become white.

As mentioned in Gans's analysis, whiteness is not a stable racial category. The characteristics and qualities of one's appearance are not always enough to account for who is or is not white. In *White by Law: The Legal Construction of Race*, Ian Haney López documents the many of the legal trials where Irish, Italian, and Jewish immigrants appealed to the courts in order to become recognized in the United States as white citizens in the early to mid-twentieth century. Many of the decisions granting and denying whiteness were subjective and arbitrary at best. The courts sometimes decided whether or not a person was white on the basis of either appearance (biological) or the local understanding of whiteness (social/political). There were times that some people would be denied the status of whiteness, while others with similar appearances, immigrating from the same nation, would be ascribed its rights and privileges.[10] Today, however, people from Italian, Irish, or Jewish heritage who have immigrated to the United States since the 1960s do not have to appeal to the legal system in order to enjoy the rights and privileges of whiteness. Once viewed with suspicion, people from these ethnic backgrounds would not be excluded from whiteness in today's social environment, in regards to their physical characteristics or appearance.

When we think further about Gans's analysis of race as a factor of class, one must further consider the issue or flip the question . . . to what degree does class define one's race? If we consider class beyond economic prosperity and wealth accumulation, and instead think of class as the cultural symbols and practices in addition to the possession of economic capital, we may begin to have a more nuanced approach to the relationship between race and class.

White-Being and Being White

In the first section of this chapter, I argued that the Constitution is an exclusive document that was created to protect the interests of white, wealthy aristocrats. In this section, through further class analysis, utilizing the works of Pierre Bourdieu and Hannah Arendt, I will demonstrate how the Constitution also establishes a particular type of habitus that is embedded in the minds of white citizens. In addition to race being a class category in terms of economic status, or capital, we can conduct a deeper analysis of class as practice or habitus.[11] The constitutional habitus establishes white-being.

By the time of the American Revolution, there was tremendous economic disparity within the developing American society, between white laborers and those who participated in the polis. Whether one is a laborer is also a factor in determining one's class or class status, in addition to all the previously mentioned elements of class that have been utilized to criticize and abstain from granting African American people full citizenship within American society. Descendants of enslaved Africans have been heavily ridiculed at various times throughout American history for behaviors such as speaking informal English, eating soul food, making genres of music such as the blues and rap, or wearing colorful clothing.

The factors that contribute to class can also be utilized in drawing a distinction within the category of whiteness. Pierre Bourdieu proposed that the cultural symbols and practices that make class include artistic taste, style in dress, eating habits, and language. These preferences and practices are largely embedded in the mind, unconsciously. Bourdieu named these preferences and practices *habitus*. Habitus is an internalized set of practices created by society and unconsciously imposed on its people. Bourdieu defines the habitus as a system of structured, structuring dispositions that are carried out in practice and always oriented toward practical functions.[12] According to Hugh Urban, habitus explains the relationship between the human body and the larger social body. Bourdieu advanced the claim that all cultural symbols and practices including tastes, style, eating habits, religion, science, philosophy, and language embody interests and function to enhance social distinction.[13] It is the way in which the structures of the social order are embedded into the individual body. The social inscriptions are visual in an individual's gestures, accents, dress, hairstyle, eating, walking, and talking.[14]

If we think about the historical development of the United States, there were ways in which certain class cultural and social practices constituted a habitus for white identity—a class identity. In addition, the Constitution of the United States of America reveals some of the cultural practices and rights that serve as a litmus test for whiteness and, by extension, citizenship. Those who fail to possess the status symbols held as necessary for full citizenship in the United States should be classified as non-white, regardless of their skin. Remember, the emphasis is whiteness as a class category based on particular types of social capital. This means that people, in order to be classified as white, must possess both the status symbols and the practices outlined in the Constitution for status as citizens. There are two important markers of whiteness in this regard.

The first, and most important, marker of whiteness, through the view of what the white aristocrats emphasized in the Constitution, is ownership of land. The second is the ability to live a life of leisure, or participate in the public square. The opportunity to possess free land, expand the reach of the empire, and produce wealth for individuals and the British Empire is the primary reason that many people left their homeland, England, and came to the New World. It was an effort for them, many of whom were on the fringes of English society, to make a better life for themselves by building wealth and producing capital.[15]

Although not originally constructed with race in mind, white-being as a form of habitus can be seen in the philosophy of Hannah Arendt's *The Human Condition*, viewed through the lens of Pierre Bourdieu's habitus, unconscious practices, preferences, habits, and actions. Arendt hierarchically arranges *viva activia*, "human life in so far as it is actively engaged in doing something."[16] Arendt suggests that there are three activities related to the *viva activia*: labor, work, and action.

Labor is the human activity that is related to the physical and chemical processes of the material body. Those who labor are caught up in a perpetual cycle of using their bodies in order to meet the necessities of life.[17] They are consumers who neither add anything to the world through the creation of human artifacts nor participate in the polis, contributing to the history of humankind. In other words, laborers' contributions are limited to the private realm, their households. They utilize their bodies to work with the materials nature gives in order to consume those materials for the sake of survival. Like animals, laborers are not truly free because they spend all of their time utilizing their bodies for the purpose of survival and consumption.[18]

Work is the activity of human life that creates a world that both shows evidence of human existence and allows human beings to exist outside of nature. Work goes beyond labor because it is a production of things produced by those who work, and it creates a world that will outlast the life of the individual humans who created the world of the things. The worker, or *Homo faber*, is a toolmaker who invents tools and implements them in order to create a world, not to help the human life process continue.[19] Work, however, is not the goal of human worthiness or human activity. Although it many leave the evidence of human existence, and tell us something about human activity, it does not bear the same weight or produce human history. It is an activity that can be underestimated in comparison to action. Many archaeologists have discovered evidence of *Homo faber*, and have been forced to decide how civilized or advanced cultures of the past were in terms of civilization and society in comparison with today's known societies and cultures.

Although work is considered more important than labor in Arendt's political philosophy, action is the highest level of human engagement. For Arendt, action is rooted in the public realm and represents humans acting among one another within the context of society. For her, this signifies the greatest and most important human activity possible. It is action that creates history. It is the action of men among other men that transcends. Action is meaningful life in the polis, the sphere of freedom.[20] According to Arendt, action is a critical human activity.[21] Through human action, men are able to create their own self-made conditions which produce a power equal to nature in terms of conditioning humankind. Humans who take action in the polis are able to create and produce a life that is not dependent upon survival or dependent upon other human relationships.

Taking Arendt's political philosophy into consideration, it is important that we understand how the rights that are established in Constitution are also class rights. They are the rights of those who are considered human actors. They were originally established for white, wealthy men and establish the parameters for white-being, the true white man who is able to interact with other men in the polis. This can only be done if one has the kind of lifestyle that allows one to actively participate in the polis, or public square. Analyzing the issues addressed in the Constitution clues us in on the debates, arguments, and concerns of the creators of our system of government and the nation's initial laws. Remember, the Constitution is the second organizing document in the nation that has become the United States of America. The first was the Articles of Confederation, which organized the nation under a union with subtle federal power. In this regard, we can view the Constitution as a document that was also designed to correct the issues that were present in the Articles. The authors of the Constitution must have considered both the strengths and the weaknesses of the Articles of Confederation, especially in the interest of forming a union that could defend itself against outside invaders.

The wealth disparities within the society were also obvious by observing the habits and the practices of the founding class. Many of the Founding Fathers displayed their wealth through dress, wearing expensive clothing with collars and cuffs, which was hard to launder. They often hired manual laborers to clean their clothes on a regular basis. In addition, the Founders owned large estates and filled their houses with other materials that represented their cultural capital such as fine china, silver, mahogany furniture, and clocks. They were also men of leisure, often enjoying dancing, dinner parties, and paintings. Many of them prided themselves on being conversationalists.

Although they resisted the hereditary control of the British monarchical society, they imitated the luxury and leisure.[22]

The leisurely lifestyle and the financial practices that enabled the Founding Fathers and others in their class to live this way became a pressing point that led to one of the early protests and armed uprisings in the Colonies. This in turn sparked the discussions behind what eventually led to the discussions that resulted in the penning of the Constitution. During the 1780s, the class divide came to an irruption in a protest by the agrarian class. At the time, small farmers made up the majority of the population.[23] After the Revolutionary War, during the transition from British colony to an independent, international trading partner, the aristocrats and merchants in Boston were under pressure to do business in gold and silver, since English currency was no longer a valid means of exchange. The British merchants demanded they exchange gold and silver on the market. The Boston merchants passed those demands of exchange onto the small farmers in rural parts of the new nation. When the farmers could not meet the demands of the urban merchants, who financed both the war for independence and the farming operations, the merchant class, who were also leaders in politics, imposed taxes on the farmers which allowed them to foreclose on the agricultural property. The merchant class, the aristocrats, were able to transfer even more wealth to themselves.[24] In addition to taxes, the farmers were indebted to the merchant class for personal loans. Between 1784 and 1786, one-third of the farmers in western Massachusetts were sued for slow defaulting on personal loans.[25]

These disparities between the white laborers and those who participated in the polis led to a historical event that highlighted the inherent conflict between the two classes and shaped the development of the Constitution, Shays' Rebellion. Many of the farmers, who were laborers and fabricators, had neglected their farms to fight in the interest of freedom from the British and unfair taxation on their labor and the products they produced. Postwar America was full of broken promises and deferred dreams as it tried to make the transition from British colony to independent trading partner. The country's action class constantly made things more difficult for the farmers, the laborers and fabricators. This class of New World hopefuls found themselves becoming the victims of the new Boston-based money economy, in which they had little interest and poor prospects for survival. They felt their traditional way of life and their dependence on their own work and labor fleeting. The promise of the New World became like salt on their tongues.

Unlike the laborer or fabricator classes, the Founding Fathers were "the well-bred, the well-read, and the well-wed."[26] In short, they were the full focus of the laborious farmers of Shay's Rebellion. Their major concerns were: a) prohibiting states from issuing their own currency, and also preventing any currency other than gold and silver as acceptable means for paying debt; b) authorizing Congress to quell domestic insurrections; c) compelling states to extradite fugitives; d) preventing state laws that might invalidate contracts, making jubilee debt laws unconstitutional; and e) strengthening the federal government's ability to raise funds and maintain an army.[27]

Many of the Constitution's framers were self-serving aristocrats. The majority of them had personal economic interests to protect and they made sure those interests were given attention at the Constitutional Convention. According to Eric Black:

> Of the 55 delegates at the convention, 40 owned government bonds that had depreciated dramatically under the Articles of Confederation, and soared in value after the Constitution required the new federal government to pay them off. Twenty-four of the framers were money-lenders. The Constitution, by ensuring the sanctity of contracts and centralizing control of the money supply, shored up the value of their loan portfolios. At least 16 owned slaves. The Constitution improved the legal and political position of slaveholders. Many owned land in the Western territories. A strong central government was a key to making those investments pay off. All were members of the upper class—George Washington was one of the richest men in America—and that class did well in the aftermath of the convention and has prospered ever since . . . The framers spoke of democracy as a menace and of the masses as untruthworthy.[28]

In the end, the Founding Fathers made certain to secure the rights of property against the passions of the farmers and other working-class people. As Black explains:

> George Mason of Virginia proposed a property-owning qualification for the Senate. James Madison proposed nine-year terms, so that senators could be shielded from democratic pressure. Two South Carolina delegates wanted the relative wealth of states to be reflected in their power in Congress.[29]

White Narcissistic Rage

So far, we have argued that the Constitution is an exclusive document that protects the interests of white, wealthy citizens. Through its traditions and concerns, it also establishes a white-being, a habitus for white citizens who enjoy its full rights and benefits. In this section, I will argue that failure of white-being is one of the reason white, working-class citizens respond with rage to black progress.

Black and brown bodies, especially in regards to political life and sociopolitical action, have been excluded from participation in American society. White rage, according to Carol Anderson, is a response to black progress that not only functions through open, physical violence, but is affectively exercised through the creation of laws that restrict and regulate black bodies.[30] Because the Constitution is designed for protection and inclusion of white bodies, whites often experience black uplift, political progress, or social activism, as an embodied invasion of physical and spatial boundaries. Their religious commitment to the Constitution as a sacred document and the experience of black uplift as a type of invasion causes white laborers to respond to perceived black progress and uplift viscerally and physically, by any means, in order to maintain the boundaries of their ideals, social space, economic environment, and bodies. Ultimately, white, working-class people are casualties of the white-being established in the Constitution.

Although the Constitution was written to protect the interests of the Founding Fathers, those who have become ethnically white still aspire to live a life of white-being. That is, they want to possess private property, and participate in the polis. Although skin color may dominate the most common perception of white-being and being white, many white folks, who dwell in the pride of whiteness, often fail at it because they do not live up to white-being. They are just being white. To explain this another way, white-being, if we consider whiteness as not only a condition of skin color but also a condition of action and class, is both a race and a class category. Some white folks fail at being white, or white-being. They fail at acquiring private property, moving into the action class, and/or enjoying a life and leisure in the polis. Failure at white-being is the foundation for white nervousness and/or white rage.

Black progress being a trigger for white psychological disease is not a new concept in the mental health world. Around the end of the Civil War, white citizens were diagnosed with mental disorders such as neurasthenia, a nervous condition. The condition was brought on by the rapid change in the social order, which made whites question the stability of the country and their future role in control of black and brown bodies.[31] According to Veronica Watson:

> Race is a factor in the overall environment of white nervousness in America. Some physicians diagnosed white people with neurasthenia as a legitimate medical diagnosis also, after the Civil War. This mental disease was brought into the discourse of white superiority. Although African Americans might suffer from a number of physiological and psychological ailments, they were rarely diagnosed as neurasthenic. Because of the changing social climate,

with black people experiencing more freedom and social mobility, white citizens were forced to adapt ... "Neurasthenia emerges when the outer environment demands a level of adaptability and flexibility that a personality is not able to accommodate or manipulate, when changes in the social world challenge one's inner sense of comfort, stability, and power." In other words, when the white personality does not experience the ease, comfort, and power that it has come to expect and upon which it relies, it experiences a crisis, a disintegration of personality.[32]

More than a form of nervousness, however, white-being is a form of primary narcissism for working-class, white Americans. According to Heinz Kohut, primary narcissism is established in the infant stage of development, when the child views the mother and him/herself as united as one. In this stage, the child believes that s/he has complete control of the parent's body as if it was his/her own body. This explains why infants often feel free to grab and pull on the mother's body at any given point, or why an infant may reach for the mother's breast to feed even at inconvenient or inappropriate times. The parent is also ascribed qualities of omniscience and omnipresence.[33] The child cannot tell that there is a separation between the mother and him/herself. As the child realizes that the mother and s/he are separate, or as the child realizes that the mother or parent is not perfect, s/he experiences narcissistic disturbances. How the child deals with narcissistic disturbances is through the formulation of an idealized parent imago. In this process, the self develops an ego ideal. This ego ideal is experienced as God. These disturbances continue throughout life in various intensities.[34]

Instead of the primary love object being a parent, I am suggesting that the myth of the Founding Fathers and the penning of the Constitution function as idealized parent imagos for white, working-class Americans and contribute to their ego ideals. Among the rights and freedoms functioning inside the ego is the right to take land or possess large amounts of territory to create wealth, and the right to control or own others, especially so-called minorities, as property. The latter point is the residue of the master-slave relationship which the Constitution assumes as part of the social culture. The inability to do either one of these things sparks narcissistic rage.

Cheryl Mattias, in analyzing white narcissism, has outlined several emotional responses by white people when they are confronted about racism or challenged by a non-white person in the public arena. The first possible response she outlines is guilt and reaffirmation. The response signals narcissism because if a white person feels a sense of racial guilt, they ultimately recenter hegemonic whiteness by announcing what good they personally do in society in order to erase, smother, or stamp out the guilt. The second response is a performance of racial ignorance. This reaction is problematic, however, because it relinquishes racial culpability and centers white emotionality. An example of this is when after being confronted by the effects of racism, a white person asks the person who pointed out the problem, "What do you suggest we do to fix the problem?" Placing the burden of fixing a problem caused by racism and white supremacy on the victims of oppression fails to hold whites accountable for their individual, group, or structural involvement in racism and oppression. A third reply that displays the fragility of the white ego is self-victimization. This is when whites compare the impact of racism on white people to its impact on people of color as if white people are also victims. Although whites are affected by racism, they are often the beneficiaries of it. The effect on them can never truly be compared to those in oppressed communities. Finally, the fourth emotional retort is blatant disrespect. This is a way of dismissing any claims of white wrongdoing.[35]

People with narcissistic personality disorder and racist individuals share some of the same characteristics, especially a lack of empathy for others.[36] C. C. Bell lists several of the characteristics: a) a grandiose sense of self; b) a preoccupation with fantasies of ultimate levels of power, success, beauty, intelligence; c) demands for constant admiration or attention; d) responding to the indifference of others, critique, and defeat with either indifference, shame, inferiority, humiliation, or rage; and e) any various of lack of empathy, entitlement, interpersonal exploitation, overidealization or devaluation of relationships.[37]

Any of these various narcissistic responses, as outlined by Mattias and Bell, are forms of white rage. As Carol Anderson argues, ultimately, the trigger for white rage is black advancement. Whether there is an increase in the population of black bodies, a display of black ambition, or a demand for equal citizenship, white rage attempts to maintain the upper hand and keep others, especially black bodies, in their place.[38] This is accomplished not only through physical violence, but also through regulations and laws, access to resources, and the judicial system.

Kelly Brown Douglas explains the relationship between narcissism and white rage as she attempts to understand why whites have gunned down so many black people, including youth. Despite what some may see as an easy case to prosecute, many of the white shooters have subsequently avoided conviction, and in some cases indictment, for killing black people by using "stand your ground" laws as a legal defense. Douglas traces the roots of American "stand your ground" laws to the myth of Tacitus's *Germania*, a book that identifies Germanic tribes who fended off the Roman Empire in the first century as aboriginal people who were free from all taint of intermarriages. They were an unmixed race of people, distinct and unique. *Germania* described these people as having "fierce blue eyes, red hair, huge frames."[39] The ideas in this book became part of the religious myth of Anglo Saxon American exceptionalism, the construction of whiteness/white supremacy, and the idea of cherished property.[40]

The Anglo-Saxon myth of exceptionalism is also the ideological grounding for ideas that hold black bodies inferior. According to Douglas, the central conception of the black body, which grounds all other negative, harmful depictions of black bodies, including black bodies as criminal and hypersexualized, is the black body as chattel. "Chattel" means that black people did not have the rights to possess their own bodies, other black bodies, or the bodies of their own children. In contrast to cherished white bodies that should be protected at all costs and could never be commodified, black bodies could only hope to be seen as valued property of whites.[41]

Douglas furthers her argument to discuss the idea of the dangerous black body. Because black bodies are seen as chattel and meant to be the property of whites, any black body that is free is deemed dangerous because it threatens the established social order of Anglo-Saxon exceptionalism by entering white space and challenging the idea of white supremacy. This is because, according to the myth, freedom is a right and property of whiteness and thus, if a black body possesses freedom, it possesses something that it does not have a right to—something that belongs to whites. Because of the inherent danger to whites, black bodies must be restricted, corralled, and restrained, keeping them from coming in contact with white cherished bodies.[42] In order to show how the freedom of black physical bodies has been restrained, Douglas traces several laws and traditions, including black codes, vagrancy laws, lynching, redlining and other housing policies during the New Deal, which were designed to segregate black bodies and white bodies and maintain a mental balance for white narcissism.[43]

Part Two

White Religious Fervor, Religious Ideology, and White Identity

SEVEN

KKK Christology: A Brief on White Class Insecurity

Paul Easterling

Don't you say nothing about my Daddy! What he fought for was dignity in defeat. And against the unconditional surrender. We weren't foreign barbarians pounding on the city walls! We were your brothers. We deserved dignity in defeat.[1]

–Chris Mannix

The angels that have anxiously watched the reformation from its beginnings, must have hovered about Stone Mountain and shouted hosannas to the highest heavens.[2]

–William Joseph Simmons

Praise White Jesus![3]

–Kalinga

Introduction

The Ku Klux Klan is an organization that has a particular vision of itself and of history. This vision is rife with historical and religious symbolism that creates a particular set of images in the minds of white Americans who sympathize with the movement and its ideals. Images of a glorious American past, where wild people and wild lands are tamed and made useful for the European race. As well, images of a God who not only condones the subjugation of (so-called) inferior peoples and lands but is actively engaged in the process of enslavement and genocide for the sake of his people, the white race. Nonetheless, despite the posturing and mythos, the KKK is simply an organization that developed from a sense of economic and social class insecurity.

The Klan began as a social club for veterans after the Civil War who were concerned about their own position in American society vis-à-vis the position of African Americans, immigrants and Catholics.[4] Hatred for black people and black progress was (and remains) one of their most central tenets. The anti-black sentiment of the KKK is matched only by the group's fervent commitment to their interpretation of Christianity. For them, the white Anglo-Saxon Protestant race are God's chosen people and all other groups of people are inferior, best suited to serve the white race, nothing more. As a Christian group, one is forced to wonder what their version of Christ looks like physically and philosophically. The Christ figure comes in many colors and iterations. It only follows that the Christ of the KKK also has a particular tone and texture.

This chapter will work to develop a character sketch of the KKK Christ. Being that the Klan is an organization of primarily working-class individuals and families, this chapter will highlight concerns focused around class insecurity. Moreover, it moves from the point of departure that the KKK is in fact a Christian organization with a unique Christology that must be studied in order to better understand the root of its hate. It makes use of Christian symbols and biblical texts, and argues that its mission is a holy charge bestowed upon it by the Christian God. Given this, we are forced to question the assumed benevolence of the Christ figure itself, much like William Jones challenged the assumed righteousness of God.[5]

The Malleability of the Christ

Before delving into the KKK's understanding of the Christ figure, it must first be made clear that Jesus Christ is an extremely malleable religious icon. That is, the image and gospel of the one touted as the savior of humanity has been and continues to be shaped and molded to serve a number of different purposes for a number of different racial, ethnic, cultural, philosophic, religious, and gendered groups. Moreover, there has been a tendency of those who develop and discuss varying Christologies to focus on the redemptive aspects of the gospel; however, the Christ is not always redemptive to all. His image can and has been used to maintain notions of white supremacy. This is the Jesus Christ of the KKK. A Christ that is only here to save the white race. A Christ whose light shines only from the burning crosses of Klan rallies. A Christ whose light burns brightest when black bodies are used as kindling.

Despite the long history of the Christ being used to oppress African American people, America's formerly captive population managed to develop redemptive notions of the Christ figure. This was no easy task. But, as a result Black Jesus "has been a mainstay of African American Christian thought; in fact, it has been the central theological category used to frame the nature of meaning of human engagement with/in the world."[6] But there are problems with Christ the redeemer for the African American community, such as the normalization of suffering.[7] By extension, Christ the redeemer has done very little to change the oppressive circumstances of African American life, thereby directly contributing to the continued maintenance of the American racial hierarchy and white supremacy. In fact, the argument could be made that an African American Christ does more to maintain racial structures by simply being a colorized Christ, not a deity that transcends color consciousness. In other words, the development of Christologies does little to deconstruct the problematic power structure of race or "otherness" in America but instead simply replaces a white face with a "colored" one.[8] This effort only works to reinforce the existing power structure under a different name and face.[9] Anthony Pinn supports: "Even this Christ-like black body is a symbol of the social system and therefore power continues to define and shape it."[10]

History of the Ku Klux Klan and the Development of Class Insecurity

Class insecurity is as much a part of the fabric of America as racism is. As a matter of fact, class insecurity has fed (and continues to feed) into racist ideas. In the early Americas, poor white migrants did not come to these lands simply to be free, they came yoked as any other beast of burden.[11] They needed to work and be made useful as the fledgling nation developed. That is to say, those who occupied the upper crust of American society needed enslaved Africans, Native Americans and poor whites to build the nation.[12] For a time, these poor populations worked side by side for affluent landowners. But, as the population of Africans grew and the Native American population became more hostile to the European presence, poor whites would become most useful as a human wall to protect affluent whites and their lands and property. In addition, as history progressed and the country developed, poor whites would be used in every conflict that threatened the dealings of the upper crust of American society. This was most true for the American Civil War.

During the Civil War thousands of poor whites on both sides were forced to the front lines as conscripts in a conflict that would ultimately offer them no real benefit.[13] At the conclusion of this conflict, poor Confederate soldiers were not left with much; even their pride was stripped from them as the Northern army demanded unconditional surrender. As a result, many resorted to robbery, piracy, stealing, and killing simply to eat. Some found work, but many were not skilled laborers, like formerly enslaved Africans, resulting in a deep sense of class insecurity for white men.[14] In this midst of this mire former Confederate soldiers decided to develop an organization which would benefit those of like mind, constitution, and social circumstance: the Ku Klux Klan.

The history of the KKK can be discussed in three phases: postbellum (between 1865 and 1871), the early twentieth century (between 1915 and 1925) and the mid-twentieth century (from the 1950s to the 1970s). The first phase of the Klan began shortly after the signing of the Emancipation Proclamation, sometime between December 1865 and April 1866 in Pulaski, Tennessee. The movement was founded by six former Confederate officers, but was not particularly well organized or uniformed in any substantive fashion. Instead, it was a loose group of individuals whose primary concern was keeping freemen and -women (emancipated African Americans) from achieving any semblance of power or peoplehood. Despite the fact that the first phase of the Klan was not well organized, it was extremely disruptive and hostile to any notion of black progress. Routinely, members intimidated, assaulted, and murdered African Americans and their white allies. They saw themselves as vigilantes, fighting for the honor of their fallen Confederate generals and the sanctity of white women. However, the real concern of the KKK was the loss of white power, particularly economic power. Now that African Americans were free, and could become wage earners and landowners, they represented competition in a budding American economy.

As the KKK grew in power during the first phase of its development, it became problematic to the federal government. Not only were its members intimidating and killing freemen and -women, it also kept progressive Republicans looking over their shoulder. As such, the federal government intervened, making the KKK an illegal terrorist organization in 1871. Despite this, the Klan was reignited in the early twentieth century at a time when Africans in America were again working to establish a sense of peoplehood. The second iteration of the Klan was founded atop Stone Mountain (just outside of Atlanta, Georgia) in very ceremonious fashion by William Joseph Simmons. Simmons and his compatriots organized this movement from the memories of old Confederates and antiquated documents of the original Klan chapters.[15] During the second phase of the KKK, the organization was larger, better organized, and by extension, much more lethal than before.[16]

The insecurity felt by economically disenfranchised white men at the turn of the twentieth century prompted the second iteration. To elaborate, leading up to the refounding of the Klan, African Americans saw a modicum of advancement during the Great Migration period and represented enough of an economic threat to fan the flame of white hate throughout the South, thus leading to the spark that ignited the light of the Klan atop Stone Mountain. Moreover, the second manifestation of the Klan was not only better organized, it was well funded and more violent than the original Klan.[17] Membership was represented in every legal facet of Southern society, from the police to juries, lawyers, and judges, making it nearly impossible to prosecute any murder or terrorist act they committed. Their power during the second iteration was virtually unquestioned.

Economically, this era of the Klan was also a period of dubious prosperity for the movement and its members. Between membership dues, businesses and auxiliary movements, the KKK was a powerful economic entity in American society. Membership grew tremendously during this period. As well, members of the Klan worked together to economically support each other. They also focused their energy on slowing or stomping out any effort of African Americans working to achieve economic independence. For the Klan, greater internal economic support and development was prompted in part by the African American push for greater economic prosperity, but it was also due to a lingering sentiment of economic insecurity brought on by centuries of abuse at the hands of affluent whites.[18] However, within the organization there were many opportunists who only joined the KKK because it offered them an economic support group of like-minded individuals. These opportunists siphoned resources from the Klan for their own personal use and contributed very little to the cause.[19] Problems such as these and a growing distaste for the Klan's extreme activities eventually, once again, led to the decline of the movement.

The third iteration of the Klan developed almost hand-in-hand with the civil rights movement. African Americans' effort to secure more civil rights and humane treatment prompted the Klan to push back. During the third manifestation of the KKK, despite its downfall in the 1930s, the organization seemed to pick up right where it left off in previous decades. Were it not for the notion of black progress being inexplicably linked to white loss, the third iteration of the Klan, arguably, would not have had the teeth it needed to feed and grow.[20] Nonetheless, during this resurgence the Klan again sought and gained the support of thousands throughout the South.[21] It was not an organization to be taken lightly, infiltrating all aspects of American life and having far-reaching support, much of it carried over from the previous generation.[22]

Each iteration of the KKK was sparked by the notion of black progress.[23] The initial founding came on the heels of the Emancipation Proclamation. The second wave of the movement developed as a response to the advances made by African Americans in the 1910s and 1920s. (This is also a period in American history when the lynching of African Americans peaked.) The third wave of the movement rose in tandem with the civil rights movement. Given this, it can be argued that the KKK was organized to essentially address a sense of loss felt by white men.[24] This sense of loss is centered on the perceived disintegration of power through the physical freedom of African Americans and subsequent pushes for social advancement. In essence, the history of the KKK is a reactionary history of poor white men organizing themselves against populations of people who were themselves impoverished and powerless.

KKK Christ—The Problem of White Jesus

The Christ figure has been employed as a symbol of white male supremacy for centuries. Simply having an image of a deity that is white and male can distort and has distorted the image of what is good or right in the world. Not included in the image of Jesus are all the "othered" peoples of the world. Women, people of African descent, Native Americans, Latinx people, Asians, and the LGBT community have all been excluded from the historically popular image of Jesus. Christologies developed from divergent communities work to disrupt the white male image of Christ so that people on the margins are able to locate themselves. However, the dominant image of Jesus is that of the White Christ.

The Christ in human hands is a shapeshifting entity. His face comes from the imaginings of the powerful and his words are recycled through human experience. In short, Jesus Christ is a pliant and potentially precarious idol of human design, nothing more. One issue that is highly problematic with the malleability of Christ is the fact that the image and philosophy of this deity can be and has been used to justify a great number of atrocities. The genocide of the indigenous population of the Americas; the enslavement of African people; the colonization of Africa, the Americas, and Asia; the subjugation of women: these are just some of the atrocities committed in the name of White Jesus. That being said, the assumption of the benevolence of the White Christ is a fallacy at best and a nefarious lie used to control humanity at worst.

The Christ figure is a slave to the people who own it at any particular time and space. Meaning, Christ is reflective of the people who call his name and nothing more. Yes, the Christ figure has redemptive qualities and traits that are to be considered modest, honest, valiant, and salvific. But these attributes can be twisted to serve a truth shared by people who are cowardly liars, murderers, and rapists, whose only concerns are self-serving and denigrating. Just as a sword can be used to protect or to pillage, the

Christ figure can be used in the same ambidextrous fashion. On the one hand, on the one hand the Black Christ rose out of a yearning for physical, mental, and spiritual liberation when freedom in American society was not a reality for enslaved Africans; on the other hand, the Christ of the KKK was also developed out of a particular yearning, a yearning of white men who were deeply insecure about their place in American society.[25]

The Christ symbol does a number of things for the KKK as a movement. First, to claim Christ as the philosophical center of the movement makes it extremely palatable to the white American cultural psyche, without which the movement would have never made the impact that it did. For the KKK, Americanism and the ethical foundation of Christianity go hand-in-hand. In addition, for the KKK, America is a Christian nation founded on the principles of Protestantism. Catholics, Jews, and Muslims are threats to the American way of life and antithetical to the supremacy of white men. Second, the Klan Christ provides white people with a sense of chosen-ness; that is, a feeling that white Protestants are a special people hand-picked to bring the white light of Jesus into the world.[26] This sense of being chosen is not unique to the KKK as it seems to be a general feeling shared by white Americans in a very broad sense. How else have they justified the atrocities of the last four centuries, but through a sense of divine mandate? Lastly, from this sense of chosen-ness they are justified by White Jesus in any action they carry out for the sake of the white race. Therefore, they will not be punished in the afterlife for their works here on Earth, but instead rewarded.

Again, the Christ figure does not operate independent of the imagery supplied by human beings. This imagery is extremely powerful. Not only has this image fueled the KKK in their charge to keep America white, but the image is enduring. To this day, many poor white Americans, who have much more in common with their poor black and brown counterparts, are still being driven by the false imagery of a pure white American past that works to their economic, political, and social detriment. Linda Gordon argues: "In Klan theology, evangelical Protestantism was what the founding fathers had imagined and decreed—an entirely false and ahistorical rendering, of course, of their eighteenth-century religious creeds."[27] In this sense history also becomes a shapeable entity that becomes more myth than fact. For a KKK Christology, like Klan theology, history is merely a manifestation of the white supremacist imagination but it does nothing to address the problematic power dynamics that poor white people suffer under.

Critical queries that come from this discussion of a KKK Christ are: Can we speak of a white Christ that does not closely resemble the Christ of the KKK? Is there any difference between the White Christ and the Christ of the KKK or are these two beings the same? And, is there a redemptive and righteous white Christ for all humans, given the history of white people? The KKK by themselves are not the only tormentors of African people. To be quite clear, the KKK are a bit late in the game when discussing the history of African American oppression. Further, they were extremely reactive in their approach, only arising out of a sense of class insecurity following points in history that represented African American advancement: the Emancipation Proclamation, the Great Migration and the civil rights movement. Simply put, racial oppression at the hands of white American Christians is much older than the KKK. So, what is the White Christ without white supremacy?

As a black philosopher of religion and theologian, William Jones was not satisfied with the assumption of other black theologians that God was on the side of the oppressed.[28] In part, his work *Is God a White Racist?* was aimed directly at the ideas put forth by James Cone, who argued that Christianity was a redemptive religion meant for the oppressed.[29] Jones simply queried: Given the history of power dynamics in the world, how do we know that God is on the side of the oppressed? If we are to judge this challenge based on God's works, evidenced by the unfolding of human history, then it is clear, that God is not on the side of the oppressed. From that perspective the same query can be asked of the KKK Christ. The KKK believe that Christ is on their side, that he has designated America as the chosen land for the white race; given the history of this country, we are forced to wonder: Where's the lie? Furthermore, this query can be extended to question the benevolence of the White Christ the world over. Wherever the White Christ has shown his face, those of a different hue have caught hell in the name of Jesus.

The mental gymnastics one would have to execute in order to separate white Christianity from the horrors of the modern world are beyond Olympian. It cannot be done. But instead of simply writing off the belief system as dangerous and useless, it is more logical to simply concede that Christianity has no power but that which is bestowed upon it by humans. There is no doubt that Christianity has the qualities of being a redemptive love-based religion; however, it is not pragmatic to assume it is *only* a religion of love. The hands of the user will dictate its purpose, like a sword. By extension, to wrestle with the KKK Christ or any other problematic notions of what a particular religious icon means, it is critical to constantly to challenge ourselves to be mindful of what we put into the image of our gods, whoever they may be.

Every religion must confront the reality of its history. The KKK Christ has a particular origin story, as does the Black Christ. The KKK Christ is Protestant and American. He came to the Earth with a message of salvation for white Americans, a salvation whose foundation is the broken bodies of undesirable populations of human beings. To be clear, this is the reality of the White Christ in a very general sense. Given the manner in which the White Christ was employed during the colonial period of Africa, Asia, and the Americas this is a worldwide reality, not just an American one. In addition, European American Christianity cannot be studied independent of the atrocities committed by white people across the globe. Therefore, the KKK Christ must be confronted as a global phenomenon, not just a postbellum American oddity. Instead the KKK Christ, this deity of class insecurity, separation and hate, is best studied as the true face of White Jesus.

Conclusion—Using the Master's Tools

This chapter opened with three quotes I felt were extremely pertinent to this conversation. The first was from the character Chris Mannix in Quentin Tarantino's *The Hateful Eight*. This quote captures the essence of the Southern frustration with being treated like the illegitimate stepchildren of America after the Civil War. Part of the reason for the development of the KKK is based on the frustration many poor Southerners felt by being treated as second-class citizens in their own country, directly contributing to the feelings of class insecurity (a feeling many African Americans also identify with).

The second quote came from the founder of the second manifestation of the Klan, William Joseph Simmons. This quote addresses the connectedness of the Klan to their understanding of Christianity. They truly believe they are God's chosen and that they are carrying out the will of this deity. As such, they need to be taken at their word. That is to say, to address and ultimately confront their hate, White Jesus will have to be confronted as well. Lastly, the quote from the film *I'm Gonna Git You Sucka* comprises three words which adequately sum up the thesis of this essay: White Jesus is very real for some, and he is not on the side of the oppressed.

Class insecurity is still a very critical issue for white America. During and after the presidency of Barack Obama, sentiments of white social insecurity increased in intensity, evidenced by the rise of alt-right leaders and groups. As well, on the rise are terrorist activities executed by individual white terrorists and white nationalist terrorist groups. The Ku Klux Klan, Neo-Nazis, and Aryan Nations have a history of terrorist activities; however, in the present zeitgeist, these activities are not as closely tied to particular groups but to individuals who are sympathetic to the groups.[30] Additionally, in Trump's America, class insecurity seems to be the fuel for a building fire. The Tiki-torchers of 2017 are a clear example that white class insecurity is still something tangible. The slogan "You will not replace us!" was the war cry of the Tiki-torchers, a slogan that clearly connects to notions of class insecurity that seethes within American white men. Admittedly, there is no clear connection of the Tiki-torchers to the Ku Klux Klan, but to put this in the context of the historical patterns presented in this chapter, the pushback of insecure white men in today's political and social climate clearly came on the heels of the Obama presidency, a perceived period of advancement for African Americans.

White American male class insecurity is also clearly a large factor in the ongoing national conversation of the border wall. While couched in the notion of national security, again it seems that poor white men are simply afraid of being replaced or losing their position in the American hierarchy. While the KKK does not seem to have the same presence it has had in the past, perhaps there is something to be said about the MAGA Christ. "Make America Great Again" is again built on notions of a mythical American past, a past where white men were in charge and "colored" populations knew their place. A MAGA Christ would closely resemble the KKK Christ, which is itself merely a manifestation of white supremacy. Sadly, this Christ will continue to wreak havoc across the globe until it is properly identified and problematized as the destructive force that it is. Until then, humanity will continue to suffer under the white-hot light of White Jesus.

EIGHT

Black People and White Mormon Rage: Examining Race, Religion, and Politics in Zion

Darron T. Smith, Brenda G. Harris, and Melissa Flores

In 2019, the island nation of New Zealand suffered the worst terrorist attack in its history when one hundred Muslim worshipers were gunned down in the middle of Friday prayers (*jummah*) at two mosques in the city of Christchurch, leaving fifty-one dead. This brazen terrorist attack was streamed live on social media for millions to view.[1] The suspect in these slayings, Brenton Tarrant, a 28-year-old self-proclaimed white supremacist from Australia, was eventually apprehended by authorities. While shackled and in custody, waiting for justice to be served for his horrific crimes, Tarrant defiantly brandished the "white power salute" to a world audience.[2]

The suspected killer's international hand display was the public's first glimpse of his twisted motives. Just minutes prior to the massacre, however, he posted a link on social media to his lengthy manifesto of hate-filled tropes and rants about mass immigration. Significantly, his screed referenced Trump as a "symbol of renewed white-identity."[3] The murderer is not the first person to invoke Trump's anti-immigrant, pro-white declamations to justify his rampage. Indeed, he is not even the most recent.[4] In the age of Trump, it has become commonplace for working-class white men to embrace the president's obstinate conduct and enact bloody violence in its name.

This link between the normalization of white supremacy and difference intolerance can be directly correlated with the current U.S. president, though this deadly association has not fazed Trump's colleagues or constituents. That so many Trump supporters and surrogates either choose to not "see" or simply do not care that the president is a bigoted difference-monger is especially troubling given the loud continuous identification with Christianity and Christian principles declared by these same Trump acolytes. Most Christians would agree, to be a believer in Christ is to adhere to and be guided by a comportment of beliefs, attitudes, and behaviors founded on the Christian principles of charity, long suffering, and the requisite command to love thy neighbor as one's self. If Trump and his supporters are Christian and use Christian principles to guide their lives, how is it possible for Trump rhetoric to be used in the service of justifying pro-white violence and murder? There is a clear disconnect here. And as black folk attempt to insert themselves among the white members, they find an environment that is hostile to their emotional, physical and spiritual wellbeing.

The purpose of this chapter is to examine the ways in which the Republican Party platform and white evangelical Christian Protestant nationalism, specifically Mormon racial theology, interact to keep black people on the periphery of a faith that proclaims, "All are alike unto God."[5] We theorize that the apparent contradictions of injustices realized from white Mormon beliefs involve complex entanglements between the white racial frame, conservative political ideology and white European religious thought, as they apply to people of African heritage. These socially constructed frames of race, religion, and politics influence the understandings and actions of individuals and groups, sometimes to the detriment and violent harm of innocent others. This nexus of race, religion, and politics applied to contemporary race relations is readily seen within the microcosm of the Church of Jesus Christ of Latter-Day Saints (LDS Church), which has a long and troubling racist history itself.

Current Day Politics

When the forty-fifth president of the United States, Donald J. Trump, came onto the American political scene unprepared and unfit for the office he currently holds, he was and remains completely unchecked by members of the Republican establishment, notwithstanding the flurry of legal action against him. Since his stunning victory in 2016, Trump's unfiltered banter, endless tweets, and extemporized interviews with media outlets such as Fox News and Breitbart News Network have given him an enormous megaphone through which to spew his brand of white nationalism to include the defense of "Christian heritage."

In this land of "freedom and equality," Trump has shown an unabashed and unrestrained disregard for those different from himself. This list of those relegated by to date Trump includes blacks, immigrants, Muslims, women, veterans and prisoners of war, Gold Star families, the disabled, Mexicans, and the LGBTQ community.[6] Further, the Trump administration's inaction on denouncing hate has consequently had a chilling effect on extremists and disaffected working-class white men in the U.S. and around the world. The U.S. president's failure to publicly address domestic white terror as a serious threat to national security has become a kind of symbolic justification of white identity politics against all those deemed not white.[7] Leading the pack in support for the U.S. president are white Christian Protestants on the far right of the political spectrum.

Few will argue the fact that Trump's behavior, judgement, and rhetoric are expressly anti-Christian, from many claims of sexual assault against him to the attacks on and condescension of those he considers different from himself. But research analysts suggest that the more devout one is to one's religious beliefs, the stronger the correlation with xenophobia, racism(s), and, certainly in the United States, Islamophobia.[8] Case in point regarding connections between religious views and difference-based oppressions: When asked by Joe Heim of the *Washington Post* if there was anything that Trump could do that would cause him to lose the support of evangelical leaders, Liberty University president Jerry Falwell, Jr., responded with a clear "No."[9] Christian conservatives either fully endorse the racist, sexist beliefs of the leader of the free world or are willing to turn a blind eye to the damage he is causing as long as their agenda(s) (traditional marriage, prayer in school, limited gun laws, capitalistic gains over environmental sustainability, etc.) are met. Thus, despite Trump's questionable character, he has become a potent ambassador of affirmation for white conservative Christian causes in the United States. And in return, they have become his most ardent supporters.

One of the more politically conservative denominations in the United States is the Church of Jesus Christ of Latter-Day Saints (the LDS Church or Mormons), many of whose members practice strict devotion to what they call the "Standard Works," which include both the Bible and the Book of Mormon as sacred, religious texts. The Mormon Church is a U.S.-based religion that emerged from nineteenth-century white Christian fundamentalism.[10] "It is the only world-recognized religion to have been born in the United States during the modern age (e.g. the age of the printing press)."[11] As a uniquely American-derived tradition, Mormonism has inherited and reflects the dominant cultural conditioning of what it means to be American, as defined by characteristics, interests, values, and more associated with white male economic and societal domination.[12]

Trump's language, his objectification of women, and his unprecedented actions against people of color, the disabled and immigrants are all seemingly antithetical to many of the teachings found in the LDS faith. Still, the mostly white and LDS population of Utah voted Trump into office at a whopping rate of 61 percent, and he maintains a favorable job approval rating in the state.[13] What is it about Trump (and the Republican Party, for that matter) that would cause LDS members to vote en masse for someone who does not espouse the wholesome, chaste and clean-cut image that they typically wish to portray and maintain? What's more, how does this support among the majority white LDS congregation sit with those in the faith who are the racial Others, marginalized by the conservative right, and how then do those black people navigate this space, worshiping alongside their white brethren who likely voted for Trump? To understand these questions, the authors will use a critical phenomenological framework to explore the connections between race, religion and right-wing identity politics.

Christianity: The Unity of Religion and Race

To follow Jesus, according to the Bible, the greatest commandment is to love one's neighbor as oneself, regardless of ethnic, religious, and social differences.[14] And yet, the most segregated day of the week remains Sunday, as Americans readily gather in their respective silos of worship.[15] The juncture of race and religion has a long and arduous history going as far back as the Crusades. As religious affiliation became less and less "visible" through the conversion process, physical features, like skin tone, eye shape, and hair texture, for example, became an easy way for humans to sift through people as "us" or "them."[16] White religious observance(s) would use binary language, thinking and doing, like white over black, light over darkness, gentile over heathen, as a way to organize and give epistemic meaning to the world. Using these white racial frames, Mormonism would come to provide the backdrop needed to separate the world into discrete races and to justify brutality.

While the practice of Christianity advanced into places like India and Africa, so did the racial frame of whiteness as "pure," "innocent," and "celestial" while blackness was associated with "evil" and "cursed."[17] Christianity reinforced these race-based narratives through art, literature, and culture, and it was of vital importance that Christ be as far removed as possible from anything suggestive of darkness. Indeed, "the entire history of Western painting bears witness to the deliberate whitening or bleaching effort that transformed Christ from a Jew to an Aryan person."[18]

Social stratification by race accelerated in North America as white Christian Puritans and pilgrims arrived in New England in the sixteenth century.[19] In no uncertain terms, as the economic and social foundation for the United States was laid, Christianity (more specifically, white Christianity) influenced the development of racial identity formation. After the first Africans arrived on the shores of Jamestown, Virginia, in 1619, elite white men interpreted the gospel of Christ in exclusionary terms, as a way to distinguish between themselves and black Africans and native peoples.

In the English settlements, "Anglo-Virginians created whiteness during the 17th century and Christianity as a religion of white people."[20] In 1667, Virginia law allowed slave owners to baptize their slaves while maintaining the ceremony brought no promise of freedom. This encouraged white slaveholders to instruct their slaves to embrace Christianity along with their debased status as servants to the white man. In fact, many preached that their status in life was predestined; this was especially helpful for profiteers in the service of the growing slave economy.[21]

Researchers have argued that colonialism and slavery produced racism; once this form of oppression emerged in human history, it became a foundational aspect of Western culture.[22] Thus, it is safe to conclude that in the United States, the "birth of racism [began] with religiously justified exploitation, massacre, and war with the Native Americans—although an explicit racist ideology ... did not fully develop until after the abolition of slavery"[23] with black codes, Jim Crow laws, and systemic de jure and de facto racial discrimination. These white supremacist narratives were buttressed in Christianity with respect to the way it has produced racial discourse ascribed to the bodies of black men and woman as cursed by God.[24]

Throughout time and across the developing world, indigenous peoples were forcibly introduced to Christian theology: first, to love God, and second, to love one's fellow man.[25] Decidedly, Christianity is the *sine qua non* of inhumanity in the gross mistreatment of native peoples and African slaves. In defense of human bondage, Christians suggested black skin was a divine punishment from God and argued Africans were a type of "subhuman," if human at all. In condoning the massacre and displacement of Indigenous Americans, white Anglo Christians developed the concept of "manifest destiny," an ideology of a "chosen people" led by the Almighty to grab land and resources from coast to coast, even if it meant genocide. These mental activities would ensure a lasting social, economic, and political structure that enabled and protected whiteness while disenfranchising people of color, African Americans more specifically, for centuries to come.

The Rage of the Christian Right

For about 90 percent of U.S. history, influential white men (clergy, lawyers, wealthy merchants and landowners, etc.) worked collaboratively and individually to promote their shared interests in white male capitalist patriarchy. This white racial framing of skin color produced social hierarchies, making it difficult for stigmatized minority groups in the U.S. to secure full freedom and opportunity long denied. As some elements of systemic racism became less accepted in the public domain, the link between conservative politics and religious group identity strengthened.

Indeed, the Grand Old (Republican) Party, commonly known as the GOP, became synonymous with white Christianity in America. As a result, the white political establishment then relied on the word of God to subjugate African Americans and enforce white supremacy through political party affiliation. The resulting laws and policies guaranteed white privilege and white male domination through education, health care, mass incarceration, housing, and the economy as well as entertainment, art, and music for years to come.

With white supremacy at the helm of the Republican Party, naturally, social justice has taken a back seat to wealth and power. Enraged white conservative politicians who perceived a threat to their race-based entitlements learned to use the law to maintain their privileges at the expense of others. Rage is not always reflected in outward acts of physical violence. More often, it is subtle, operating through white-controlled institutions, policies, and white-imposed laws designed to disenfranchise black people at the local, state, and federal levels of government. These same white conservatives found allyship in the arms of the evangelical Christian church, as clergy would use religious pronouncements to confuse and further divide the American people.

According to the GOP website, their platform declares that they are "the party of the Declaration of Independence and the Constitution."[26] As Americans, we rely on the Constitution as a blueprint outlining our system of government and its rules of law. Although the Constitution never mentions "God" in the text, the Republican Party consider the document as divinely inspired, nevertheless. They fail to recognize the text as a document written by elite white men interested in preserving their property, assets, and legacy. When religiosity intersects with politics, inevitably those in positions of power end up writing laws from their myopic perspective of God and country.

Although the GOP platform declares they are for human equality, denouncing "bigotry, racism . . . and religious intolerance," their legislative initiatives and policies have consistently favored the rich and powerful at the expense of less fortunate Americans, many of whom are non-white. In particular, these legal agendas have devastating consequences on black and brown communities who typically lack the financial resources to buffer the aftermath of these GOP-instituted laws. For example, the recent repeal of important measures in the Voting Rights Act and the practice of state-sanctioned gerrymandering has allowed, even perpetuated, the enrichment of one group with more political space to enhance its own vote, effectively keeping whites in power and blacks at the bottom of the well.[27] Further, GOP lawmakers routinely manipulate their mostly white constituency in stoking racial fears and anxieties of white extinction. These political tactics confuse and incite rage from the working class to the far-right extreme elements of the party as they embrace, rather than denounce, racial bigotry and religious intolerance.

Despite its claims that "all are alike unto God," the Mormon faith is a community of believers not immune to a legacy of racial bigotry toward people of African heritage. There are elements within Mormonism such as the concept of and belief in industry, the hard work ethic, and education/literacy as well as white male patriarchy, faith in God, and family values; the "American dream" bootstraps narrative wrapped up in the American experiment in democratic rule. But this romanticism of the "American dream" metaphor is also precisely what makes it so white. And because of that, Mormonism echoes the country's long-standing negative racial history in that the position of black LDS members in the Church remains inconsequential.

Mormon Rage against the Black Body

The rage of the GOP toward difference is shared by the Mormon Church. For more than a century, the LDS Church would not allow black males to hold the priesthood or black women to receive priesthood benefits including temple endowments. These embodied rituals are critical to being a "good" member in full standing in the church. On June 9, 1978, then-Mormon president and prophet Spencer W. Kimball reversed the 130-year ban. The Mormon Church's reversal of its anti-black doctrine was widely praised as significant progress, away from its vestiges of institutional racism and toward racial inclusiveness. For black Mormons, the long-promised day initiated by Kimball was an answer to prayer. This historic LDS policy reversal set to affect the transformation of the Mormon faith from a racially divisive, parochial institution into a worldwide, universal and "color-blind" church. The universality of LDS doctrine as it pertains to blacks, however, remains paradoxical, especially when considering how little effort has been put into removing its large corpus of racist teachings and commentary from its early history.

In the ensuing four decades since June of 1978, the expectant jubilation surrounding the Church's official but ostensible commitment to the full acceptance and fellowship of black folk has borne the spoiled fruit of interpersonal psychic turmoil, as some express their spiritual needs from deft white leadership while permitting the teachings of them as cursed. To understand the contradiction between unfulfilled religious expectations of acceptance in the LDS Church and the cold reality of our contemporary racial dilemma, it is necessary to deconstruct the calculated alliance between white Christianity and the majority white Republican Party, as it has become one in the American mind.

Like Christian conservatives, the LDS Church believes that a traditional marriage between man and woman is the only proper and ordained marriage in the eyes of God. Likewise, the Republican Party platform promotes this religious view of marriage and takes political and legal action to maintain this definition of marriage, thereby excluding a group of people from the civic rights and benefits that flow from a legally recognized marriage. Simply put, a traditional marriage leads to the traditional family—a model that includes gender roles and norms where the woman's place is in the home, rearing children. Because women are thought to be incapable of controlling their emotions and making rational decisions in a patriarchal society, conservative evangelical men (holy men) have determined they must intercede with regressive politics to limit a woman's choice in most aspects of her life. In declaring their stance on these issues and others as God's values, the Republican platform is seen by its followers as sanctioned by the Divine—compliance with which constitutes commitment to the first great commandment, to love God. Religion then becomes a prism or filter through which people see and understand the world.

Like politics, religious organizations become the place where white anger and rage foment. Institutions like the LDS Church further extend this rage through racist beliefs, rituals, and practices that incite symbolic violence against blacks. Mormon racial attitudes toward African Americans are both patronizing and patriarchal; and when confronted with past racism within the faith, white Mormon elders launch into a diatribe of scriptural justifications in defense of their bigoted views in an attempt to silence black voices—and arguably their pain—in favor of quiet compliance with doctrine.[28]

The LDS Church is an authoritarian organization of top-down leadership consisting entirely of men, more than 90 percent white and less than 2.5 percent black. Authoritarianism is expressly anti-black. The expectations are that blacks subscribe to norms and beliefs of the Church that certainly marginalize. Whereas religion is supposed to liberate them, the politics of the church oppresses, punishes, and penalizes black people simply for being black, even when—and arguably because—they are devout. Part of Mormon anger involves embracing Republican political views of the world and conflating them with the sacred. Although antithetical to Christ's mission and the LDS tenets of brotherhood, unity, peace, harmony, and love, the white resentment and rage inflicts deep wounds on the spirits of those individuals and groups perceived as the racial Other.

Although various white Christian denominations began to distance themselves from the racist rhetoric and teachings of their faith, the LDS Church nevertheless persisted teaching its members through white racist frames well beyond the Civil Rights era. While the white Catholic Church, and Protestant-based faiths—Episcopal Church, United Methodist Church, Southern Baptist, Lutheran—have since acknowledged their racist past and issued public regrets for their role in black African slavery, Jim Crow racism, and their participation in the mistreatment of African Americans, no apology has been issued from the Mormon faith.[29] After the tragedy at Charlottesville, Virginia, in August of 2017 which led to the death of Heather D. Heyer, the Church released a formal statement, in part stating that "white supremacist attitudes are morally wrong and sinful, and we condemn them."[30] While this statement was welcomed, it stopped short of addressing the Church's long-standing and complicated relationship with race and racism. Indeed, the LDS Church remains officially convinced that its exclusionary policies related to its central doctrine and practices were divinely inspired, and therefore, in need of no apology.

The LDS Church participated in the production and use of religious-based racist tropes. There are volumes of evidence to be found in official Church publications, including books, magazines, conference sermons, video, and other forms of communication.[31] This coupling of conservative religious beliefs with regressive political ideologies becomes a toxic space for black Americans to occupy, particularly when it is within their own flock. Matters of faith are not only ethereal in nature but are bound up in community, culture, and tradition. These social constructs generate a sustainable household of faith, a community of devotees with similar norms and orientation of the Divine. As these racist dogmas spill over into civic life, some black people who convert to Mormonism find themselves in a quandary, worshiping alongside white people who vote for conservative policies that harm and persecute people of color. Therefore, it defies logic how African Americans could find solace and comfort in an austere environment. As such, the politico-religious atmosphere of the LDS Church affects its black members differently than its white members in a multitude of ways, most especially by means of psychic violence that has visceral consequences invisible to the naked eye.

Racial Battle Fatigue: Blacks in the Politically Conservative LDS Church

The old adage "Sticks and stones may break my bones, but words will never hurt me," in practice, could not be further from the truth. We utter this phrase to ease the sting of interpersonal rejection from those whose opinions matter most. But, in actuality, humans are extremely sensitive to criticism, and we seek approval from others to validate ourselves. Our species is hardwired to curry favor in order to gain acceptance from other *Homo sapiens*.

Ancient *sapiens* learned to work together through mutual cooperation, following rules and abstaining from unwanted behaviors to fit in within hunter-gatherer societies.[32] These relationships were formed outside of the family unit and included strangers, even rivals from other groups, who joined together in an effort to survive and flourish.[33] The evolution of such prosocial behaviors (i.e., sharing, empathy, trust) enabled our early ancestors to share knowledge and skills in an effort to further the species' prosperity. Those ancestors unwilling or unable to work toward the mutual benefit of the whole found themselves cast out from the group and left to fend for themselves against the elements and megafauna, which meant certain death. As a result, *sapiens* developed emotional sensitivities to feelings of shame, isolation and rejection, which can give rise to physiological effects inside the body that precipitate negative health outcomes.[34]

In today's time, these same ostracized individuals may not experience physical banishment, but they remain socially excluded from the very society in which they live. Social exclusion is a type of behavior where humans reject one another from participation in forming important social bonds and attachments needed for survival. Because of this evolutionary history and the acknowledgement that our existence is dependent upon social connection, social rejection is perhaps the worst form of human suffering.

In the context of the LDS Church, the desire of black Mormons to fit in among their white congregants can exact a heavy mental toll within their faith. These feelings are a result of centuries-old white supremacy in which blacks in the Church resign themselves to accept some aspects of European ways of knowing and being at the expense of their own sense of self-worth and emotional wellbeing. The pervasive privileging of white people and their interests, histories, narratives, accomplishments, values, and perspectives on the world and about God creates a lived experience viewed as the "norm" among Saints while black Mormons are positioned as interlopers in the LDS community. This practice of marginalization, intentional or not, by the majority white conservative membership affects the minds of black members, leaving many vulnerable to self-doubt and feelings of isolation. It is this dissonance that has led some black LDS members to leave Mormonism or linger skeptically on the fringes. Those who stay are more prone to racial microaggressions, which can lead to racial battle fatigue.[35]

"Racial battle fatigue" (RBF), a term coined in 2008 by William A. Smith, describes the negative and racially charged experiences all people of color in the United States experience.[36] Building on psychiatrist Chester M. Pierce's research on microaggressions,[37] Smith posited that these subtle racial dismissals, both intentional and unintentional, inflict real pain, confusion, and lifelong consequences on blacks and other people of color.[38]

Smith defines RBF as a natural response to race-related stress that people of color experience at the hands of racially dismissive, insensitive, hostile, and demeaning racial individuals and environments.[39] RBF presents itself as the "psychological, physiological, emotional, and behavioral toll placed on People of Color who are responding to daily racial macro and microaggressions"[40] and taken in totality can have a devastating effect on the mental and physical health of those who experience it. In fact, it is so damaging that it has been said to be a form of psychological warfare. This warfare has lifelong mental, physical, and emotional consequences. Over time, these microaggressions render black Americans vulnerable to disease. Cortisol, a stress hormone, has been well documented as closely correlated with the body's response to stressful stimuli. As a result of experiencing RBF, consistently high levels of cortisol flow through the body and produce significant wear and tear on vital organs including the brain, kidneys, eyes, and heart. Smith identifies the symptoms of RBF as an increase in stress levels that result in psychological symptoms of anger, anxiety, helplessness, hopelessness, and fear (to name a few) and physiological symptoms such as chest pain, high blood pressure, fatigue, insomnia, and muscle pains.

Unlike other trauma-induced mental pathology, such as post-traumatic stress disorder, where the person has escaped the stress-inducing event and can begin to process it, African Americans are not able to escape the trauma-inducing experience of RBF because they will always be black and they will always face micro and macroaggressions from individuals as well as society at large. In this context, even in this religious space—a space that is supposed to be the most welcoming, the most supportive, and the most loving—black men and women remain in a state of heightened vigilance against the prospect of racial insults and other negative interactions by whites. Over lifelong membership in the LDS Church, black men and women seldom, if ever, get to experience a real sense of quiet peace that white members are privileged to feel. In fact, extended, ongoing proximity to whites can have negative consequences for their health—quite literally, in some cases, leading to premature death.

Thus, the LDS Church has made little progress with respect to proselytizing and retaining black people. Blacks in the Mormon faith incessantly endure passive-aggressive white rage while pledging fealty to white male ecclesiastic authority. That rage manifests through automatic or implicit assumptions of black inferiority and deficiency, which then triggers acts of violence upon the black psyche and body within a house of worship and elsewhere. Some of the more common interactions involve hair touching, second-guessing someone's ability to perform a task or role at church, or invoking narratives about the cursing of blacks as descendants of Noah's errant son, Ham.

Be it white contempt or pity, black people receive dehumanizing messages and insults. Importantly, the relentless nature of racial microaggressions directed against black folk who are regularly in close proximity to whites at church, work, or elsewhere has produced profound negative consequences for the lives of black people over generations. Specifically, existing in a near-constant state of anticipation to fight, flee, or freeze in response to white racial microaggressions (as well as social exclusion) means that many black Americans, irrespective of socioeconomic status, become susceptible to RBF.

Mormonism is a religion that creates the privileging of white people's significance in the universe, but simultaneously withholds that same affirmation of black Mormons' significance in the faith. A number of blacks that continue to worship within the LDS Church have acquiesced to their white leaders on matters of race, instead downplaying the racial history and mythology or ignoring it altogether. For those black members who remain active within the Church and against the overwhelming whiteness of Mormonism, they typically find ways to augment their practice by seeking outside spiritual fulfillment and engagement with what Stephen Finley refers to as an "expanded ecclesiology," which is a desire to maintain cultural ties with the black community.[41] Regardless of their religious position on race, members that observe and obey the LDS canon ultimately subject themselves to repeated abuse. It then becomes clear how white racial aggressions, which diminish, demean, erase, and/or marginalize blacks, are so profoundly deadly for black Americans today.

Conclusion

Following Charles Long,[42] we define religion as "the process of coming to terms with the ultimate significance of one's place in the world," and white people have been conditioned to believe that they are the rightful owners and rulers of the planet. The social identity of white people, as individuals and groups, in the U.S. and around the world, has been lived through the systemic privileging of the histories, cultures, achievements, normative values, and interests associated with Europeans and European Americans. This glorification of whiteness positions white people—either individually or collectively—to see themselves as the literal and justified owners of the world, past and present.[43] This belief in oneself as superior when coupled with xenophobic mendacity has led to the suffering of stigmatized minoritized peoples, as whites used religion to justify laws that further marginalized already disenfranchised black Americans from full social, political and economic participation in American life, keeping whites in positions of power.

As a society, the white male power elite has done little to alter the current trajectory of white supremacy. Politically conservative white people most assuredly lack the presence of mind to understand the rich complexity of race. Calling into question any of these overarching frames has historically triggered the fragile white mind to fly into rage in defense of its ego in an emotionally charged survival mode that activates the body's "fight or flight response." Failure to see and teach that systemic racism is as American as apple pie leads to profound white solipsism, to the ongoing detriment of blacks—especially black males—and their exclusion from all facets of society. This glaring omission of our nation's racist past and contemporary realities is not accidental.

Racial division intensified in the U.S. after the 1870s as white labor felt increasingly threatened by job displacement of newly freed cheaper black labor. Ordinary landless whites were made to believe that the source of their suffering in a forced slave economy was the slaves themselves, rather than white male oligarchy. Rage in this context is misguided, bordering on insanity, as people of color have no power that white men are bound to respect. Disregard for black life boils down to chicanery adopted to divert white suffering away from its true underlying cause—white supremacy. Political initiatives were mobilized after the Civil War to protect white labor from white capitalist greed looking to undermine their labor power to the lowest bidder.

Over the next century, white politicians and the clergy used religion and politics to their advantage. Better-educated conservative whites regularly conflate religion, politics and race as "God's errand," which less-educated whites are obliged to consume through social media and Fox News and in white conservative religions.[44] In addition, the GOP base tends be mostly undereducated or uneducated working-class whites who are literally "dying of whiteness" through regressive policies they blindly support from the top 1 percent of Americans.[45] In truth, the 1-percenters are doing all they can to preserve wealth, power, and influence. This uneven system is partially maintained through white religious conservative propaganda, like conflating patriotism with godliness, that stokes white religious rage among its constituency. These uncritical notions of the mind have informed generations of white Americans (whether conscious or unconscious) and their descendants to the present day. White male capitalist patriarchy laid the groundwork for a stratified society by race, class, religion, and gender.

Systemic white racism has touched every major corner in society, including the sacred word and faith communities and religious traditions, not excluding Christianity. African Americans, in turn, have responded by forging sanctuaries of their own for religious and secular devotions. Presently, about 90 percent of African Americans worship in predominately black churches across the country, segregated from whites and racially different others. The Black Church has been an important institution in the African American community overall because it has reimagined a more socially just representation of Jesus Christ. Black Christian churches, thus, have recast white Christianity—with its debasing views of black people—in ways that speak to overcoming white supremacy. One way they do this is by worshiping in ways that socialize blacks to see the benefit of the group over a false narrative of individualism and the bootstraps metaphor. But the Western religious ideology of individual salvation departs sharply from black cultural expressions and practices of community-based group uplift. As white people try to fit black folk into a box, many push back, but some capitulate. And that submission comes at a steep price, as it takes an exorbitant amount of emotion work to be accepted by white people.[46]

Those few black faces found in predominately white churches, like the LDS Church, face a particular form of rage that is passive-aggressive in nature and seen when blacks speak out against racist teachings and ideas in church settings and functions. White (male) LDS rage stems from the perception that black men are now in equal standing with regard to the priesthood, which also extends the opportunity to have relations with white Mormon women. This baseless rage took hold during the Second Great Awakening when fire-and-brimstone religious thought permeated colonial America. White preachers, pastors and ministers reinforced the politics of fear, leading to contemporary racial anxiety and fear that white people would become irrelevant. This is demonstrated by their attempts to police the boundaries of black bodies, behaviors and actions. It is in this politico-religious no-(black)-man's land where black Mormons find themselves—in a faith that largely supports a party whose policies do not benefit blacks as a group.

Black Latter-Day Saints exist within a sphere of reality where their voices are drowned out by the cacophony of racist beliefs and extreme misinterpretations of blackness in reference to God's plan of salvation. One common assumption from white members is that melanin is only a temporary "condition" that will be rectified in the afterlife, the presumption being that after death black skin will miraculously transform into white skin, the way it supposedly was before a Divine cursing fell upon the so-called "black race." There is not much room to negotiate these toxic views of blacks passed off as religious instruction. In this space, some black LDS have challenged the veracity of Mormon racial folklore, taking the risk to speak truth to power, further jeopardizing their standing in the church. But the constant need to address and reframe conservative white salvific interpretations, particularly without redress, is physically taxing and emotionally draining as well. Hence, whatever stratagems blacks rely on to reconcile Mormon racist attitudes and beliefs take a toll on mental and emotional reserves.

NINE

Anatomizing White Rage: "Race is My Religion!" and "White Genocide"

Kate E. Temoney

Introduction

Listing a few notable exceptions,[1] Michael Minkenberg avers that "in academic debates, religion remains conspicuously absent in concepts of the radical right; instead, it is usually treated as a strategic ploy or superficial issue."[2] The radical right is a self-described political movement, but this alone does not seem to account for the scholarly inattentiveness to the role of religion. The answer may lie in the "notable exceptions" Minkenberg lists, which are treatments of the radical right in a European (and in particular, western European) rather than a North American, and more specifically, U.S. context. In this context, the radical right is often discussed as an iteration of a white supremacy movement with a legacy that has both embraced racialized Christianity and eschewed it.[3] Nonetheless, Minkenberg does hit the mark when he writes that

> religious beliefs may not be a core element of the radical right ... however, religion functions as a relevant context factor and frame for political mobilization ... even in secularized societies, against the perceived threat of rapid sociocultural change and its (alleged) agents and protagonists.[4]

What Minkenberg's framing provides is an opportunity to wrestle with, but not be mired in, definitional arguments about "religion" and "genocide." Moreover, this framing also enables an analysis of how and why these terms are an important part of the discourse of white nationalism—a racist, separatist movement that aims to create a territory for the "white race." Therefore, we need not be primarily constrained by whether the radical right's or white nationalists' references to religion and genocide are consistently faithful to particular definitions in order to pursue the larger question of the tactical value that the invocation of "religion" and "genocide" seem to provide. Put another way, we need not be preoccupied with whether whiteness should or should not "count" as a religion or whether religion can be meaningfully disentangled from other spheres of life for study. What is most important is "what types of things are authorized by either saying [something] is or saying [something] isn't [a religion],"[5] and analogously, what is or is not a genocide. The form of analysis in this chapter is both phenomenological and hermeneutical. It is phenomenological insofar as rigorous description will be in the form of direct quotes from white nationalists that espouse "my race is my religion" and reference "white genocide." It is hermeneutical in that I attempt to interpret these quotes in order to discern their strategic value to the white nationalist agenda and their centrality to white rage.

For the purpose of this chapter, "radical right," "extreme right," "white supremacy," "alt-right" and other various groups will all be subsumed under the term "white nationalism," even if spokespersons and affiliates of these groups and movements do not self-describe as such. The reason for this is that all of these groups, regardless of their stated aims and religious affiliations, share a common aspiration: racial segregation through the establishment of an ethnostate. Per the Anti-Defamation League:

> "Extreme right" is used to describe right-wing political, social and religious movements that exist outside of and are more radical than mainstream conservatism. In the United States, the extreme right consists primarily of two large, slightly overlapping spheres. In one sphere is the white supremacist movement, including its various submovements, such as neo-Nazis, racist skinheads, and the alt right, among others.[6]

One way of unpacking the religion of white rage in North America—the animus of whites against non-whites, including black people in the United States, due to the perceived correlates of white disenfranchisement and black progress—is to historically and conceptually situate the project of modern white nationalists. As an avenue for parsing out the interrelationships among whiteness, religion, and labor that underpin contemporary white rage, I propose anatomizing the project of white nationalists as epitomized by two banner phrases: the assertion that "my race is my religion" and the claim of an ongoing "white genocide." This approach provides an opportunity to address, from a historical perspective, 1) the circumstances that forged religiosity, supremacy, and labor as constitutive of white identity, and 2) a chronology of developments among white supremacist movements that contextualizes the uses of "religion" and "genocide" in contemporary racist discourse. This approach also 1) affords an examination of the rhetorical efficacy of the invocation of "religion" and "genocide" by white nationalists and 2) provides a working framework for decoding how and why immigration, shifting demographics, and the uplift of people of color are experienced as an existential crisis. Guided by Charles Long's understanding of religion as a "comprehensive and orienting outlook" and Paul Tillich's conceptualization of religion as "ultimate concern" accompanied by an "ultimate fulfillment," I conclude that the constructs of "white" and "religion," and their elision, functionally allow "whiteness" to stand as a single and singular group consciousness for negotiating the world and creating ultimate meaning in that world and beyond it. Created from this group consciousness is an imagined community whose fragility, victimhood, and ideological heterogeneity are subsumed under the pressing imperative to collectively combat "white genocide" or the extinction of white culture as the dominant and normative American way of life.

The chapter is organized into three sections. First, I briefly trace three ideological shifts in white supremacist movements in order to provide a context for why religion and genocide are functionally important and potent in white nationalist discursive practices. These shifts are the construal of whiteness from a geographically bound identity to a global identity; transition of white supremacy from a Christian movement to a religious but not a Judeo-Christian faction to a religiously tolerant movement; and the transformation of the violent, hate group of white supremacists into a non-violent, victimized group of white nationalists. Second, in both scholarly treatment and the vernacular of white supremacists, race as a religion has multiple meanings. I outline three interrelated notions of "whiteness as a religion" or "the religiosity of whiteness," which I capture with the language of the historical origin of whiteness as both religious and industrious, features and practices of whiteness as religious, and whiteness as functionally and foundationally religious (with an emphasis on the third). In the last section, I aver that the trigger sentiments "my race is my religion" and "white genocide" serve the same three strategic purposes in the campaign of white nationalists. The invocation of religion and genocide concretize an imagined group through the promotion of tribalism (unification); legitimize and mainstream their message through familiar, resonant, and reasoned arguments (standardization), and raise the stakes and significance of the endangerment of whites in order to motivate them to act to defend their embattled group (mobilization).

Using Charles Long's conception of "religion" as a comprehensive and orienting outlook and Paul Tillich's definition of religion as an "ultimate concern" with a correlative "ultimate fulfillment" elucidates that "whiteness as a religion" is tantamount to believing that what is uncritically accepted as markers of whiteness—such as privilege, work, and numerical and cultural dominance—are constitutive of a white life world. Hence if the hegemony of whiteness is challenged, it renders white nationalists incapable of orienting themselves in the world in any meaningful way, and thus whiteness must be defended with all of the ferocity that religious zealotry affords—a defense that is akin to what Damon T. Berry coins as "racial protectionism."[7] Repeated references to religion and genocide have the rhetorical advantage of imparting the gravity of white imperilment, but more specifically, both terms are the bases for concretizing the abstract concept of "whiteness" as a homogenous victim group and motivating inured whites to band together and work to secure their rightful place in the present and eschatological world order.

Three Ideological Shifts in White Nationalism

A Rebranding of White Supremacy: White Nationalism and a Global Identity

Damon T. Berry refers to the writings of Michal O'Meara—a white supremacist and scholar of the European New Right who "has written one of the most thorough descriptions of white nationalism from within the community"—and notes O'Meara's observation of a "terminological change" in the 1990s among his ilk.[8] In *Toward the White Republic*, O'Meara writes that "many who previously identified themselves as White Power advocates, segregationists, separatists, supremacists, survivalists, neo-Confederates, biological realists, etc. started calling themselves 'white nationalists.'"[9] According to O'Meara, this shift began with an acknowledgment by Francis Parker Yockey—an American fascist, Nazi sympathizer, and Holocaust denier—who lamented the failure of the post-1945 project to "maintain the integrity of America's racial character and prevent alien races from intruding," forcing racist advocates to reconsider the binary approach of rescuing the United States from impurity or abandoning it.[10] The failed attempt to stave off the invasion of non-whites resulted in a name change to "white nationalists," and despite what the name implies, the focus of white nationalism then became the preservation of the "white race as a global identity" based on an "imagined biological and cultural connection" that was not circumscribed by national borders.[11] This conjured community would prove indispensable to the movement in its evolution from geographically isolated groups of white people to a pan-whiteness that could corporately come under assault anywhere in the world. "Imagined" or "conjured" are not the same as "unreal," however, but denote a sense of community among people who, as Benedict Anderson writes, are members who "will never know most of their fellow-members, meet them, or even hear of them, yet in the minds of each lives the image of their communion."[12] The years that followed the end of World War II and the Holocaust ushered in a bevy of human rights instruments and conventions designed to protect Jewish communities and other vulnerable groups—most notably the 1948 Universal Declaration of Human Rights and, in the same year, the United Nations Convention on the Prevention and Punishment of the Crime of Genocide. Ironically, fifty years later, neo-Nazis would first claim to be victims of a white genocide coordinated by the conspiratorial Jews of a Zionist Occupation Government.

The Dynamic Relationship between Religion and White Nationalism

Another shift in the white nationalist movement is treated by Berry in his 2017 book *Blood and Faith: Christianity in American White Nationalism*. At times driven by chronology and at other times by critical biographies, he delineates the attitudes of white nationalists toward Christianity in particular and religion more broadly.[13] White nationalists and scholars of white nationalism alike, albeit in different ways and for different purposes, draw metahistorical and historical links, respectively, between white supremacy and Christianity. Seemingly forgoing this well-trodden material, Berry does not rehash the well-knit relationship between white supremacy and Christianity, or more specifically Protestant Christianity, but instead begins with a pivotal figure in white nationalism who would eventually reject Christianity. Berry opens his book by excavating the life and works of Revilo Pendleton Oliver, who Berry notes is beloved by white nationalists and embodies the transition "of the old racist Right during the height of the Cold War into a new racial activist Right after World War II."[14] In the 1950s and early 1960s Oliver supported both American conservatism and Christianity as central to the preservation of Western (read, "white") civilization; however, by 1969 he rejected both as "equally detrimental to the cause of white racial survival."[15] Oliver also noted the problematic and intolerable connection between Christianity and Judaism, as captured by the increasingly popular use of the liberal term "Judeo-Christianity" at that time.[16]

Ben Klassen, author of *Nature's Eternal Religion*, first published in 1973, also personifies this shift from embracing Christianity to rejecting it for the same reasons enumerated by Oliver, writing that "many religions have been notoriously bad for the races that have embraced them, as for example the

White Race having embraced Christianity . . . Yes, we are cursed with the Jewish religion of Christianity, whether we like it or not." [17] Even while expressing his contempt for Christianity, Klassen disagrees with Oliver's atheism as a solution and asserts "that religion and the affinity of mankind for religion is an inborn trait with which Nature has endowed us, and is inbred in our genes."[18] In this vein, Klassen founds the Church of the Creator, later the Creativity Movement or Church of Creativity and now the World Church of the Creator,[19] and other racialized religions that are critical of Christianity emerge, such as Cosmotheism and Odinism. In the changing religious landscape of white nationalism, from being intertwined with Christianity, followed by a disavowal of Judeo-Christianity but not religion per se, the last and still evolving phase now seems to be an identification of the modern alt-right with non-belief supplemented by a policy of toleration of Christian and non-Christian religions in the interest of white solidarity.[20]

The Road to Non-violence and Victimhood

We end where we began, with a brief treatment of the third ideological shift among white power activists pertinent to the discussion of the intersections of whiteness, religion, and genocide, by revisiting the rebranding of white supremacists as "white nationalists." In a 2018 interview with Terry Gross of National Public Radio's *Fresh Air*, Derek Black, the heir apparent of Don Black—a former Ku Klux Klan grand wizard who created the white nationalist website Stormfront in 1995—disavowed his father's beliefs and commented on how Don Black catapulted the term "white nationalists" into common, public discourse. Derek Black explained that his "dad popularized . . . the term 'white nationalism,'" and that in their quest for ethnostates the white nationalists

> really did believe they were not doing bad things to other people, that the accusations of violence and hatred and racism were just insults put towards them and that they really did just want what's best for white people and then, by extension, other people.[21]

This ideological shift in white nationalism facilitated a transformation from violent white supremacists that lynched black people to beleaguered white separatists facing extinction who advocated segregation for the betterment of all races. Black divulges that the creation of white victimization "was a long process,"[22] and the promulgation of the inflammatory white genocide narrative was less dramatic than it sounded, pointing more to an "attack on whiteness" and loss of "white privilege" than to a loss of life.[23] Nonetheless, viewing whiteness as a religion or as the focal point for interpreting and navigating the world reveals that an attack on whiteness and a loss of white privilege are commensurate with a social death of existential proportions.

Three Conceptualizations of Whiteness as a Religion

Whiteness as Ineliminably Religious and Industrious

The "religiosity of whiteness" or construing "whiteness as a religion" seem to emphasize different aspects of religion for both white nationalists and the researchers who study them: 1) the *historical origin* of whiteness as coarising with the invention of religion and incubated in religious institutions, 2) the *sociological and performative features* of whiteness as manifest through common belief and ritual, and 3) the *function* of religion as central to building and navigating a life world. The first is a historical claim, that the very identity of "whiteness" from its inception in the United States was forged within an institutional, Christian (often Protestant) context. This origin-of-whiteness approach is paradigmatic of Eric Weed's "theo-historical work," *Religion of White Supremacy in the United States*; here "religion" refers to the institutional practices, dogmas, signs, and symbols that contributed to the formation and promotion of a white identity as a Christian identity. In addition, Jeannine Hill Fletcher, inspired by Michael Omi and Howard Winant's concept of "racial projects"[24]—the idea that "race is not a concrete or static reality, but an imaginative construct always created in particular times and places with specific material influences and impacts"— discusses the fabrication of whiteness as a theological construct as a "religio-racial project."[25]

In *The Sin of White Supremacy: Christianity, Racism, and Religious Diversity in America*, Fletcher writes that "Christianity and Whiteness [were] bound together [in a] religio-racial project [linking] Christian Supremacy, White Supremacy, and Whiteness."[26] This project began with the "discovery" of the Americas by Christian Europeans in the fifteenth century and developed into the colonial practices of conquest and the religious conversion of inferior indigenous peoples, making whiteness ineliminably religious as well as elitist. A modern and typifying encapsulation of this heritage is succinctly summarized by a white supremacist who, in an interview conducted by Betty A. Dobratz, inverts the slogan my "race is my religion" slogan:

> While lots of organizations use that statement . . . Michael Teague, Church of Jesus Christ Christian/Aryan Nations Headquarters Staff Leader and head of security[,] stated, "I would say that my religion is my race. Instead of my race is my religion. Yahweh God is my race. We are sons and daughters of the

most high God . . . . As far as myself being Christian Identity . . . it's the whole basis of my racial beliefs."[27]

It is also important to note here that another feature of "whiteness" that emerged as early as the fifteenth century was that of white industriousness in opposition to non-white fecklessness. For example, Europeans construed the environment-sustaining practices of native people of the Americas, such as limited hunting and coplanting—preventing animal extinction and the nitrogen depletion of soil—as evidence of a disinterest in raising animals and a haphazard, lazy approach to planting. Similarly, enslaved black people were stereotypically construed as lazy and usurpers. David R. Roediger's thesis is that

> whiteness in the USA "was a way in which white workers responded to the fear of dependency on wage labor and to the necessities of capitalist work discipline, with racial identity and definitions of freedom becoming intertwined in the forced contrast with a variety of other racial and ethnic groups."[28]

In other words, the construct of "whiteness" was inextricably linked to work while other racial groups were associated with indolence, an association that persists in coded, contemporary language.

> Race and class politics interface and overlap in the U.S. Individuals and groups interpret their conditions of existence and their subjective experiences in ways which draw upon both racially based and class-based meanings . . . Thus the new right grafts together issues of race and issues of class. New right publisher William Rusher provides an apt illustration [in his criticisms of big government welfare systems by] blaming unemployment among minorities for parasitism at the expense of "productive" [white] workers.[29]

The seamless and unchallenged fusion of religious superiority and hard work as inherent to the advent of whiteness in the United States helps us better understand the invention of the white laborer and their attending white rage—whereby whiteness and white privilege as *the* American experience and cultural norm are challenged in the face of black uplift.

Whiteness as Belief and Ritual

Moving away from particular religious traditions and institutions toward a general and conventional understanding of religion more broadly, whiteness may be construed as a religion because exercises in asserting whiteness exhibit social features that are commonly understood as religious. Relying on a definition of religion proposed by sociologist George Ritzer, Stephen C. Finley and Lori L. Martin write:

> We argue that whiteness itself is a religion. A conventional definition of religion defines religion "as a social phenomenon that consists of beliefs about the sacred; the experiences, practices, and rituals that reinforce those beliefs; and the communities that share similar beliefs and practices."[30]

Finley and Martin conclude that whiteness is a religion, for example, by citing the primacy of lynching black bodies as ritualistic reconstitutions of white superiority and the perpetuation of "sacred values" construed as peculiar to whites, in this case, "justice, freedom, fairness, and democracy."[31] This rendition of religion does not seem to necessitate that those who enact these rituals and hold these beliefs consider themselves as participants in religious praxis or members of a confessional organization. Rather, this construal of "whiteness itself as a religion" is an operative claim that assesses the sociological processes and effects of whiteness as religious in form and force—the enshrinement of an exclusive community and group consciousness resistant to external critiques of its internal logic.

Whiteness as Orientation and Ultimate Concern

Last, and the characterization of whiteness as a religion that most clearly elucidates the claim of "my race is my religion" and the urgency of a "white genocide," is the interpretation of whiteness as an "orientation," per Charles H. Long. In *Significations: Signs, Symbols, and Images in the Interpretation of Religion*, Long writes:

> As a historian of religions, I have not defined religion in conventional terms... For my purposes, religion will mean orientation—orientation in the ultimate sense, that is, how one comes to terms with the ultimate significance of one's place in the world.[32]

Long's reference to "ultimate significance" is reminiscent of Paul Tillich's description of faith. Tillich asserts that faith is "the state of being ultimately concerned ... [and this] demands the total surrender of him who accepts this claim, and it promises total fulfillment even if all other claims have to be subjected to it or rejected in its name."[33] Tillich himself uses this definition as an explanatory model for "extreme nationalisms," whereby "all other concerns, economic well-being, health and life, family, aesthetic and cognitive truth, justice and humanity, [must] be sacrificed"; otherwise, ultimate fulfillment, such as securing the "'greatness' of one's nation," will be denied.[34]

Analogously, the emphasis on whiteness as the single and paramount referent for ordering one's life, and the tandem, unconditional loyalty that this demands of whites in order to achieve the most significant and destined goal that whiteness affords, is encapsulated by several tenets of the "Five Fundamental Beliefs" and "The XVI Commandments," found on the home page of the Church of Creativity website, Creativity Alliance. The first of the Beliefs is "I. WE BELIEVE that our Race is our Religion,"[35] while three of the Commandments are "IV. The guiding principle of all your actions shall be: What is best for the White Race? VI. Your first loyalty belongs to the White Race [and] XVI. We, the Racial Comrades of the White Race, are determined to regain complete and unconditional control of our own destiny.[36] Applying Long's and Tillich's concepts of religion and faith to the religiosity of whiteness reveals several crucial functions of whiteness. One function is that of whiteness as the primary and most significant referent from which all experiences are made intelligible; "everything is centered in" whiteness.[37] Another is that, as an all-encompassing outlook, a religiosity of whiteness requires that all actions and aspects of life be subsumed under whiteness as a matter of teleology.

"My Race is My Religion" and "White Genocide"
Unification: Religion

"Race is my religion!'"[38]
–Tom Metzger, avowed atheist, former Ku Klux Klan grand dragon, and founder of the White Aryan Resistance

The sketch of several prominent ideological shifts among white supremacists and three notions of whiteness as a religion helps bring into relief how and why the mantras of "my race is my religion" and "white genocide" are effective tools for advancing the interests of white nationalists. The invocation of "religion" and "genocide" 1) concretizes an imagined group through the promotion of tribalism, 2) legitimizes and mainstreams their message through familiar yet resonant vocabulary, and 3) mobilizes whites as an embattled entity by raising the stakes and significance of their endangerment. Despite the loosely coordinated, and at times even antagonistic, North American white nationalist movements, an increasing number of contemporary white supremacists are claiming "their race is their religion," downplaying the divide among the collectively racialized theologies of pro-Christian white supremacists and non-Christian religious movements and the atheistic bend of anti-religion alt-right members.[39] Promoting "race as my religion," despite the fact that race is constructed, reinforces the notion that whiteness translates to a criterion of group membership. This fosters group cohesion among various stripes of white nationalists by encouraging them to rally around, per Long, a common racial identity as the ultimate source of meaning, and per Tillich, the pursuit of an "ultimate fulfillment" that is valued above all other personal and group commitments, including adherence to Christianity. Furthermore, Dobratz avers:

> Some in the movement seem to be arguing that the statement "My race is my religion" should be incorporated in the master frame. William J. Murray . . . also saw religion as divisive and wanted religion to be an individual concern: "Because of the diversity of religious beliefs in this Movement, there has been a great deal of infighting. I believe we should all agree on one thing, and that is that our Race is our religion!"[40]

Not only does the appeal to "whiteness as a religion" convey the centrality of whiteness to the outlook and life world of white nationalists, but the call for absolute allegiance to the white race and the subordination of "individual concerns" to whiteness is also a practical concession in the interest of not alienating white supremacists who are conventionally religious. In this vein, "whiteness as a religion" is not a veneer designed to attract whites who are religious to the white cause, as such a tactic is highly unlikely to attract anyone who is not already sympathetic to the white nationalist agenda. Rather, it signals a softening of anti-Christian rhetoric and toleration for all current and potential white nationalists, regardless of religious inclination. For example, Dobratz writes that

> Matt Hale of WCOTC [World Church of the Creator], in reply to my question about the expression "My race is my religion," said he believed that Ben Klassen had coined this expression. Hale proclaimed: "Our basic view is that a religion that promotes one's people is a good religion and one that denies is a bad religion. Now there are some sincere Christians out there that believe that Christianity promotes the white race and certainly while we disagree with them, we can appreciate them."[41]

Despite the increasingly atheistic trajectory of white supremacy as illustrated by the alt-right, as Murray and Hale's statements exemplify, the use of the term of "religion" is still seen as rhetorically useful for building solidarity among white nationalists and as a gesture toward not estranging like-minded whites.

Unification: Genocide

> We must secure the existence of our people and a future for white children.[42]
> –David Lane, white supremacist and member of the terrorist group the Order

The shorthand reference to the above slogan is the "14 Words," and it "is the most popular white supremacist slogan in the world," reflecting the "primary white supremacist worldview in the late 20th and early 21st centuries: that unless immediate action is taken, the white race is doomed to extinction by an alleged 'rising tide of color' purportedly controlled and manipulated by Jews."[43] Despite any religious differences, white nationalists are united in the common causes of the defense of the religiosity of white privilege and the preservation of a dominant white culture in the face of extinction—a "white genocide." Proclaiming that white people are facing a radical decline also encourages solidarity. It concretizes the racial construct of white or whiteness by defining whites as a group based on the collective threat posed by an increasing non-white demographic. In essence, this encourages anyone who identifies as white, regardless of whether they embrace white supremacist ideology or not, to view themselves as a fellow people besieged. Moreover, an accusation of genocide presupposes the existence of a "national, ethnic, racial or religious group"; the 1948 Convention on the Prevention and Punishment of the Crime of Genocide reads:

> Genocide means any of the following acts committed with the intent to destroy, in whole or in part, a national, ethnic, racial or religious group, as such: (a) Killing members of the group; (b) Causing serious bodily or mental harm to members of the group; (c) Deliberately inflicting on the group conditions of life calculated to bring about its physical destruction in whole or in part; (d) Imposing measures intended to prevent births within the group; (e) Forcibly transferring children of the group to another group.[44]

Hence, the mere reference to genocide by white nationalists implicitly confers, or takes for granted as a social fact, that whites enjoy a racial group status, a status that defies geographical borders and is global in scope.

Standardization: Religion

What follows may not sound religious to those who are only familiar with traditional religions, but it is religious and also philosophical and plays a

> large part in the belief system of some of us and is how we view all of existence and all living things, including human beings and the different races.[45]
> –Martin H. Millard, better known as H. Millard, white nationalist author, columnist, and frequent contributor to Council of Conservative Citizens, Western Spring, National Vanguard, and New Nation News websites

Whiteness as a religion foments unity, but as Berry claims, "for white nationalists, even those who are atheists, religion plays an important role in how they are attempting to work together and mainstream their positions on immigration and other issues."[46] Rather than marginalizing religion, a range of beliefs and unbelief among white nationalists has forced a "rethinking [of] what 'religion' means to the movement":

> The rise of the "Alt-Right" . . . may be seen as representing the explicit turn to the "political" and the effacement of the more recognizably "religious." But I argue that this does not mean they are neglectful of "religion." Rather, they are rethinking what "religion" means to the movement, especially as they try to rebuild long broken bridges back to the conservative mainstream . . . They are also trying to ensure that the history of hostility toward Christianity within white nationalism does not poison efforts to woo the predominantly Christian right. But religious diversity among the racist right is only one part of the challenge that white nationalists face in their efforts to influence the political mainstream.[47]

"Mainstream" is multivalent in this context, as it refers both to the religious right as a politically viable coalition of conservatives from mainline religious traditions and to the mainstream, or wider citizenry, that white nationalists are attempting to reach by influencing and infiltrating public discourse using religious language. This latter notion of "mainstream" is the subject of Carol M. Swain's book *The New White Nationalism in America: Its Challenge to Integration*, as demonstrated by her comment on a tenor change among white supremacists' leadership. In contrast to

> the older racist right, the new white nationalism seeks to expand its influence mainly through argument and rational discourse aimed at its target audience of . . . embittered or aggrieved . . . white Americans . . . Unlike the Klan and Nazi movements, white nationalism is aggressively seeking a mainstream audience . . . it is preeminently a movement of discourse, persuasion, and ideas.[48]

Reasoned argumentation is the hallmark of the alt-right, and former white nationalist Derek Black confirmed this an interview when he indicated he wanted to prove he could win the majority of the vote in a local election using white nationalist talking points.[49] The slogan "my race is my religion" keeps the importance of religion at the forefront of the white nationalist strategy. It is a conduit for communicating the importance of the white cause through using the familiar yet potent word "religion" as pointing toward the importance of a dedication to whiteness without necessarily being bogged down by the extremism of white supremacy and attempting to present that whiteness as a religion is a reasonable, and even scientifically sound, judgment.

Standardization: Genocide

> ALL white countries are being flooded with millions and millions of non-whites . . . This deliberate and obvious program to force blend whites out of existence is GENOCIDE under international law.[50]
>
> –FightWhiteGenocide.com

The tack of mainstreaming, in the sense of making claims credible and likely to find wider appeal, is also exemplified by attempts to substantiate the claim of a white genocide and to sanitize an ethnostate solution. This four-step approach involves citing data that the white population is declining in number in the United States, asserting that genocide is afoot in Africa, maintaining that these occurrences are orchestrated to deliberately destroy the white population—thus meeting the legal threshold of genocide per the 1948 Genocide Convention—and proposing homogenous states for all races as a banal, commonsense solution. White supremacists attribute the numerical decline of whites to various mechanisms, such as immigration, miscegenation, high birth rates among non-whites, and low birth rates among whites; and their cultural and economic decline to race-preferential programs and emphases on the value of multiculturalism.

Empirical data supports white nationalist claims that the U.S. white population is shrinking; the U.S. Census Bureau predicts that the "nation will become 'minority white' in 2045. During that year, whites will comprise 49.7 percent of the population."[51] However, white nationalists purport that this demographic shift is the culmination of a purposeful Jewish/government conspiracy, in league with other current minority populations, to extirpate whites and their culture. In addition, in 2018 a white nationalist global campaign insisted that white farmers in South Africa "are being targeted and killed, that the government is seizing their land, they are being discriminated against by affirmative action programmes and that their language is being sidelined," a repeat of the genocide in Zimbabwe.[52] White nationalists believe these events portend future genocides and should be the concern of all whites everywhere. Aligning these events with the Genocide Convention furthers the portrayal of these events as genocidal. A petitioner, only identified as A.D., implored President Obama in 2012 to, as the title of the petition makes clear, "Stop White Genocide by halting MASSIVE third world immigration and FORCED assimilation in White countries!"[53] The petition opens with the interrogative form of what has been widely proposed by white nationalists as the only ostensibly rational remedy to white genocide: "Africa for Africans, Asia for Asians, White countries for EVERYBODY?" Moreover, a grassroots movement, the White GeNOcide Project, cites the Genocide Convention to support its white nationalist claim:

> "Deliberately inflicting on the group . . . conditions of life calculated to bring about its physical destruction in whole or in part." Under that definition, the White Genocide Project's website states that a "combination of mass immigration (of different groups of people) plus forced assimilation would qualify as genocide."[54]

Mobilization: Religion

> "Do not deny the eternal struggle; become a conscious and active director of it in your own small sphere of existence and you may survive and prosper in the here and now and beyond the grave."[55]
>
> –H. Millard

Both Mark Juergensmeyer and Bruce Lincoln locate the potency of religion in its capacity to heighten the stakes of conflict and court violence because transcendent and sacred referents invite an extraordinary defense commensurate with the protection of a community's most fundamental values.[56] As Tillich reminds us, religion as "ultimate concern" includes the twin correlate of "ultimate fulfillment"; whiteness as a religion places whites at the center of all considerations in pursuit of securing a destined this-worldly and otherworldly existence, "in the here and now and beyond the grave."[57] Minkenberg and Berry recognize the motivating potential that the invocation of religion has, as religion of whiteness "elevates whiteness itself as a transcendent mode of valuation, a means of identification, and a motivating moral trope."[58] Religious discourse is a powerfully resonating mechanism for amplifying the degree of danger a group believes it is facing, and can be parlayed into an obligation to act. Following Long's definition of religion as orientation, a threat to whiteness is nothing short of an existential threat.

Mobilization: Genocide

"Screw your optics, I'm going in . . . They're [Jews are] committing genocide to my people."[59]
–Robert Bowers, gunman who carried out what is believed to be the deadliest attack on Jews on American soil, killing eleven people at the Tree of Life Synagogue in Pittsburgh on October 27, 2018

Pointing to the vitriolic anti-Semitic and anti-immigrant rhetoric of white nationalists "coupled with demagogic anti-immigrant rhetoric from many ostensibly mainstream media sources and public figures," the Anti-Defamation League website reads that "it is not hard to imagine that such hateful rhetoric may have played a role in tipping Bowers . . . into allegedly committing a violent and hateful act.[60] A proclamation of a "white genocide" conveys the peril whites are facing and establishes their victimhood, reversing the image of whites as perpetrating violence against brown bodies and instead presenting them as a target of violence by virtue of the increased presence of brown bodies and eventual eclipsing of white privilege and cultural domination presumed to accompany the nation's demographic landscape.

Nonetheless, the mantra of white genocide conveys an urgency that does more than spurn petitions; it serves as a pretext for preemptive violence. Robert Powers, and others before him, such as Dylann Roof—who massacred nine black parishioners of the Emanuel African Methodist Episcopal Church in Charleston on June 17, 2015—whether they believed it or not, justified their murderous actions as necessary for the preservation of the white race. Kathy Gilsinan remarks that "what's notable about the manifesto's meditation on white victimhood [by Roof], and the spread of the paradigm and its vocabulary of self-defense, is their power to motivate violence, even as white-nationalist leaders insist they condone nothing of the kind."[61]

Conclusion

Three key shifts in the development of white nationalism chart a course for comprehending why "race is my religion" and "white genocide" are effective slogans for advancing white nationalist interests. These shifts are the expansion of "whiteness" from a U.S. identity to a global identity, from a Christian to a non-Christian movement to a religiously tolerant movement, and from an aggressive group that instigates violence to an embattled group that must defend itself against violence. The strategic employment of "religion" and "genocide" in white nationalist rhetoric encourages whites to see themselves, regardless of religious affiliation or non-membership, as a concretized, common people *united* by the group conscious of a religiosity of whiteness, whose duty is to combat genocide, regardless of where they reside in the world. Religion and genocide are familiar yet powerful ideas that are points of departure for *mainstreaming* a white nationalist agenda and *mobilizing* whites to act. White nationalists recognize the importance of not appearing antagonistic to religions and of presenting reasoned arguments—as opposed to promoting outwardly racist premises for their stances—as a practical matter of recruiting people to their cause and convincing others that, per the Genocide Convention, whites are victims of an unfolding genocide. Last, casting the decline of the white population and white dominance as of this- and otherworldly significance and proportions is designed to further motivate whites to stop white genocide and can be a pretense for preemptive violence against black people and other similarly marginalized groups.

The elision of "whiteness" and "religion" as exemplified in the phrase "my race is my religion," where religion is understood as an orientation or outlook, renders whiteness as *the* ultimate concern of the group and its primary identity marker for making meaning, being in the world, and fulfilling any telos or ultimate end. This conceptualization of the *function* of religion as elemental to a life world illuminates why white nationalists experience threats to whiteness—an increase in the minority population in the United States and real and perceived black community uplift—as constituting an existential crisis that manifests as terror and anger. However, the other two conceptualizations, understanding whiteness as religion as *historical* and *sociologically performative* claims, are both crucial to unveiling the content of white rage. The historical process of constructing whiteness consisted of defining whiteness over and against the black bodies Europeans encountered in the Americas and deemed shiftless and heathens, beginning the process of a racial project that would make work and Christianity, extrinsic to whiteness. Church institutions contributed to the endurance of white elitism by providing a theological basis for white superiority, and the performative acts of belief and ritual—conventional components of the sociological conception of religion, such as ritual in the form of lynching—confirmed and reaffirmed white privilege as an incontrovertible social fact. Hence, people of color numerically eclipsing whites as the dominant population and as a normative culture—through both the birth rates of non-white Americans and the influx of immigrants—and the perceived loss of employment and privilege to black people and other people of color do not translate to a fear of plurality or a mere change in status but to an intentional and organized assault on the very essence of what it means to be white.

TEN

Exorcising Blackness: Calling the Cops as an Affective Performance of Gender

Biko Mandela Gray

When average people participate in racist acts, they demonstrate a profound misreading of the subjects they encounter.[1]

–Sharon Patricia Holland

In the first instance, performativity must be understood not as a singular or deliberate "act," but, rather, as the reiterative and citational practice by which discourse produces the effects that it names.[2]

–Judith Butler

What I am offering is a theory of passion not as the drive to accumulate . . . but as that which is accumulated over time. Affect does not reside in an object or sign, but is an effect of the circulation between objects and signs.[3]

–Sara Ahmed

When Good Days Go Bad: BBQ Becky, Permit Patty, and Cornerstore Caroline

April 29, 2018, Oakland, California. The day was chilly, but the sun was out. People were strolling on the sidewalk; every once in a while, someone would speed by on rollerblades or, perhaps, a skateboard. The lake was in clear view. It was a beautiful day in the park, in the place where families and friends gather to enjoy weather. It was what Ice Cube might have called "a good day." Or at least it could've been.

But Jennifer Schulte wasn't having it. Donning a blue jacket and aviator shades, Schulte spotted an infraction: a group of people were grilling outside, but they were using *charcoal*. And this was too much.

[911 dispatcher]: Oakland Police, how may I help you?
["BBQ Becky"]: Um, yeah, I would like to report that someone is illegally using a charcoal grill in a non-designated area . . . I'd like it dealt with immediately, so that coals don't burn more children and we don't have to pay more taxes.[4]

Maybe this really was about just the charcoal. Schulte, after all, has a PhD from Stanford in chemical engineering.[5] This could have been about the environment, about the hazards and dangers of fossil fuels. And maybe it was.

But there are two curious moments that nullify this line of thinking. You see, Schulte didn't make one, but *two* calls to the police: the first call, which starts with the above conversation, takes a racial turn, transmuting environmental concerns into an instance of environmental(ly inspired) racism.

[Dispatcher]: And the person that's using the grill, I need a description of them—what race are they?
[BBQB]: African American.
[Dispatcher]: And how old are they?
[BBQB]: I'd say about forty—late thirties.
[Dispatcher]: And what color clothes is he wearing?
[BBQB]: He is wearing dark black pants and a black sweatshirt, um, with an orange logo on it—I have a picture of it.
[Dispatcher]: And how tall is he, approximately?
[BBQB]: He's sitting down, I'm not sure.
[Dispatcher]: And is he thin, medium, or heavy build?
[BBQB]: Uh, he's heavier build. He's muscular.[6]

The conversation turned, and turns, on the race of the purported griller, a "muscular," "African American" man. By invoking the man's build and "muscularity," Schulte unwittingly (or intentionally) invokes the recent history of other "muscular" black men like Michael Brown and Terrence Crutcher, Tamir Rice and Alton Sterling. They were larger, of heavier build, and they, too, were seen as violating the law. All of them resonate in the interstices of this call, making an environmental complaint feel like something far more serious.

It's still possible, however, to dismiss this reading. Maybe Schulte identifies the man's race because she was prompted to do so. Maybe she was just following instructions; after all, the logic of race in the United States remains coded in and through how one's body is perceived. The man was "African American" because he was perceived as such, and the officers needed an identifying set of markers—along with his clothes and his build—to ensure that the man they would hail is actually the man who has allegedly transgressed the law.

But then the second moment happens. Schulte may have readily identified the man's race and build, but when asked to identify her own racial identity, she puts up a fight.

> [Dispatcher]: You're gonna have to tell me what race you are, how old you are, and what you're wearing—[the police] will never find you [if you don't identify yourself]...
> [BBQB]: I am wearing a dark navy-blue sweatshirt with jeans, and I have dark brown hair, about shoulder length. And I have people harassing me—
> [Dispatcher]: What race are you? And how old are you?
> [BBQB]: My race doesn't matter![7]

Having wanted to only racialize others, Schulte now had been called upon to racialize herself. Just two hours earlier, Schulte had no problem identifying the man's race. However, when the gaze turned upon her, she was no longer interested in engaging these racial dynamics. Her "race," which is to say, her whiteness, had moved from being "the background to experience" to becoming a phenomenological object of analysis.[8] This encounter is no longer (solely) about charcoal. This isn't about children burning themselves. Whatever ecological concerns Schulte may have expressed have now fallen to the periphery; what was—what *remains*—on the table is the question, the problematic, the *problem*, that is race. So much for the environment. Schulte's phone call was recorded, and she goes viral, earning a nickname on Twitter: *BBQ Becky*.

*　*　**

We move forward a few months, and we head to San Francisco. It's June 23rd, and another scene, shorter in duration, but no less fascinating (or terrifying?) occurs. Alison Ettel sits in her apartment, running a small business selling cannabis for dogs. It's not a global corporation, but it's something: perhaps she proudly wears the title of feminist, with this business being evidence of her own quest for equality. It's a small victory, but, again, it's *hers*.

The window is open. The day is beautiful, and sunlight is always better than other forms of light. And then she hears it: *Cold water! One dollar each!* It's a minor annoyance, so she keeps working. But the shouting continues; what started as an annoyance has now become a full-on distraction. As a worker, she can no longer work. The shouting is too much. (The irony, of course, is that she lives near a busy sidewalk; extraneous noise is ever present.)

So she pretends to calls the cops. It's not clear when she realizes that the offender is Jordan Rodgers, a young girl, but no worries; she's *persistent*. She stays on the phone even after she realizes who's doing the shouting. Rodgers's mother confronts her. Ashamed, she tries to hide, but *she stays on the phone*. In an act of what cannot be called anything other than psychic terrorism, Alison Ettel pretends to call the cops on a young eight-year-old girl for "illegally selling water without a permit."[9] She becomes another internet sensation: *Permit Patty* sticks, and she goes on a host of interviews to clear her name and offer non-apologies.[10]

* * *

Story three: even shorter, but no less potent. A young black family—a mother, a son, and a daughter—is in a convenience store in Flatbush, New York City. As they leave, the son's backpack brushes against Teresa Klein's backside. Klein becomes outraged; she calls (or she claims to have called) NYPD to report sexual assault. Voice raised, Klein angrily screams into the phone, "I was sexually assaulted by a child." The young child, named Jeremiah Harvey, can be seen crying as the threat of the police looms large; the police never show, but the terroristic and psychological damage has been done. Klein, like her two predecessors, earns her own nickname: *Cornerstore Caroline*.

* * *

Schulte, Ettel, and Klein were not alone; there are multiple reports of other women calling the police on black people for the most minor of alleged infractions.[11] But what holds them together is that each of them enact what Sharon Patricia Holland calls acts of "profound misreading"; in each of these cases, these women (among many more) overdetermine the meaning of black life and black activity in an attempt to put black people back in their supposed places. Schulte, Ettel, and Klein may not have gotten the legal reprieve they wanted (or pretended to want), but the very act of calling the notoriously, historically, and violently anti-black institution that is the police solidifies them as the ones for whom making such calls are legitimate and encouraged actions. In other words, this isn't about the law, but instead about the anti-blackness that is at the heart of the law—and more specifically, how this anti-blackness sustains white subjectivity.[12]

In this chapter, I draw from poststructuralist and affect theories to suggest that the very action of calling the cops on black people solidifies oneself as a normatively gendered subject.[13] Multiple thinkers have demonstrated that blackness solidifies and supports norms through violence enacted against it.[14] This chapter is my attempt to add to those discourses through an affective-oriented analysis. Ultimately, my goal in this chapter is to show how normative subjects establish themselves through anti-black affect. If, as Ben Highmore stresses, "affect gives you away," then the heightened emotions that colored these women's interactions with both the police and the people they surveilled give them away as subjects who benefit from what Hortense Spillers might call the "potential for gender differentiation."[15] In other words, what is "given away" is not simply one's internal state; it is also, always and already, how one's internal state invokes, sustains, or critiques the normative structures—in this case, the normative structure of womanhood—that make subjects possible in the first place.

In the first section of this chapter, I show that anti-blackness is steeped in and structured by what Brian Massumi calls the "logic of threat." Threat is an affective structure; it flows in, through, and between people, announcing one's capacity to "affect and be affected." As an affect, threat is a structure of legitimation; threat justifies preemptive violence as well as the specific emotions that motivate such violence. In this regard, the specific emotion is rage: if the etymology of rage is connected to the excessive aggression of rabies, then I want to suggest that it is excessive *sensitivity* that characterizes rage. The logic and the expression justify one another; when someone expresses rage at a threatening black object, rage becomes normal. It becomes *normative*, establishing the one who rages as the one who *can* and *should* express rage.

The second section articulates the normativity of gender through the performance of affect. In a riff off of Simone de Beauvoir by way of Hortense Spillers, I might suggest that one "becomes" a woman by enacting anti-black violence on the basis of anti-black *affect*. The flushed faces, streaming tears, and heightened voices, therefore, are expressions of what we might call an affective economy of anti-blackness. Drawing from Sara Ahmed and Judith Butler, the second section reads these women's actions as what we might call affective performances of gender: having established the affective and emotional context of the calls, this section shows how these women perform their gender by trafficking in anti-black rage. By expressing emotional and affective anti-blackness, these women establish themselves as normatively gendered subjects; they re-establish themselves as women *through* their anti-black rage.

In the final section, I turn to the religious dimensions of these calls. I demonstrate that these acts, as well as the institutional mechanisms put in place to support and justify them, articulate a theodicean logic that sediments and rationalizes the rage enacted against blackness. In other words, these women's rage is justified *because* the black objects of their rage are always and already coded as rage-inducing in the first place. The tears, the screams, the hiding, and the frustration name an affective desire to exorcize the threat of blackness from their midst; by calling the cops, these women enact what I call *affective exorcisms*: these women attempt to purge (evil and threatening) blackness from the (normative and good) white public. Whether or not these exorcisms are successful has no bearing on the fact that these attempts to expiate blackness suffer few to no legal or institutional repercussions. In hailing the law, these women show themselves as above reproach. They are, and cannot help but be, innocent.

We begin, therefore, with the affective and emotional dimensions of anti-blackness.

Blackness as Rage-Inducing Threat

In "The Future Birth of the Affective Fact," Brian Massumi offers the following observation:

> The felt reality of threat legitimates from preemptive action, once and for all. Any action taken to preempt a threat from emerging into a clear and present danger is legitimated by the affective fact of fear, actual facts aside. Preemptive action will always have been right. This circularity is not a failure of logic. It is a different logic, operating on the same affective register as threat's self-causing.[16]

Threat, then, traffics in a different kind of circular logic, producing preemptive actions on the basis of *potential* violence. The logic is what Massumi calls the "double conditional"; threat operates as a feeling of *if one could, one would*. In other words, there need not be any empirical evidence that something ominous or dangerous is actually imminent. Instead, one need only *feel* that the *possibility* of imminent threat can and will be actualized. Shoot first and ask questions later, so the logic goes.

Although Massumi draws from the 9/11 attacks to discuss his claim, I want to suggest here that blackness itself is ensnared by this affective logic. In other words, given the well-documented historical framing of black people as violent brutes, black people contemporarily, contemporaneously, and (phenomeno)logically show up as constant threats. In a riff off of Massumi, we might suggest that if *black people* could enact violence, they would.

We need not go too far back in time to demonstrate this "affective fact." The recent, widespread, and prevalent occurrences of officers shooting or physically harming unarmed black people—men *and* women—continually enact this logic. Tamir Rice had a "gun"; Jonathan Ferrell "ran through" tasers; Michael Brown demonically and maniacally "ran through" bullets; and Alton Sterling continually "reached for a gun" before, during, and after he was shot. Upon encountering what they perceive as a threat, police constantly reference "waistbands" and life-threatening fear as the reason for discharging their weapons. In each of these cases, the assumptive logic takes hold; the potentiality of violence justifies preemptively enacting *lethal* violence. Massumi puts it this way:

> The could-have/would-have logic works both ways. If the threat does not materialize, then it just goes to show that it still always would have if it could have. If the threat does materialize, then it just goes to show that the future potential for what happened had really been there in the past."[17]

Again: shoot first, and ask questions later.

Massumi lays out the logical dimensions of threat. In other words, Massumi's logic is what he might call *affective*: this logic allows for us to see what he himself might call the "trans-" or "pre-personal" ways that bodies encounter one another. The structure of threat can be deeply personal, but it gains its steam through continued circulation, through the perpetual movement and diffusion of various signs and symbols that legitimate blackness as a threat. Despite the fact that there is little evidence to suggest that black people can and will actually attack police, the logic of threatening blackness nevertheless takes and has taken hold within the context of U.S. sociocultural and sociopolitical life.

As Frantz Fanon told us long ago, and as Achille Mbembe elaborates, black people are phobogenic objects whose contemporary presence invokes a history and mythology of threatening black monstrosity: Alton Sterling was a "devil" according to Blane Salamoni, and Terrence Crutcher, who had his hands *raised in the air* when he was killed, looked "like a bad dude" according to the police officer in the helicopter.[18] These lapses in perception, these "profound misreadings," occur on the basis of an affective structure that is lodged in the specific people who enact them even as it exceeds their specific individuality.

But Massumi's account of threat is still *logical*. His accounting of threat lacks the phenomenological complexities that unfold when threat's logical structure takes hold. The experience of threat can take various forms, and while fear is the most prevalent, what I want to suggest here is that, when it comes to antiblackness, the logic of threat emotionally manifests itself as *rage*.

We often think of rage as the hyperexpression of anger. And often, it is: reddened faces, raised voices, and possibly physical violence all fall under rage's banner, providing us with a physical and phenomenological expression of rage as the intense and excessive explosion of emotion in the face of a rage-inducing object. In other words, rage is what occurs when one's intentional attention terminates in an entity (be it subject or object) that demands an excessive response. To riff off of Sara Ahmed's discussion of happiness, rage is neither lodged in the object nor the subject, but is, instead, the effect of an intense connection between perceiving subjects and what these subjects perceive. Rage adheres perceiving subjects to the "objects" of their rage; in other words, rage sticks, and is sticky.

However, if, as Eugenie Brinkema points out, specific affects carry specific formal qualities, then I want to suggest here that rage's formal structure is one of *excessive sensitivity*. The etymology of the word "rage" carries a deep connection to rabies, a disease that produces cognitive dysfunction and excessive aggression. If rage is etymologically connected to rabies, then what I would like to suggest here is that rage appears to us as excessive, as *too much*. And central to this is not the anger, but instead the *excess*: rage shows up as improper outbursts or over-the-top explosions; it manifests through inordinate expressions of emotion; it signals to us that whatever induced the rage does not quite deserve the emotional explosion that erupted in the moment of encounter. In short, rage expresses *hypersensitivity*; and this can be both physical and emotional—in fact, the two are connected.

Consider it: Schulte called the cops because she *sensed* charcoal and saw black people; Klein mistook someone brushing past her as someone grabbing her backside. And Ettel *heard* screaming on a noisy street and *pretended* to call the cops to stop the screaming. All of these responses are unsettling in their inordinate excessiveness, but Ettel's sustained juridical pretense *after* realizing the identity of the "screamer" is so excessive that it borders on psychic torture. These were instances of violent and violating hypersensitivity, of inflamed sensation and terrifyingly inflammatory reactions in the face of the most quotidian of activities. Anger need not be present; mere annoyance can and will do. Rage, then, is structured by and through excess—excessive sensitivity, excessive reactions.

We might want to understand rage—especially Ettel's rage—as irrational, as exceeding the normative boundaries of what counts for appropriate reactions. However, when read through Massumi's logic of threat, such "irrationality" manifests itself as proper and appropriate within the racialized context of the United States. While many may want to excoriate these three women—and the horde of other women and men who follow in their wake—for being irrational in their actions, the unfortunate and terrifying fact remains: These actions are only "irrational" to the extent that they are not deemed appropriate by the larger order.

Because black bodies are understood as phobogenic objects—because they would if they could—there is never an inappropriate time to rage out on them. The excessiveness might be excessive, but it's warranted through the logic of threat. Cops already preemptively kill black people. Therefore, because police officers shoot black people first and ask questions later, there is nothing irrational about hailing police to do what they already do. The logic of threat legitimates rage, allowing for its intensity to circulate not as abnormally excessive but instead as normatively *appropriate*. Call the cops on black people, and they usually come—unless, of course, you want to simply scare black people back into their place. Either way, the only person who should be scared is the person who the call is about.

White Women's Tears: Gender, Performativity, and Affect

Legitimacy, then, is the name of the game. The excessiveness of rage becomes reasonable and encouraged when it is incorporated into the double-conditional logic of black threat; put more simply, emotion (rage) is legitimated by the flow of affect (the logic of black threat). And this structure of emotional legitimation can, will, and does have gendered implications. Through the legitimated rage that motivated these (pretend) phone calls, these women also solidified themselves *as* women, as happily ensconced and ensnared in gender's grammar and logic; these events are just as much gendered as they are affective.

I want to read the enraged act of calling the cops on threatening blackness as an affectively gendered performance, wherein the enactments of "the reiterative and citational practice by which discourse produces the effects that it names" are reiterating and citing normative gender (in this case, "woman") through emotional expression.[19] Put simply: these women established themselves as *white women* by enacting legitimated rage.

Consider, for example, Teresa Klein, a.k.a. "Cornerstore Caroline." Amid Jeremiah Harvey's tears, Klein can be heard loudly telling the police, "That's right—the son grabbed my ass, and [the mother] decided to yell at me." Surveillance footage would eventually show that Jeremiah did no such thing; as he walked out of the store, his backpack brushed against Klein—which she misread as "grabbing."

The misreading of a brush for a grab is part of the excessiveness of rage. Phenomenologically, the touch of a backpack feels different from a grabbing hand—which means that what Klein felt wasn't necessarily a "grab" but instead the mere *touch* of blackness. A "profound misreading" occurs—again. And the "again" is crucial; Klein misreads this incident because it's part of the long history of such misreadings. It makes sense and is made possible *because* it has been done before, because it is not abnormal for white womanhood to invoke black touch as a threat to its gendered and bodily integrity.

Such moves exceed the intentions of the subject who invokes them. The enactment itself, and the effects that this enactment engenders, are what reify Klein as a white woman; whether or not she is actually a white supremacist is irrelevant in the face of a historical and contemporary set of gender norms that are built and sustained by white supremacy.[20] Klein needed not be racist to emotionally and affectively channel and perform the racism of normative gender. "Performativity is," Butler writes, "not a singular 'act,' for it is always a reiteration of a norm or set of norms, and to the extent that it acquires an act-like status in the present, it conceals or dissimulates the conventions of which it is a repetition."[21]

Klein's call didn't simply reiterate the gender norms; it also continued to traffic in what we might call an affective economy of anti-blackness. Regarding affective economies, Sara Ahmed writes:

> Emotions work as a form of capital: affect does not reside positively in the sign or commodity, but is produced as an effect of its circulation ... the movement between signs or objects converts into affect ... Affect doesn't reside in an object or sign, but is an effect of the circulation between objects and signs ... Signs increase in affective value as an effect of the movement between signs: the more signs circulate, the more affective they become.[22]

Klein enacts a "profound misreading" of the situation because there is already a symbolic and historical connection between black bodies and hypersexuality: black bodies have become signs of encroaching threat, and the more these signs continue to circulate, the easier it is to detach the emotional feeling of threat from a cognizant and intentional enactment of white supremacist violence. The history of lynchings, many of which occurred on the basis of white women leveling (or at least not refuting) charges of sexual assault, reverberates in and through Klein's outrage, turning the black male body into a sign of threat, and therefore transmuting arbitrary contact into a potential site of state-sanctioned violence.[23] In other words, the logic of black threat gains its steam from an affective economy of anti-blackness. Black bodies accumulate affective threat over time, and this accumulation operates in service of subjective norms—one of which is gender. Klein reinforced her gender identity *by* identifying Jeremiah Harvey as the perpetrator of her assault.

We need not stay at the level of the (hetero)sexual, however; Ettel's pretended phone call invokes a history of relationships between white women and black women steeped in constitutive exclusion. In other words, white women have historically established their womanhood through the exclusion of black women from the category of woman. The historical circulation of such relations develops an affective economy of misogynoir, ultimately rendering black women the constitutive outside of (white) womanhood. As another chapter in this volume contends, the history of women's suffrage, for example, was propped up by a mutually exclusive racial logic that rendered white women deserving of the vote *by excluding black people*, particularly black women. If, as Spillers suggested, black women are "ungendered" subjects of the flesh, then white women draw from the violence enacted against "black female flesh" to establish and maintain their normative gendered identities. Or, as Judith Butler once put it:

> [The] exclusionary matrix by which subjects are formed thus requires the simultaneous production of a domain of abject beings, those who are not yet subjects, but who form the constitutive outside of the domain of the subject. The abject designates here precisely those "unlivable" and "uninhabitable" zones of social life which are nevertheless densely populated by those who do not enjoy the status of the subject, but whose living under the sign of the "unlivable" is required to circumscribe the domain of the subject.[24]

Ettel's "phone call," then, reproduces an affective set of relations that inscribe and reify Jordan Rodgers as an abject entity. By trafficking in the excessiveness of rage legitimated through the anti-black logic of black threat, Ettel's act of psychic terror reifies and inscribes Jordan's fundraising as a threat to the "peacefulness" of this (white) public space.

All of these incidents are connected—not simply because they have the same structure, but also because they are steeped in affects and emotions that exceed the specific *thought* of the one who enacted the violence. You don't need to "be" racist to enact racism. All you have to do is feel it.

Conclusion: Affective Exorcisms as the Religious, Racialized, and Gendered Performance of Innocence

We've now established that gender can and will sediment through the performance of rage. These women re-established themselves as women through their outraged expressions; they sedimented their gender identity by trafficking in the logic of black threat. In this final section, I simply want to suggest that these performances were also religious, that they articulated the religious dimensions of white supremacy *through* the affective performance of gender.

As many scholars in religious studies know, there is a close historical relationship between affect and religion.[25] And it is precisely this close relationship that produces what I want to call here an affective theodicy of whiteness—one that, in this case, articulates the divinity of white womanhood as unquestionable. As many in the history of philosophy know, theodicy is not simply the philosophical problem of evil; it is also the *response*, the reaction to the perpetual announcement and presence of what has been deemed evil in this world. Theodicy, in short, justifies the goodness of the divine in the face of evil.

However, when thought about in conversation with questions of racism, theodicean forms of rationalization move from the realm of the merely theological into the existential, the sociopolitical, and the social-ontological. To ask about God's goodness in the face of an earthquake is one thing; to ask about God's goodness in the face of black suffering is another. It is precisely when the focus moves away from what Anthony Pinn and others classified as "natural evil" to questions of social violence and suffering that we find ourselves asking the age-old question that William Jones once asked: *Is God a white racist?*

Here, I am not asking that question so much as drawing from its diagnostic power to analyze white women's constant preoccupation with hailing the police on black people. As Stephen Finley and I have written elsewhere, the very enactment of anti-black violence within the context of the United States invokes a theodicean—and therefore *religious*—structure premised upon the deification of the whiteness that the state seeks to protect.[26] As Lewis Gordon once put it:

> Blacks and whites are caught in a futile situation in an antiblack world. The black is always *too black*. The white, on the other hand, is *never white enough*—except from the standpoint of the black. For the black, to be white enough is to be a human being and hence one step closer to God. But since such a goal is out of his [sic] reach, he [sic] might as well regard whiteness as divine. If the black *is* human, and whiteness is above blackness, then to be white is tantamount to being a god.[27]

In another essay, Gordon draws this line of thinking to its social-ontological and sociotheological conclusion: "Blackness is fundamental to the formation of European modernity as it is one that imagines itself legitimate and pure through the expurgation of blackness. It is, in other words, *the theodicy* of European modernity."[28] To think with Gordon, then, is to see whiteness, and therefore white people, as enacting, maintaining, and protecting the divinity they farcically embody *through* the constant denigration, submission, and expiation of blackness—and therefore black people.

In other words, when BBQ Becky, Permit Patty, and their horde of copycat callers carry out their brutal acts of hailing, they are engaging in *theodicean* acts—acts that prop up their innocence and unquestionable status *through* the constant surveillance and accusation of black people. Put simply, by hailing the state to "address" minor legal infractions (or, in the case of someone like Cornerstore Caroline, to address no legal infraction at all), these women perform what I'd like to call *affective exorcisms*: by attempting to have black people removed or punished, these women attempt to exorcize the threatening danger of blackness from the putatively good white public—and they do so through the gendered performance of rage.

Many of the chapters in this volume have articulated religion as ultimate orientation, and named white supremacy as precisely the ultimate orientation toward whiteness. As I conclude this chapter, I simply want to add to that chorus of voices by naming affective exorcism as an expression of the religion of white rage. What these women show is that one does not need to harbor specific feelings of hatred or specific pride in one's gender to be anti-black. Ettel, for example, made it clear that she "wasn't racist" during an interview, and Klein, for what it's worth, apologized to Jeremiah Harvey (in his absence) upon realizing what had actually happened. Schulte, to my knowledge, has yet to apologize.

But that's precisely the point, isn't it? In the wake of affective exorcisms that solidify one's gender through the performance of rage against black threat, white women can and will further re-establish their identity through *apology*. They were already innocent when the (pretend) calls were made; they further solidify that innocence through an apology that cannot help but ring hollow in the wake of the potential lethality of their calls. All exorcisms aren't successful. But the ones who perform them are always read as "good," as in the service of "God," and therefore free of any guilt. Success or failure, mistake or mark, intentional or inadvertent, these enactments of rage will always and already mark these women as *white innocent women*. Apologize or don't; it doesn't matter, because one has already been deemed normative—and therefore innocent. These women were framed as damsels in distress. They re-established themselves as women through the performance of affective exorcisms. They were innocent because they were already supposed to be innocent, because the affective economy of anti-blackness, mixed with the grammar of gender, established these women as unmistakably innocent. And, despite the public shaming and possible professional repercussions, no amount of mistaken identity, unintended racism, or apology can change that.

ELEVEN

White Power Barbie and Other Figures of the Angry White Woman

Danae M. Faulk

Though the term unarmed black man may be literally accurate, it doesn't tell the whole story in most cases. In a number of cases, if the victim ended up being unarmed, it certainly wasn't for lack of trying. Grabbing an officer's gun or using other equipment to beat the police doesn't give you a free pass. Oh, but heaven forbid someone be critical of this movement . . . For someone who wants equal rights, it sure sounds like you'd prefer special treatment. It sure sounds like you'd like a gold star at the end of the day, just for being born. Get over yourself. You're not a humanitarian. You're not a unifier. You're not teaching black children to go forth and conquer. You're teaching them to feel sorry for themselves. Nice work, and how 'bout you sit down. Those are my final thoughts. God bless and take care.[1]

–Tomi Lahren

Political commentator Tomi Lahren has built a career around sharing her "final thoughts"—a segment that blends the temperament and tone of popular white male political commentators like Bill O'Reilly with an Anne Coulter-esque taste for controversy. Joining the ranks of other conservative media figures who see themselves as bravely transgressing the taboos of political correctness, Lahren reflects a form of white frustration and aggression that codes any challenge to white normativity as a threat to the nation's wellbeing: Colin Kaepernick's protest is anti-America; Black Lives Matter supports black supremacy; Jesse Williams perpetuates a war on cops. "It's not white people working to divide America," Lahren asserts, "it's you!"[2] *You. You* people. *Black* people. It's not hard to hear how the refrains of white supremacy punctuate Lahren's outrage.[3]

In light of these refrains, critics have given Lahren the (dis)honorary title of "White Power Barbie"—a name that, all at once, connects Lahren's indignation to anti-black racism. The adjective "white power" gestures to the white supremacist sensibilities which bubble just beneath the surface of Lahren's appeal to national unity and the nation's wellbeing. Moreover, "white power" speaks to how Lahren's outrage conjures blackness as the "real" threat to America, reflecting how the threat to white dominance returns, reverberates, and resonates as a threat to the nation. To then add "Barbie" is to pair this type of white aggression and moral outrage with the popular image of the famous blonde-haired plastic doll, known best for her anatomically impossible measurements and her controversial role in shaping young children's understanding of ideal womanhood.[4] Thus, Lahren's moniker "White Power Barbie" asks us to consider how the outrage of white women, particularly those considering themselves patriotic and pro-working class, plays a role in the production and sustenance of white (supremacist) America.

In this chapter, I argue that Lahren is emblematic of an ongoing tradition of angry white women who define and negotiate their gendered experiences *as* white women affectively through, rather than against, white supremacist and anti-black sentiments. I argue that the reception of such women both generates and is mediated by *the figure of the Angry White Woman*: a woman whose anger is read as attributable, positive, and morally correct. Such a figure, I argue, is rooted in the historical association of white femininity to moral authority within white supremacist thought. This strong link between white womanhood and morality has a twofold effect: on the one hand, it subjects white women to the responsibility of protecting the goodness of whiteness; on the other hand, it enables whiteness to be "good" through the supposed moral superiority of white women. This twofold effect hinges on affect.

Anger, specifically morally inflected anger, indexes the role of white women as guardians of America. As protectors of the nation's morality and wellbeing within white supremacy, white women's anger functions as a defense against moral decay, which often is code for the imagined encroachment of blackness. In this way, white women's anger operates as a switch-point in the larger affective economy of white dominance, inciting and amplifying an affective investment in white America. While this relationship is made explicit within communities holding a desire for and belief in the social and political superiority of white people (white supremacy), the figure of the Angry White Woman also circulates in supposedly neutral and even anti-racist spaces. In the latter, the figure operates to uphold the normativity of white women's experiences and histories, such that whiteness operates unmarked (white normativity).⁵ Thus, white women's anger often serves an indispensable role in the generation, circulation, and sustainment of white supremacist sensibilities, even if unconscious, unaware, or unintended.

Figuring Angry (White) Women

The white supremacist potential of white women's anger arises from the specific way that the figure of the Angry White Woman configures, disfigures, and transfigures white womanhood. Modes of figuring can organize bodies and affects (configuration) as well as take them apart (disfiguration) and can always move beyond or across them (transfiguration). To focus on figuration of white women is thus to draw attention to the construction and consequences of specific iterations of white womanhood and anger. Certainly white women who become angry or express anger can also be exposed to charges of irrationality, hysteria, and other forms of entangling women with the source of their anger.⁶ My point here is not to erase those histories or accuse white women's anger of always intentionally contributing to the maintenance of white supremacy and white normativity in the U.S., but to consider those moments where white women's anger, particularly in the form of moral outrage, is capacitated by and capacitates whiteness. To this end, this chapter serves as genealogy of the Angry White Woman, tracing the sociocultural and affective connections that form the grounds through which the figure is both legitimated and drafted to serve the whims of white normativity and white supremacy in the United States.⁷ To accomplish this, I draw from Sara Ahmed's work on emotion and figures.

In her interrogation of happiness, Ahmed, a feminist philosopher and cultural critic, asks us to consider what figures and emotions do, what associations they secure, what things they stick together, and how they shape the ways that specific bodies show up. She argues, for instance, that the figure of the Angry Black Woman can shape the ways that black women are received and experienced by others in feminist circles:

> You might be angry *about* how racism and sexism diminish life choices for women of color. Your anger is a judgment that something is wrong. But then in being heard as angry, your speech is read as motivated by anger. Your anger is read as unattributed, as if you are against *x* because you are angry rather than being angry because you are against *x*.⁸

In this example, black women are encountered by their white feminist interlocutors as killjoys of feminism. The figure organizes the silencing of black women's anger by securing a history of associations that enable black women to not be *heard* as angry about something, but only be *received* as angry.⁹ Thus for Ahmed, anger does not emanate from or belong to a person, nor does it reference a subjective or psychological state of being, but rather "is produced as an effect of circulation."¹⁰ Similarly, albeit with a different trajectory in mind, this chapter considers: what does the figure of the Angry White Woman do? What work does the circulation of white women's anger do? What associations do such figures of white women bring with them? How do these figures and emotions shape bodies? And from what historical landscapes do they emerge? Rather than centering on psychological states of specific women or providing a historical account, this chapter links with Ahmed's scholarship to consider the ethical and political work that the Angry White Woman and her anger do.

The specific configuration of white womanhood that animates the Angry White Woman is articulated through the figure of the *True Woman*. In her famous analysis, Barbara Welter argues that the True Woman upheld four virtues: purity, submissiveness, domesticity, and piety. "Without them, no matter whether there was fame, achievement or wealth, all was ashes. With them she was promised happiness and power."¹¹ This promise to power came as a set of contradictions about the role women should play in securing the nation's future. On the one hand, she was something that demanded male protection. On the other hand, her proximity to those four virtues meant that she must "uphold the pillars of the temple with her frail white hand," acting as protector of the nation's wellbeing.¹² Thus, the True Woman offered a path for some to lay claim to a legitimated role in the nation-state's development as guardians of the religious, moral, and familial spheres of American life, even if such a role demanded that these women transcend their humanity to become an angel in the house.

True Womanhood was a white patriarchal demand on women, but this very demand provided some women with the potential for political and social access within a white-dominated society. Operating within the same logic that argued for the necessity of True Women, a white woman could make exacting criticisms of white men as threats to the nation's wellbeing. Within this logic, such criticisms would need to be responded to tactically by white men, given that they were argued through a set of values central to arguments of white superiority. To disagree with a white woman mediated by the figure of the True Woman could potentially disrupt the authority of whiteness, if one yielded to the assumption that white femininity was a crucial pillar in upholding a white-dominated society.¹³ For this reason, historian Nancy Hewitt argues that while some women resisted True Womanhood, "many more women manipulated the ideals as a means of expanding their sphere and their influence."¹⁴ The True Woman afforded a viable strategy for some white women to critique white men and patriarchal society, negotiating their position within whiteness through the very arguments of white superiority.

While the True Woman is not the only model of womanhood in the nineteenth-century United States, I use the term in this chapter to name a specific configuration of white femininity, moral authority, and responsibility to the nation that resurfaces repeatedly throughout the twentieth century. From Mary Elizabeth "Tipper" Gore's quest to protect American children from "dangerous" music with "Parental Advisory" labels to Miley Cyrus's repudiation of the hip-hop scene as too sexist, the same sensibilities that facilitated the True Woman's authority can be felt animating the contemporary ways white women enter into discussions about morality. While neither Gore's nor Cyrus's criticisms of historically black cultural productions like rap and hip-hop were particularly angry, the True Woman nevertheless provides the grounds of possibility for the Angry White Woman, legitimating those moments when moral criticism turns to moral outrage by casting more aggressive emotions as reactive, attributable, and morally correct, and by playing off the gendered logics of white superiority. Thus, a morally inflected anger would come to shape two of the more popular figurations of the Angry White Woman: the *Suffragette* and the *Handmaid*.

The Suffragette

> To every woman who gave birth to every taxpayer and citizen of this nation, we have fought for everybody else's equal rights ... It's our time to have wage equality once and for all and equal rights for women in the United States of America.[15]
>
> –Patricia Arquette

In 1978, white suffragist Susan B. Anthony was chosen as the first representation of an American woman to be minted on a U.S. coin. Reflecting on the choice, President James Carter wrote:

> The life of Susan B. Anthony exemplifies the ideals for which our country stands. The "Anthony dollar" will symbolize for all American women the achievement of their unalienable right to vote. It will be a constant reminder for the continuing struggle for the equality of all Americans.[16]

Yet for many, Anthony is hardly a symbol of "all American women." The choice to mint the Anthony dollar derives from an ongoing racial coding of the suffragist as white within the U.S. sociohistorical imaginary that erases the labor, presence, and influence of women like Sojourner Truth, Ida B. Wells, and Mary Church Terrell while occluding the white supremacist grounds upon which many white suffragists made their claims for enfranchisement. This continual flattening of the diversity of historical actors within the suffrage movement transfigures the suffragist to the *Suffragette*—a white woman, often bourgeois, whose outrage at the plight of women forces her to speak out and march in the name of equality.

As seen with the True Woman, the Suffragette circulates with a set of assumptions which it emerges from and upholds. The most enduring of these is the perpetual masquerade of "white woman" as "woman." This collapse of woman with whiteness coincides with the covert and overt use of anti-black sentiments for the negotiation of women's suffrage, particularly after emancipation. As Angela Davis argues, the issue was not the emancipation of slaves, but the sense that giving black men the right to vote would elevate them in society, making them superior to white women.[17] Thus, a number of white suffragists argued for the necessity of women's suffrage (read: white women's suffrage) for maintaining the wellbeing of the democracy in a world where black men could vote.

The arguments of white suffragists were contradictory, simultaneously evoking both the power and vulnerability of white women while positioning blackness as weak and also threatening to the nation's wellbeing. Anthony's collaborator and fellow suffragist Elizabeth Cady Stanton did precisely this in her response to abolitionist Wendell Phillips's claim that women's rights needed to wait:

> The representative women of the nation have done their uttermost for the last thirty years to secure freedom for the negro, and so long as he was lowest in the scale of being we were willing to press his claims; but now, as the celestial gate to civil rights is slowly moving on its hinges, it becomes a serious question whether we had better stand aside and see "Sambo" walk into the kingdom first. "This is the negro's hour." Are we sure that he, once entrenched in all his inalienable rights, may not be an added power to hold us at bay?[18]

Stanton resented the suggestion that women, especially white women, should not receive the vote if white men were willing to extend it to "a degraded, ignorant black one."[19] Negotiating within white supremacist sentiments, Stanton evoked the goodness of white women as a necessity in the face of the defilement and endangerment of U.S. society from "a vile and festering mass of voters who degrade the ballot."[20] Thus, Stanton exemplifies how the Suffragette's impetus to agitate for the vote and for equality arises from and, as discussed later, carries forward white supremacist sensibilities.

If Stanton exemplifies the historical context from which the Suffragette emerges, Rebecca Latimer Felton shows us how such figures can affectively censor and amplify the expressions of frustration and moral indignation of the white women from which they emerge. Felton, the first woman to serve in the U.S. Senate, was even more violent in her deployment of blackness as threat than Stanton. Playing into the racist assumptions of "black men's uncontrollable sexual desire for white women" through the figure of the "black rapist," Felton's 1897 address to the Georgia Agricultural Society justified extralegal violence precisely this way, appealing to the image of a vulnerable white, rural working woman:

> When there is not enough religion in the pulpit to organize a crusade against sin; nor justice in the court house to promptly punish crime; nor manhood enough in the nation to put a sheltering arm about innocence and virtue—if it needs lynching to protect woman's dearest possession from the ravening human beasts—then I say lynch, a thousand times a week if necessary.[21]

While the larger context for Felton's justification of lynching included an indictment of Southern white men for corrupting the democracy, society would only return to order, she argued, as soon as white men extended civil rights to white women and ended their mistreatment of black men.[22]

Felton's critiques of white men, however, would be drowned out by her own words. *Then I say lynch, a thousand times a week if necessary. I say lynch, a thousand times a week. Lynch a thousand times a week.* What had been a call for equality within white communities circulated in newspapers as a call *to* lynch from a respectable white woman, amplifying the pervasive feelings of threat and vulnerability looming in many white Southern communities post-emancipation. Thus, the Angry White Woman disfigured the complexities of Felton's address for equality within a white supremacist America into a flat call for violence against black men.

Despite their differing and complex relations to black equality, what sutures Felton and Stanton together as suffragists is their appeal to democracy as a salve for the nation's troubles. The Suffragette inherits this faith in the possibility of the democratic nation-state, albeit in a different register. The white supremacist sentiments that enabled the simultaneous portrayal of "white women suffragists as victims of male privilege on the one hand and inheritors of white privilege on the other—as both oppressed and oppressing"[23]—resonate in some present-day evocations of the need for gender equity by white women. The refrains of Elizabeth Cady Stanton's frustration about "the negro's hour" are uncannily heard in Patricia Arquette's Oscar acceptance speech one hundred and fifty years later. Like the Suffragette, Arquette is incensed that women continue to be unequal in a supposedly democratic nation-state. Yet Arquette's evocation of "our" is revealing of the ways that women's equality translates to a heteronormative, cis-gendered, white women's equality, as non-white, trans, and queer women stand in the vast space between "women" and "everyone else." Arquette's speech upholds the unmarked association of whiteness (white normativity) with womanhood by calling forth an image of the compassionate, selfless white woman who protects the goodness of the nation for others, tapping into and maintaining the affective connection between white femininity and the moral uplift of the nation. Thus, the Suffragette, even without the explicit white supremacist sentiments of suffragists like Felton and Stanton, functions to uphold and maintain an investment in white America.

The Handmaid

"Women are the n-word of the world." Raped, beaten, enslaved, married off, worked like dumb animals; denied education and inheritance; enduring the pain and danger of child birth and life IN SILENCE for THOUSANDS of years. They are the most disrespected creatures on earth.[24]

–Bette Midler

While the Suffragette gives us the figure of a woman's frustrated resentment and anger with a less-than-democratic democratic society, the Handmaid is a permutation of the Angry White Woman enraged and violated by injustice. In 2017, a television adaptation of Margaret Atwood's *The Handmaid's Tale* revived interest in a class of women in Atwood's novel called Handmaids as metaphor for women's experiences in the twenty-first century. Set in a dystopian future where the United States government has been overtaken by the theocratic Republic of Gilead and women are reduced to their reproductive function, the story has been lauded as "relevant forever," a timeless depiction of "a creeping sort of sexism that American women are all-too familiar with" and "a dystopic articulation of rape culture in the United States."[25] Politics of anger are central to many of these appraisals of the show, with one reviewer arguing that its success comes from its ability to "[capture] a moment in time and successfully [funnel] its rage outwards at a world in which women are indeed silenced, controlled and killed by men."[26] The stifled rage of women's oppression is acutely felt during the show's depiction of Particicution—a type of group execution used in Gilead.

Surrounding by men with guns and kneeling before a stage, a group of Handmaids are addressed by an Aunt—a class of women in Gilead whose job it is to train and indoctrinate Handmaids:

> Duty is a hard-tasked mistress, and it is in the name of duty that we are here today. This man has been convicted of rape. As you know, the penalty for rape is death. This disgusting creature has given us no choice . . . But that is not the worst of it. Now you know that I do my very best to protect you. The world can be quite an ugly place. But we cannot wish that ugly away. We cannot hide from that ugliness. This man raped a Handmaid. She was pregnant. And the baby died.

Following her speech, the Aunt blows her whistle to signal the beginning of the Particicution. The Handmaids break into an enraged frenzy. The red-cloaked women beat the accused man, throwing his body about, tearing at his hair and flesh, screaming through their own tears, staining their faces and hands with his blood. A quick shot to the Aunt's trembling face suggests even she is moved by the terror of the scene.

Oscillating between brutal rage and maddening release, the scene articulates the moment in Gilead where the women's anger is allowed to surface and amplify, albeit only through the figure of a dutiful citizen. Just as Tomi Lahren justifies her aggressive critiques of black folks as a response to acts of ill-will toward the nation-state, the Handmaid's rage is allowed to surface only when such anger can be tethered to her sensitivity to moral injustice, with morality understood in the show as the normative ethics of the theocratic state. Despite the conditions that give rise to a Handmaid's anger, the Particicution functions to direct the flow of anger toward those objects legitimated as the cause of injustice. Thus, the Handmaids' violent rage is justified by the affective regime of Gilead, just as the Handmaids' brutality justifies the regime. This scene, therefore, illustrates precisely how the anger of oppressed women can amplify support for the same system that oppresses them through such notions of justice, duty, and righteousness.

Despite its penetrating analysis of sexism and violence, the adaptation of *The Handmaid's Tale* trades in the same configuration of white womanhood, morality, and responsibility that has historically silenced women of color. One of the most significant changes in the adaptation was the producer's decision to populate the book's white supremacist theocracy of Gilead with a diverse cast—a choice that acknowledged the problematic optics of using an all-white cast in 2017.[27] Such a decision reimagines the very grounds of women's oppression. It is no longer a white supremacist Protestant patriarchy where race, ethnicity, sexuality, class, age, religion, and reproductive capacities all play significant roles in differently shaping the structures of gender oppression. Instead, in this post-racial patriarchy, women's oppression is an extension of being categorized as a woman.[28] Critic Angelica Jade Bastién notes that this type of "color-blind casting" merely ignores the racialized experiences of the characters of color and universalizes the particular experiences of white women.[29] In refusing to substantively engage with the racial dynamics that white women introduce, *The Handmaid's Tale* "is more concerned with the interiority of white women at the expense of people of color who recognize that Gilead isn't a possible horrifying future, but the reality of what America has always been."[30] It imagines a fantasy of violence that evokes the continuing horrors of white supremacy and coopts the experiences of women of color for the purpose of offering a narrative vehicle for white women's anger arising from their own position within white patriarchy, similar to when white women like Bette Midler coopt histories of black oppression by applying a racist slur to their own experiences of injustice. Furthermore, it recalls the white supremacist fear that the nation's wellbeing is tethered to its valuation and protection of white womanhood since, as writer Catherine Morse notes, in the Atwood novel, the violation, degradation, and enslavement of white women serves as the evidence of Gilead's dystopic state.[31]

What differentiates the Handmaid from the Suffragette is this appeal to justice for the injured rather than equality for the excluded.[32] The red robe and white bonnet of the Handmaid has become a powerful protest image of sexual and reproductive violence, even appearing outside of North America.[33] She shows up at demonstrations and marches, supporting Planned Parenthood and protesting Brett Kavanaugh's Supreme Court nomination. Many women of color have reclaimed the red robes and white bonnets not to reflect the fantasy of white women's enslavement, but instead to call attention to the ongoing experiences of women of color that the fantasy of the Handmaid derives from.[34] I suggest that these deployments of the red robe and white bonnet tap into the affective force of the show's use of the figure of the vulnerable, violated, and injured white woman who organizes injustice, oppression, and outrage in such a way as to index anger as justified. In other words, rather than entangling the person with whatever they are angry about, as Sara Ahmed would say, the Handmaid as an iteration of the Angry White Woman prevents such entanglement by allowing for a woman to be perceived as angry *because* of something.[35] This formation operates within the same white supremacist sensibilities that construct white womanhood as morally sensitive and vulnerable, i.e. the legacy of the True Woman. The Handmaid's anger is not only attributable, but also justified to the degree that it can be attributed to an injustice or wrongdoing.

Priestess White Power Barbie

> As an American who values safety, security, sacrifice and the rule of law, there is no single endorsement that means more to me than the International Union of Police Associations . . . [the Democrats' standpoints are] absolutely disgraceful and all a part of their felon-coddling, anti-law, and anti-law enforcement agendas that seek to normalize law-breakers while demonizing the men and women who put on that badge and uniform every single day to protect and defend our communities . . . Few presidents in our nation's history, and especially in the last ten years in the thick of the war on cops, have supported our brave law enforcement officers quite like President Donald Trump . . . Though, let's be frank, it's not hard to be more pro-law enforcement than Barack Obama.[36]
>
> –Tomi Lahren

In all her permutations—White Power Barbie, Suffragette, Handmaid—the Angry White Woman carries with her the legacy of the True Woman. Through the twentieth and twentieth-first century, white women like Tomi Lahren, Bette Midler, and Patricia Arquette have answered the call of True Womanhood to "uphold the pillars of the temple" not just with their virtues, but with their anger. White women's anger, expressed as a form of moral critique, plays a crucial role in upholding an affective economy that sustains white America as sacred. To this degree, the affective investment in white America functions similarly to how Charles Long understands religion. Religion, he argues, is "how one comes to terms with the ultimate significance of one's place in the world."[37] To frame the anger of white women as religious is to see such anger as sustaining white dominance and white superiority as ultimate orientation. Thus, white women's anger plays a role in ordering the world according to white supremacist sensibilities.

For White Power Barbie and her followers, a major source of concern and outrage is the "war on cops," a notion that frames the criticism of police officers as tantamount to an act of violence against the state. The logic follows that to not support police officers is to not support America, making one's identity as an American predicated on one's attachment to and investment in the nation as embodied by police officers. This tracks with Lahren's explanation of her support for police in the face of anti-police brutality movements: "Not because I'm white, or conservative but because I'm an American."[38] Yet, as the moniker "White Power Barbie" reminds us, white supremacist sensibilities percolate through Lahren's anger, especially when such anger ties together the desire for less police brutality with "felon coddling" and dangerous police hating.

Take for instance her encounter with black musician John Legend. In 2018, Legend tweeted: "Please stop calling the police on black people who are just trying to live. Please. Stop. Police shoot us for no fucking reason at all. Please. Stop." Lahren responded to Legend on Twitter, writing: "According to the FBI Police shot more unarmed white men in 2016. Black people commit 50%+ of crime in America & we are only 13%." *Black people commit 50%+ of crime. Black people commit crime.* Lahren would take this a step further later, stating: "It's anti-cop rhetoric from people like John Legend and Colin Kaepernick that put our officers at risk. Just last week, two officers were ambushed at a restaurant—why? Because the war on cops is real and it's deadly." *John Legend and Colin Kaepernick put our officers at deadly risk. John Legend and Colin Kaepernick are deadly risks.* In this exchange, Lahren not only isolates blackness as criminal, but also frames the black criticism of police brutality as a deadly threat. For White Power Barbie, blackness is criminal, threatening, and deadly for cops, which means blackness is criminal, threatening, and deadly for the nation.

As Sara Ahmed reminds us, objects are not feared because they are something to be truly fearful of. White communities do not fear blackness because it is fearsome, but rather "through the circulation of signs of fear, the black other 'becomes' fearsome."[39] In this way, white women's anger has not just functioned to protect the borders of white supremacy, but rather makes those borders "by establishing objects from which the subject, in fearing, can stand apart, objects that become 'the not' from which the subject appears to flee."[40] Lahren's anger transfigures the criticism of police by anti-racist black movements and leaders into a war on national unity, articulating that black "law breakers" rather than erethic cops are the national problem. Thus, instead of invoking the promise of democracy or violence of injustice, White Power Barbie's anger appeals to patriotism and loyalism, which in this case is the unqualified support of police brutality and virulent anti-blackness, both of which uphold white supremacy in the U.S., as salves for the nation's woes. Consequently, despite their appeal to patriotism rather than democracy or justice, White Power Barbie, the Suffragette, and the Handmaid all intensify a religious orientation toward whiteness that can be either a negative attachment to blackness as threatening or a wholesale erasure of blackness all together. The Angry White Woman does religious work to the degree that her deployment of democracy, justice, and patriotism operates as an affective mechanism for supporting and upholding white America.

What enables Tomi Lahren's anger at anti-police brutality movements and policies to shape blackness, and more generally non-whiteness, as the cause of anger and as enraging, is the figure of the Angry White Woman. In the case of White Power Barbie, her anger matters to the degree that white womanhood is invested in as a moral alarm system for the nation. Simultaneously, her moral outrage intensifies an investment in a white supremacist America that relies on white womanhood to mark and protect white moral superiority. Following Long's work, the True Woman resonates within the Angry White Woman to form something like a religion of white women's anger, where such religion is understood as an orientation to a white supremacy that uses anger to create, amplify, and sustain the boundaries of white America over and against the imagined encroachment of blackness.

TWELVE

Weaponizing Religion: A Document Analysis of the Religious Indoctrination of Slaves in Service of White Labor Elites

E. Anthony Muhammad

For some observant Americans, the candidacy and subsequent presidency of Donald Trump have blurred the boundaries between racism[1] and the conventional view of religion. Despite Trump's history of housing discrimination, of referring to blacks as "too stupid" to vote for him, of making racist remarks against Haitians and Nigerians, and of labeling neo-Nazis as "very fine people,"[2] the record of support of Donald Trump by white evangelicals[3] is part of a long-standing, historically intertwined relationship between religion and racism. This history is emblematic of decades of research documenting the relationship between high religiosity and racism.[4]

In an effort to document one particular manifestation of the interplay between religion and racism, this chapter will engage in a document analysis investigation of the Christian indoctrination of enslaved blacks in America from 1620 to 1862. In this analysis, a brief history of racism within the Christian tradition will be explored. Next, the fluctuating history of religious fervor in America will be discussed to contextualize the shifting positions both for and against the religious instruction of slaves. After that, rationales for the religious indoctrination of slaves, including both material and spiritual profits of the white clergy and planter class, will be presented as well as the means by which said indoctrination was administered to slaves.

While the overall theme of this analysis focuses on the use of religious indoctrination as mitigation against loss,[5] the guiding framework of the current study is the broad, ontological understanding of religion as discussed by Charles H. Long. According to Long, religion is, simply, a matter of orientation; of "how one comes to terms with the ultimate significance of one's place in the world."[6] By enlisting historical documents, the current study will highlight the way white evangelicals and the white labor elite (planters/slave owners) conspired to devise a systematic and deliberate form of religious instruction as a means of orienting both themselves and enslaved blacks. These socially constructed, religiously anchored orientations served to insulate the white clergy and labor elites from spiritual, material, physical, and economic loss at the expense of enslaved blacks' "place in the world."

Christian Anti-Blackness

One of the best-known examples of racist orienting in Christian doctrine is the curse of Ham. Documented in the ninth chapter of Genesis, the biblical story depicts Noah's curse upon his son Ham for failing to cover his nakedness during a wine-induced sleep. In actuality, Noah's curse was laid upon his grandson Canaan, Ham's son. The Bible informs us that the curse consisted of Canaan being condemned to be a servant of his uncles Shem and Japheth, Ham's brothers. Over the years, the curse morphed into being marred with black skin and the ordained servitude of black people. Fittingly, the "curse of Ham" became one of the primary justifications for the enslavement, dehumanization, and subjugation of blacks during the Atlantic slave trade.[7]

While David Whitford located the source of the Hamitic curse to the "early modern era" (during the sixteenth century),[8] the Christian demonization of black skin extends back much further. According to Jeffrey Burton Russell, "the Devil's color is usually black, in conformity with Christian tradition and almost worldwide symbolism."[9] Russell's reference to the "Christian tradition" is perhaps a nod to the Council of Toledo where in 447 AD the official description of Satan himself was determined to be "a large, black, monstrous apparition with horns on his head, cloven hooves, ass's ears, claws, fiery eyes, gnashing teeth, huge phallus, and sulphurous smell."[10] Here, the greatest force of evil in the universe and the arch-enemy of God himself is depicted as having black skin and possessing the stereotypical "huge phallus."

Even lesser-known Christian traditions have incorporated anti-blackness into their religious doctrines. In the Book of Mormon, we meet with a tradition similar to that of the Hamitic curse in the Bible. In detailing the curse levelled against the Lamanites, we are told in the 2nd Book of Nephi,

> Wherefore, the word of the Lord was fulfilled which he spake unto me, saying that: Inasmuch as they will not hearken unto thy words they shall be cut off from the presence of the Lord . . . And he had caused the cursing to come upon them, yea, even a sore cursing, because of their iniquity. For behold,

they had hardened their hearts against him, that they had become like unto a flint, wherefore, as they were white, and exceedingly fair and delightsome, that they may not be enticing unto my people the Lord God did cause a skin of blackness to come upon them.[11]

Each of these examples from Christian traditions laid the groundwork for the justification and subsequent use of religion in the subjugation of black bodies in America. While the use of religion against enslaved blacks has a long and definitive history, agreement on whether to teach slaves Christianity was far from unanimous.[12]

White Religious Fervor and the Christianizing of Enslaved Blacks

Support for the religious conversion of enslaved blacks from their traditional "heathen" religions to Christianity waxed and waned over the course of American history. Opposition was due, in large part, to the pervasive notion of "hereditary heathenism," the idea that "religion is an essential characteristic, inborn, and determinant of future ideas and attitudes."[13] The futile nature of Christianizing African "pagans" was due as much to the notion of hereditary heathenism as it was to the foreign beliefs and practices that enslaved Africans brought to American shores. Despite traditional African religions sharing with Christianity John Mbiti's five components of religion, namely 1) beliefs, 2) practices, ceremonies, and festivals, 3) religious objects and places, 4) values and morals, and 5) religious officials or leaders,[14] the prevailing view toward converting enslaved Africans was that "the gross bestiality and rudeness of their manners, the variety and strangeness of their languages, and the weakness and shallowness of their minds render it in a manner impossible to make any progress in their conversion."[15]

Despite this general feeling, there proved to be a concomitant relationship between white religious fervor and support for the religious instruction (indoctrination/conversion) of slaves. For whites, religious fervor manifested throughout early American history as seeking increased spiritual renewal, increased spiritual zeal, increased membership in religious denominations, and a spike in attendance at popular religious revivals.[16] For enslaved Africans, the religious fervor of whites translated into an increase in the establishment of churches for slaves, Sabbath schools for the formal religious instruction of slaves, and targeted, systematic efforts of religious conversion through routine plantation meetings.[17] That is to say, as white religious fervor gained traction, so too did the idea of giving religious instruction to black slaves. As a brief overview of history will show, arguments for and against the religious indoctrination of slaves were always buttressed by factors that were thought to have some perceived impact on the fate of the white community.

In keeping with the document analysis methodology of the current study, this overview is drawn from historic, archival documents. Spotlighting an early twentieth-century analysis by C. V. Bruner, the historical writings of Charles C. Jones (a Presbyterian pastor, a slave owner, and "the preeminent advocate of religious instruction of the Negros"),[18] and an exemplar from Cotton Mather (the prolific New England pastor and slave owner), the following discussion outlines the fluctuating tides of white religious fervor and attitudes toward the religious instruction of slaves. In what follows, I deliberately utilize these historic writings to lay the foundation for white religious fervor as a context for religious instruction as a means to circumvent perceived losses on the part of clergy, the labor elite, and ordinary white workers. In doing so, the following overview also serves as its own document analysis of important historical texts.

First Period

According to Bruner, there were five distinct periods in American history where slaveholders, clergy, and society in general actively considered the religious conversion of slaves.[19] The first period, from 1619 (the year the first group of African slaves entered and were settled in the colonies) until 1740, was marked by religious indifference on the part of slaveholders and religious institutions. Slaveholders deemed converting slaves to Christianity a risky endeavor for various reasons. For one, the allegiance of the "original stock" of Africans to their "absolute Heathenism" was viewed as a barrier to conversion.[20] Other reasons contributing to the lack of conversions among slaves during the first century of colonial history include the assumption that the slaves were incapable of comprehending Christian beliefs, the lack of concern on the part of slaveholders for their own Christian salvation, let alone the salvation of their slaves, and, most importantly, the prevailing belief at that time that a Christian could not be held in bondage.[21] According to Edmund Morgan, "Before the 1660s it seems to have been assumed that Christianity and slavery were incompatible. Negroes and Indians held in slavery who could prove that they had been baptized sometimes sued for their freedom and won it."[22] While some Christianizing of slaves did indeed take place during this era, the perceived loss of black labor due to slave conversions to Christianity was an effective deterrent to mass conversion efforts on the part of white planters.

The trepidation that existed in the minds of slave owners due to the fear that Christianized slaves would seek their freedom under laws that prevented the enslavement of Christians would soon be removed. Eventually, "as slavery became more profitable, the assembly moved to protect masters by building a wall between conversion and emancipation."[23] As a result, slaveholder fears of losing property were forever put to rest by the passage of laws preventing the manumission of slaves upon conversion. Once slaveholders' fears of the loss of slave labor were allayed, the push for the religious instruction of black slaves was once again outwardly professed in a most vigorous manner under the guise of saving souls in accord with one's religious duty. However, in an effort to reinforce in the mind of the slave the reality that conversion, for them, did not mean manumission, some slaves who converted to Christianity were made to profess the following declaration:

> You declare in the Presence of God and before his Congregation that you do not ask for the holy baptism out of any design to free yourself from the Duty and Obedience you owe to your Master while you live, but merely for the good of Your Soul and to partake of the Graces and Blessing promised to the Members of the Church of Jesus Christ.[24]

The Negro Christianized

Early in the first period of black conversion there were some attempts and arguments, though limited, for the Christianizing of slaves. Emblematic of the position to Christianizing slaves during this period was a pamphlet produced by Cotton Mather, the influential, slaveholding, Christian pastor of Boston, Massachusetts. His pamphlet, *The Negro Christianized*, published in 1706, details several arguments in favor of Christianizing efforts (see Figure 12.1). Broadly, Mather presented four detailed arguments for the Christianizing of slaves and offered rebuttals to common arguments against their religious instruction. A recurring theme throughout the pamphlet was the duty of Christian slave owners: their duty to God and their duty to their servants entrusted to them by God. The paternalistic tone of Mather was rich in appeals to scripture, historians, and philosophers. His arguments hinged upon the responsibility endowed upon Christian slave owners because of their "belief in Christ." Interspersed between Mather's faith-based appeals were indications of his views of blacks in general. In various portions of the pamphlet he described black slaves as "the blackest instances of blindness and baseness" and "the most brutish creatures on Earth," and he acknowledged that "the state of your Negros in this world must be low, and mean, and abject; a state of servitude."[25] Despite the aspersions cast on blacks, Mather used their salvation to invoke a doctrine of perceived spiritual loss in an effort to spur the mass Christianizing of

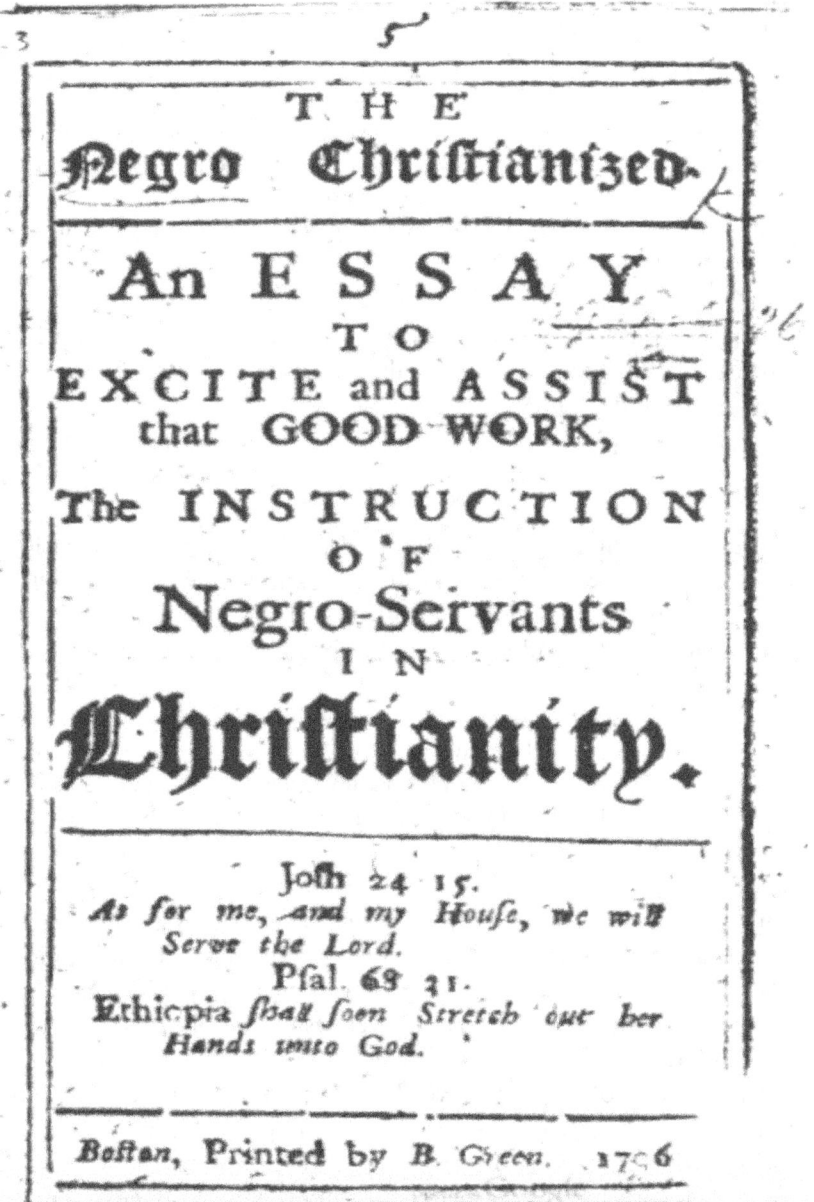

Figure 12.1 Cotton Mather, *The Negro Christianized*

slaves. In doing so, he admonished Christian slave owners who neglected Christianizing their slaves by saying:

> The blood of the souls of your poor Negroes, lies upon you, and the guilt of their barbarous Impieties, and superstitions, and their neglect of God and their souls: If you are willing to have nothing done toward the salvation of their souls . . . If you withhold knowledge from your Black people they will be destroy'd. But their destruction must very much ly [sic] at your doors; you must answer for it.[26]

In Mather's view, the loss of the white labor elite's own salvation in the hereafter was the cost of neglecting their Christian duty to Christianize the slaves in servitude to them.

Second Period

According to Bruner, the second period dealing with the conversion of slaves lasted between 1740 and 1790. This period saw a deliberate effort to bring religion to whites and slaves alike. This was due in large part to the Great Awakening.[27] Cynthia A. Rice described the Great Awakening as

> a spiritual renewal movement that was targeted at the common man and woman, rich and poor, black and white, male and female, all were welcome, they [white Christians] emphasized the importance of each individual and they simplified the gospel message to make it more accessible and applicable to everyday life.[28]

While there is disagreement among historians regarding how many awakenings there actually were, it is generally accepted that what are termed the Great Awakenings occurred during the eighteenth and nineteenth centuries and these movements impacted every aspect of religious, societal, and political life in America.[29]

The embrace of religious fervor by whites and the subsequent conversion of enslaved Africans were themes running through all of the major Christian denominations of the era.[30] In the South, the first to undergo the awakenings were the Presbyterians, followed by the Baptists, and then the Methodists.[31] After the Revolutionary War, all three denominations simultaneously pushed for converts and their proselytizing efforts included enslaved Africans.[32] The religious zeal spurred by the Great Awakening and the idea of equality and independence brought on by the Revolutionary War greatly increased the number of slaves converted to Christianity. Fueled by the wave of equality and independence that came on the heels of the Revolutionary War, Christianized slaves during this period appeared to achieve a degree of progress in their being seen as spiritual equals with whites and in their ability to establish several self-governing, slave-only congregations.

Third Period

The third period, from 1790 to 1830, was marked by a disregard for, then a subsequent resurgence in, the conversion of slaves. Bruner notes that, despite the proliferation of religious sentiment among whites during the second period instigated by the Great Awakening, the third period saw an increase in atheism throughout the colonies of America, brought on by the French Revolution.[33] This led to yet another period of waning religious interest on the part of slaveholders that, in turn, led to decreased religious attention being given to their slaves.

Bruner points out that also happening during the era were the increased activity of anti-slavery movements and the occurrences of notable slave rebellions. It's significant that the two most noteworthy planned rebellions of the era, those of Denmark Vesey and Gabriel Prosser, were both initiated by slave preachers and were devised during the religious meetings of the slaves.[34] This critical point encompasses one of the primary fears of white society when considering converting slaves to Christianity, that is, the engendering of a spirit of radical independence. In the case of Vesey, despite white clergy and planters attempting to "peddle their vision of a proslavery God to black congregants,"[35] Vesey "fashioned a theology of liberation that fused the demanding faith of the Israelites with the sacred values of Africa," and in so doing, "his lessons were employed as a means by which to produce a profound sense of racial identity among his adherents."[36] Rebellions like Vesey's reinforced in the minds of white clergy and white workers (the planting elite and white workers in general) the potential loss of property, wealth, and even life that comes with the Christianizing of slaves. The gains that were believed to have accrued to enslaved blacks (their spiritual equality and a radical sense of personhood) were unintended consequences of Christianizing slaves that were to be avoided at all costs.

Fourth Period

Bruner notes that the fourth period of slave conversion, spanning from 1830 to 1845, "was in some respects a repetition of the preceding period, beginning with another reaction but closing with a very decided recovery and an increase in interest and religious activity that surpassed that of the former periods."[37] The decline in slave conversions came on the heels of the rise in radical abolitionist activity throughout the South. In addition to the affront that they caused to slaveholding society, the abolitionists were thought to have added fuel to the fires of slave insurrections, culminating in the deadly revolt by Nat Turner, another slave preacher. The increased abolitionist activity and the perceived link between slave insurrections and religious instruction led to sweeping legislative action in the South restricting the education, religious teaching, and spheres of activity of slaves. The close of the fourth period, however, saw the birth of the Association for the Religious Instruction of the Negroes, in Liberty County, Georgia (ARIN), and various other plantation missions. The religious clergy behind these organizations attempted to convey to slaveholders/planters that Christianizing slaves, rather than jeopardizing their material wellbeing, would in fact serve to buttress the "peculiar institution" by making slaves more "orderly and obedient."[38] While slave rebellions had been used as evidence against the religious instruction of slaves, clergy began using the rebellions as evidence of the need for the *proper* religious instruction of slaves. The ARIN and other organizations ultimately won the support of slaveholders by showing the economic and managerial benefits that came with the proper, Christian indoctrination of slaves. The religious fervor ignited by this religious response to slave rebellions set the stage for the most active period of Christian indoctrination efforts directed at slaves.

Fifth Period

The fifth and final period of slave instruction, from 1845 to 1860, was "a period of remarkable religious development among the Negroes. Slave owners displayed a far greater interest in the work than ever before."[39] Bruner details four principal reasons for this dramatic increase in white religious fervor around Christianizing slaves. First, given the split over slavery between the churches of the North and South, the abolitionist strain had been removed from Southern churches. Second, slaveholders became convinced of the value of religiously educated slaves. Third, "civilizing" the slaves with religion would undermine a core tenet of abolitionist rhetoric, that the institution of slavery fostered paganism among the slaves. And fourth, slaveholders determined that material benefit could come from happy and content slaves. It was these events that served as accelerants for the white, religious fervor directed toward Christianizing slaves and, as we'll see, the religious response of indoctrination was to be the tool of choice in the production of both a submissive workforce and the material benefit that comes from their effective management.

* * *

To summarize this section, fluctuations in the desire to Christianize slaves during the various periods of history share a common theme. In addition to religious trends in white society, opinions on religiously indoctrinating slaves were also influenced by perceptions of loss on the part of white labor elites (slave owners) and white religious leaders. The losses in question were both spiritual (such as the spiritual damnation described by Cotton Mather) and material. At varying points throughout history, the perceived losses associated with converting slaves included 1) the loss of property (slaves) upon conversion in accord with colonial law, 2) the perceived insubordination of slaves brought on by their equal spiritual standing as Christians, and 3) the loss of white life due to slave revolts inspired by liberation-themed biblical interpretations. In an effort to shield themselves against these losses, white evangelical and white labor elites used codified laws as well as the religious mechanism of theological indoctrination to inhibit both the physical and the spiritual progress of Christianized slaves while simultaneously exacerbating black mental, spiritual, and psychological inferiority. But while evangelicals canvased the South extolling the virtue and responsibility of Christianizing enslaved blacks, the use of religion in the "management" of slaves in order to maximize profits was more quietly acknowledged in publications directed toward slaveholders.

The Charleston Meeting of 1845

In the writings of their proceedings and minutes of their meetings, evangelicals in their organizations and denominations constantly appealed to the religious duty of bringing souls to Christ. Their use of scripture and their suggestions to slaveholders on their religious duties to their slaves, as well as the particulars of working, educating, clothing, feeding, disciplining, and allowing for the social upkeep of slaves, all buttressed the institution of slavery. But in the proceedings of a particularly influential meeting of slaveholders in Charleston, South Carolina, in 1845, a glimpse into the more salient motivation for the religious instruction of slaves is uncovered (see Figure 12.2).

The Charleston meeting in 1845 was described by Bruner as "a very significant meeting of planters . . . which had been called for the purpose of discussing the religious instruction of the Negroes."[40] Bruner writes further

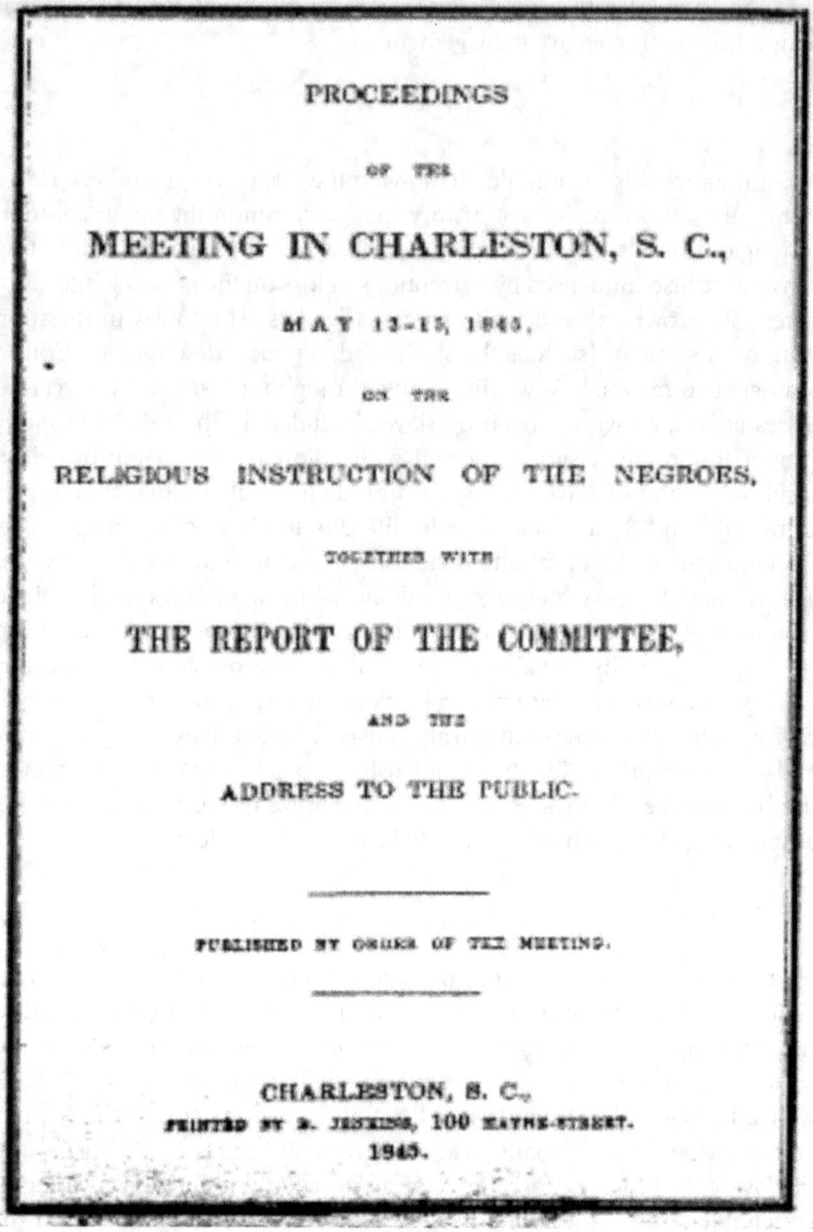

> PROCEEDINGS
>
> OF THE
>
> **MEETING IN CHARLESTON, S. C.,**
>
> MAY 13-15, 1845,
>
> ON THE
>
> RELIGIOUS INSTRUCTION OF THE NEGROES,
>
> TOGETHER WITH
>
> **THE REPORT OF THE COMMITTEE,**
>
> AND THE
>
> ADDRESS TO THE PUBLIC.
>
> ───────
>
> PUBLISHED BY ORDER OF THE MEETING.
>
> ───────
>
> CHARLESTON, S. C.,
> PRINTED BY B. JENKINS, 100 HAYNE-STREET.
> 1845.

Figure 12.2 Front cover of *Proceedings of the Meeting in Charleston, S.C., May 13–15, 1845 on the Religious Instruction of the Negroes* (Library of Congress, Rare Book and Special Collections Division)

that "reports of planters to a questionnaire which had been sent out before the meeting were almost unanimous as to the wisdom of training slaves in religious matters and as to the general interest in the movement."[41] In a section of the meeting's proceedings entitled "Address to the Holders of Slaves in South-Carolina," slaveholding labor elites are told:

> A wise management would combine kindness with discipline; and aim at making labour effective, and the labourer happy. But these ends can only be effected by moral causes; causes that act upon character—that form, or reform the moral being. Would we most naturally look for effective labour, in the dissolute, the unprincipled, and the discontented; or in those who are godly and honest, regular in their habits, and satisfied with their condition?[42]

In this section alone we see the emergence of a very pertinent theme. First, there is the framing of the discussion in terms of establishing a process of "wise management." Such management is focused squarely on the goal of making "labour" (the slaves) both "effective" (profitable) and "happy" (content with their condition as slaves). Going further, it is declared that the most sensible means of finding both an effective and a happy labor force is in those who are "godly and honest, regular in their habits, and satisfied with their condition."

Continuing with their discussion, slaveholders were briefed on the type of doctrine that would adequately facilitate such a "wise management." In identifying Christianity as the ideal source of this teaching, slaveholders were assured that it would instill in the slave

> precepts that inculcate good-will, forbearance and forgiveness; that enjoin meekness and patience under evils; that demand truth and faithfulness under all circumstances; a teaching that sets before men a righteous judgment, and happiness or misery in the life to come, according to our course of faith and practice in the life that now is, must, unless counteracted by extraordinary causes, so change the general character of persons thus taught.[43]

Association for the Religious Instruction of the Negroes (ARIN)

The meeting of slaveholders in Charleston was not alone in its quest to justify and orchestrate the systematic indoctrination of enslaved blacks as a means of maintaining the social order and limiting the possibility of black progress in any form. By 1845 virtually every religious denomination was committed to the goal of Christianizing slaves. Organizations, missionaries, committees, associations, and pastors channeled the wave of religious fervor into an industry of "plantation missions" charged with bringing what would prove to be a customized and weaponized form of Christianity to the slaves in an effort to mitigate any spiritual, material, and financial loss to whites. Organizations like the Association for the Religious Instruction of Negroes, in Liberty County, Georgia, worked tirelessly to set up processes and procedures for the "salvation" of slaves. The proceedings of their annual meetings detailed progress reports on Sabbath schools founded for the instruction of slaves, membership tallies of converted slaves, reports on the conversion of slaves throughout the various counties in Georgia, and the continued development of the religious and economic justifications for bringing slaves to the faith. Slaveholders and denominations alike were so committed to converting the slave to Christianity that "even after the outbreak of the Civil War the efforts of the Southern churches on behalf of the slaves continued; and when the Confederacy was threatened with bankruptcy the appropriations for Negro missions were scarcely diminished."[44] As with the proceedings of the 1845 meeting in Charleston, publications of the ARIN also detailed their motivations for Christianizing slaves with no ambiguity.

In their thirteenth annual report the association made sure to remind slave owners of the dire need and incalculable value that came with religiously indoctrinating their slaves. Regarding the relation of slaves to their owners they write:

> They are . . . "your money." They are the source, the means of your wealth; by their labour do you obtain the necessaries, the conveniences and comforts of life. The increase of them is the general standard of your worldly prosperity; without them you would be comparatively poor. They are consequently sought after and desired as property, and when possessed, must be so taken care of and managed as to be made profitable.[45]

Leaving nothing to the imagination, the association identified religious instruction as the means by which slaves could be "managed as to be made profitable." In a section outlining the "desirable purposes" of the association, they identify one of their goals as demonstrating to slave owners that the religious instruction of slaves "would diminish the pain and trouble of their management, and by making them better servants and better men, tend directly to promote the peace and prosperity of owners and communities."[46]

Both the Charleston meeting and the ARIN exemplify, in clear language, the motivations for the religious instruction of enslaved blacks. These documents, and countless others, highlight the role of perceived loss in the white labor elites' drive to indoctrinate slaves into Christianity. This loss, be it the loss of their salvation for not bringing the gospel to the "heathens" under their care, or the loss of material "conveniences and comforts of life" due to the loss of the labor of black bodies, was the driving force in their use of a weaponized form of Christianity, a form that simultaneously reinforced white supremacy and black inferiority.

The Catechisms: White Labor Elites' Weaponized Religious Doctrine

To this point this chapter has documented the motivations for using religion as a tool in the mitigation of perceived loss on the part of the white evangelicals and the white labor elites (planters/slave owners). This loss, perceived as both spiritual and material, was abated through the religious indoctrination of slaves into Christianity via a particularly virulent doctrine. This type of doctrine had to be designed and delivered in a way that instilled white supremacy as well as black inferiority. The identification and analysis of such a doctrine is the focus of the final section of this chapter. Under investigation are two catechisms, one meant for white adherents and the other for enslaved blacks. Through an analysis of the content and themes in each catechism a clear picture of the indoctrination of slaves with a weaponized doctrine of Christianity becomes apparent.

The Protestant Episcopal Catechisms of the Confederacy

The primary documents under analysis are two catechisms published in 1862 by the *Church Intelligencer,* a periodical of the Protestant Episcopalian Church in the Confederate states. The first is an eight-page document entitled *The Catechism of the Protestant Episcopal Church in the Confederate States* (hereafter referred to as the White Catechism) (see Figure 12.3). A second document, published in the same year and by the same organ, had a more specialized audience. Entitled *A Catechism, to Be Taught Orally to Those Who Cannot Read; Designed Especially for the Instruction of the Slaves, in the Prot. Episcopal Church in the Cofederate* [sic] *States* (hereafter referred to as the Slave Catechism), this document, at forty-eight pages, was six times the size of the White Catechism (see Figure 12.4).

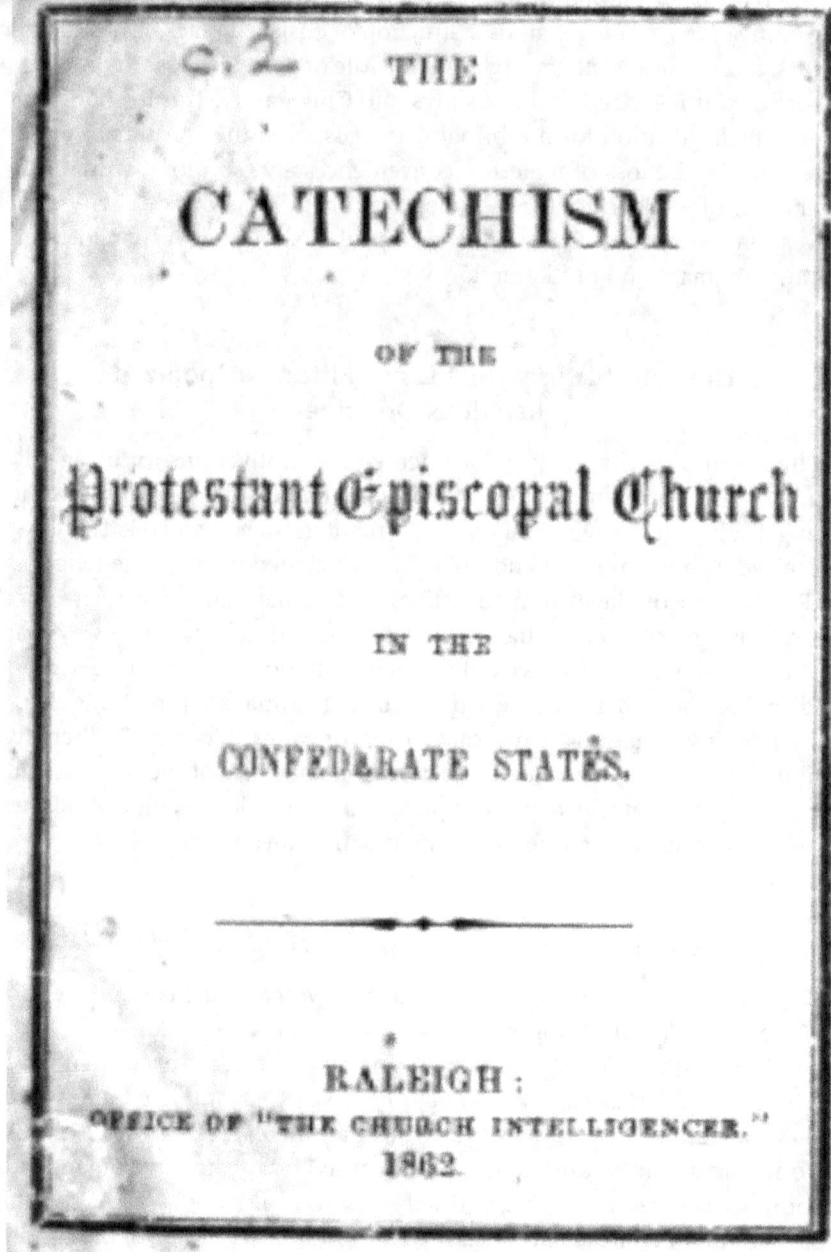

Figure 12.3 *The Catechism of the Protestant Episcopal Church in the Confederate States*

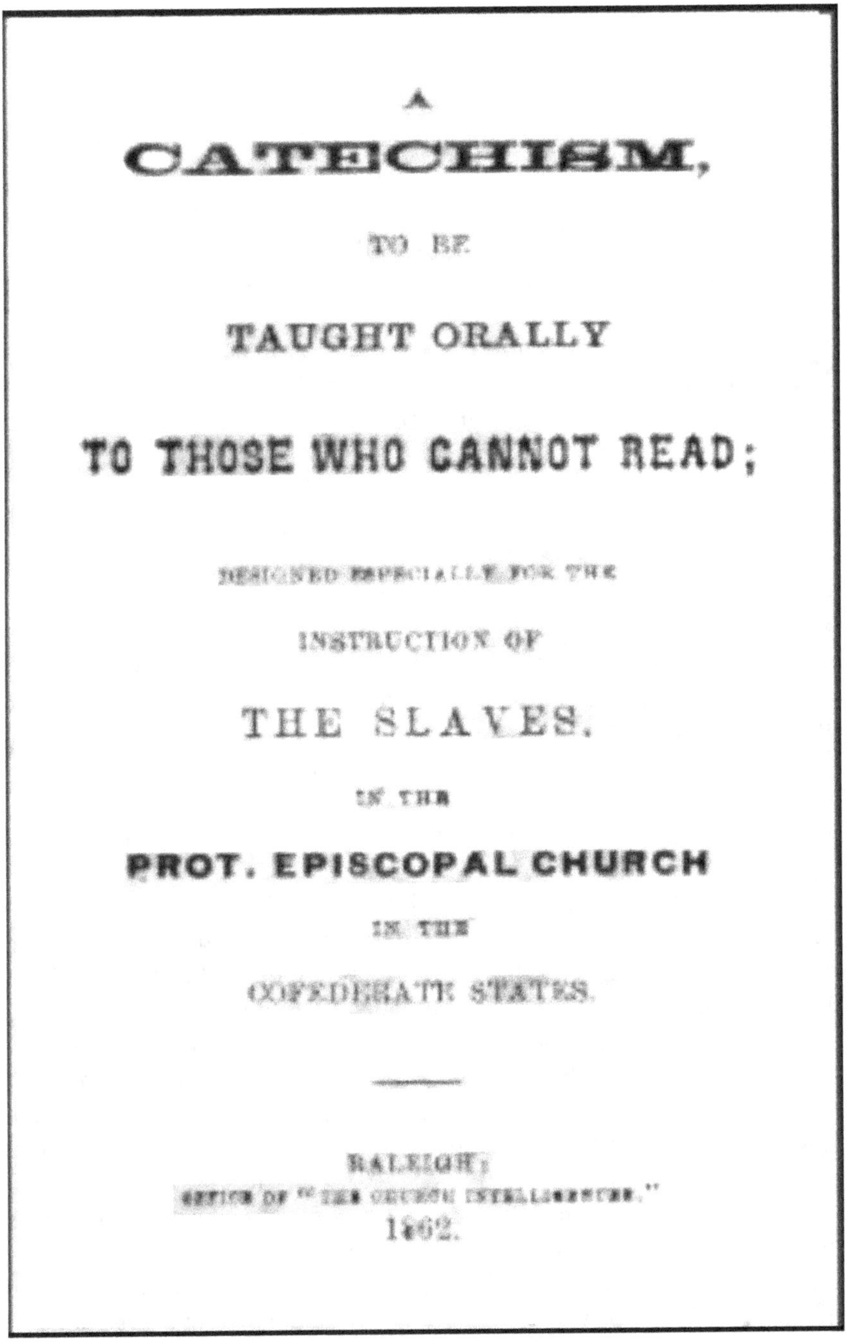

A

CATECHISM,

TO BE

TAUGHT ORALLY

TO THOSE WHO CANNOT READ;

DESIGNED ESPECIALLY FOR THE

INSTRUCTION OF

THE SLAVES,

IN THE

PROT. EPISCOPAL CHURCH

IN THE

CONFEDERATE STATES.

———

RALEIGH:
OFFICE OF "THE CHURCH INTELLIGENCER."
1862.

Figure 12.4 *A Catechism, to Be Taught Orally to Those Who Cannot Read*

Content

Upon investigation, the makeup of the Original Catechism is a straightforward question and answer format emblematic of catechisms. The tenets of the faith are clearly foregrounded. Questions regarding the Trinity, the Ten Commandments, the sacraments, baptism, the Lord's Prayer, and other core concepts of Christianity are asked and answered in a straightforward, matter of fact way. Taken together, the contents of the White Catechism are a succinct embodiment of the major beliefs of the faith and how they are to be understood.[47]

The Slave Catechism, on the other hand, presents itself as a completely different document altogether. Throughout its forty-eight pages, recurring themes revolve around God's omniscient and ever-watchful eye, sin and the wages of sin, Christ bringing salvation from sin, seeking eternal life, engaging in chaste behavior, obeying and the consequences of disobeying, guarding against the influence of the devil, how to act in order to get to heaven, doing God's will, interpretations/applications of the Lord's Prayer, and, the most prominent themes of the forty-eight pages, having no malice of thought, harboring no ill will, and constantly exercising forgiveness.[48]

The difference in length of the two documents is exceptionally interesting. Conventional wisdom in the antebellum South was that blacks were intellectually inferior to whites. In fact, many Christian missionaries, when charged with the task of giving religious instruction to slaves, communicated their disbelief in the effectiveness of such an endeavor. Generally, black slaves were thought to be "slow of apprehension, of dull understanding, and soon forgetting what they learned," and particularly, it was deemed "difficult for black men to understand the principles of education."[49] The duplicitous nature of this belief is exposed by the forty-eight pages of the slave catechism. Why would a catechism for those of "dull understanding" contain six times the content of the catechism for presumably superior whites?

Also, given the supposed inability of blacks to understand "the principles of education," why does the Slave Catechism cover a much wider range of complex religious concepts? Some of the articles covered in the Slave Catechism address fairly complex examples of religious thought, like the meaning and praxis of the Lord's Prayer. The discussion of the sacrament is yet another example of a complex principle being taught to a supposedly inferior people. As discussed in the Slave Catechism, the sacrament is described as the "outward visible sign of an inward spiritual grace."[50] The discussion of the "visible" as opposed to the "inward" manifestations of the sacrament was also included in the White Catechism. The inclusion of this discussion in both documents is just one example that belies the conventional idea of a supposedly inferior people being unable to digest and comprehend complex religious thought.

Emerging Themes: Personalization, Forgiveness, and God's Watchful Eye

From the very first page of each catechism, we see other differences emerge. In the White Catechism, we see that almost immediately the adherent is personalized by the asking of their name. The adherent states their name and subsequently recites the titles "member of Christ," "child of God," and "inheritor of the kingdom of heaven,"[51] all of which were bestowed upon them after the act of baptism. Contrast this with the first page of the Slave Catechism. We see no such personalization, there is no asking of their name. Even if the slaves chose to find themselves in the text of the first page under the generalized description of "men," we find that "men" is linked with such non-human entities such as "trees," "water," and "cattle." Also of note, in response to the question "What were you made of?" the slaves respond with "Of the dust of the ground."[52] In religious symbology, the dust of the ground is often a metaphor depicting the insignificance of a thing. For example, scriptural references to "dust" have been used as "a symbol of man's frailty," as an expression of "deep humiliation, abasement or lamentation," and to denote a "state of lowliness."[53] So here, from the very beginning of each catechism, we see whites personalized and adorned with lofty titles while slaves are grouped with cattle and reminded of their insignificant and lowly origins.

But eventually (and by "eventually" is meant nearly halfway through their catechism) the slave is made aware of their becoming a member of Christ and child of God upon baptism, but with a catch. Here we see the question asked "Were you a child of God when you were born?" To which the slaves are directed to respond "No, I was the child of the wicked one." Next, they're asked "What is it then to be made a child of God in holy baptism?" To which the slave responds "It is to be taken out of the family of the wicked one and put into the family of God."[54] Here, the Slave Catechism is highlighting the "wicked," pre-baptismal nature of slaves, but in the White Catechism we find no mention of a wicked pre-baptismal nature whatsoever.

Likewise, there are things that appear in the White Catechism that don't appear in the catechism for slaves: for example, a biblical reference to being freed from bondage. When asked about the Ten Commandments, the white adherent answers by describing them as "the same which God spake in the twentieth chapter of Exodus, saying, I am the Lord thy God who brought thee out of the land of Egypt, out of the house of bondage."[55] The conspicuous absence of this reference in the Slave Catechism could be explained by one of the previously discussed arguments made against the religious instruction of slaves. As we saw, it was thought that exposing slaves to the Bible and biblical stories about God's emancipation of slaves was bound to put the wrong ideas in their heads. The rebellion of Nat Turner (who killed over sixty whites) and the planned rebellion of Denmark Vesey, for example, both turned the tide against the religious instruction of slaves. This sentiment was exemplified by the residents of Charleston, South Carolina, who opposed the establishment of a Negro church because they "were fearful that an independent Negro congregation would create another Vesey or Nat Turner insurrection, and it was their duty to prevent this from happening by refusing to permit the church to exist in the city."[56]

Within the Slave Catechism, we find a host of other telling themes. Take, for instance, the idea of self-regulation of thoughts. For nearly a full page the Slave Catechism insists that the slave harbor "no bad thoughts," mind their words and actions, and never hate, never "wish to hurt anybody," or never "wish to do any wrong."[57] Contrasted with these self-regulatory instructions in the Slave Catechism, outside of one sentence about bearing "no malice or hatred in my heart, to keep my hands from picking and stealing, and my tongue from evil speaking, lying and slandering,"[58] we find no extensive treatment or emphasis on admonishing the thoughts, words, or wishes of the white adherent within the White Catechism.

Along with the regulation of "harmful" thoughts, forgiveness is another theme we find heavily stressed in the Slave Catechism. In response to the question "How do others sin against you?" the slave responds "By cursing me, telling lies about me, or striking me," all of which slave masters were frequently prone to do.[59] From there we read:

Q: What must you do to those who thus sin against you?
A: I must forgive them.
Q: What if you do not forgive them?
A: Then God will not forgive me.
Q: Why?
A: Because, I pray to Him to forgive me, just as I forgive others.
Q: How are you to forgive others when they trespass against you?
A: I am not to hurt them because they hurt me—but I must pray for them and try to do them good.
Q: What if you do to them just as they do to you?
A: Then God will not forgive my sins, but will punish me.[60]

In the White Catechism, we find three significant references to forgiveness. The first appears in the recitation of the Lord's Prayer ("*forgive* us our trespasses as we *forgive* those who trespass against us") and the second is a reference to God's forgiveness of sins.[61] Contrasted with the full page of instruction given to slaves on forgiveness, in the White Catechism, the references to whites showing forgiveness are more limited, as in the case when the white adherent recites, "I believe in the Holy Ghost; the holy Catholic Church; the Communion of Saints; the Forgiveness of sins; the Resurrection of the body; And the Life everlasting. Amen."[62]

Yet another significant theme interspersed throughout the Slave Catechism is the omniscience and omnipresence of God. In these entries, we see how important it is for the slave to know that God can see persons "when they are alone in some secret place" and that God "knows everything," "sees everything," and "is always everywhere."[63] It absolutely had to be stressed to the slave that God "sees into our hearts, and knows all the thoughts we think."[64] The omniscience and omnipresence of God is critical to establish in the mind of the slave because, at all costs, the slave must come to know that, even if they think they might get away with disobeying the slave master, they will never really escape damnation because "God knows it; for God always sees" them.[65] In comparison, no such discussion of the ever-watchful, omniscient, and omnipresent God is found anywhere in the White Catechism.

Conclusion

The Christian religious tradition is rife with anti-black references and iconography. This tradition includes representing the devil as black and associating black skin with vileness, servitude, and divine damnation. Given this tradition, Christianity was well suited as a tool for the religious subjugation of black slaves in America. Guided by the fluctuating trends in white religious fervor throughout early American history, white evangelicals, white labor elites, and even ordinary white workers ultimately enacted a systematized and specialized program of religious instruction for slaves, especially in the South. Specifically geared toward the mental, physical, and spiritual subjugation of slaves, and simultaneously constructed to both maximize the profitability of slaves and minimize any black progress whatsoever, this customized doctrine's ultimate purpose was the mitigation of material, spiritual, and economic loss to whites at the expense of black life and religiosity. In the current study, through the use of primary sources (original catechisms and the proceedings of a pro-slavery organizations), both the rationale and exemplars of this "weaponized" form of Christianity were uncovered and discussed. By highlighting the deliberately pernicious doctrine given strictly to slaves, the current study spotlighted the self-serving interests of white clergy, white labor elites, and ordinary white workers in their proselytizing efforts. It is hoped that this analysis would engender a more critical disucssion of black Christian endorsement, and in so doing, replace the "taken for grantedness" that seemingly accompanies aspects of black Christian expression today.

THIRTEEN

The Religions of Black Resistance and White Rage: Interpenetrative Religious Practice in the 1963 Civil Rights Struggle in Danville, Virginia

Tobin Miller Shearer

The violence exhibited on the evening of June 10, 1963, in Danville, Virginia, revealed the religion of white rage at work. In a town known as the "city of churches," where more than one hundred congregations served a population of only 46,500 residents, officials attacked a group of fifty praying demonstrators.[1] The police, firefighters, and deputized sanitation workers who broke the African American demonstrators' bones, lacerated their skin, and contused their bodies did so while Rev. H. G. McGhee led the kneeling protestors in prayer. After the batons stopped swinging and the fire hoses ceased gushing, forty-eight of the demonstrators required hospitalization.[2]

The events in Danville in 1963 reveal the interpenetrative nature of black and white religion in the South in the early 1960s and show how those closely connected religious practices simultaneously undermined and strengthened white hegemony even while fostering white rage. The prayer postures, pious injunctions, and faith-based organizing by African American activists enlivened and empowered the black community to challenge segregationists while also intensifying white backlash and weakening, at least temporarily, black resistance to Jim Crow. This particular religious expression of white rage, bolstered by formal, sanctioned, civil religious prayers and dedications, helped create the conditions in which a large group of black religious activists peacefully engaged in a prayer vigil at the city hall on June 10, 1963, came under attack from firefighters, police, and deputized garbage men armed with fire hoses and night sticks. The rage of the white assailants emerged from the religious practices they shared with the black community, not those that were unfamiliar to them. Amid those common traditions, white rage erupted in response to a black resistance marked by disciplined calm.

The civil rights historians who have discussed the events in Danville and others like them have typically treated white and black religious practices as separate and largely unrelated phenomena. Scholars have documented the mass revival that sustained black activists throughout numerous Southern cities.[3] They have examined black music and its relationship to protest, the black church's affiliation with groups like the Southern Christian Leadership Conference (SCLC), and the homiletics that inspired individuals to march, sacrifice jobs, and put their homes up for bond security.[4] Only more recently have scholars turned their attention to the religious practices of the white segregationists who responded with such violence in cities like Danville.[5] As a whole, this body of scholarship has treated the respective religious communities as distinct, discrete religious practices.

The events in Danville demand a more unified approach. An emerging group of scholars have begun to note the connections between and among white and black religious practitioners during the civil rights movement.[6] The well-established argument that race and religion are inextricably connected in U.S. history makes it possible to reshape the segregated narrative of black and white religion in the civil rights movement by exploring how those affectively disparate religious practices interpenetrated in public space.[7] Sites of formal religious practice such as those found in sanctuaries will thus be set aside in order to examine the public expression of religion in the midst of conflict and contestation.

In this way, labor history becomes not just a means of studying worker-management conflict but also a means to explore profound religious formation. White laborers—the police, firefighters, and sanitation workers—drew a paycheck for their violent crackdown on black protestors. They were working as they broke bones and cracked heads. That violence-infused labor took place in a sacred context. They attacked religious practitioners knowing that the targets of their rage were in the midst of practicing their religion. Whether they originally intended for this to be the case or not, their actions became infused with religion the second they turned fire hoses on praying protestors.

The study of that religious formation turns on a definition of religion. African American religious studies scholar Charles Long defines religion in part as "how one comes to terms with the ultimate significance of one's place in the world."[8] Although the formal participation of Danville city officials in local religious communities is without question, under Long's definition, those officials also engaged in religious practices every time they sought to maintain their "place in the world." When the Danville protestors knelt on the pavement in the midst of protest—or indeed any time that they pushed back against the segregationist and white supremacist practices of the day—they challenged the arrangement of the local "place." And they did so by simultaneously claiming that they had an equal right to ultimate significance both socially and religiously. Common religious forms and common religious practices made the point plain. The white community had no more hold on religious significance and the means to determine it than they did on social significance and the means to determine that.

The struggle to determine religious significance emerged within a highly Christian context. While the more than one hundred congregations in Danville spanned the denominational spectrum, as was the case in much of the South, Baptists predominated. Within that heavily Protestant environment, Sacred Heart served the Catholic community even as Beth Sholom and Aetz Chayim served respectively the Jewish members of Danville's small Reform and Orthodox communities.[9] The religious resources most commonly brought into public venues during the Southern civil rights struggle—prayer, vestments, song, liturgy, and the bodies of the believers themselves—stemmed from Protestant, Catholic, and Jewish practices. In the Danville civil rights struggle, as suggested by the heavy preponderance of Protestant churches, Protestant forms predominated. Although religious communities also provided social networks, logistical support, leadership training, moral grounding, financial backing, and meeting spaces, the particular religious resources that activists brought into public space prompted the most conflict and revealed the most about the relationship between the religions of black resistance and white rage.

These two religious modalities carried distinct affective and compositional markers. As religious phenomena, both white rage and black resistance emerged from, received sustenance through, and were formed by religious organizations, in this case white and black Protestant congregations in Danville. The religion of white rage—expressed in public through righteous indignation, unchecked invective, and brutal assault—echoed the ire and vexation of Old Testament prophets and wore a similar mantle of theological certitude. White public officials claimed a fundamental right to express their segregationist conviction with righteous anger because, in part, their religious community supported them in doing so and offered an ideological framework that gilded their obloquy with respectability. The religion of black resistance—expressed in public through measured oration, reserved appeals, and disciplined non-violence—knew no less moral certainty but, in the context of Danville in 1963, tempered the prophets' spleen with restraint. Black movement leaders came from, met in, and depended upon the black church—an institution defined at the time by a consistent and thorough degree of unanimity. Like their white adversaries, they too gained good repute from their Christian identity but did so in a context where the white community demanded that black respectability not challenge the status quo.

The emotional content of the two religious expressions offers a stark and somewhat counterintuitive contrast. The racialized community with the most economic and political power expressed the most public indignation and anger; the one with the least economic and political resources expressed the least public fury. Absent the racial constrictions of the era, one might expect the reverse if for no other reason than that the black community had far more wrongs to be righted. But even though both communities drew on similar theological precepts, worship forms, and religious assumptions, the white community's religious formation rarely challenged the free expression of all the anger white members in Danville chose to vent. Religious formation in the black community, however, often demanded a more circumspect emotional array.

The religion of white rage, at least as it was expressed in the middle of the 1960s in a former seat of the Confederacy, must furthermore be understood as one fully nested in, shaped by, and in close conversation with the religion of black resistance. Just as white and black racial identities in the United States have from their inception been formed in contrast to and with knowledge of the other, so too have racially distinct expressions of religion. The religion of white rage took on form and expression in the midst of the project of white leaders like those in Danville seeking to hold onto their status, control, and supposed supremacy in their social worlds. Their anger emerged when they began to realize that not all shared their bedrock belief of their right to be in charge, a realization that most often emerged in the midst of interactions with the black community. The religion of black resistance formed and coalesced as leaders of the African American community like those in Danville expressed their right to full citizenship, equal access to goods and services, and unfettered participation in local government. Their resistance emerged when they saw signs of just how entrenched the white community was in holding onto their positions of power.

Danville makes this examination particularly fruitful. Although not as prominent as other places in the national narrative of the civil rights movement—or for that matter in civil rights movement historiography—Danville drew the attention of the country and of movement activists at the time. While a first-year student at Oberlin College in 1963, Kathleen Cleaver, who would later go on to become the Black Panther Party's first female executive leader, heard a speaker describe police brutality and community activism in Danville. She later described the experience as "eye-opening."[10] Martin Luther King, Jr., and his associates seriously considered choosing Danville as their next organizing site after Birmingham, and King spoke in Danville before an appreciative crowd. The attention paid by movement activists mirrored that of the national press. The *New York Times*, for example, featured articles that mentioned the struggle in Danville 164 times in 1963 alone.

While the violence and conflict in Danville drew national attention both within and without the movement, the prominence of religious practitioners and their use of religious resources in demonstrations and marches made this former seat of the Confederate government an especially rich research site. As was the case in many other civil rights struggles, male clergy dominated the ranks of the movement leadership. At least one white minister spoke up about racial injustice, and members of the city council, mayor's office, police department, fire department, and sanitation division either attended white congregations or were familiar with the forms and patterns of Christian religious practice by virtue of living in a city packed with churches. But, even more importantly, as the opening anecdote demonstrates, religious practices mattered in how the civil rights movement unfolded in the city. Given the protracted nature of the struggle, activists kept praying, singing, and wearing religious vestments in public, thereby offering multiple sites in which to explore the interactive nature of the religion of white rage and the religion of black resistance.

The story of civil rights activism picks up in 1960 when a group of leaders decided they needed a new organization to more effectively push back against the segregationist tide. Although an NAACP chapter had been active in Danville since 1918, four leaders deemed that organization too conservative. And so, in 1960, Rev. Lawrence G. Campbell, Rev. Alexander I. Dunlap, Julius E. Adams, and Arthur Pinchback founded the Danville Christian Progressive Association (DCPA) as an affiliate of King's SCLC.[11] Rev. Lendall W. Chase then became president of the organization and began to promote a much more aggressive agenda.

Religious practices and protest tactics intertwined for Danville activists even when outside their community. A little over a year after the founding of the DCPA, a group of ministers from Danville travelled to the town of Hopewell about 150 miles to their northeast. At the behest of the statewide SCLC, they joined a group of 200 clergy who marched in full clerical robes to the Hopewell courthouse. There they gathered in the courtroom where Rev. Curtis Harris was on trial for contempt. Confronted with several hundred robe-wearing clergy, the presiding judge postponed the trial. Upon hearing the news, the president of the Virginia SCLC, Dr. Milton Reid, led a spontaneous public prayer. In response, all of the white court officials—including the judge—stopped talking and mirrored the reverent postures of the clergymen.[12]

If they did not know it previously, the Danville contingent experienced first hand the power religious resources brought into public space. Rather than being held in contempt themselves, the clergy walked unaccosted out of the courthouse and back through Hopewell. The court officials knew what was happening when Dr. Reid began praying. They recognized the religious posture he used. Even though most of the white witnesses had almost certainly never set foot inside a black church, they knew the practice of prayer. They assumed similar postures, maintained a similar silence, and showed a similar deference. In the highly formalized but no less public courtroom where religious attire mirrored judicial garb and a preacher's oratory echoed that of a bailiff's, prayer forestalled both violence and court action. In light of the violence that followed, the deference shown by the judiciary to a prayer form familiar to them suggests that the specific nature of the public space where activists brought their religious resources to bear mattered. Prayer mediated power quite differently in the courtroom than on the streets.

The actions by the clergy assembled in Hopewell in 1962 did not immediately prompt parallel actions in Danville. Religious leaders there first sought redress through formal channels. Through the remainder of 1962, the Reverends Campbell, Chase, and Dunlap along with Julius Adams—all of them from the DCPA—not only appeared at city council meetings to demand an end to segregation, but by August those same four men filed a federal suit seeking the complete integration of Danville's schools, hospitals, public buildings, cemeteries, teaching assignments, public housing, and city employment.[13] In keeping with well-tested Gandhian-based strategies, the leaders first used official, legal options to seek their goals.

The Danville movement then took to the streets. Drawing once again on black church leaders, the first illegal action saw the five founding members of the DCPA arrested on January 1, 1963, after they refused to leave a segregated Howard Johnson's restaurant.[14] A series of marches soon followed. Even though a visit by King in March did not result in street action after the national SCLC leader refused to lead a march, from May 31 to June 5, Rev. Campbell and Rev. Dunlap led daily downtown demonstrations.[15] The police and the press first ignored the marchers.[16] What little press they did receive showed them singing "Ain't gonna let nobody turn me around" while ascending the municipal building steps.[17]

The city's passive response turned aggressive on June 5. On that day, a group of students along with two members of the clergy held a sit-in in the mayor's office. After the police attempted to remove them, one of the students struck an officer. Police then arrested the entire group.[18] The next day another group of protestors stopped traffic when they sat down in the middle of a downtown main street. Police asked Judge Archibald Aiken to order the demonstrators to disperse. The activists refused. Aiken then issued a temporary injunction aimed at prohibiting the civil rights activists from obstructing traffic or business entrances, disturbing the peace with loud language, inciting mob violence, or assembling.[19]

The legal action that followed Aiken's injunction had its roots in an earlier attempt by the white community to quell what it saw as an act of rebellion. Even though the temporary injunction later became permanent, its scope was insufficient for the full extent of the repression sought by Aiken. Aiken also swore in a special grand jury on June 7 that proceeded to indict three ministers for inciting to riot. The jury, presumably acting under Aiken's direction, invoked a statute passed in 1859 in the aftermath of John Brown's takeover of Harper's Ferry. The 1859 statute made it illegal for "conspiring to incite the colored population of the State to acts of violence and war against the white population."[20] The statute made evident that the white leadership in Danville felt under attack. The grand jury set bail at $5,500 for each of the ministers.

The events of June 10 that followed thus played out on a national stage filled with religious actors and lit up by white rage. Although details of the attack on the activists kneeling in prayer differ from account to account, all those involved confirm the basic plot. Late in the day, a Monday, after a series of protests, Rev. H. G. McGhee and a group of some fifty demonstrators marched around the jail and sang hymns as police, firefighters, and deputized sanitation workers watched. Student Nonviolent Coordinating Committee (SNCC) worker Bob Zellner, a white field secretary with his own history of encountering segregationist violence, took pictures until E. G. McCain, the chief of police, smashed Zellner's camera. An enraged McCain then ordered the marchers to disperse.[21]

Like Bull Connor in Birmingham, McCain was prone to such public displays of anger. In a sermon to his congregation, Rev. Campbell quoted chief McCain as having shouted "I am tired of you niggers eating off me like leeches, eating off this community like leeches."[22] But McCain's anger erupted most sharply in the face of black defiance. He could become irate while quelling even the most peaceful protest with little fear of social or political censure as long as white dominance remained intact. Rather than leave the alley where McCain stopped them, the marchers dropped to their knees. Rev. McGhee prayed out loud that divine forgiveness be granted to the police who, McGhee intoned, "know not what they do."[23] In this less formal, outdoors, highly visible setting, as in many other displays of street-placed piety during civil rights actions across the country, the "performative prayer" invited violence rather than forestalled it.[24] McCain shouted "Let 'em have it," and the police with the help of deputized sanitation workers turned fire hoses on the demonstrators.[25]

The violence that followed was intense. A young participant in the demonstration said that being struck by water from a fire hose was "like drowning standing up." He added, "The hoses make you helpless, then they beat you up."[26] Having been smashed to the tarmac by the high-pressure streams, the marchers then sought refuge under parked cars as the police and the sanitation workers began to beat them with batons. The forty-eight who found refuge in Rev. Campbell's Bible Way Church then sought treatment at Winslow Hospital, the only option available for African Americans in Danville, for lacerations, contusions, and broken bones.[27]

The African American community continued to draw upon its devotional practices as the anger displayed by the white city officials increased. The following day Mayor Julian Stinson warned, "We will hose down the demonstrators and fill every available stockade."[28] Police then again turned fire hoses on a crowd of 150 gathered at the courthouse. That same day, another group of 200 protestors led by Rev. Chase marched to the city hall to demand a meeting with the mayor. Unsuccessful in that attempt, Rev. Chase led a group 250-strong the following day, June 13, only to find the city hall doors locked. After remaining for nine hours, the group finally retreated in the face of another fire hose threat.[29] A video clip from that evening shows Mayor Stinson berating Rev. Chase after the group had dispersed and then agreeing to meet the next morning as long as Chase did not bring any "criminals" with him.[30] The demonstrators assembled that night at Rev. Campbell's church for a mass meeting as police armed with submachine guns searched cars going to and from the church.[31]

Eleven days later, the police gave evidence of their further disregard for the church's historic sanctuary role. Having placed additional restrictions on demonstrations, city officials began to indict protest leaders under the John Brown statute.[32] Focusing on fourteen leaders from the DCPA as well as the SNCC and SCLC, Judge Aiken not only placed $5,000 bonds on each individual but would not allow the legal counsel representing the accused to call witnesses on their behalf.[33] Several of those leaders—Bob Zellner, Avon Rollins, and Daniel Foss—had taken refuge in the High Street Baptist Church. Mayor Stinson then ordered police officers to apprehend the activists. They did so on June 23 by entering the church, kicking down an office door, and carrying the protestors to waiting cars. All three men were placed in jail, again with $5,000 bonds.[34]

The end of the summer proved challenging for the Danville movement as mass meeting attendance waned. When August opened, the total amount assessed in bail bonds had reached $300,000, stretching the resources of the community as more than 300 individuals awaited trial.[35] Even though a federal judge placed limits on prosecuting those charged with violating the 1859 statute, Judge Aiken proceeded with trials of those indicted for lesser offenses, sentencing most to a fine and no more than five days in jail while immediately suspending those sentences under appeal.[36] Despite fresh arrests, a high school sit-in, and an invitation to those travelling to the March on Washington to stop in Danville, attendance at evening mass meetings waned.[37] Daily reports to the attorney general's office by the FBI claimed that as few as thirty people participated in one of the meetings with attendance averaging in the forties, a significant drop from the hundreds that had shown up when the movement first started.[38]

In response, Rev. Lawrence Campbell again brought religion outside the sanctuary. Drawing on the modalities of Baptist practice, Rev. Campbell led a worship service in which participants sang and chanted with the same energy and fervency common to a Sunday gathering. In this instance, however, rather than a sermon, testimonies about police abuse anchored the event. Campbell supported those who stood in public to denounce the violence supported by Mayor Stinson and the city council.[39]

Even without evidence of city or state officials preparing to integrate public offices or private establishments, the African American community rallied additional support, yet again drawing on their religious resources to do so. On September 15, 250 high school students held a short, fifteen-minute prayer vigil at the entrance to the federal post office during which they mourned the death of six children in Birmingham as well as the murder of NAACP field secretary Medgar Evers in Jackson, Mississippi.[40] To prepare for further protests and sit-ins, organizers offered daily workshops in non-violence at the High Street Baptist Church.[41] A smaller group of three returned to the post office on September 23 and held an extended sit-in, again requesting federal intervention.[42] Through networks built up during church services and other religiously organized events, local African Americans banded together in support of those arrested. The $300,000 they had raised in property bonds represented not only a community bound tightly through the practices and structures of the church but a community aligned with a great degree of unity against a tide of unrelenting racism from the white power structure. This was the religion of black resistance mounted in the face of the religion of white rage.

Amid this resistance and rage, the executive director of the Virginia Council of Human Relations, Heslip M. Lee, visited Danville from September 16 to 17 to assess the white response. Principal among Lee's observations was that the white community was as fractured as it was unified. As was the case in many other parts of the South, massive resistance to integration obscured significant internal divisions. Groups like the SCLC took full advantage.[43] Lee described a city council split between "racists" and "somewhat moderates" and identified "other leaders aligned" with the racist group and "other community leaders aligned with the moderates."[44] In particular he noted the power of city council member and avowed segregationist John Carter to block moderates' attempts to meet at least some of the protestors' demands. Lee also encouraged moderates to attempt to influence Mayor Stinson, the swing vote open to outside pressure.

Another white visitor filed a report focusing on the white community a few weeks later. Benjamin Muse, a liberal journalist, also emphasized the tensions present within the white community. On one end of the spectrum of white response, Muse mentioned in passing that members of a white Methodist congregation censored their pastor for statements he had made in support of the integrationists' efforts.[45] Yet, white liberal affirmation of the African American demonstrators remained rare. According to Muse, "most of the white leadership" felt to some extent that "Danville [had been] on the way to race relations reform last spring when a group of Negroes, with some criminals and many children among them, suddenly launched a series of violent and unprovoked demonstrations."[46] They blamed outsiders and a few key black clergymen for disrupting progress.

Muse's most telling comments about the white community came not from his description of division but rather from his identification of white rage. According to Muse, the "Danville problem, though grave and threatening, is one more of emotion than of substance."[47] He claimed that white leaders and officials—as well as the broader public—wanted to see the black community "punished" for the demonstrations that had unfolded during the summer. From the perspective of white community leaders, the black community should not be "rewarded with concessions" but rather retaliated against. The sense of aggrievement went so deep that those white people who came out in favor of a biracial committee found themselves accused of being "nigger-lovers."[48]

To be certain, Muse also assessed black responsibility for the lack of movement toward the stated goals. He suggested that African Americans in Danville wanted to "get even" with white people, noting the deep-seated anger present in the community for the brutality of the police and the arrogance of those white officials who had refused to even appoint a biracial committee. More than impatience with white intransigence, Muse felt that black leaders likewise wanted a measure of retaliation. He also noted strategic missteps taken such as putting forward a black candidate to the city council and thereby drawing votes away from moderate white candidates as well as boycotting white businesses that employed black staff.[49]

Muse's assessment, however, misses a central issue. The only violence that had been expressed in the Danville saga came from angry white people carried out on the bodies of peaceful black people. Despite claims from white Danville residents that the police had shown great restraint in responding to the "wild" protestors, all of the evidence points to indiscriminate, sustained, and brutal violence on the part of the officers toward the non-violent demonstrators.[50] At one point a single protestor did strike back, but other than that, local testimonies, newspaper accounts, and television footage show protestors either going peacefully with those who sought to arrest them or going limp, the latter strategy eventually resulting in stringent fines.[51] Both sides did express anger and may have desired revenge or retaliation, but the prevailing power imbalance allowed only the white community to express those emotions through state-sponsored violence exercised without censure.

Those local organizing efforts did yield results despite the reports of waning numbers at the evening mass meetings and tapped-out bail reserves. The pressure that King and his emissaries brought to bear on the Danville struggle from the outside had helped shift city council opinion in the direction of cooperation rather than further resistance.[52] Following behind-the-scenes negotiations involving the local DCPA, SCLC staff, and city officials, the city hired its first black police officer and firefighter by October.[53] By November, the city announced the adoption of a non-discriminatory hiring policy.[54] Although a number of local businesses did not change their hiring practices, prompting additional protests by the DCPA, on December 16 Rev. Chase responded to the passage of the fair employment clause by stating, "The Negro has made one step further in being included in the democratic process at Danville."[55]

Perhaps most significantly for the long-term future of the integration movement in Danville, the efforts of the DCPA brought more black voters to the polls. A December report from the integrationist group stated that a five-month registration effort had resulted in 1,200 black voters added to the rolls. In the previous six years, only 200 black voters had registered, thus indicating a six-fold increase in African American voting power. The report also documented that the previous election had counted a mere 2,249 votes. A show of force by the black community could result, claimed the anonymous author of the report, in "a Negro candidate" being "elected to something of importance."[56] Even though a white segregationist ticket triumphed at the city council elections in 1964, a black city councilman won a seat two years later.[57] By 1970, the public schools were fully integrated. A decade later, in 1980, the city of Danville elected its first black mayor, Charles Harris.[58]

The white rage so evident in Danville during the events of June 10, 1963 demonstrated again that the publicly stated point of segregation had failed. Historians have already shown how integrated many domestic spaces were as black cooks, nannies, gardeners, and maids found employment in white households.[59] While worshiping communities had remained uniformly segregated since the end of the Civil War, worship practices and many of the central theological commitments in both black and white churches remained similar.[60] Segregation of worship place was not segregation of worship practice. White people and black people recognized, usually respected, and participated in the same stuff of religion. And that was the fuse that could so easily set white rage afire.

Thus not only did the religion of white rage recognize the prayer forms employed by the religion of black resistance, but the former remained emotionally tethered to the latter. White rage could only make sense in the white-framed emotional logic of the day in the face of black serenity. By itself, absent a black stimulus, the white rage looked unhinged. Precisely because they maintained non-violent discipline, black protestors offered white officials and the laborers they employed a reason to be enraged.

The city of churches had made plain its commitments. On one level the irony was all too apparent, easy to criticize, morally bankrupt. In a manner no different than other Southern towns where white Christian affiliation dominated civic life and social space, religious leaders and the town officials who populated their pews employed their religious resources to bolster the status quo. No record has yet surfaced of a sermon, public pronouncement, or collective action by a white minister, congregation, or assembly publicly and unequivocally denouncing the violence visited upon the integration activists. Recognition of religious forms did not lead to condemnation of religious attacks.

In this, there should be little more to expect than what took place. With only the rarest of exceptions, to be white and Christian in the South in the 1960s was to be on the side of segregation or at least to be content to allow fellow Christians to perpetuate the status quo. That the mayor, most members of the city council, the police chief, the rest of the police force, local merchants, at least two newspaper publishers, and deputized sanitation workers would come together to protect white supremacy is just one instance of a pattern reproduced thousands of times across the South. Discussion of those events as emblematic of white segregation bears little promise of new insight.

What does bear promise is reconsidering the events from the perspective of a religious process driven much more by commonality than difference. Scholars in the womanist tradition have long reminded us of the importance of examining the dynamics of privilege and oppression from more than one vantage point.[61] We have also learned from several generations of civil rights scholarship that it does a disservice to understanding the full historical record to describe all integrationists as nothing but heroic and morally superior and all segregationists as nothing but cowardly and ethically bankrupt. Casting aside this moral dichotomy reveals a contest in which the adversaries knew each other, understood each other's foundational religious commitments, and followed similar forms. The derision and acrimony evident in the various confrontations disclosed once again that, at least in this instance, familiarity had indeed bred contempt. Ironically, that familiarity showed an underlying disjuncture. At base the white segregationists rejected the prevailing message of Christian unity preached from both white and black pulpits.

The story of the Danville civil rights struggle in 1963 reveals how the interpenetrative nature of black and white religion in the South in the early 1960s simultaneously undermined and strengthened white hegemony even while fostering white rage. At points the fact that white officials and enforcers recognized and practiced the same kind of religion as did the black protestors created a space where the religion of black resistance was amplified and strengthened. Such was the case in more formal settings such as when white officials at the Hopewell courthouse in early February of 1962 stopped their conversations, bowed their heads, and took no steps to halt the ministers as they marched back out of town. In other less formal, more exposed settings, the knowledge and practice of shared religious forms amplified the rage of those tasked with maintaining the status quo. The pervasive power of the white community in all its expressions of racial supremacy showed its strength with particular ferocity when members of the black community dared to demonstrate that they shared the same religion. Whiteness scholar James Perkinson observes that whiteness "functions as a kind of silent *prophylaxis*, policing the borders between (its) more privileged lifeworlds and the social conditions it identifies as 'black' and 'dangerous.'"[62] He might as well have been writing about Danville.

The events in Danville are just one example of hundreds in which black civil rights activists and their allies brought religious resources to public spaces during the black freedom struggle. Clergy also wore ministerial collars. Groups of protestors together recited the Lord's Prayer. Others sang religious songs, quoted scripture, or donned stoles, habits, and vestments. But the most common religious practice brought into protest space was prayer, usually fully embodied, often kneeling. And, as the most common protest practice with religious roots, it also became the most likely to evoke a violent white response.

The reasons for the linkage between prayer and violence are likewise multiple and varied. Vulnerable, kneeling bodies were easy targets, ones that often then received beatings. The rhetoric of prayer could be antagonizing even in the midst of divine appeal. Prayers were uttered at the moments of most intense conflict and thereby became associated with violence simply because protestors offered prayers at the very point when they intuited violence was about to erupt. But the events at Danville also suggest that another element particular to the practice of religion was at play.

The most striking aspect of the events as they unfolded in Danville is the sharp contrast between the public responses of white church leaders and black ones. In the immediate aftermath of the June 10 events and for months to come, the pages of the local newspapers made no mention of any response from the many primarily white institutions in the city. By contrast, the newspapers were filled with quotations from and references to the black ministers and their congregations who participated in and most often led the demonstrations underway. In 1963, in the churches of Danville, Virginia, where members of the white community gathered, the public rage and violence directed at the black community was covered over, supported, and validated by silence. The one reference that bubbled to the top of the historical record notes the backlash visited upon a white minister who offered a measure of support to the black demonstrators. The silence spoke volumes.

That silence can be traced to a brand of evangelicalism that read divine intent in the actions and pronouncements of elected officials, that separated religious belief from social action, and that embraced a long history of deliberate and intentional racial segregation as a matter of both social practice and theological commitment. Others have delved deeply into the historical and theological complexities of that brand of evangelicalism and its parallel expressions in mainline denominations and other Christian communities.[63] What this study offers is a suggestion—limited by time, geography, and an imperfect historical record, and contingent upon further study and analysis of the individual white congregations themselves—that the public expression of racial violence exercised in support of white supremacy was as dependent upon the silence of the white religious community as it was upon their vocal participation. The religion of white rage in this instance depended upon the absence of a religious soundtrack as much as the religion of black resistance depended upon the presence of the same, the latter expressed in passionate prayers, rousing songs, and somber dress and the former in nothing more than the echoes of words not uttered.

CONCLUSION

Race, Religion, and Labor Studies: The Way Forward

Lori L. Martin, Stephen C. Finley, and Biko Mandela Gray

> No refuge could save the hireling and slave
> From the terror of flight or the gloom of the grave,
> And the star-spangled banner in triumph doth wave
> O'er the land of the free and the home of the brave.
> –Francis Scott Key, "The Star-Spangled Banner" (3rd verse)[1]

Race, Religion, and the American Religio-Necropolis

The third verse of the American national anthem is *apropos* for the argument and discussion that follows. It illustrates the ontological distinction between the white worker and the African American, whose correlation refuses reduction to class, or even to class and race, *contra* David Roediger in *The Wages of Whiteness*. If race is—as is popularly the case—understood as simply a construct rather than a set of structural positions, inculcated and sedimented through the structures of religion (to which race is tied and in which it must be understood), then the black, as modernity's not-quite-human and America's resident non-citizen, could never be represented in terms of "class" but, rather, as the Afropessimists contend, as perpetually outside the coordinates of the human and the citizen but within the trajectory of slavery's afterlife.[2] The Afropessimists are slightly off here, too, since for them—in particular Frank Wilderson—race, not economics and class, is the existential base for African Americans.[3] Given how intertwined race and religion are in modernity—which has been documented multiple times in this volume—it would only be proper to say that race and religion constitute the base for black people. As such, slavery—or the position of the slave—was not an event but a non-contingent ontological status, whose association white people avoided through linguistic maneuvers.[4]

In fact, the term "white worker" may have its origins in the late eighteenth and early nineteenth centuries with white people who were being hired as "help" or "hands," which is to say "domestic workers," in order to distinguish themselves from the status of "slaves" or "niggers."[5] The notion of "servant," for instance, was so deeply connected to the *slave*, which, in turn, signified *black* in America, that whites who found themselves working for wages developed a lexicon by which they would be understood as qualitatively distinct from the slave. Entire indexes of terms having to do with white labor—*boss*, for instance, as a term of Dutch origin to differentiate the white worker from *master*, which was part of the lexicon of slavery—emerged from this context.[6] The term "hireling," which makes its appearance in the national anthem, was another such term. In this case, however, it was a derogatory category of white labor that, while distinct from the slave, connoted "prostitution," in that a white person would work for wages regardless of the type of work that was involved and because it went against the notion of independence that was a hallmark value of the fledgling American republic.[7] Set against the War of 1812, the hireling was blasphemous, since the term referred to the hatred of the white worker, who would fight for pay, alongside the slaves, who fought for their freedom, with the British in the war against America. The language of the national anthem must be understood in this historical context.

Francis Scott Key is familiar as the author of "The Star-Spangled Banner," but less so are the additional verses of the song, particularly verse three, which serves as the epigraph for this chapter, and in which is found the line "No refuge could save the hireling and slave." Rarely read are the verses beyond verse one that is the sacred ode to the putative "land of the free and the home of the brave," which is sung at sporting, educational, political, and religious events in America. Key was a slave owner from Maryland, who was ostensibly conflicted about the institution of slavery. While owning slaves, whom, like Thomas Jefferson, he never manumitted, he was also a founding member of the white Christian American Colonization Society, which sought repatriation of African Americans to Africa for missionary purposes, and, as the name of the organization indicates, for colonial interests. Key, undeniably, despised the slave; and, in this case, he hated the treasonous hireling. Yet, there was no egalitarianism in the hatred of the two, no equal class status. One position was permanently ontological while the other—that of the hireling—was a socially and historically contingent event. This conceptual fact animates our conclusion.

The collection of chapters in *The Religion of White Rage* points to the importance of conducting research about *race, religion, and labor studies*. Research in one of these areas seldom includes consideration of the others, and rarely are all three considered simultaneously. We argue that one cannot properly consider one without the others within labor studies and American religion in the United States, and furthermore, what it *means* to be American, and we contend that this intersecting area study is the way forward for the future of labor studies. Scholars are already considering the mutual development of race and religion and the ways they co-constitute one another and remain forever linked and, in many ways, indistinguishable from the other.

At this juncture, scholars have built upon the notion that race is a social construction which casts a diversity of social meanings, and they have weighed in on debates about whether culture or structure best explains persistent racial inequalities on a host of outcomes. Going further than the idea of race as a social construction and the important debate about structures and cultures, however, we observe that race and religion are constitutive elements of modernity, which does not exist without them. The relationship between race, religion, and modernity means that modern notions of democracy, for example, require and produce the death of black people in *apparent* contradiction to its values of freedom, equality, individual rights, and agency. That death of some as a necessary condition in American democracy for the freedom and flourishing of [white] others is not a contradiction, but its very nature has rarely been interrogated. Antonia Michelle Daymond's recent article, "Can These Bones Live?: Addressing the Necrotic in U.S. Theo-Politics," agrees.

Following Achille Mbembe, Lewis Gordon, and Stephen C. Finley and Biko Mandela Gray, Daymond explores the relationship between race, religion, and the American state, which imbues its apparatus and culture with black-death requiring, black-death necessitating, and black-death normalizing in American state ideology, in which the state could accurately be framed in the present chapter as a *religio-necropolis* (or perhaps a "theo-necropolis").[8] Apprehension, which is to say intellectual perception, of this fact has been obfuscated due to the misrecognition or omission of race and religion, not only as conjoined conceptions, but as concepts that are necessary for the very meaning of modernity itself and its products, such as democracy. Theodore Vial reiterates many of the conclusions that Charles Long drew in his *Significations* four decades earlier, which are addressed above and elsewhere in this book, namely that race and religion are co-constitutive elements of modernity. What Vial contributes to the conversation in *Modern Religion, Modern Race*—already perhaps settled in numerous scholarly texts on race and religion—is that one cannot and should not end with that insight, since race and religion continue to function in our "post-Enlightenment" age.[9]

That is, one cannot make sense of state-sanctioned anti-black violence such as the extrajudicial police killings of Michael Brown, Freddie Gray, Eric Garner, and others without the "conjoined twins" of race and religion.[10] These categories, Vial argues, affect how bodies are arranged in academic departments and how the very categories of study themselves evince the force of these notions. Similar to what we and other contributors have argued in the pages of *The Religion of White Rage*, Vial contends that "religion, like race, organizes our personal experience, our social and political relations, and our academic work" and, therefore, "like race, religion is not simply a taxonomic parlor game played out on real and metaphoric sidelines; it does real work in today's world."[11] Indeed it does, and Vial would like us to see the relation between race and religion as a present one and not simply in the historic and distant past. Vial offers this push beyond the past, which would entail a focus on post-Enlightenment Germany, as an extension of and critique of Charles Long, Cornel West, and others.[12] Race and religion continue to live and develop in this present age.

Scholars who study race and religion such as Long, West, and Vial have also sought to decouple erroneous notions of religion—found primarily in the social sciences—as uniquely institutional and move toward the view of religion found in these pages as orientations that may have secondary or tertiary institutional expressions. In the American context, the notion of labor has played a significant role—along with race and religion—in constituting *the* American, inevitably white and frequently male. Because labor studies has, by many accounts, failed to expand as an area study (as has religion in America), some scholars have concerns about the future of the field.[13] In the conclusion to this chapter, we outline what we consider some of the major challenges facing labor studies and describe how linking race, religion, and labor presents an opportunity for not only making the area of study more relevant but also saving it from extinction. In this way, it might potentially be a force for social change. There is a critical need to understand the linkages between race, religion, and labor studies. Such an understanding will allow us to make sense of the times in which we live and develop strategies for addressing persistent racial inequalities and injustices.

One major challenge is reaching consensus on the definition of labor studies. We contend that such a definition must move the field beyond a focus almost exclusively on unions and labor movements. This has meant that the work has been mostly sociological and descriptive history, both of which have relied heavily on Marxist and neo-Marxist methodologies, which privilege class analysis to the subjugation of race and the near-absolute exclusion of religion. Having done so, labor studies fails to reach consensus regarding the definition of the white worker or the white working class—terms that are often used interchangeably. There are no labor studies without the white worker and the white rage they direct toward black people. White workers are aided by other whites with both lower and higher socioeconomic status. Moreover, labor studies would benefit from a canonical set of texts, which provides a range of theories and methodological approaches for asking and answering important research questions that delineate and animate the field. These important works, we will argue, must draw not only from the social sciences, which has historically been the case, but also from the humanities, including from Africana philosophy and the study of African American religion. We highlight a few recent—and some "classical"—studies that might fit into the area of study we are proposing with some important modifications.

Defining Labor Studies

A number of labor scholars have tried to define labor studies in an effort to identify and perhaps to locate its place in the academy. In the shadow of such disciplines like sociology, labor studies has been defined by scholars such as Helmut Golatz as the "integrating principle of a new body of knowledge among the social sciences, the focus of which [is] the study of the total labor effort according to the insights of the various traditional disciplines."[14] Labor studies scholar Al Nash has defined labor studies as "an orientation."[15]

By most definitions, labor studies is closely tied with unions and the labor movement.[16] In his work, Michael Parsons described a number of factors impacting unions that also impact labor studies. These issues include cultural, economic, intellectual, political, and social change factors.[17] Culturally, support for unions has declined steadily since the mid-1930s. Likewise, labor studies programs have fallen victim to budget crises on campuses where they have been formally excised from college curricula. A primary criticism of labor studies programs is that they are anti-intellectual and that "political fortunes of labor studies and the union movement are one and the same."[18] Accordingly, political pressures, Parsons notes, have exerted a consistent set of political force over time.[19] Businesses place pressure on labor studies to teach new industrial relations. Industrial relations calls upon labor studies to focus on it. Regarding labor studies, unions call into question its usefulness, especially when the membership seeks to challenge incumbent leaders or policy.

We agree with and extend Nash's and Golatz's understanding of labor studies with some important changes. A more apt definition for labor studies is as *an orientation and a body of knowledge among the social sciences and the* humanities *according to the insights of various traditional disciplines that includes the racial, symbolic, and mythological meaning of the worker/laborer.* Among the "traditional disciplines," we recommend, are Africana philosophy and African American religion, disciplines which enhance our understanding of another challenge facing labor studies: how best to define the white worker.

Defining the White Worker

Definitions of the white worker vary. The very term "white workers" is often used interchangeably with the term "white working class." Some scholars, both inside and outside the area of labor studies, attempt to define white workers quantitively by their educational level. "Moderately educated white workers," for instance, are defined as white people who tend to work with their hands, completed high school, and do not have a college degree.[20] W. Bradford Wilcox and his colleagues argued, for example, that the white working class has experienced changes in economic opportunities and family formation over the past several decades, which has led many to loosen their ties to religious institutions. Wilcox and colleagues also argue that white workers construct a moral world that is centered around the disciplined self, which is to say that white workers claim to value hard work and providing for their partners and offspring as virtuous.[21]

The inability to live up to their own ideals and failures to model white middle-class lifestyles, whatever that might be perceived to entail, has driven white workers away from churches and toward individuals and organizations they understand as addressing their classed concerns, related to their perceived declining condition.[22] This trend was particularly evident in the gravitation of *white workers* toward Donald Trump's presidential campaign in 2016.[23] Nearly 70 percent of white workers—moderately educated white workers—voted for Trump, and this included the majority of white women. Michèle Lamont, Bo Yun Park, and Elena Ayala-Hurtado explained the many ways that Trump's political rhetoric resonated with the moral matrix of the white workers. This matrix includes understanding boundaries between white workers and the people perceived to be above them and below them. The people above them, namely affluent white people, don't really matter to white workers given that white workers demonstrate a relative ambivalence toward the group, in contrast to the hate and rage that white workers demonstrate toward people who are perceived to be below them, especially

Conclusion: Race, Religion, and Labor Studies / 233

black people. As a matter of fact, Lamont, Park, and Ayala-Hurtado insist that white workers tend to view black people as poor, lazy, undisciplined, always in search of something for nothing.[24]

Indeed, some labor scholars, such as Victor Devinatz, linked Trump's tactics and appeal to white workers to those of noted segregationist George Wallace.[25] Devinatz observed that 2016, the year Trump was elected, was the first time many union members, mostly white workers, didn't support their leaders' pick for president, U.S. senator Hillary Rodham Clinton. Instead, they supported Donald Trump.[26] Part of Clinton's problem, according to Devinatz, was her campaign's failure to center the white worker and focus on class, rather than focusing on coalition building between people of color and white voters with college degrees.[27] The few unions and union leaders that officially backed Trump were, like the many supporters of Wallace, fans of *law and order* tropes and members of unions made up of law enforcement officials, ranging from local police officers to customs and border patrol. Devinatz also mistakenly defined white workers as "non-college educated whites."[28] Like Wallace, Trump's "election rhetoric took advantage of fears generated by race."[29] That is, white worker votes were motivated by racism.

Although sociologists may use education to determine one's socioeconomic status, a combination of income, education, and occupational prestige is more commonly used.[30] Nevertheless, these indicators do not consider race or religion, which is, the force exerted by one's sense of one's place in the world. Research since the mid-1990s has called upon scholars to direct their attention more toward wealth, given that individuals and households with similar income, education, and levels of occupational prestige may have very different wealth levels, which has introduced race and racial wealth inequality into ongoing debates about which matters more: race or class.[31] Income and wealth are not one and the same, and class, regardless of how it is measured, is heavily steeped in anti-black sentiments by custom and by law.[32] White wealth is a product of policies and practices that exploit black bodies for others' gain. Access to liquid assets, for example, is particularly important during times of economic crises, such as the loss of employment or a prolonged health care crisis. Lack of access to financial resources to weather an economic storm is a persistent problem that is exacerbated by enduring racial inequality.[33] Black workers fare far worse than white workers where both income and wealth are concerned, regardless of how one defines the white.[34] Nonetheless, labor studies would benefit from a definition of white workers that not only takes into account sociological and economic factors, but captures the psychological and public benefit, which more clearly reveals the fact that the white worker may best be understood as sociological, economical, philosophical, metaphorical, and/or religious, given the context.

The work of W. E. B Du Bois from the late nineteenth century through much of the first six decades of the twentieth century provides some much-needed guidance for understanding white workers more broadly, including their connection to other white people, including wealthy white elites (although, as we have shown, "white worker" as a mythology and metonym signifies all white people). Du Bois wrote, for example, about the relationship between politics and industry in 1909. He described the process of transforming workers into voters as a trend in modern thought, and he warned of the dangers of preferring white workers over and above "black workers." Du Bois said that one could not train two sets of workers in economic competition and make one set voters (white workers) and deprive the other (black workers) of participation in government. Schools, including those focused on industrial training, not only increase economic competition by race, but also "accentuate race prejudice."[35] "When a whole community, a whole nation pours contempt on a fellow man it seems a personal insult for that man to work beside me or at the same kind of work."[36] Another consequence is that black people in general, and black workers, in particular, are viewed "as unworthy and dangerous," not only in the workplace but in in areas of public accommodation (public transportation, theaters, neighborhoods, lectures, church, etc.).[37] Du Bois concluded that "this the southern white working man is industriously taught from the cradle to the grave."[38] White workers have the power to act, power that makes it

> possible for the inefficient and lazy white workman to be able to crush and keep down his black competitor at all hazards, and so that no black man shall be allowed to do his best if his success lifts him to any degree out of a place in which millions of Americans are being taught to stay.[39]

A few decades later, Du Bois was no more optimistic about the possibilities for racial reconciliation among black and white workers for a number of reasons. For one, Du Bois stated, "whereas white workers were willing to lynch and starve Negroes and crush them in ignorance, white capitalists furnished the work for education and police protection."[40] Du Bois forecasted the future of racial hatred, saying, "Race hate will persist in the United States even when the lines of class struggle are closely defined."[41] One cannot adequately define or understand white workers, their relationship to unions and the broader labor movement, and labor studies without seriously considering race and religion or what Du Bois famously described as the religion of whiteness.

In Search of a Canonical Set?

Another challenge facing labor studies is the lack of an established canonical set of texts that accurately represent the work and boundaries of the field.[42] While the absence of a set of sacred books may be viewed positively because the absence may indicate an openness and appreciation for diverse themes, the creation of a canonical set does not necessarily limit the potential expansiveness of labor studies. Conversely, a canonical set provides a shared foundation for scholars of labor studies. The literature should reflect dominant theorists and schools of thought. Selected works by Du Bois, who Eric Larson calls one of the greatest labor scholars, should be required reading for all current and future scholars of labor studies.

The Third Rail and the Future of Labor Studies

Almost thirty years ago, Parsons outlined two possible outcomes for labor studies given the challenges he outlined and the challenges we outlined previously.[43] Parsons described the optimistic track as involving the separation of labor studies from the future of the labor movement.[44] For Parsons, this would include a more academic structuring of labor studies that also maintains a labor perspective.[45] The more likely and more pessimistic route, according to Parsons, would be characterized by a decline in labor studies that coincides with a decline in the labor movement.[46]

It is our contention that there is a third possible track, one that some labor studies scholars have already decided to take. The third track, support for an area of study we call race, religion, and labor studies, foregrounds the structural dynamics of race, religion, and class as it relates to the white worker. The area of studies we propose restores agency to workers and calls for critiques of white workers as subjects and black workers as objects. Recognizing that race, religion, and labor are "mutually constitutive" is critical.[47]

This third track involves the understanding that the notion of a labor movement assumes the centrality of whiteness and ignores the labor movements centered on the experiences of black people and other people of color. It does not call for a total separation from the labor movement but an expansion of how labor movements are understood. It is possible, we argue, to have a more academic structure, while maintaining a commitment to activism and social justice issues. Reaching a consensus about how to define labor studies, which includes scholars from both the humanities and the social sciences, will play an important role in facilitating support for race, religion, and labor studies within the academy and from the public. It will also help to expand labor studies, saving it from extinction, and provide for a wide range of themes in meaningful, as opposed to token, ways.

We find evidence of recently published studies that with some modifications would fall nicely under the umbrella of what we are calling race, religion, and labor studies because each understands labor studies as both an orientation and a body of knowledge. Each understands white workers as more than just a group sharing similar levels of education, income, and occupational prestige, but also symbols of who and what matters in America and in what ways. The studies selected consider the matrix of privilege and oppression that is essential to understanding white workers in and of themselves and in relationship to others, especially toward black people. The studies also use a variety of methodological techniques, including both qualitative and quantitative approaches. Finally, each study also evokes theories and/or methods that draw from, build upon, and/or expand on existing theories and/or methods in both the humanities and the social sciences.

Heidi Gottfried has praised two studies, one by Howard Kimeldorf and one by Ching Kwan Lee, for blurring the lines between the humanities and the social sciences; for focusing on workers as active subjects; and understanding class as an aggregate of lived experiences and not merely abstract structures.[48] Black-white intergroup relations were not the primarily focus of the two books.

Cedric de Leon's work on the labor movement throughout the U.S., but also in the city of Chicago, in the nineteenth century is another example of the type of work we envision for the future of race, religion, and labor studies.[49] De Leon describes how racial exclusion led to segregated social movements. A labor movement was established and involved largely white workers, and black workers retreated and established a civil rights movement. De Leon draws upon methodological techniques from the humanities to discuss what he lists as three processes contributing to biracial unionism, which he contends began in the late 1860s.[50] The first process was discursive. The second he calls institutional and the third local. De Leon highlights how insulting it was for white workers to assume that civil rights matters were resolved during the Civil War and that the next battlefield was wage labor, thereby minimizing, dismissing, and ignoring the ongoing discrimination and anti-black sentiments aimed at black workers, in general, and black people as a whole.[51]

Despite de Leon's careful attention to the significance of race and the religious response of white workers to the experiences of black workers, his work implies that black workers abandoned labor issues and/or saw them and experienced them as separate from civil rights issues. As early as the late 1880s, we find evidence of black people addressing both issues, seeing them as interrelated and interdependent.⁵² One need only look to the codification of the politics of respectability as an example. Evelyn Brooks Higginbotham wrote about the ways black women tried to reclaim their image, determine their own fate, and improve their economic standing as marginalized workers.⁵³

Venise Wagner's study of steelworkers and racial wealth inequality is appropriate for race, religion and labor studies.⁵⁴ Wagner wrote about bankruptcies following the 1959 steelworkers' strike.⁵⁵ White and black workers were out of work for at least four months without pay. When the strike ended, workers came back based upon seniority. White workers had more seniority than black workers, which meant that many African Americans were out of work for up to seven months without pay. Black workers disproportionately filed for bankruptcy during the four to seven months following the start of the strike. Furthermore, an analysis of the bankruptcy records reveals that black workers were disproportionately targeted for predatory lending. Many were the victims of usury loans in addition to the challenges they faced because of redlining, an apartheid mortgage system, and contract buying. Wagner concluded that "whiteness was wealth, while non-whiteness in real economic terms was blight, a negative that subtracted value."⁵⁶ Wagner provided an interdisciplinary approach to highlight the multiple ways that white workers are privileged within and outside of the workplace, which undermines the belief that white workers are most at risk.⁵⁷ Neither benefits nor risks are equally shared, and the benefits to white workers and the risks to black workers are far-reaching and have the potential for intergenerational wealth transfers. Afropessimism and Africana philosophy would be useful here in understanding meaning and the black body.

Finally, Eric Larson's work on the potential for labor education in bridging the labor movement and the Black Lives Matter movement is well suited for race, religion, and labor studies.⁵⁸ Larson places race at the center of his analysis.⁵⁹ He does not describe the reactions of white workers to the Black Lives Matter movement as religious (as Biko Gray does in his work), but we understand it in that way.⁶⁰ It helps explain white workers' refusal to recognize the root causes of unfairness and injustice in the criminal justice system. Larson drew from labor history, Du Bois' concept of the wages of whiteness, black history, and black feminist thought, for example, to address the politics of bridge building between these two movements. Larson's interdisciplinary approach facilitated his ability to show the role of unions in facilitating mass incarceration, for example, and the phenomenon of private prisons.⁶¹ He observed, "Black lives, in these structures, are the 'collateral consequences' of white jobs and institutional stability."⁶² We believe Larson is overly optimistic about the potential of labor education to bridge the divide between white workers and black workers critical of the criminal justice system. Part of understanding white rage as religious involves understanding an unwillingness on the part of white workers to accept empirical evidence that is counter to the dominant narratives about black people that are constructed in their own imaginations and incorporated in key American social institutions.

Labor relations between black and white have never been about class. The only way one can reduce relations between workers to class is if one begins with that assumption. Then, claims of white workers voting against their interests, for example, have currency. But this becomes wholly irrelevant if one begins with the *white worker* as a mythological site. Purported class distinctions between white people fall away in importance because they embrace the mythic white worker. As with Kavanaugh and Trump, the white worker becomes a universally white symbol, which points to a myth of beginnings. Hard work, ingenuity, grit, which valorizes the historic white American frontier life, gets concretized in the American notion of meritocracy. An origin story, tied to the very (whitely) foundations of the American narrative of hardship and overcoming, of discovery and development, of chosenness and manifest destiny, ties white people to American civil religion in a way it never could with Africans, indigenous communities, and Mexicans.

The white worker, then, does not vote against his/her interests. Class isn't the ground of being. It isn't the base. Religion, intertwined with race, is for whites. Whiteness is their foundational orientation. It is what gives them meaning. It is their interface with the world. It structures relations, affect, motivations, institutions, individual relations, etc. As a result, there is no contradiction between white workers voting Republican (or for conservative Democrats in Louisiana) if one understands what their priority is, their ultimate orientation. It is neither jobs nor economic concerns. It is about the meaning of their place in the world as *white*. And their perception is that their world, their whitely place in it, is in jeopardy—their potential loss of place, because of their perception that black people and others want to live in this world as full human beings and American citizens, threatens them and gives way to rage.

Labor studies has not had a clear way forward because it has been grounded in institutional activities as the focus of its scholarship, in the function of unions, for instance, rather than in the primary meaning of the white worker, and it has been grounded by insights from the humanities such as religious studies and philosophy. Albeit an ostensible conflict, this does not represent a contradiction. Seen through a grounding mythology in a larger orientation, the choices of white workers—which many have seen as racist—make perfect sense. The *white worker* is America; and is *American*. The data and facts of history becomes secondary. Genocide and slavery become obscured in lieu of the legend. And this legend, this myth—the white worker—becomes the site of *eternal return*. It is the central and orienting mythology among other mythologies—both civil religious and Christian—that ground their being and animate their world.

This is why Kavanaugh could refer to the myth of the white worker despite evidence in his experience and privilege to the contrary. History and sociology become secondary to mythology and theology—a theology of whiteness to which whiteness seeks return in times of perceived loss. This is why "Make America Great Again" resonates with so many, while African Americans and people of color ask, "When was that; when was America ever great?"

We seek to subvert the notion of class as a secondary consideration at best. As a neo-Marxist, Roediger wants to recognize the agency of white workers to cocreate whiteness with elite whites, and we're saying that whiteness is just a white creation that ultimately undercuts class distinctions when seen through the appropriate lenses of religion and race simultaneously. Whereas labor scholars want to see class as objectively real and quantitative, which we dispute (especially across racial fields), and religion as a construct, we argue that "class" via its dominant symbol, the white worker, is just as mythical a construct.

NOTES

INTRODUCTION / "The Souls of White Folk": Race, Affect, and Religion in the Religion of White Rage

1. George D. Kelsey, *Racism and the Christian Understanding of Man* (New York: Charles Scribner's Sons, 1965).
2. W. E. B. Du Bois, *Darkwater: Voices from within the Veil* (Mineola, NY: Dover, [1920] 1999), 18.
3. "Brett Kavanaugh's Opening Statement at Senate Hearing," CBS News/YouTube, September 27, 2018, https://youtu.be/eahnOcp883k (accessed February 19, 2020).
4. "Brett Kavanaugh's Opening Statement at Senate Hearing."
5. Charles Long, *Significations: Signs, Symbols, and Images in the Interpretation of Religion* (Aurora, CO: Davies Group, [1986] 1995), 7.
6. Dan MacGuill, "Did Donald Trump Encourage Violence at His Rallies?" *Snopes* (no date), https://www.snopes.com/fact-check/donald-trump-incitement-violence (accessed February 19, 2020).
7. We might hear in this statement Durkheim's notion of collective effervescence. For more on this, see Kathryn Lofton, *Consuming Religion* (Chicago: University of Chicago Press, 2017).
8. Christopher Driscoll, *White Lies: Race and Uncertainty in the Twilight of American Religion* (New York: Routledge, 2016), 26.
9. Driscoll, *White Lies*, 26–7.
10. Lewis Gordon, "Race, Theodicy, and the Normative Emancipatory Challenges of Blackness," *South Atlantic Quarterly* 112, no. 4 (2013), 725.
11. William Jones, *Is God a White Racist? A Preamble to Black Theology* (Boston: Beacon Press, [1973] 1986).
12. Gordon, "Race, Theodicy," 726.
13. Sara Ahmed, *The Cultural Politics of Emotion* (New York: Routledge, 2004).

14. George Yancy, *What White Looks Like: African American Philosophers on the Whiteness Question* (New York: Routledge, 2004), 7–8.
15. Biko M. Gray, Stephen C. Finley, and Lori L. Martin, "'High Tech Lynching': White Virtual Mobs and Administrators as Policing Agents in Higher Education," *Issues in Race & Society: An Interdisciplinary Global Journal* (2019); Stephen C. Finley, "Signification and Subjectivity: Reflections on Racism, Colonialism, and (Re)Authentication in Religion and Religious Studies," *International Journal of Africana Studies* 19, no. 2 (2019), 15–35; Stephen C. Finley and Lori L. Martin, "The Complexity of Color and the Religion of Whiteness," in Lori L. Martin, Hayward D. Horton, Cedric Herring, Verna M. Keith, and Melvin Thomas (eds.), *Color Struck: How Race and Complexion Matter in the "Color-Blind" Era* (Rotterdam: Sense, 2017), 179–96; Long, *Significations*, 75–124; Du Bois, *Darkwater*.
16. Yancy, *What White Looks Like*, 2.
17. Long, *Significations*, 85–6, 96–8, esp. 95.
18. Mircea Eliade, *The Myth of the Eternal Return, or Cosmos and History*, trans. Willard R. Trask (Princeton, NJ: Princeton University Press, [1954] 2005).
19. Long, *Significations*, 78.
20. Long, *Significations*, 79.
21. Long, *Significations*, 79.
22. Long, *Significations*, 79.
23. Du Bois, *Darkwater*, 18.
24. Du Bois, *Darkwater*, 17–29.
25. Du Bois, *Darkwater*, 23–4.
26. Du Bois, *Darkwater*, 24. Furthermore, Du Bois refers to all the people of the colonies not only as "darkies" but as "niggers," indicting that at the base of all such treatment is anti-blackness.
27. Long, *Significations*, 96–106.
28. Long, *Significations*, 94.
29. Long, *Significations*, 96.
30. Du Bois, *Darkwater*, 17.
31. Du Bois, *Darkwater*, 28.
32. Du Bois, *Darkwater*, 18–20, 21–9.
33. Du Bois, *Darkwater*, 29.
34. Du Bois, Darkwater, 28.
35. E. Franklin Frazier, "The Pathology of Race Prejudice," *The Forum* 77 (1927), 856–61; Bobby E. Wright, *The Psychopathic Racial Personality and Other Essays* (Chicago: Third World Press, 1984).
36. Du Bois, *Darkwater*, 28.
37. Du Bois, *Darkwater*, 25.
38. Du Bois, *Darkwater*, 27.
39. Du Bois, *Darkwater*, 28.
40. Du Bois, *Darkwater*, 19.
41. Du Bois, *Darkwater*, 17.
42. Du Bois, *Darkwater*, 22.

43. Yancy, *What White Looks Like*, 4.
44. Sara Ahmed, "A Phenomenology of Whiteness," *Feminist Theory* 8, no. 2 (2007), 149–68.
45. Ahmed, "A Phenomenology of Whiteness," 150.
46. Ahmed, "A Phenomenology of Whiteness."
47. Chandelis Duster, "Gov. Andrew Cuomo Uses 'N-Word' to Make Point about Derogatory Terms against Italians," CNN Politics, October 15, 2019, https://www.cnn.com/2019/10/15/politics/andrew-cuomo-racial-slur/index.html (accessed February 20, 2020). The article redacts the term.
48. Alissa Wilkinson, "Chris Cuomo Said 'Fredo' Is Like the 'N-Word' for Italians. It's... Not," *Vox*, August 13, 2019, https://www.vox.com/culture/2019/8/13/20804039/chris-cuomo-fredo-godfather (accessed February 20, 2020).
49. Gregory J. Seigworth and Melissa Gregg, "An Inventory of Shimmers," in Melissa Gregg and Gregory J. Seigworth (eds.), *The Affect Theory Reader* (Durham, NC: Duke University Press, 2010), 2.
50. Ben Highmore, "Bitter After Taste: Affect, Food and Social Aesthetics," in Gregg and Seigworth (eds.), *The Affect Theory Reader*, 118.
51. Debra Thompson, "An Exoneration of Black Rage," *South Atlantic Quarterly* 116, no. 3 (2017), 457–81.
52. Thompson, "An Exoneration of Black Rage," 463.
53. Carol Anderson, *White Rage: The Unspoken Truth of Our Racial Divide* (New York: Bloomsbury, 2016), 5.
54. Jordanna Matlon, "Racial Capitalism and the Crisis of Black Masculinity," *American Sociological Review* 81, no. 5 (2016), 1014.

ONE / "Make America Great Again": Racial Pathology, White Consolidation, and Melancholia in Trump's America

1. To William B. Parsons, with great respect.
2. Frantz Fanon, *Black Skin, White Masks*, trans. Charles Lam Markmann (New York: Grove Press, 1967), 151.
3. Fanon, *Black Skin, White Masks*, 109.
4. Robert E. Hood, *Begrimed and Black: Christian Traditions on Blacks and Blackness* (Minneapolis: Augsburg Fortress, 1994), xi.
5. Martin Luther King, Jr., *Where Do We Go from Here? Chaos or Community?* (Boston: Beacon Press, 1968), 88–90. ßKing was very clear in his writings on the "white backlash" that white conservatives and liberals were equally culpable and that the effectiveness of a backlash required both—or all—segments of the white populace.
6. Robert E. Terrill, "The Post-Racial and Post-Ethical Discourse of Donald J. Trump," *Rhetoric and Public Affairs* vol. 20, no. 3 (2017), 499. Terrill points out how Trump's racial discourses are "dog whistle," in that they do not explicitly use racial language but they have racial consequences for his audiences. Yet, in my estimation, and probably for the author, they hear concealed racial tropes and respond in racialized ways.

7. King, *Where Do We Go from Here?*, 68.
8. Francine Uenuma, "The Massacre of Black Sharecroppers That Led the Supreme Court to Curb the Racial Disparities in the Justice System," *Smithsonian Magazine*, August 2, 2018, https://www.smithsonianmag.com/history/death-hundreds-elaine-massacre-led-supreme-court-take-major-step-toward-equal-justice-african-americans-180969863 (accessed February 20, 2020).
9. Uenuma, "The Massacre of Black Sharecroppers."
10. James W. Perkinson, "The Ghost in the Global Machine: White Violence, Indigenous Resistance, and Race as Religiousness," *CrossCurrents* 64, no. 1 (2014), 71.
11. Perkinson, "The Ghost in the Global Machine," 59–60.
12. W. E. B. Du Bois, *Darkwater: Voices from within the Veil* (Mineola, NY: Dover, [1920] 1999), 18.
13. Perkinson, "The Ghost in the Global Machine," 64.
14. Hood, *Begrimed and Black*, 1.
15. Celia Brickman, *Aboriginal Populations in the Mind: Race and Primitivity in Psychoanalysis* (New York: Columbia University Press, 2003), 1–12; cf. Ranjana Khanna, *Dark Continents: Psychoanalysis and Colonialism* (Durham, NC: Duke University Press, 2003), 1ff.
16. Fanon, *Black Skin, White Masks*, 151–2.
17. Brickman, *Aboriginal Populations in the Mind*, 9.
18. Fanon, *Black Skin, White Masks*, 160–1.
19. See, for instance, Rudolf Otto, *The Idea of the Holy*, trans. John W. Harvey (London: Humphrey Milford, 1923); cf. Stephen C. Finley, "The Supernatural in the African American Experience," in Jeffrey J. Kripal (ed.), *Religion: Super Religion* (Farmington Hills, MI: Macmillan Reference USA, 2017), 233–4.
20. Fanon, *Black Skin, White Masks*, 160–1.
21. Fanon, *Black Skin, White Masks*, 161 n. 25; cf. Jacques Lacan, *Ecrits: A Selection*, trans. Bruce Fink (New York: W. W. Norton, 2002), 1–9.
22. Lacan, *Ecrits*, 3–5.
23. Sigmund Freud, *Civilization and Its Discontents*, trans. James Strachey (New York: W. W. Norton, 1961), 29, 35, 51, 59.
24. Fanon, *Black Skin, White Masks*, 170.
25. Fanon, *Black Skin, White Masks*, 177.
26. Fanon, *Black Skin, White Masks*, 165.
27. Charles H. Long, *Significations: Signs, Symbols, and Images in the Interpretation of Religion* (Aurora, CO: Davies Group, [1986] 1995), 120–1, 180, 184.
28. Long, *Significations*, 180.
29. Long, *Significations*, 180.
30. Long, *Significations*, 180.
31. Doug Criss, "This is the 30-Year-Old Willie Horton Ad Everybody Is Talking About Today," CNN Politics, November 1, 2018, https://www.cnn.com/2018/11/01/politics/willie-horton-ad-1988-explainer-trnd/index.html (accessed February 21, 2020).

32. Robin J. DiAngelo, *White Fragility: Why It's So Hard for White People to Talk about Racism* (Boston: Beacon Press, 2018), 91.
33. Fanon, *Black Skin, White Masks*, 161 n. 25.
34. Fanon, *Black Skin, White Masks*, 154.
35. Sigmund Freud, *Introductory Lectures on Psycho-Analysis*, trans. James Strachey (New York: W. W. Norton, 1966), 423. "It is plausible to suppose that the fixation and regression are not independent of each other. The stronger the fixations on its path of development, the more readily will the function evade external difficulties by regressing to the fixations. . ."
36. Sigmund Freud, "Mourning and Melancholia," in *The Standard Edition of the Complete Psychological Works of Sigmund Freud, Volume XIV (1914–1916): On the History of the Psycho-Analytic Movement, Papers on Metapsychology and Other Works*, trans. James Strachey (London: Hogarth Press, [1957] 1964), 237–58; John E. Baker, "Mourning and the Transformation of Object Relationships: Evidence for the Persistence of Internal Attachments," *Psychoanalytic Psychology* 18, no. 1 (2001), 55–73.
37. Peter Homans, *The Ability to Mourn: Disillusionment and the Social Origins of Psychoanalysis* (Chicago: University of Chicago Press, 1989), 24–6.
38. Long, *Significations*, 89–106.
39. Anne Anlin Cheng, *The Melancholy of Race: Psychoanalysis, Assimilation, and Hidden Grief* (New York: Oxford University Press, 2001), 11.
40. E. Franklin Frazer, "The Pathology of Race Prejudice," *The Forum* 70 (1927), 856–62; Bobby E. Wright, *The Psychopathic Racial Personality and Other Essays* (Chicago: Third World Press, 1984).
41. Homans, *The Ability to Mourn*, 4.
42. Cheng, *The Melancholy of Race*, 8; see D. W. Winnicott, *Playing and Reality* (London: Tavistock, 1971), 1–34.
43. Mircea Eliade, *The Myth of the Eternal Return, or Cosmos and History*, trans. Willard R. Trask (Princeton, NJ: Princeton University Press, 1954).
44. Eliade, *The Myth of the Eternal Return*, 33–4, 44, 108.
45. Sigmund Freud, *Three Essays on a Theory of Sexuality*, trans. James Strachey (New York: Basic, [1962] 2000), 84.
46. See other studies: Kate White (ed.), *Unmasking Race, Culture, and Attachment in the Psychoanalytic Space* (London and New York: Karnac, 2006); Christopher Lane (ed.), *The Psychoanalysis of Race* (New York: Columbia University Press, 1998).
47. Fanon, *Black Skin, White Masks*, 110.
48. Otto, *The Idea of the Holy*, 9.
49. Otto, *The Idea of the Holy*, 10; cf. Otto, *The Idea of the Holy*, 21.

TWO / You Will Not Replace Us! An Exploration of Religio-Racial Identity in White Nationalism

1. Vice News, "Watch the 'Vice News Tonight' Episode 'Charlottesville: Race and Terror,'" *Vice*, August 14, 2017, https://www.vice.com/en_us/article/433vkq/

watch-the-vice-news-tonight-episode-charlottesville-race-and-terror (accessed February 21, 2020).
2. Thomas Chatterton Williams, "The French Origins of 'You Will Not Replace Us,'" *New Yorker*, December 4, 2017, https://www.newyorker.com/magazine/2017/12/04/the-french-origins-of-you-will-not-replace-us (accessed February 21, 2020).
3. Christopher Sebastian Parker, "Race and Politics in the Age of Obama," *Annual Review of Sociology* 42 (2016), 217–30.
4. Jared Taylor, a prominent white nationalist, discusses this phenomenon as the incentive undergirding the need for "race realism" and race consciousness in whites. Jason Wilson, "'Young White Guys Are Hopping Mad': Confidence Grows at Far-Right Gathering," *The Guardian*, July 31, 2017, https://www.theguardian.com/us-news/2017/jul/31/american-renaissance-conference-white-identity (accessed February 21, 2020).
5. Richard Hofstadter, *The Paranoid Style in American Politics and Other Essays* (New York: Vintage, [1965] 2008).
6. Robert P. Jones, *The End of White Christian America* (New York: Simon & Schuster, 2016).
7. Hofstadter, *The Paranoid Style in American Politics*, 14.
8. Hofstadter, *The Paranoid Style in American Politics*, 23–4.
9. Christopher Driscoll, *White Lies: Race and Uncertainty in the Twilight of American Religion* (New York: Routledge, 2016), 65–117.
10. Kelly Brown Douglas, *Stand Your Ground: Black Bodies and the Justice of God* (Maryknoll, NY: Orbis, 2015).
11. Shannon Sullivan, *Revealing Whiteness: The Unconscious Habits of Racial Privilege* (Bloomington: Indiana University Press, 2006).
12. Hofstadter, *The Paranoid Style in American Politics*, 30.
13. Jeet Heer, "Trump's Cult of Personality Takes Paranoia to the Next Level," *New Republic*, January 26, 2018, https://newrepublic.com/article/146786/trumps-cult-personality-takes-paranoia-next-level; Thomas B. Edsall, "The Paranoid Style in American Politics is Back," *New York Times*, September 8, 2016, https://www.nytimes.com/2016/09/08/opinion/campaign-stops/the-paranoid-style-in-american-politics-is-back.html (both accessed February 21, 2020).
14. Hofstadter, *The Paranoid Style in American Politics*, 37.
15. Matthew C. MacWilliams, "Who Decides When the Party Doesn't? Authoritarian Voters and the Rise of Donald Trump," *PS: Political Science & Politics* 49, no. 4 (2016), 716–21.
16. Charles H. Long, *Significations: Signs, Symbols, and Images in the Interpretation of Religion* (Aurora, CO: Davies Group, [1986] 1999), 163.
17. Sylvester A. Johnson, *African American Religions, 1500–2000: Colonialism, Democracy, and Freedom* (New York: Cambridge University Press, 2015), 88.
18. See Michael Kimmel, *Angry White Men: American Masculinity at the End of an Era* (New York: Nation, 2013), 31–68.
19. Hofstadter, *The Paranoid Style in American Politics*, 30.

20. Hofstadter, *The Paranoid Style in American Politics*, 53.
21. Keri Leigh Merritt, *Masterless Men: Poor Whites and Slavery in the Antebellum South* (Cambridge, England: Cambridge University Press, 2017), 177.
22. Merritt, *Masterless Men*, 179–215.
23. Nancy Isenberg, *White Trash: The 400-Year Untold History of Class in America* (New York: Penguin, 2017), 230.
24. See also J. D. Vance, *Hillbilly Elegy: A Memoir of a Family and Culture in Crisis* (New York: Harper, 2016).
25. Arlie Russell Hochschild, *Strangers in Their Own Land: Anger and Mourning on the American Right* (New York: New Press, 2016).
26. Daniel Cox, Rachel Lienesch, and Robert P. Jones, "Beyond Economics: Fears of Cultural Displacement Pushed the White Working Class to Trump," PRRI, May 9, 2017, https://www.prri.org/research/white-working-class-attitudes-economy-trade-immigration-election-donald-trump (accessed February 21, 2020).
27. Douglas, *Stand Your Ground*, 48–89.
28. "Black Boys Viewed as Older, Less Innocent than Whites, Research Finds," American Psychological Association, March 6, 2014, https://www.apa.org/news/press/releases/2014/03/black-boys-older.aspx (accessed February 21, 2020). See also P. A. Goff, M. C. Jackson, B. A. L. Di Leone, C. M. Culotta, and N. A. DiTomasso, "The Essence of Innocence: Consequences of Dehumanizing Black Children," *Journal of Personality and Social Psychology* 106, no. 4 (2014), 526–45.
29. Tommy Curry, *The Man-Not: Race, Class, Genre, and the Dilemmas of Black Manhood* (Philadelphia: Temple University Press, 2017).
30. Henri Bergson, *The Two Sources of Morality and Religion*, trans. R. Ashley Audra and Cloudesley Brereton (Notre Dame, IN: University of Notre Dame Press, [1935] 1977). See also Mary Douglas's interpretations in *Purity and Danger* (New York: Routledge, [1966] 2002).
31. Long, *Significations*, 7.
32. Damon T. Berry, *Blood and Faith: Christianity in American White Nationalism* (Syracuse, NY: Syracuse University Press, 2017), 3.
33. Judith Weisenfeld, *New World A-Coming: Black Religion and Racial Identity during the Great Migration* (New York: New York University Press, 2016).
34. Michael Barkun, *Religion and the Racist Right: The Origins of the Christian Identity Movement* (Chapel Hill: University of North Carolina Press, 1994), viii–ix.
35. Gordon Kaufman's constructive theological perspective cites "God" as symbolic of human imaginative efforts to create world coherence and continuity, and thus, tethers to this symbol ultimacy and finality as constitutive of the human telos.
36. Christopher Ingraham, "Two New Studies Find Racial Anxiety Is the Biggest Driver of Support for Trump," *Washington Post*, June 6, 2016, https://www.washingtonpost.com/news/wonk/wp/2016/06/06/racial-anxiety-is-a-huge-driver-of-support-for-donald-trump-two-new-studies-find; Michele Norris, "As America Changes, Some Anxious Whites Feel Left Behind," *National Geographic*, April 2018, https://www.nationalgeographic.com/magazine/2018/04/race-rising-anxiety-white-america (both accessed February 21, 2020).

37. Emile Durkheim, *The Elementary Forms of Religious Life*, trans. Carol Cosman (Oxford: Oxford University Press, 2001), 6–7.
38. Durkheim, *The Elementary Forms of Religious Life*, 88.
39. Jared Taylor, *If We Do Nothing: Essays and Reviews from 25 Years of White Advocacy* (Oakton, VA: New Century, 2017).
40. "14 Words," ADL website, https://www.adl.org/education/references/hate-symbols/14-words (accessed February 21, 2020).
41. "The Year in Hate: Trump Buoyed White Supremacists in 2017, Sparking Backlash among Black Nationalist Groups," Southern Poverty Law Center, February 21, 2018, https://www.splcenter.org/news/2018/02/21/year-hate-trump-buoyed-white-supremacists-2017-sparking-backlash-among-black-nationalist (accessed February 21, 2020).
42. Paul Gilroy, "Scales and Eyes: 'Race' Making Difference," in Sue Golding (ed.), *The Eight Technologies of Otherness* (London: Routledge, 1997), 190–6.
43. Willie James Jennings, *The Christian Imagination: Theology and the Origins of Race* (New Haven, CT: Yale University Press, 2010), 250, 290–91; Johnson, *African American Religions*, 2–8.
44. See also Brian K. Bantum, *The Death of Race: Building a New Christianity in a Racial World* (Minneapolis: Fortress Press, 2016).
45. Bernard Lonergan, *Insight: A Study of Human Understanding* (Toronto: University of Toronto Press, 1992).
46. M. Shawn Copeland, *Enfleshing Freedom: Body, Race, and Being* (Minneapolis: Fortress Press, 2010), 13.
47. Copeland, *Enfleshing Freedom*, 14.
48. Copeland, *Enfleshing Freedom*, 94.
49. Copeland, *Enfleshing Freedom*, 98.
50. Copeland, *Enfleshing Freedom*, 126–8.

THREE / "I AM that I AM": The Religion of White Rage, Great Migration Detroit, and the Ford Motor Company

1. Carol Anderson, *White Rage: The Unspoken Truth of Our Racial Divide* (New York: Bloomsbury, 2016), 3.
2. This chapter refers to thought and events from a variety of periods in U.S. history. The preferred referent for black Americans has been dynamic, including variations such as "Negro," "black," and "African American." In general, here, the term "black" in reference to the racial group, is used interchangeably with the term "African American" with three contextual considerations: First, where "whites" or "white" has been used, we attempt to be consistent in using "black" as a parallel construction; second, we have retained the term used by an author in his/her original text—unless in a direct quote, the term "Negro," preferred in its historical period, has been dropped for one of the contemporary preferences; and third, where the contextual reference is one of culture or citizenship, the term "African American" has been used to lay claim to cultural identity and/or citizenship rights.

3. August Meier and Elliot M. Rudwick, *Black Detroit and the Rise of the UAW* (New York: Oxford University Press, 1979), 94. The phrase "great white father" carries symbolism and meaning. It hearkens to Native American spirituality. The "Great Grandfather" or "Great Spirit" is a reference to the power of the Creator of humankind which, in the structure of spirituality of many indigenous peoples, connected them relationally to one another. Natives see themselves as children of the Great Spirit. Merriam-Webster reports that as far back as 1806, the "great white father" referred to the president of the United States, especially in reference to relations with indigenous North Americans. A second meaning in this dictionary extends the term to refer to any person of authority. See "Great White Father," Merriam-Webster, https://www.merriam-webster.com/dictionary/Great%20White%20Father (accessed February 21, 2020); Troy Johnson, "Native American Indian Spirituality," in Elizabeth M. Dowling and W. George Scarlett (eds.), *Encyclopedia of Religious and Spiritual Development* (Thousand Oaks, CA: Sage, 2006), 314–15; "Proclamation: To the Great White Father and All His People," *Anthropology News* 11, no. 2 (1970), 2–12.
4. Charles H. Long, *Significations: Signs, Symbols, and Images in the Interpretation of Religion* (Philadelphia: Fortress Press, 1986), 7.
5. Paul Tillich, *Dynamics of Faith* (New York: Harper & Brothers, 1957), 1.
6. Long, *Significations*, 7.
7. Emile Durkheim, *The Elementary Forms of Religious Life*, trans. Karen E. Fields (New York: Free Press, 1997). Originally published 1912.
8. Durkheim, *The Elementary Forms of Religious Life*, 9.
9. Durkheim, *The Elementary Forms of Religious Life*, 9.
10. Gordon Lynch, *The Sacred in the Modern World: A Cultural Sociological Approach* (Oxford: Oxford University Press, 2012).
11. Lynch, *The Sacred in the Modern World*, 42.
12. Walter H. Capps, *Religious Studies: The Making of a Discipline* (Minneapolis: Fortress Press, 1995), 161.
13. Robert N. Bellah, *The Broken Covenant: American Civil Religion in Time of Trial*, 2nd edn. (Chicago: University of Chicago Press, 1992), 1. Originally published New York: Seabury Press, 1975.
14. Bellah, *The Broken Covenant*, 19.
15. Nell Irvin Painter, *The History of White People* (New York: W. W. Norton, 2010), 104.
16. Painter, *The History of White People*, 104. Free white females, other free persons—regardless of sex—and slaves were placed in separate categories.
17. Jim Wallis, *America's Original Sin: Racism, White Privilege, and the Bridge to a New America* (Grand Rapids, MI: Brazos, 2016), xii, 37–8.
18. Wallis, *America's Original Sin*, 33–4.
19. Dwight N. Hopkins, "Slave Theology in the 'Invisible Institution,'" in Cornel West and Eddie S. Glaude, Jr. (eds.), *African American Religious Thought: An Anthology* (Louisville, KY: Westminster John Knox Press, 2003), 799.

20. Jeffrey C. Alexander, *The Meanings of Social Life: A Cultural Sociology* (Oxford: Oxford University Press, 2003), 3–4.
21. Bellah, *The Broken Covenant*, 1.
22. Meredith B. McGuire, *Religion: The Social Context*, 5th edn. (Belmont, CA: Wadsworth Thomson Learning, 2002), 26–32.
23. Painter, *The History of White People*, 104, 106.
24. Painter, *The History of White People*, 105.
25. Painter, *The History of White People*, 106.
26. Douglas Brinkley, *Wheels for the World: Henry Ford, His Company, and a Century of Progress, 1903–2003* (New York: Viking, 2003), 3.
27. Brinkley, *Wheels for the World*, 14.
28. Brinkley, *Wheels for the World*, 259–64, 451.
29. Brinkley, *Wheels for the World*, 444.
30. Brinkley, *Wheels for the World*, 177.
31. Beth Tompkins Bates, *The Making of Black Detroit in the Age of Henry Ford* (Chapel Hill: University of North Carolina Press, 2012), 43.
32. Meier and Rudwick, *Black Detroit and the Rise of the UAW*, 94.
33. Brinkley, *Wheels for the World*, 151.
34. Brinkley, *Wheels for the World*, 154.
35. Brinkley, *Wheels for the World*, 154.
36. Brinkley, *Wheels for the World*, 156–7.
37. Brinkley, *Wheels for the World*, 158.
38. Brinkley, *Wheels for the World*, 159.
39. Thomas Sugrue, *The Origins of the Urban Crisis: Race and Inequality in Postwar Detroit* (Princeton, NJ: Princeton University Press, [1996] 2014), 34.
40. Meier and Rudwick, *Black Detroit and the Rise of the UAW*, 6. See also Brinkley, *Wheels for the World*, 159.
41. Brinkley, *Wheels for the World*, 159, 174.
42. Brinkley, *Wheels for the World*, 172.
43. Brinkley, *Wheels for the World*, 162.
44. Brinkley, *Wheels for the World*, 161–5, 275–8. Especially when up to half of the Ford workforce were immigrants, these and other Sociological Department activities were aimed at their Americanization.
45. Meier and Rudwick, *Black Detroit and the Rise of the UAW*, 9. Several references list variations on the civic organizations that played a role in preparing African Americans for industrial employment and/or screening and recommending candidates. See Angela D. Dillard, *Faith in the City: Preaching Radical Social Change in Detroit* (Ann Arbor: University of Michigan Press, 2007); see also John Brueggemann, "The Power and Collapse of Paternalism: The Ford Motor Company and Black Workers, 1937–1941," *Social Problems* 47, no. 2 (2000), 220–40; Sugrue, *The Origins of the Urban Crisis*; Bates, *The Making of Black Detroit in the Age of Henry Ford*.
46. Bates, *The Making of Black Detroit in the Age of Henry Ford*, 5, 7, 75–6.
47. Meier and Rudwick, *Black Detroit and the Rise of the UAW*, 9–10.

48. This chapter highlights black male Great Migrants, but members of Second Baptist regularly staffed the Detroit train station looking for young women arriving from the South. They sought to offer young women assistance before less savory figures had an opportunity to unwittingly recruit them into criminal enterprises, including prostitution. See Victoria W. Wolcott, *Remaking Respectability: African American Women in Interwar Detroit* (Chapel Hill: University of North Carolina Press, 2001).
49. Brueggemann, "The Power and Collapse of Paternalism," 223.
50. Bates, *The Making of Black Detroit in the Age of Henry Ford*, 6.
51. Meier and Rudwick, *Black Detroit and the Rise of the UAW*, 94.
52. Brueggemann, "The Power and Collapse of Paternalism," 221.
53. Brueggemann, "The Power and Collapse of Paternalism," 221.
54. Brueggemann, "The Power and Collapse of Paternalism," 221, quoting Edna Bonacich, "Advanced Capitalism and Black/White Race Relations in the United States: A Split Labor Market Interpretation," *American Sociological Review* 41, no. 1 (1976), 42. Brueggemann argues that white workers abandoned loyalty to Ford in search of greater autonomy through collective labor efforts. Initial unionization efforts failed. Union organizing efforts at Ford were the most difficult in the industry, and finally succeeded when organizers appealed to the black upper class and black Ford workers.
55. Sugrue, *The Origins of the Urban Crisis*, 122.
56. Sugrue, *The Origins of the Urban Crisis*, 122.
57. Sugrue, *The Origins of the Urban Crisis*, 122.
58. Sugrue, *The Origins of the Urban Crisis*, 122.
59. Joyce Shaw Peterson, "Black Automobile Workers in Detroit, 1910–1930," *Journal of Negro History* 64, no. 3 (1979), 177.
60. Anderson, *White Rage*, 3.
61. Catherine Bell, *Ritual Theory, Ritual Practice* (New York: Oxford University Press, 1992), 197.
62. Bell, *Ritual Theory*, 8.
63. Bell, *Ritual Theory*, 206.
64. Brueggemann, "The Power and Collapse of Paternalism," 221.
65. Brinkley, *Wheels for the World*, 385.
66. Scott Martelle, *Detroit, A Biography* (Chicago: Chicago Review Press, 2014), 115.
67. "National Labor Relations Act," National Labor Relations Board website, https://www.nlrb.gov/how-we-work/national-labor-relations-act (accessed February 24, 2020). The National Labor Relations Act became law in 1935.
68. Bell, *Ritual Theory*, 221.
69. Brinkley, *Wheels for the World*, 390. See also Bates, *The Making of Black Detroit in the Age of Henry Ford*, 159–63.
70. Brinkley, *Wheels for the World*, 429.
71. Meier and Rudwick, *Black Detroit and the Rise of the UAW*, 39–40.
72. Brinkley, *Wheels for the World*, 430.
73. Dillard, *Faith in the City*, 7.

74. It took longer to include blacks in the leadership of most labor unions.
75. Brueggemann, "The Power and Collapse of Paternalism," 225.
76. Jonathan M. Metzl, *Dying of Whiteness: How the Politics of Racial Resentment is Killing America's Heartland* (New York: Basic, 2019), 11.
77. Metzl, *Dying of Whiteness*, 4.
78. Metzl, *Dying of Whiteness*, 4.
79. We have intentionally not specified black workers or white workers; the religion of white rage can lead to death for either group because of the worker-friendly policies that do not get enacted for the sake of white rage.

FOUR / American (Un)Civil Religion, the Defense of the White Worker, and Responses to NFL Protests

1. Jonathan Intravia, Alex Piquero, and Nicole Leeper Piquero, "The Racial Divide Surrounding United States of America National Anthem Protest in the National Football League," *Deviant Behavior* 39, no. 8 (2018), 1058–68.
2. Robert Bellah, "Civil Religion in America," *Dædalus* 96, no. 1 (1967), 1–21.
3. Bellah, "Civil Religion in America."
4. Bellah, "Civil Religion in America."
5. Bellah, "Civil Religion in America."
6. Jürgen Heideking, "The Federal Processions of 1788 and the Origins of American Civil Religion," *Soundings: An Interdisciplinary Journal* 77, no. 3/4 (1994), 367–87.
7. Bellah, "Civil Religion in America."
8. Bellah, "Civil Religion in America."
9. Jermaine M. McDonald, "A Fourth Time of Trial: Towards an Implicit and Inclusive American Civil Religion." *Implicit Religion* 16, no. 1 (2013), 47–64.
10. Charles H. Long, *Significations: Signs, Symbols, and Images in the Interpretation of Religion* (Aurora, CO: Davies Group, [1986] 1999), 7.
11. Long, *Significations*, 7.
12. Lori Latrice Martin, Hayward Derrick Horton, Cedric Herring, Verna M. Keith, and Melvin Thomas (eds.), *Color Struck: How Race and Complexion Matter in the "Color-Blind" Era* (Rotterdam: Sense, 2017).
13. Tunji Adeyinka, "The Role of Patriotism in Sports Sponsorship," *Journal of Sponsorship* 4, no. 2 (2011), 155–62.
14. Long, *Significations*, 163.
15. Matteo Bortolini, "The Trap of Intellectual Success: Robert N. Bellah, the American Civil Religion Debate, and the Sociology of Knowledge," *Theory and Society* 41, no. 2 (2012), 187–210; Phillip E. Hammond, Amanda Porterfield, James G. Moseley, and Jonathan D. Sarna, "Forum: American Civil Religion Revisited," *Religion and American Culture: A Journal of Interpretation* 4, no. 1 (1994), 1–23.
16. Hortense Spillers, "Martin Luther King, Jr. and America's Civil Religion," *Nanzan Review of American Studies* 29 (2007), 44.

17. Grace Y. Kao and Jerome E. Copulsky, "The Pledge of Allegiance and the Meanings and Limits of Civil Religion," *Journal of the American Academy of Religion* 75, no. 1 (2007), 121–49.
18. George Docherty, "Under God," sermon preached February 7, 1954, transcript available at http://www.christianheritagemins.org/articles/UNDER%20GOD.pdf (accessed February 24, 2020).
19. Docherty, "Under God."
20. Docherty, "Under God."
21. Docherty, "Under God."
22. Docherty, "Under God."
23. Kao and Copulsky, "The Pledge of Allegiance," 125.
24. Dylan Weller, "Godless Patriots: Towards a New American Civil Religion," *Polity* 45, no. 3 (2013), 372–92.
25. John Kitch, "Football as American Civic Religion," *Law and Liberty*, February 2, 2018, http://www.libertylawsite.org/2018/02/02/football-as-american-civic-religion (accessed February 25, 2020).
26. Rick Porter, "The 100 Highest-Rated TV Programs of 2017: 60% Sports, 40% Everything Else," *TV by the Numbers*, December 28, 2017, https://tvbythenumbers.zap2it.com/more-tv-news/the-100-highest-rated-tv-programs-of-2017-60-sports-40-everything-else (accessed February 25, 2020).
27. Porter, "The 100 Highest-Rated TV Programs of 2017."
28. Michael L. Butterworth, "Ritual in the 'Church of Baseball': Suppressing the Discourse of Democracy after 9/11," *Communication and Critical/Cultural Studies* 2, no. 2 (2005), 107–29.
29. Michael L. Butterworth and Stormi D. Moskal, "American Football, Flags, and 'Fun': The Bell Helicopter Armed Forces Bowl and the Rhetorical Production of Militarism," *Communication, Culture & Critique* 2, no. 4 (2009), 413.
30. Butterworth and Moskal, "American Football, Flags, and 'Fun,'" 414.
31. Derek Thompson, "Which Sports Have the Whitest/Richest/Oldest Fans?" *The Atlantic*, February 10, 2014, https://www.theatlantic.com/business/archive/2014/02/which-sports-have-the-whitest-richest-oldest-fans/283626 (accessed March 12, 2020).
32. Jonathan Berr, "NFL's Tangled Ties with National Anthem Don't Run Deep," CBS News, May 28, 2018, https://www.cbsnews.com/news/the-nfls-tangled-ties-with-the-national-anthem-dont-run-deep (accessed February 25, 2020).
33. Brian Britt, "Taking a Knee as Critical Civil Religion," University of Chicago Divinity School, January 5, 2017, https://divinity.uchicago.edu/sightings/taking-knee-critical-civil-religion (accessed February 25, 2020); Laura Rene McNeal, "From Hoodies to Kneeling During the National Anthem: The Colin Kaepernick Effect and Its Implications for K-12 Sports," *Louisiana Law Review* 78, no. 1 (2017), 146–96.
34. Samuel G. Freedman, "When White Sports Fans Turn on Black Athletes," *The Guardian*, October 5, 2017, https://www.theguardian.com/commentisfree/2017/

oct/05/white-sports-fans-nfl-black-athletes-race-protest (accessed February 25, 2020).

35. Carole Lynn Stewart, "Civil Religion, Civil Society, and the Performative Life and Work of W. .E. B. Du Bois," *Journal of Religion* 88, no. 3 (2008), 322.
36. Eric Woodrum and Arnold Bell, "Race, Politics, and Religion in Civil Religion Among Blacks," *Sociological Analysis* 49, no. 4 (1989), 353–67.
37. W. E. B. Du Bois, *The Souls of Black Folk* (Chicago: A. C. McClurg, 1903); Micah E. Johnson, "The Paradox of Black Patriotism: Double Consciousness," *Ethnic and Racial Studies* 41, no. 11 (2018), 1971–89; Stewart, "Civil Religion, Civil Society, and the Performative Life and Work of W. E. B. Du Bois."
38. Craig A. Forney, *The Holy Trinity of American Sport: Civil Religion in Football, Baseball, and Basketball* (Macon, GA: Mercer University Press, 2007); Tamir Sorek and Robert G. White, "American Football and National Pride: Racial Differences," *Social Science Research* 58 (2016), 266–78; Michael Stein, "Cult and Sport: The Case of Big Red," *Mid-American Review of Sociology* 2, no. 2 (1977), 29–42.

FIVE / The Color of Belief: Black Social Christianity, White Evangelicalism, and Redbaiting the Religious Culture of the CIO in the Postwar South

1. See Tona J. Hangen, *Redeeming the Dial: Radio, Religion, and Popular Culture in America* (Chapel Hill: University of North Carolina Press, 2002). For the Knoxville episode, see Elizabeth Fones-Wolf and Ken Fones-Wolf, "'Termites in the Temple': Fundamentalism and Anti-Liberal Politics in the Post-World War II South," *Religion and American Culture* 28, no. 2 (2018), 167–205.
2. Memo about Klan public meeting, Knoxville, TN, May 18, 1946 (nine-page typescript), Stetson Kennedy Papers, reel 1, New York Public Library.
3. Michael K. Honey, *Southern Labor and Black Civil Rights: Organizing Memphis Workers* (Urbana: University of Illinois Press, 1993); Jarod H. Roll, *Spirit of Rebellion: Labor and Religion in the New Cotton South* (Urbana: University of Illinois Press, 2010); Alison Collis Greene, *No Depression in Heaven: The Great Depression, the New Deal, and the Transformation of Religion in the Delta* (New York: Oxford University Press, 2016).
4. John Egerton, *Speak Now Against the Day: The Generation before the Civil Rights Movement in the South* (Chapel Hill: University of North Carolina Press, 1994), 185–97; Mark Fannin, *Labor's Promised Land: Radical Visions of Gender, Race, and Religion in the South* (Knoxville: University of Tennessee Press, 2003) 254–309; Paul Harvey, *Freedom's Coming: Religious Culture and the Shaping of the South from the Civil War through the Civil Rights Era* (Chapel Hill: University of North Carolina Press, 2005).
5. Elizabeth Fones-Wolf and Ken Fones-Wolf, "Sanctifying the Southern Organizing Campaign: Protestant Activists in the CIO's Operation Dixie," *Labor: Studies in Working Class History* 6, no. 1 (2009), 6–7.

6. Robert H. Zieger, *The CIO, 1935-1955* (Chapel Hill: University of North Carolina Press, 1995), 124.
7. Jack R. McMichael, "The New Social Climate in the South," *Social Questions Bulletin*, May 1945, 4-5; William Holmes Borders, "The Spiritual and Economic Basis for Democracy in the South," *Christian Frontiers*, April 1947, 114-20; "Welcome Labor Unions!" *Christian Frontiers*, November 1946, 277-8.
8. This biblical passage was perhaps the favorite of anti-union employers and their religiously inclined supporters, especially conservative evangelical ministers. See Elizabeth Fones-Wolf and Ken Fones-Wolf, *Struggle for the Soul of the Postwar South: White Evangelical Protestants and Operation Dixie* (Urbana: University of Illinois Press, 2015), ch. 4.
9. Barbara Dianne Savage, *Your Spirits Walk beside Us: The Politics of Black Religion* (Cambridge, MA: Belknap Press, 2008); Bettye Collier-Thomas, *Jesus, Jobs, and Justice: African American Women and Religion* (New York: Alfred A. Knopf, 2010); Gary Dorrien, *The New Abolition: W. E. B. Du Bois and the Black Social Gospel* (New Haven, CT: Yale University Press, 2015).
10. John Hayes, *Hard, Hard Religion: Interracial Faith in the Poor South* (Chapel Hill: University of North Carolina Press, 2017), 195.
11. Wayne Flynt, "Religion for the Blues: Evangelicalism, Poor Whites, and the Great Depression," *Journal of Southern History* 71, no. 1 (2005), 11-12.
12. David Burgess, "The Fellowship of Southern Churchmen: Its History and Promise," *Prophetic Religion*, Spring 1953, 3-11; Anthony P. Dunbar, *Against the Grain: Southern Radicals and Prophets, 1929-1959* (Charlottesville: University Press of Virginia, 1981), 59-61, 74-5.
13. Dunbar, *Against the Grain*, 28-33; Fones-Wolf and Fones-Wolf, *Struggle for the Soul of the Postwar South*, 114-28. For books treating Taylor's disciples, see Robert F. Martin, *Howard Kester and the Struggle for Social Justice in the South, 1904-77* (Charlottesville: University Press of Virginia, 1991); James J. Lorence, *A Hard Journey: The Life of Don West* (Urbana: University of Illinois Press, 2007); Erik S. Gellman and Jarod Roll, *Gospel of the Working Class: Labor's Southern Prophets in New Deal America* (Urbana: University of Illinois Press, 2011).
14. Horace Huntley and David Montgomery (eds.), *Black Workers' Struggle for Equality in Birmingham* (Urbana: University of Illinois Press, 2004), 5-12; Honey, *Southern Labor and Black Civil Rights*, 117-40.
15. Zieger, *The CIO*, 74-8.
16. Spicer quoted in Carletta A. Bush, "Faith, Power, and Conflict: Miner Preachers and the United Mine Workers of America in the Harlan County Mine Wars, 1931-1939," PhD dissertation, West Virginia University, 2006, 205.
17. Frank Bonds interview with Patty McDonald, March 21, 1979, Samford University Oral History Collection, Samford University, Birmingham, AL.
18. Eula McGill interview with Jacquelyn Hall, February 3, 1976, Southern Oral History Collection, University of North Carolina, Chapel Hill.

19. Henry Wade interview with Douglas Flamming, July 12, 1985, Crown Oral History Project, Special Collections, Virginia Polytechnic Institute and State University, Blacksburg.
20. Earl Lewis, *In Their Own Interests: Race, Class, and Power in Twentieth-Century Norfolk, Virginia* (Berkeley: University of California Press, 1991), 152.
21. Morris Benson interview with Peggy Hamrick, June 8, 1984, Working Lives Oral History Project, University of Alabama, available at http://purl.lib.ua.edu/54289 (accessed February 25, 2020).
22. Earl Brown quoted in William H. Chafe et al. (eds.), *Remembering Jim Crow: African Americans Tell about Life in the Segregated South* (New York: New Press, 2001), 272.
23. Lucy Randolph Mason, "The CIO and the Negro in the South," *Journal of Negro Education* 14, no. 4 (1945), 552–61.
24. Wayne Flynt, *Alabama Baptists: Southern Baptists in the Heart of Dixie* (Tuscaloosa: University of Alabama Press, 1998), 361–3.
25. Flynt, *Alabama Baptists*, 373–6; Oral History Memoir of Acker C. Miller, August 5, 1971, Baylor University Institute of Oral History, Waco, TX.
26. Greene, *No Depression in Heaven*, 116.
27. D. Witherspoon Dodge, *Southern Rebel in Reverse: The Autobiography of an Idol-Shaker* (New York: American Press, 1961).
28. Fones-Wolf and Fones-Wolf, *Struggle for the Soul of the Postwar South*, 132–4.
29. *Proceedings of the Fifty-Fourth Annual Session of the National Baptist Convention* (1934), 152–3.
30. "Address of L. K. Williams," *Proceedings of the Fifty-Seventh Annual Session of the National Baptist Convention* (1937), 258–9.
31. *Proceedings of the Fifty-Sixth Annual Session of the National Baptist Convention* (1936), 330, 339.
32. Gary Dorrien, *The New Abolition: W. E. B. Du Bois and the Black Social Gospel* (New Haven, CT: Yale University Press, 2015), 393.
33. Jessie Grace interview with Cliff Kuhn, July 16, 1984, Working Lives Oral History Project.
34. Samuel Andrews interview with Peggy Hamrick, July 17, 1984, Working Lives Oral History Project.
35. Lucy Randolph Mason, "Memo Memphis, April 25, 1941," Operation Dixie Records, reel 64, Rare Book, Manuscript, and Special Collections Library, Duke University, Durham, NC.
36. Barry Hankins, *God's Rascal: J. Frank Norris and the Beginnings of Southern Fundamentalism* (Lexington: University Press of Kentucky), 41–3; Matthew Avery Sutton, *American Apocalypse: A History of Modern Evangelicalism* (Cambridge, MA: Belknap Press, 2014), ch. 8; Robert Fuller, *Naming the Antichrist: The History of an American Obsession* (New York: Oxford University Press, 1995), ch. 5; Greene, *No Depression in Heaven*, ch. 5.
37. Matthew Avery Sutton, "Was FDR the Antichrist? The Birth of Fundamentalist Antiliberalism in a Global Age," *Journal of American History* 98, no. 4 (2012), 1052–74.

38. Fuller, *Naming the Antichrist*, 153.
39. Fones-Wolf and Fones-Wolf, "Termites in the Temple," 177.
40. "Johnston, Parson Jack" file, Stetson Kennedy Papers, reel 2, New York Public Library; Fones-Wolf and Fones-Wolf, *Struggle for the Soul of the Postwar South*, 49.
41. Stetson Kennedy, *Southern Exposure* (Garden City, NY: Doubleday, 1946), 232–8.
42. Davis reminiscence in Huntley and Montgomery (eds.), *Black Workers' Struggle for Equality in Birmingham*, 116.
43. Earl Brown quoted in Chafe et al. (eds.), *Remembering Jim Crow*, 265, 268; Leon Alexander interview with Peggy Hamrick, July 8, 1984, Working Lives Oral History Project.
44. Honey, *Southern Labor and Black Civil Rights*, 140.
45. *Proceedings of the Fifty-Ninth Annual Session of the National Baptist Convention* (1939), 72.
46. *Georgia Baptist*, April 1, 1939, 5.
47. Excellent overviews of the situation are found in Zieger, *The CIO*, 90–110; and Melvyn Dubofsky, *The State and Labor in Modern America* (Chapel Hill: University of North Carolina Press, 1994), 137–67.
48. The standard work is: Nelson Lichtenstein, *Labor's War at Home: The CIO in World War II* (New York: Cambridge University Press, 1982).
49. William P. Jones, *The March on Washington: Jobs, Freedom, and the Forgotten History of Civil Rights* (New York: W. W. Norton, 2013), 27–40.
50. *Proceedings of the Sixty-First Annual Session of the National Baptist Convention* (1941), 289 (Burroughs quote); *Proceedings of the Sixty-Second Annual Session of the National Baptist Convention* (1942), 58 (Jemison statement).
51. *Atlanta Daily World*, April 25, 1942, 2.
52. William Stuart Nelson, "The Christian Imperative and Race Relations," *AME Zion Quarterly Review* 54, no. 2 (1944), 79.
53. Michael Keith Honey, *Black Workers Remember: An Oral History of Segregation, Unionism, and the Freedom Struggle* (Berkeley: University of California Press, 1999), 65–80 (quote at 71).
54. Honey, *Black Workers Remember*, 97.
55. Huntley and Montgomery (eds.), *Black Workers' Struggle for Equality in Birmingham*, 35–6.
56. Huntley and Montgomery (eds.), *Black Workers' Struggle for Equality in Birmingham*, 213–23.
57. Alexander interview, July 8, 1984; Benson interview, June 8, 1984.
58. John Garner interview with Cliff Kuhn, July 20, 1984, Working Lives Oral History Project.
59. Robert Rodgers Korstad, *Civil Rights Unionism: Tobacco Workers and the Struggle for Democracy in the Mid-Twentieth-Century South* (Chapel Hill: University of North Carolina Press, 2003).
60. Huntley and Montgomery (eds.), *Black Workers' Struggle for Equality in Birmingham*, 9; Rosemary Feurer, *Radical Unionism in the Midwest, 1900–1950* (Urbana: University of Illinois Press, 2006), 146–51.

61. James T. Sparrow, *Warfare State: World War II Americans and the Age of Big Government* (New York: Oxford University Press, 2011), p. 58. For more on the Double V, see also Neil A. Wynn, *The African American Experience During World War II* (Lanham, MD: Rowman & Littlefield, 2010).
62. Danielle L. McGuire, *At the Dark End of the Street: Black Women, Rape, and Resistance—a New History of the Civil Rights Movement from Rosa Parks to the Rise of Black Power* (New York: Alfred A. Knopf, 2010), 28.
63. Robert H. Zieger, *For Jobs and Freedom: Race and Labor in America since 1865* (Lexington: University Press of Kentucky, 2007), 132.
64. McGuire, *At the Dark End of the Street*, 26–7.
65. Sparrow, *Warfare State*, 97–99, quote from the U.S. Employment Service memo, dated August 18, 1942, at 99. For additional information on the Eleanor Clubs, see Bryant Simon, *A Fabric of Defeat: The Politics of South Carolina Millhands, 1910–1948* (Chapel Hill: University of North Carolina Press, 1998), 219, 224.
66. *Baltimore Afro-American*, January 29, 1944, 3. See also Michael Perman, *Pursuit of Unity: A Political History of the American South* (Chapel Hill: University of North Carolina Press, 2009), 255–7.
67. Sparrow, *Warfare State*, 98; *Atlanta Daily World*, November 30, 1944, 1.
68. *Atlanta Daily World*, June 22, 1945, 1.
69. *Atlanta Daily World*, July 5, 1951 (on Smith); Andrew M. Manis, "'City Mothers': Dorothy Tilly, Georgia Methodist Women, and Black Civil Rights," in Glenn Feldman (ed.), *Politics and Religion in the White South* (Lexington: University Press of Kentucky, 2005), 125–56; Jacquelyn Dowd Hall, *Revolt against Chivalry: Jessie Daniel Ames and the Women's Campaign against Lynching* (New York: Columbia University Press, 1979).
70. Fones-Wolf and Fones-Wolf, *Struggle for the Soul of the Postwar South*, 52, 185.
71. Fones-Wolf and Fones-Wolf, *Struggle for the Soul of the Postwar South*, 107–8.
72. John S. Nurser, *For All Peoples and All Nations: The Ecumenical Church and Human Rights* (Washington, DC, Georgetown University Press, 2005), 12, 147.
73. Jane Dailey, "The Theology of Unionism and Antiunionism," *Labor: Studies in Working-Class History* 14, no. 1 (2017), 83–5.
74. Nurser, *For All Peoples and All Nations*, 147. For one such attack on FCC spokespersons, see Fones-Wolf and Fones-Wolf, "Termites in the Temple," 181.
75. "Lynchings, Sept. 2, 1945 (V-J Day) thru September, 1946," typescript memo, Southern Conference for Human Welfare Collection, Box 1, folder 10, Archives and Special Collections, Robert Woodruff Library, Atlanta University Center, Atlanta, GA.
76. Press release, undated, SCHW Collection, Box 3, folder 1.
77. Quote from Kevin M. Kruse, *White Flight: Atlanta and the Making of Modern Conservatism* (Princeton, NJ: Princeton University Press, 2005), 34.
78. Letter from a group of ministers to Rev. Clifton J. Allen, February 17, 1945, Clifton J. Allen Papers, Box 49, folder 35, Southern Baptist Historical Library and Archives, Nashville, Tennessee. For more on the Christian Americans, see Kennedy, *Southern Exposure*, 251–5.

79. Memo of article from *Greenville Piedmont*, November 19, 1945, Stetson Kennedy Papers, reel 1; Kruse, *White Flight*, 34.
80. *Religious Herald* (Richmond, VA), May 30, 1946, 3; letter to Rev. Allen, February 17, 1945, Clifton J. Allen Papers.
81. *The Defender* (Wichita, KS), November 1946, 35; *Pentecostal Evangel* (Springfield, MO), June 16, 1945, 8, June 29, 1945, 16, January 19, 1946, 8.
82. Carl McIntire, "Private Enterprise in the Scriptures," *Sword of the Lord*, September 21, 1945, 1, 4; Carl McIntire, "The Modernist-Communist Threat to American Liberties," *Sword of the Lord*, September 14, 1945, 1, 6.
83. Joel A. Carpenter, *Revive Us Again: The Reawakening of American Fundamentalism* (New York: Oxford University Press, 1997), 153.
84. *United Evangelical Action*, March 15, 1946, 12.
85. *Evangelicals Move Forward for Christ*, pamphlet published in Indianapolis, National Association of Evangelicals Records, Box 99, Billy Graham Center, Wheaton College, Wheaton, IL.
86. "The Story behind the Race Conflicts," *United Evangelical Action*, October 25, 1943, 3.
87. There is an immense literature on the CIO's Operation Dixie and its failure to navigate the multiple goals and expectations of the Southern working class. See Egerton, *Speak Now against the Day*, 185–97.
88. Fones-Wolf and Fones-Wolf, *Struggle for the Soul of the Postwar South*, 93–104. See also Carpenter, *Revive Us Again*, 161–74; Darren Dochuk, *From Bible Belt to Sunbelt: Plain-Folk Religion, Grassroots Politics, and the Rise of Evangelical Conservatism* (New York: W. W. Norton, 2011), 53–66.
89. *Militant Truth*, special labor edition (no date, ca. 1946), Southern Labor Archives, Georgia State University, Atlanta; Stetson Kennedy, "Preachers of Disunity," and "Johnston, Parson Jack" file, unpublished typescripts, ca. 1947, Stetson Kennedy Papers, reel 2.
90. Vernon W. Patterson, "Where Does the 'Social Gospel' Road End," *Sword of the Lord*, July 25, 1947, 2.
91. Fones-Wolf and Fones-Wolf, *Struggle for the Soul of the Postwar South*, chapter 4.
92. *Pentecostal Evangel*, August 2, 1947, 12, November 1, 1947, 10.
93. *Sword of the Lord*, June 20, 1947, 4.
94. Glenwood Blackmore, "What's Wrong with FEPC?" *United Evangelical Action*, September 15, 1949, 5–6.
95. See "Asks Webber Surrender Credentials," *Zion's Herald*, June 19, 1946, 588; "Labor Chaplain," *Zion's Herald*, July 24, 1946, 712; "Chaplain to Labor Causes Dispute," *Zion's Herald*, September 3, 1947, 848.
96. *Wesleyan Christian Advocate*, August 19, 1948, 7, November 8, 1946, 2, December 20, 1946, 2.
97. Fones-Wolf and Fones-Wolf, *Struggle for the Soul of the Postwar South*, 107.
98. J. E. Flow, "The Federal Council and Race Segregation," *Southern Presbyterian Journal*, May 15, 1946, 9–10.
99. *Religious Herald*, August 15, 1946, 11.

100. This is the argument we made in our book *Struggle for the Soul of the Postwar South*, based on archival research in the records of those active in and against the CIO's Southern Organizing Campaign as well as reading more than 200 oral histories of Southern white workers. Since that book was published, we have been reading oral histories of African American workers and are convinced that they shared many of the same religious beliefs.
101. "The Monroe Incident," *Wesleyan Christian Advocate*, August 9, 1946, 6.
102. "Southern Baptists Study Race Relations," *Religious Herald*, September 1, 1949, 15.
103. Gilbert James, "What's Right with FEPC?" *United Evangelical Action*, September 15, 1949, 3–4.
104. Jane Dailey, "Sex, Segregation, and the Sacred after Brown," *Journal of American History* 91, no. 1 (2004), 119–44.

SIX / Constitutional Whiteness: Class, Narcissism, and the Source of White Rage

1. Eric Black, *Our Constitution: The Myth That Binds Us* (Boulder, CO: Westview Press, 1988), x.
2. Keri Leigh Merritt, *Masterless Men: Poor Whites and Slavery in the Antebellum South* (Cambridge, England: Cambridge University Press, 2017), 46.
3. Jamie L. Bronstein, *Two Nations, Indivisible: A History of Inequality in America* (Santa Barbara, CA: Praeger, 2016), 8.
4. Black, *Our Constitution*, x.
5. Black, *Our Constitution*, xii.
6. Black, *Our Constitution*, xiii.
7. Bronstein, *Two Nations*, 3.
8. Bronstein, *Two Nations*, 3.
9. Herbert J. Gans, "Race as Class," *Contexts* 4, no. 4 (2005), 18.
10. Ian Haney López, *White by Law: The Legal Construction of Race*, 2nd edn. (New York: New York University Press, 2006), 74.
11. Pierre Bourdieu, *Distinction: A Social Critique of the Judgement of Taste*, trans. Richard Nice (Cambridge, MA: Harvard University Press, 1984), 101.
12. Pierre Bourdieu, *The Logic of Practice*, trans. Richard Nice (Stanford, CA: Stanford University Press, 1990).
13. David L. Swartz, "Bridging the Study of Culture and Religion: Pierre Bourdieu's Political Economy of Symbolic Power," *Sociology of Religion* 57, no. 1 (1996), 72.
14. Hugh Urban, "Sacred Capital: Pierre Bourdieu and the Study of Religion," *Method & Theory in the Study of Religion* 15, no. 4 (2003), 358.
15. Merritt, *Masterless Men*, 38–9.
16. Hannah Arendt, *The Human Condition*, 2nd edn. (Chicago: University of Chicago Press, 1998), 22.
17. Arendt, *The Human Condition*, 7.
18. Arendt, *The Human Condition*, 84, 134.

19. Arendt, *The Human Condition*, 139–51.
20. Arendt, *The Human Condition*, 30.
21. Arendt, *The Human Condition*, 7.
22. Bronstein, *Two Nations*, 4.
23. Black, *Our Constitution*, 3.
24. Black, *Our Constitution*, 3–4.
25. Black, *Our Constitution*, 4.
26. Black, *Our Constitution*, 8.
27. Black, *Our Constitution*, 8.
28. Black, *Our Constitution*, 21.
29. Black, *Our Constitution*, 22.
30. Carol Anderson, *White Rage: The Unspoken Truth of Our Racial Divide*, paperback edn. (New York: Bloomsbury, 2017), 3–4.
31. Veronica T. Watson, *The Souls of White Folk: African American Writers Theorize Whiteness* (Jackson: University Press of Mississippi, 2013), 59.
32. Watson, *The Souls of White Folk*, 58–59.
33. Heinz Kohut, "Forms and Transitions of Narcissism," *Journal of the American Psychoanalytic Association* 14, no. 2 (1966), 246.
34. Kohut, "Forms and Transitions of Narcissism," 249.
35. Cheryl E. Matias, *Feeling White: Whiteness, Emotionality, and Education* (Rotterdam: Sense, 2016), 70–1.
36. C. C. Bell, "Racism: A Symptom of the Narcissistic Personality Disorder," *Journal of the National Medical Association* 72, no. 7 (1980): 662.
37. Bell, "Racism," 662.
38. Anderson, *White Rage*.
39. Kelly Brown Douglas, *Stand Your Ground: Black Bodies and the Justice of God* (Maryknoll, NY: Orbis, 2015), 5.
40. Douglas, *Stand Your Ground*, 44.
41. Douglas, *Stand Your Ground*, 53–4.
42. Douglas, *Stand Your Ground*, 68–9.
43. Douglas, *Stand Your Ground*, 116–32.

SEVEN / KKK Christology: A Brief on White Class Insecurity

1. Quentin Tarantino (dir.), *The Hateful Eight* (Los Angeles: Visiona Romantica, 2015).
2. DeNeen L. Brown, "The Preacher Who Used Christianity to Revive the Klan," *Washington Post*, April 10, 2018, https://www.washingtonpost.com/news/retropolis/wp/2018/04/08/the-preacher-who-used-christianity-to-revive-the-ku-klux-klan (accessed February 26, 2020).
3. Keenan Ivory Wayans (dir.), *I'm Gonna Git You Sucka* (Los Angeles: Ivory Way Productions, 1988).
4. Daryl Johnson, "Hate in God's Name: Religious Extremism and Its Relation to Violent Conflict," Southern Poverty Law Center, September 25, 2017, https://

www.splcenter.org/20170925/hate-god's-name (accessed February 26, 2020). "White supremacists believe mainstream religions, including Christian denominations and their institutions, have fallen astray from God and are under the control and influence of Satan. As a result, white supremacists interpret scriptures and spiritual parables through the lens of racial discrimination and hate. In this way, they can justify their beliefs (which are vile and deplorable) as good, moral and responsible."

5. William Ronald Jones, *Is God a White Racist?: A Preamble to Black Theology* (Garden City, NY: Anchor Press, 1973).
6. Anthony B. Pinn, "Looking like Me?: Jesus Images, Christology, and the Limitations of Theological Blackness," in George Yancy (ed.), *Christology and Whiteness: What Would Jesus Do?* (Abingdon, England: Routledge, 2012), 173. Kindle.
7. Pinn, "Looking like Me?" 173.
8. "Colored" in this case will include the different racialized Christs as well as sexually and gender-flexible Christs. See James H. Cone, *A Black Theology of Liberation* (Philadelphia: Lippincott, 1970); Dolores S. Williams, *Sisters in the Wilderness: The Challenge of Womanist God-Talk*, 20th Anniversary Edition (Maryknoll, NY: Orbis, 2013); Mercy Amba Oduyoye. *Introducing African Women's Theology* (Cleveland: Pilgrim Press, 2001); Maryanne Stevens (ed.), *Reconstructing the Christ Symbol: Essays in Feminist Christology* (Eugene, OR: Wipf & Stock, [1993] 2004); Ellen K. Wondra, *Humanity Has Been a Holy Thing: Toward a Contemporary Feminist Christology* (Lanham, MD, University Press of America, 1994); Viki Soady, review of Benjamin Valentin (ed.), *In Our Own Voices: Latino/a Renditions of Theology*, Journal for Peace and Justice Studies 25, no. 2 (2015), 193–5; Alicia Vargas. "The Construction of Latina Christology: An Invitation to Dialogue," *Currents in Theology and Mission* 34, no. 4 (2007), 271; Thomas Bohache, "Embodiment as Incarnation: An Incipient Queer Christology," *Theology & Sexuality* 10, no. 1 (2003), 9–29; Patrick S. Cheng, *Radical Love: An Introduction to Queer Theology* (New York: Seabury, 2011); Mary Elise Lowe, "Gay, Lesbian, and Queer Theologies: Origins, Contributions, and Challenges," *Dialog* 48, no. 1 (2009), 49–61; Patrick S. Cheng, *From Sin to Amazing Grace: Discovering the Queer Christ* (New York: Seabury, 2012); José M. de Mesa, "Making Salvation Concrete and Jesus Real: Trends in Asian Christology," *Exchange* 30, no. 1 (2001), 1–17; Peter C. Phan, "Jesus the Christ with an Asian Face," *Theological Studies* 57, no. 3 (1996), 399–430.
9. Jones, *Is God a White Racist?*; Yancy (ed.), *Christology and Whiteness*. George Yancy provides extremely salient points in that book that work to address this issue. He essentially asks: How do white Christians deal with the problem of their whiteness—white supremacy—in the context of a Christian God who is said to love all?
10. Pinn, "Looking Like Me?" 176.
11. Nancy Isenberg, *White Trash: The 400-Year Untold History of Class in America* (New York: Penguin, 2017), 75–6.
12. Isenberg, *White Trash*, 75–6.

13. Isenberg, *White Trash*, 127.
14. Isenberg, *White Trash*, 75–6. Nancy Isenberg argues that in the early colonies through the antebellum period there was a need for lower-class whites. Poor whites were counted among the growing population of the budding U.S. colonies; however, their presence was not valued. Unproductive poor whites were seen as waste people. They did not have the same value as enslaved Africans. This point is significant where discussed in context of land acquisition. A poor white person who finds land (even if there are squatters) represents land that is a part of U.S. land holdings and no longer under the control of the Natives.
15. David W. Griffith (dir.), *Birth of a Nation* (Thousand Oaks, CA, Epoch Producing Corporation, 1915). The film was also very important for the development of the second iteration of the KKK. This picture was wildly popular throughout the South, but what gave it (and the organization) the "bump" it needed was its endorsement by President Woodrow Wilson, who had a private showing in the White House and afterwards claimed the movie was "written with lightning."
16. "Ku Klux Klan: The Invisible Empire," *CBS Reports*, September 21, 1965, available at https://www.c-span.org/video/?433239-1/ku-klux-klan (accessed March 12, 2020). "What made the Ku Klux Klan so wildly successful in the early 1920s was an aggressive, state-of-the-art sales approach to recruitment . . . Far from reaching commercialization and the technology it brought such as radio, the Klan's system was entirely up-to-date, even pioneering, in its methods of selling."
17. Anthony B. Pinn, *Terror and Triumph: The Nature of Black Religion* (Minneapolis: Fortress Press, 2003), 48, 72. Rituals or reference for Pinn are the auction block and the lynching post. During this historical period, African Americans were lynched at the whim of the Klan's members in order to maintain Southern traditions and norms. Lynching represented the ultimate power of the Klan, meaning, not only did the Klan endorse and participate in the murder of hundreds of African Americans during its second iteration, but also their power was more greatly shown in the fact that very little was done to legally rectify the problem.
18. Isenberg. *White Trash*, 131.
19. Linda Gordon, *The Second Coming of the KKK: The Ku Klux Klan of the 1920s and the American Political Tradition* (New York: Liveright, 2017), 67.
20. Part of the mission of the KKK was to maintain (and eventually widen) the gap between poor whites and poor blacks through fraternal nepotism. Through the organization the KKK offered white men the opportunity not just to regain the glory of whiteness but as well the social comfort of a community that would reinforce that notion. As a member of the KKK, upward social, economic and political mobility was not immediate and widespread, instead the KKK as a community were able to support members socially (community development), economically (development of business and other nepotistic opportunities that would not be afforded to non-members), and politically (election of judges and other state officials who would exact policies for the benefit of white men).

21. Isenberg, *White Trash*, 135–7, Kindle. Class insecurity in the context of American white men deals directly with the effort to create a lower class of whites that most white American men occupied since the early colonial period of the U.S.
22. Isenberg, *White Trash*, 75–6, Kindle. To explain, in the early history of the American colonies the dregs of English society were some of the first to occupy the land. Many of these poor souls came to the continental U.S. as slaves themselves or indentured servants. It must be noted that many of these poor whites came to the colonies on the promise that they would work off the debt accrued during their migration. According to Isenberg the term "waste land" only meant that the land was not being used in the way "God intended." Instead of being useful as farm land or property that could earn money, waste land was lands that were untilled and remained stagnant in their most natural state. Similarly, "waste people" were individuals who did not work or earn in a way that benefited society and the church, wallowing in the deadly sin of sloth. Waste people, like waste lands, needed to be made useful to both the government and the church. Individuals who were considered waste people in the eyes of the laity and government (which went hand-in-hand) were on the lowest rung of society, lower even than the Native Americans and enslaved Africans. Native Americans were at least indigenous to the land, thus useful. And Africans were the captive workforce, again useful to the church and the representative government.
23. Ibram X. Kendi, *Stamped from the Beginning: The Definitive History of Racist Ideas in America* (New York: Bodley Head, 2017), 39–43, Kindle. According to Kendi there were two major threats brought about by the emancipation of enslaved Africans—miscegenation and black progress, particularly through employment opportunities.
24. Isenberg, *White Trash*, 56–60, Kindle.
25. The knee-jerk reaction many might feel upon reading this sentence/paragraph is very understandable. How could a person of African descent consider comparing the redemptive Black Christ to the hate-filled pseudo-philosophy of the KKK? Easy. On Sunday morning they will both call on Jesus' name: this is an inescapable truth that must be examined.
26. This is the very reason for the lighting/burning of Christian crosses.
27. Gordon, *The Second Coming of the KKK*, 42.
28. Jones, *Is God a White Racist?*
29. Cone, *A Black Theology of Liberation*.
30. Adam Bhala Lough (dir.), *Alt-Right: The Age of Rage* (Los Angeles: Alldayeveryday, 2018). There are particular individuals who are seen as leaders of the white supremacy alt-right movement. Individuals such as Richard Spencer, Jared Taylor and Milo Yiannopoulos and groups like the Proud Boys and Breitbart have rebranded white supremacy to make it more palatable for the younger generation.

EIGHT / Black People and White Mormon Rage: Examining Race, Religion, and Politics in Zion

1. Steve Hendrix and Michael E. Miller, "'Let's Get This Party Started': New Zealand Shooting Suspect Narrated His Chilling Rampage," *Washington Post*, March 15, 2019, https://www.washingtonpost.com/local/lets-get-this-party-started-new-zealand-gunman-narrated-his-chilling-rampage/2019/03/15/fb3db352-4748-11e9-90f0-0ccfeec87a61_story.html (accessed February 27, 2020).
2. Joey Garrison, "'Violent Terrorist': Who Is the White Supremacist Suspect in New Zealand Mosque Shootings?" *USA Today*, March 21, 2019, https://eu.usatoday.com/story/news/nation/2019/03/15/new-zealand-christchurch-mosque-shootings-who-brenton-tarrant/3172550002 (accessed February 27, 2020).
3. Connor O'Brien, "'I Don't Give Any Credibility' to New Zealand Shooter Citing Trump, Ambassador Says," *Politico*, March 17, 2019, https://www.politico.com/story/2019/03/17/new-zealand-shooter-trump-scott-brown-1224069 (accessed February 27, 2020).
4. Brian Todd, Christina Maxouris, and Amir Vera, "The El Paso Shooting Suspect Showed No Remorse or Regret, Police Say," CNN, August 6, 2019, https://www.cnn.com/2019/08/05/us/el-paso-suspect-patrick-crusius/index.html (accessed February 27, 2020).
5. Howard William Hunter, "All Are Alike unto God," speech at Brigham Young University, Provo, UT, February 4, 1979.
6. Philip Bump, "The People Whom President Trump Has Called Stupid," *Washington Post*, August 6, 2018, https://www.washingtonpost.com/news/politics/wp/2018/08/06/the-people-trump-has-called-stupid (accessed February 27, 2020).
7. Since the drafting of this chapter the Department of Homeland Security has identified racially based violent extremism, particularly violent white supremacy, as domestic terrorism and an abhorrent affront to the nation. See, Department of Homeland Security Strategic Framework for Countering Terrorism and Targeted Violence, Embargoed Draft Text, September 19, 2019, available at https://games-cdn.washingtonpost.com/notes/prod/default/documents/56c099f1-5905-42de-b542-69f790f02939/note/bebd1e86-e32a-40a2-892c-4a7dd4f84b25.pdf#page=1 (accessed February 27, 2020).
8. Gordon W. Allport and J. Michael Ross, "Personal Religious Orientation and Prejudice," *Journal of Personality and Social Psychology* 5, no. 4 (1967), 432–43.
9. Christina Zhao, "Evangelicals Who Don't Support Trump May Be 'Immoral,' Jerry Falwell Jr. Says," *Newsweek*, January 1, 2019, https://www.newsweek.com/evangelicals-who-dont-support-trump-may-be-immoral-jerry-falwell-jr-says-1276488 (accessed February 27, 2020).
10. By "fundamentalism," the authors refer to the belief system that emerged from the rivalistic uptick in Christianity that captured the American imagination in what religious scholars refer to as the Great Awakening. It was during this era in the 1830s in upstate New York that Mormonism emerged. Unlike

evangelical religious belief in biblical inerrancy or biblical literalism, Latter-Day Saints believe in continuing revelation from God to the prophet and leader of the church.
11. Darron T. Smith, *When Race, Religion, and Sport collide: Black Athletes at BYU and Beyond* (Lanham, MD: Rowman & Littlefield, 2015).
12. We use the myth of middle-class home ownership with possession of an American-made automobile parked in a nicely manicured driveway to signify The Dream. Such a residence would be incomplete without a white picket fence and "Old Glory" flying in the wind.
13. Jessica Martínez and Gregory A. Smith, "How the Faithful Voted: A Preliminary 2016 Analysis," Pew Research Center, November 9, 2016, https://www.pewresearch.org/fact-tank/2016/11/09/how-the-faithful-voted-a-preliminary-2016-analysis (accessed February 27, 2020).
14. David Crystal, *Begat: The King James Bible and the English Language* (Oxford: Oxford University Press, 2010).
15. Scott Williams, *Church Diversity: Sunday the Most Segregated Day of the Week* (Green Forest, AR: New Leaf, 2011).
16. From the late eleventh century to the thirteenth century, the Crusades brought contact between the peoples of western Europe and the Middle East, which led to widespread emigration and religious wars between Christians and Muslims over control of the Holy Land (Jerusalem) and other sacred sites. Karen Armstrong, *Islam: A Short History*. (New York: Modern Library, 2002).
17. David M. Goldenberg, *The Curse of Ham: Race and Slavery in Early Judaism, Christianity, and Islam* (Princeton, NJ: Princeton University Press, 2003).
18. Roger Bastide, "Color, Racism, and Christianity," *Dædalus* 96, no. 2 (1967), 312–27.
19. Winthrop D. Jordan, *White over Black: American Attitudes toward the Negro, 1550–1812* (Chapel Hill: University of North Carolina Press, 1968).
20. Rebecca Anne Goetz, *The Baptism of Early Virginia: How Christianity Created Race* (Baltimore: Johns Hopkins University Press, 2012).
21. Trevor Wallace, "God Changed His Mind about Black People: Race and Priesthood Authority in Mormonism," MA thesis, Uppsala University, 2016, available at http://www.diva-portal.org/smash/get/diva2:1048951/FULLTEXT01.pdf (accessed February 27, 2020).
22. Eduardo Bonilla-Silva, *White Supremacy and Racism in the Post–Civil Rights Era* (Boulder, CO: Lynne Riener, 2001).
23. Bosco B. Bae, "Christianity and Implicit Racism in the U.S. Moral and Human Economy," *Open Theology* 2, no. 1 (2016), 1002–17.
24. Newell G. Bringhurst and Darron T. Smith (eds.), *Black and Mormon* (Urbana: University of Illinois Press, 2004).
25. Matthew 22:36–9.
26. "A Rebirth of Constitutional Government," GOP website, https://www.gop.com/platform/we-the-people (accessed February 27, 2020).

27. John Shattuck, Aaron Huang, and Elisabeth Thoreson-Green, "The War on Voting Rights," Carr Center for Human Rights Policy, February 2019, available at https://carrcenter.hks.harvard.edu/files/cchr/files/ccdp_2019_003_war_on_voting_final.pdf (accessed February 27, 2020).
28. Darron T. Smith, "Negotiating Black Self-Hate within the LDS Church," *Dialogue: A Journal of Mormon Thought* 51, no. 3 (2018), 29–44.
29. Robert R. Weyeneth, "The Power of Apology and the Process of Historical Reconciliation," *Public Historian* 23, no. 3 (2001), 9–38.
30. "Church Releases Statement Condemning White Supremacist Attitudes," Church of Jesus Christ of Latter-Day Saints website, August 15, 2017, https://www.churchofjesuschrist.org/church/news/church-releases-statement-condemning-white-supremacist-attitudes?lang=eng (accessed February 27, 2020).
31. "Out of the Best Books? Publications Continue to Promote Folklore," *Sunstone*, March 2003, 34–5.
32. Brian Hare, "Survival of the Friendliest: *Homo Sapiens* Evolved via Selection for Prosociality," *Annual Review of Psychology* 68 (2017), 155–86.
33. C. Sue Carter, "Oxytocin Pathways and the Evolution of Human Behavior," *Annual Review of Psychology* 65 (2014), 17–39.
34. Tara L. Gruenewald, Margaret E. Kemeny, Najib Aziz, and John L. Fahey, "Acute Threat to the Social Self: Shame, Social Self-Esteem, and Cortisol Activity," *Psychosomatic Medicine* 66, no. 6 (2004), 915–24.
35. Sally S. Dickerson, Tara L. Gruenewald, and Margaret E. Kemeny, "When the Social Self Is Threatened: Shame, Physiology, and Health," *Journal of Personality* 72, no. 6 (2004), 1192–1216.
36. William A. Smith, Jalil Bishop Mustaffa, Chantal M. Jones, Tommy J. Curry, and Walter R. Allen, "'You Make Me Wanna Holler and Throw Up Both My Hands!': Campus Culture, Black Misandric Microaggressions, and Racial Battle Fatigue," *International Journal of Qualitative Studies in Education* 29, no. 9 (2016), 1189–1209.
37. Racial microaggressions are defined as "subtle, stunning, often automatic, and non-verbal exchanges which are put downs of blacks by offenders." C. Pierce, J. Carew, D. Pierce-Gonzalez, and D. Willis, "An Experiment in Racism: TV Commercials," in Chester M. Pierce (ed.), *Television and Education* (Beverly Hills, CA: Sage, 1978), 62–88.
38. William A. Smith, Man Hung, and Jeremy D. Franklin, "Between Hope and Racial Battle Fatigue: African American Men and Race-Related Stress," *Journal of Black Masculinity* 2, no. 1, 35–58.
39. William A. Smith, "Toward an Understanding of Misandric Microaggressions and Racial Battle Fatigue among African Americans in Historically White Institutions," in Eboni M. Zamani-Gallaher and Vernon C. Polite (eds.), *The State of the African American Male* (East Lansing: Michigan State University Press, 2010), 256–77.
40. Smith, "Toward an Understanding of Misandric Microaggressions and Racial Battle Fatigue."

41. Jessie L. Embry, "Oral History and Mormon Women Missionaries: The Stories Sound the Same," *Frontiers: A Journal of Women Studies* 19, no. 3 (1998), 171–88.
42. Charles H. Long, *Significations: Signs, Symbols, and Images in the Interpretation of Religion* (Aurora, CO: Davies Group, [1986] 1995), 7.
43. Joe Feagin, *Systemic Racism: A Theory of Oppression* (New York: Routledge, 2006).
44. John C. Green, "The American Religious Landscape and Political Attitudes: A Baseline for 2004," available at https://assets.pewresearch.org/wp-content/uploads/sites/11/2007/10/green-full.pdf (accessed February 27, 2020).
45. Jonathan M. Metzl, *Dying of Whiteness: How the Politics of Racial Resentment Is Killing America's Heartland* (New York: Basic, 2019).
46. Cardell K. Jacobson and Darron T. Smith, "Emotion Work in Black and White: Transracial Adoption and the Process of Racial Socialization," in Patricia Neff Claster and Sampson Lee Blair (eds.), *Visions of the 21st Century Family: Transforming Structures and Identities* (Bingley, England: Emerald, 2013), 43–75.

NINE / Anatomizing White Rage: "Race Is My Religion!" and "White Genocide"

1. Michael Minkenberg, "Religion and the Radical Right," in Jens Rydgren (ed.), *The Oxford Handbook of the Radical Right* (New York: Oxford University Press, 2018), 366. Minkenberg lists Kai Arzheimer and Elisabeth Carter, "Christian Religiosity and Voting for West European Radical Right Parties," *West European Politics* 32, no. 5 (2009), 985–1011; Tim Immerzeel, Eva Jaspers, and Marcel Lubbers, "Religion as Catalyst or Restraint of Radical Right Voting?" *West European Politics* 36, no. 5 (2013), 946–68; and Jean-Yves Camus, "The European Extreme Right and Religious Extremism," *Central European Political Studies Review* 9, no. 4 (2007), 263–79.
2. Minkenberg, "Religion and the Radical Right," 366.
3. See, for example, Damon T. Berry, *Blood and Faith: Christianity in American White Nationalism* (Syracuse, NY: Syracuse University Press, 2017); Betty A. Dobratz, "The Role of Religion in the Collective Identity of the White Racialist Movement," *Journal for the Scientific Study of Religion* 40, no. 2 (2001), 287–302.
4. Minkenberg, "Religion and the Radical Right," 367, 387.
5. William T. Cavanaugh, "The Myth of Religious Violence," in Andrew R. Murphy (ed.), *The Blackwell Companion to Religion and Violence* (Malden, MA, and Oxford: Wiley-Blackwell, 2011), 29.
6. "Extreme Right/Radical Right/Far Right," ADL website, https://www.adl.org/resources/glossary-terms/extreme-right-radical-right-far-right (accessed February 28, 2020).
7. Damon T. Berry, "Religious Strategies of White Nationalism at Charlottesville," *Religion and Culture Forum*, October 13, 2017, https://voices.uchicago.edu/religionculture/2017/10/13/religious-strategies-of-white-nationalism-at-charlottesville (accessed February 28, 2020).
8. Berry, *Blood and Faith*, 6.

9. Michael O'Meara, *Toward the White Republic* (San Francisco: Counter-Currents, 2010), 1.
10. Berry, *Blood and Faith*, 6.
11. Berry, *Blood and Faith*, 6.
12. Benedict Anderson, *Imagined Communities: Reflections on the Origin and Spread of Nationalism*, rev. edn. (New York: Verso, 2005), 6.
13. Berry, *Blood and Faith*, 19.
14. Berry, *Blood and Faith*, 19.
15. Berry, *Blood and Faith*, 19.
16. Berry, *Blood and Faith*, 19.
17. Ben Klassen, *Nature's Eternal Religion: Part One of the White Man's Bible* (Church of Creativity, [1973] 2015), 239, available at https://creativityalliance.com/eBook-BenKlassen-Nature%27sEternalReligion.pdf (accessed February 28, 2020).
18. Klassen, *Nature's Eternal Religion*, 239.
19. "Creativity Movement," Southern Poverty Law Center, https://www.splcenter.org/fighting-hate/extremist-files/group/creativity-movement-0 (accessed February 28, 2020).
20. See Dobratz, "The Role of Religion in the Collective Identity," 297; Berry, "Religious Strategies of White Nationalism."
21. *Fresh Air*, NPR, September 24, 2018; see transcript at "How a Rising Star of White Nationalism Broke Free from the Movement," https://www.npr.org/templates/transcript/transcript.php?storyId=651052970 (accessed February 28, 2020).
22. *Fresh Air*.
23. *Fresh Air*.
24. Michael Omi and Howard Winant, *Racial Formation in the United States: From the 1960s to the 1990s*, 2nd edn. (New York: Routledge, 1994).
25. Jeannine Hill Fletcher, *The Sin of White Supremacy: Christianity, Racism, and Religious Diversity in America* (Maryknoll, NY: Orbis, 2017), 5.
26. Fletcher, *The Sin of White Supremacy*, 4, 5.
27. Dobratz, "The Role of Religion in the Collective Identity," 297.
28. David R. Roediger, *The Wages of Whiteness: Race and the Making of the American Working Class*, 3rd edn. (London: Verso, 2007), 13.
29. Omi and Winant, *Racial Formation in the United States*, 126–7.
30. Stephen C. Finley and Lori Latrice Martin, "The Complexity of Color and the Religion of Whiteness," in Lori Latrice Martin, Hayward Derrick Horton, Cedric Herring, Verna M. Keith, and Melvin Thomas (eds.), *Color Struck: How Race and Complexion Matter in the "Color-Blind" Era* (Rotterdam: Sense, 2017), 185–6.
31. Finley and Martin, "The Complexity of Color and the Religion of Whiteness," 186–7.
32. Charles H. Long, *Significations: Signs, Symbols, and Images in the Interpretation of Religion* (Aurora, CO: Davies Group, [1986] 1995), 7.
33. Paul Tillich, *Dynamics of Faith* (New York: Perennial, [1957] 2001), 1–2.
34. Tillich, *Dynamics of Faith*, 2.

35. "Five Fundamental Beliefs," Creativity Alliance website, https://creativityalliance.com (accessed February 28, 2020).
36. "Sixteen Commandments," Creativity Alliance, https://creativityalliance.com/home/16commandments (accessed February 28, 2020).
37. Tillich, *Dynamics of Faith*, 2.
38. Don Duncan, "Racism on Trial—A Brutal Portland Murder and the Southern Lawyer 'Who Broke the Klan': White Supremacy on Trial," *Seattle Times*, September 23, 1990, http://community.seattletimes.nwsource.com/archive/?date=19900923&slug=1094653 (accessed February 28, 2020).
39. Kimberly Winston, "'Blood and Faith': A New Book Links White Nationalists to Christianity," *Religion News Service*, August 23, 2017, https://religionnews.com/2017/08/23/blood-and-faith-a-new-book-links-white-nationalists-to-christianity (accessed February 28, 2020).
40. Dobratz, "The Role of Religion in the Collective Identity," 297.
41. Dobratz, "The Role of Religion in the Collective Identity," 297.
42. "14 Words," ADL website, https://www.adl.org/education/references/hate-symbols/14-words (accessed February 28, 2020).
43. "14 Words."
44. Convention on the Prevention and Punishment of the Crime of Genocide, UN Doc. A/810, adopted December 9, 1948, 78 UNTS 277.
45. H. Millard, "True Religion, Meaning and Purpose Are One with and Indissolubly Linked to Our White DNA Code," Western Spring website, April 19, 2016, http://www.westernspring.co.uk/true-religion-meaning-purpose-one-indissoslubly-linked-white-dna-code (accessed March 2, 2020).
46. "Blood & Faith: An Interview with Damon T. Berry," *606*, February 15, 2018, https://sixoh6.com/2018/02/15/blood-faith-an-interview-with-damon-t-berry (accessed March 2, 2020).
47. Berry, "Religious Strategies of White Nationalism."
48. Carol M. Swain, *The New White Nationalism in America: Its Challenge to Integration* (Cambridge, England: Cambridge University Press, 2002), 4.
49. Eli Saslow, "The White Flight of Derek Black," *Washington Post*, October 15, 2016, https://www.washingtonpost.com/national/the-white-flight-of-derek-black/2016/10/15/ed5f906a-8f3b-11e6-a6a3-d50061aa9fae_story.html (accessed March 13, 2020).
50. "What is White Genocide?" "FAQ's" [sic], Fight White Genocide website, http://www.fightwhitegenocide.com/faqs (accessed March 2, 2020).
51. William H. Frey, "The US Will Become 'Minority White' in 2045, Census Projects Youthful Minorities are the Engine of Future Growth," Brookings Institution website, March 14, 2018, https://www.brookings.edu/blog/the-avenue/2018/03/14/the-us-will-become-minority-white-in-2045-census-projects (accessed March 2, 2020)
52. Farouk Chothia, "South Africa: The Groups Playing on the Fears of a 'White Genocide,'" BBC News, September 1, 2018, https://www.bbc.com/news/world-africa-45336840 (accessed March 2, 2020).

53. "STOP White Genocide, by Halting MASSIVE Third World Immigration and FORCED Assimilation in White Countries!" Obama White House Archives, December 3, 2012, https://petitions.obamawhitehouse.archives.gov/petition/stop-white-genocide-halting-massive-third-world-immigration-and-forced-assimilation-white (accessed March 2, 2020).
54. Kathy Gilsinan, "Why Is Dylann Roof So Worried about Europe? Echoes of an International Conspiracy Theory in Charleston," *The Atlantic*, June 24, 2015, https://www.theatlantic.com/international/archive/2015/06/dylann-roof-world-white-supremacist/396557 (accessed March 6, 2020).
55. Millard, "True Religion, Meaning and Purpose."
56. Mark Juergensmeyer, *Terror in the Mind of God: The Global Rise of Religious Violence* (Berkeley: University of California Press, 2001); Bruce Lincoln, *Holy Terrors: Thinking about Religion after September 11*, 2nd edn. (Chicago: University of Chicago Press, 2006).
57. Millard, "True Religion, Meaning and Purpose."
58. Berry, *Blood and Faith*, 12.
59. Abigail Hauslohner and Abby Ohlheiser, "Some Neo-Nazis Lament the Pittsburgh Massacre: It Derails Their Efforts to Be Mainstream," *Washington Post*, October 30, 2018, https://www.washingtonpost.com/national/some-neo-nazis-lament-the-pittsburgh-massacre-it-derails-their-efforts-to-be-mainstream/2018/10/30/3163fd9c-dc5f-11e8-85df-7a6b4d25cfbb_story.html (accessed March 2, 2020).
60. "White Supremacists' Anti-Semitic and Anti-Immigrant Sentiments Often Intersect," ADL website, October 27, 2018, https://www.adl.org/blog/white-supremacists-anti-semitic-and-anti-immigrant-sentiments-often-intersect (accessed March 2, 2020).
61. Gilsinan, "Why Is Dylann Roof So Worried about Europe?"

TEN / Exorcising Blackness: Calling the Cops as an Affective Performance of Gender

1. Sharon Patricia Holland, *The Erotic Life of Racism* (Durham, NC: Duke University Press, 2012).
2. Judith Butler, *Bodies That Matter: On the Discursive Limits of "Sex"* (Abingdon, England: Routledge, [1993] 2011).
3. Sara Ahmed, *The Cultural Politics of Emotion*, 2nd edn. (New York: Routledge, 2015).
4. "LISTEN: 'BBQ Becky's' Viral 911 Call Made Public," KTVU/YouTube, August 31, 2018, https://youtu.be/LgaU1h0QiLo (accessed March 2, 2020).
5. "Stanford University Reacts to BBQ Becky Calling Cops on Black People, *NewsOne*, May 16, 2018, https://newsone.com/3799344/stanford-university-allegedly-jennifer-schulte (accessed March 2, 2020).
6. "LISTEN: 'BBQ Becky's' Viral 911 Call Made Public."
7. "LISTEN: 'BBQ Becky's' Viral 911 Call Made Public."

8. Sara Ahmed, "A Phenomenology of Whiteness," *Feminist Theory* 8, no. 2 (2007), 149–52.
9. "Permit Patty Calls Police on 8-Year-Old for Selling Water without a Permit," Trish's World/YouTube, June 24, 2018, https://youtu.be/gbOkxqt_uiU (accessed March 2, 2020).
10. "Woman in 'Permit Patty' Video Speaks Out: I Feel Manipulated," CNN/YouTube, June 26, 2018, https://youtu.be/lyJOYzof9R4 (accessed March 2, 2020).
11. Antonia Noori Farzan, "BBQ Becky, Permit Patty and Cornerstore Caroline: Too 'Cutesy' for Those White Women Calling Police on Black People?" *Washington Post*, October 19, 2018, https://www.washingtonpost.com/news/morning-mix/wp/2018/10/19/bbq-becky-permit-patty-and-cornerstore-caroline-too-cutesy-for-those-white-women-calling-cops-on-blacks (accessed March 2, 2020).
12. Holland, *The Erotic Life of Racism*, 6.
13. As Afropessimist and black nihilist thinkers have shown, there are metaphysical, ontological, and political implications of a world that is grammatically, ontologically, and metaphysically structured and sustained through anti-blackness. For more on this, see Frank B. Wilderson, III, *Red, White, and Black: Cinema and the Structure of U.S. Antagonisms* (Durham, NC: Duke University Press, 2010); Jared Sexton, "The Social Life of Social Death," *InTensions* 5 (2011); Calvin L. Warren, *Ontological Terror: Blackness, Nihilism, and Emancipation* (Durham, NC: Duke University Press, 2018).
14. Holland tells us that "racism can . . . be described as the emotional lifeblood of race; it is the 'feeling' that articulates and keeps the flawed logic of racism in its place." *The Erotic Life of Racism*, 4. And Lewis Gordon claims, "It is difficult to imagine a racist who is without some form of emotional or affective response in the presence of the people whom he [sic] regards as his [sic] racial inferiors." Lewis Gordon, *Bad Faith and Antiblack Racism* (Atlantic Highlands, NJ: Humanities Press, 1995), 78.
15. Hortense J. Spillers, "Mama's Baby, Papa's Maybe: An American Grammar Book," *Diacritics* 17, no. 2 (1987), 66.
16. Brian Massumi, "The Future Birth of the Affective Fact," in Melissa Gregg and Gregory J. Seigworth (eds.), *The Affect Theory Reader* (Durham, NC: Duke University Press, 2010), 54.
17. Massumi, "The Future Birth of the Affective Fact," 56.
18. See Frantz Fanon, *Black Skin, White Masks*, trans. Richard Philcox (New York: Grove Press, 2008); Achille Mbembe, *Critique of Black Reason*, trans. Laurent Dubois (Durham, NC: Duke University Press, 2017), particularly the chapter "The Well of Fantasies."
19. Butler, *Bodies That Matter*, xii.
20. We need only think of Emmett Till's case as an apex of this dynamic. There are others—in fact the history of lynching has often been tethered to accusations of unwanted or inappropriate contact between black men and white women. For more on this, see Equal Justice Initiative, *Lynching in America: Confronting the Legacy of Racial Terror*, 3rd edn. (Montgomery, AL: Equal Justice Initiative,

2017), available at https://eji.org/wp-content/uploads/2019/10/lynching-in-america-3d-ed-080219.pdf (accessed March 2, 2020).
21. Butler, *Bodies That Matter*, xxi.
22. Ahmed, *The Cultural Politics of Emotion*, 45.
23. See note 17 above.
24. Butler, *Bodies That Matter*, xiii.
25. For more classical and philosophical treatments of affect in the study of religion, see Wayne Proudfoot, *Religious Experience* (Berkeley: University of California Press, 1985); Friedrich Schleiermacher, *On Religion: Speeches to Its Cultured Despisers*, trans. and ed. Richard Crouter, 2nd edn. (Cambridge, England: Cambridge University Press, 1996); Rudolf Otto, *The Idea of the Holy*, trans. John Harvey (New York: Oxford University Press, [1923] 1950). For a more recent treat on the relationship between religion and affect, see Donovan O. Schaefer, *Religious Affects: Animality, Evolution, and Power* (Durham, NC: Duke University Press, 2015).
26. Stephen C. Finley and Biko Mandela Gray, "God *Is* a White Racist: Immanent Atheism as a Religious Response to Black Lives Matter and State-Sanctioned Anti-Black Violence," *Journal of Africana Religions* 3, no. 4 (2015), 443–53.
27. Gordon, *Bad Faith and Antiblack Racism*, 147.
28. Lewis Gordon, "Race, Theodicy, and the Normative Emancipatory Challenges of Blackness," *South Atlantic Quarterly* 112, no. 4 (2013), 729.

ELEVEN / White Power Barbie and Other Figures of the Angry White Woman

1. "Tomi Lahren's STUPID Response to Jesse Williams' BET Award Speech about Racism," Young Turks/YouTube, June 29, 2016, https://youtu.be/FlMoC9oz8Ac (accessed March 2, 2020).
2. "Tomi Lahren's STUPID Response."
3. Lahren's vitriol is not limited to black anti-racist leaders and movements. Since the inauguration of Donald Trump, Lahren has increasingly focused on framing brown migrants as a threat to the nation and the American good life.
4. For more on the effect Barbie play has on the reinforcement of thin-ideal internalization in young girls, see Helga Dittmar, Emma Halliwell, and Suzanne Ive, "Does Barbie Make Girls Want to Be Thin? The Effect of Experimental Exposure to Images of Dolls on the Body Image of 5- to 8-Year-Old Girls," *Developmental Psychology* 42, no. 2 (2006), 283–92; Karlie Rice, Ivanka Prichard, Marika Tiggemann, and Amy Slater, "Exposure to Barbie: Effects on Thin-Ideal Internalisation, Body Esteem, and Body Dissatisfaction among Young Girls," *Body Image* 19 (2016), 142–9. For more on a child's perception of future career possibilities in relation to Barbie play, see Aurora M. Sherman and Eileen L. Zurbriggen, "'Boys Can Be Anything': Effect of Barbie Play on Girls' Career Cognitions," *Sex Roles* 70, no. 5–6 (2014). 195–208. For more on the impact of Barbie play in a transnational context, see Chinyere G. Okafor, "Global Encounters: 'Barbie' in

Nigerian Agbogho-Mmuo Mask Context," *Journal of African Cultural Studies* 19, no. 1 (2007), 37–54.

5. In this chapter, I am separating "white normativity" from "white supremacy" analytically to capture the different modalities in which an investment in white America can be articulated. While I reserve "white supremacy" in this chapter for the explicit political project of white dominance and "white normativity" for an unmarked set of assumptions about the centrality of whiteness, the two are not mutually exclusive categories. White normativity upholds white supremacy just as white supremacy upholds white normativity. For more on white normativity, see Sara Ahmed, "A Phenomenology of Whiteness," *Feminist Theory* 8, no. 2 (2007), 149–68. For a different articulation of white normativity and white supremacy, see Robin DiAngelo and Michael Eric Dyson, *White Fragility: Why It's So Hard for White People to Talk about Racism* (Boston: Beacon Press, 2018).
6. The trope of the angry feminist is ubiquitous in U.S. popular culture and is a common form of dismissal that affects feminists from all activist and intellectual traditions, albeit differently. This trope can take many shapes, including the pejorative labels "bra-burner," "social justice warrior," and "feminazi."
7. As a genealogy, my aim is not to provide an account of historically specific angry white women, but rather to trace the ways through and by which someone like Tomi Lahren is possible.
8. Sara Ahmed, *The Promise of Happiness* (Durham, NC: Duke University Press, 2010), 68.
9. For more on the racist stereotyping of black women and the trope of the Angry Black Woman, see Melissa V. Harris-Perry, *Sister Citizen: Shame, Stereotypes, and Black Women in America* (New Haven, CT: Yale University Press, 2011); Patricia Hill Collins, *Black Feminist Thought: Knowledge, Consciousness, and the Politics of Empowerment* (New York: Routledge, 2000); "The Sapphire Caricature," Jim Crow Museum website, Ferris State University, https://www.ferris.edu/HTMLS/news/jimcrow/antiblack/sapphire.htm (accessed March 2, 2020).
10. Ahmed, *The Promise of Happiness*, 120.
11. Barbara Welter, "The Cult of True Womanhood, 1820-1860," *American Quarterly* 18, no. 2 (1966), 152.
12. Welter, "The Cult of True Womanhood," 152.
13. I use the qualifier "potentially" as we know that many white men still disagreed with the criticisms of white women despite their deployment of the True Woman figure.
14. Nancy A. Hewitt, "Taking the True Woman Hostage," *Journal of Women's History* 14, no. 1 (2002), 158.
15. "Patricia Arquette Winning Best Supporting Actress," Oscars/YouTube, March 9, 2015, https://www.youtu.be/6wx-Qh4Vczc (accessed March 2, 2020).
16. "Dwight D. Eisenhower and Susan B. Anthony's Dollar: Gasparo's Portfolio," National Museum of American History website, https://americanhistory.si.edu/collections/search/object/nmah_1396076 (accessed March 2, 2020).
17. Angela Y. Davis, *Women, Race, & Class* (New York: Vintage, 1983), 112.

18. Elizabeth Cady Stanton, "This Is the Negro's House," letter to the editor, *National Anti-Slavery Standard*, December 26, 1865.
19. Stanton, "This Is the Negro's House." This attitude toward black men—black masculinity as animalistic and ignorant—coincides in Stanton's letter with a kind of maternalistic attitude toward black women, namely to save them from black men: "If the two millions of Southern black women are not to be secured in their rights of person, property, wages, and children, their emancipation is but another form of slavery. In fact, it is better to be the slave of an educated white man, than of a degraded, ignorant black one."
20. Stanton, "This Is the Negro's House."
21. Crystal N. Feimster, *Southern Horrors: Women and the Politics of Rape and Lynching* (Cambridge, MA: Harvard University Press, 2011), 127.
22. Feimster, *Southern Horrors*, 127.
23. Jen McDaneld, "White Suffragist Dis/Entitlement: The *Revolution* and the Rhetoric of Racism," *Legacy* 30, no. 2 (2013), 244.
24. Timothy Bella, "Women 'Are the N-Word of the World,' Bette Midler Tweeted. She Apologized Hours Later," *Washington Post*, October 5, 2018, https://www.washingtonpost.com/news/morning-mix/wp/2018/10/05/women-are-the-n-word-of-the-world-bette-midler-tweeted-she-apologized-hours-later (accessed March 2, 2020).
25. Jennifer Keishin Armstrong, "Why The Handmaid's Tale Is So Relevant Today," BBC Culture, April 25, 2018, http://www.bbc.com/culture/story/20180425-why-the-handmaids-tale-is-so-relevant-today (accessed March 2, 2020); Jessica Valenti, "The Handmaid's Tale Is Timely. But That's Not Why It's So Terrifying," *The Guardian*, April 27, 2017, https://www.theguardian.com/commentisfree/2017/apr/27/handmaids-tale-timely-terrifying-hulu-series-margaret-atwood (accessed March 2, 2020); Zarah Moeggenberg and Samantha L. Solomon, "Power, Consent, and The Body: #MeToo and *The Handmaid's Tale*," *Gender Forum*, no. 70 (2018), 4–25.
26. Fiona Sturges, "Cattleprods! Severed Tongues! Torture Porn! Why I've Stopped Watching the Handmaid's Tale," *The Guardian*, June 16, 2018, https://www.theguardian.com/tv-and-radio/2018/jun/16/handmaids-tale-season-2-elisabeth-moss-margaret-atwood (accessed March 2, 2020).
27. Eliana Dockterman, "The *Handmaid's Tale* Showrunner on Why He Made Some Major Changes from the Book," *Time*, April 25, 2017, http://time.com/4754200/the-handmaids-tale-showrunner-changes-from-book (accessed March 3, 2020).
28. While class, age, and reproductive capacities are shown to influence a woman's experience of oppression in Gilead, the adaptation prioritizes the mutual suffering of all women *as* women.
29. Angelica Jade Bastién, "In Its First Season, *The Handmaid's Tale*'s Greatest Failing Is How It Handles Race," *Vulture*, June 14, 2017, https://www.vulture.com/2017/06/the-handmaids-tale-greatest-failing-is-how-it-handles-race.html (accessed March 3, 2020). Bastién argues that the adaptation might have considered how histories of slavery, reproductive injustice, and lynching in the U.S. might differently shape the experiences of Handmaids of color.

30. Bastién, "In Its First Season."
31. Catherine Morse, "The Handmaid's Tale Was Always about Race—So Is the Abortion Ban," *Medium*, May 18, 2019, https://medium.com/@morseca01/the-handmaids-tale-was-always-about-race-so-is-the-abortion-ban-c2cf2aa39025 (accessed March 3, 2020).
32. Exclusion can certainly be injurious, and injury can be a form of exclusion. My choice to separate these is to differentiate between the affective and rhetorical registers that differing figures evoke when expressing moral anger.
33. Peter Beaumont and Amanda Holpuch, "How *The Handmaid's Tale* Dressed Protests across the World," *The Guardian*, August 3, 2018, https://www.theguardian.com/world/2018/aug/03/how-the-handmaids-tale-dressed-protests-across-the-world (accessed March 3, 2020).
34. Claire Valentine, "Women Show Up at Brett Kavanaugh's Hearing Dressed as Handmaids," *Paper*, September 4, 2018, http://www.papermag.com/handmaids-tale-protestors-brett-kavanaugh-2601984117.html (accessed March 3, 2020).
35. Ahmed, *The Promise of Happiness*, 68.
36. Yael Halon, "Trump Has 'Deep Love and Support' for Police, Unlike Dems: Lahren on Police Union's 2020 Endorsement," Fox News, September 24, 2019, https://www.foxnews.com/media/lahren-on-police-union-2020-endorsement (accessed March 6, 2020).
37. Charles H. Long, *Significations: Signs, Symbols, and Images in the Interpretation of Religion* (Aurora, CO: Davies Group, [1986] 1999), 7.
38. Tomi Lahren, "Tomi Lahren: I Support Law Enforcement, Not Because I'm White or Conservative but Because I'm an American," Fox News, March 12, 2019, https://www.foxnews.com/opinion/tomi-lahren-i-support-law-enforcement-not-because-im-white-or-conservative-but-because-im-an-american (accessed March 3, 2020).
39. Sara Ahmed, "Affective Economies," *Social Text* 22, no. 2 (79) (2004), 127.
40. Ahmed, "Affective Economies," 128.

TWELVE / Weaponizing Religion: A Document Analysis of the Religious Indoctrination of Slaves in Service of White Labor Elites

1. Richard Delgado and Jean Stefancic define racism as "any program or practice of discrimination, segregation, persecution, or mistreatment based on membership in a race or ethnic group." *Critical Race Theory: An Introduction*, 2nd edn. (New York: New York University Press, 2012), 171.
2. Jennifer Rubin, "Like His Lies, Trump's Racist Comments Don't Surprise, but They Should Be Counted," *Washington Post*, November 4, 2018, https://www.washingtonpost.com/news/opinions/wp/2018/11/04/like-his-lies-trumps-racist-comments-dont-surprise-but-they-should-be-counted (accessed March 3, 2020).

3. Robert P. Jones, "White Evangelical Support for Donald Trump at All Time High", PRRI, April 18, 2018, https://www.prri.org/spotlight/white-evangelical-support-for-donald-trump-at-all-time-high (accessed March 3, 2020).
4. Debra L. Hall, David C. Matz, and Wendy Wood, "Why Don't We Practice What We Preach? A Meta-Analytic Review of Religious Racism," *Personality and Social Psychology Review* 14, no. 1 (2010), 126–39.
5. Anne C. Loveland, *Southern Evangelicals and the Social Order, 1800–1860* (Baton Rouge: Louisiana State University Press, 1980), 219–56.
6. Charles H. Long, *Significations: Signs, Symbols, and Images in the Interpretation of Religion* (Aurora, CO: Davies Group, [1986] 1995), 7.
7. David Whitford, "A Calvinist Heritage to the 'Curse of Ham': Assessing the Accuracy of a Claim about Racial Subordination," *Church History and Religious Culture* 90, no. 1 (2010), 27.
8. Whitford, "A Calvinist Heritage to the 'Curse of Ham,'" 27. However, much earlier Jewish traditions recount a curse of black skin as well. The Babylonian Talmud, produced between the third and sixth centuries, also identifies black skin as the curse brought down upon Ham for sexual activities aboard the Ark.
9. Jeffrey Burton Russell, *Lucifer: The Devil in the Middle Ages* (Ithaca, NY: Cornell University Press, 1984), 68.
10. Russell, *Lucifer*, 69.
11. 2 Nephi 5:20–1.
12. Ibram X. Kendi, *Stamped from the Beginning: The Definitive History of Racist Ideas in America* (New York: Nation, 2016), 64.
13. Rebecca Anne Goetz, *The Baptism of Early Virginia: How Christianity Created Race* (Baltimore: Johns Hopkins University Press, 2012), 12.
14. John S. Mbiti, *Introduction to African Religion*, 2nd edn. (Lone Grove, IL: Waveland Press, 1991), 11–12.
15. Kendi, *Stamped from the Beginning*, 65.
16. Cynthia A. Rice, "The First American Great Awakening: Lessons Learned and What Can Be Done to Foster a Habitat for the Next Great Awakening," *International Congregational Journal* 9, no. 2 (2010), 104–5.
17. *Annual Report of the Missionary to the Negroes in Liberty County, Ga., 1833*. Charleston, SC: Observer Office Press, 1834.
18. Donald G. Mathews, "Charles Colcock Jones and the Southern Evangelical Crusade to Form a Biracial Community," *Journal of Southern History* 41, no. 3 (1975), 319.
19. C. V. Bruner, "An Abstract of the Religious Instruction of the Slaves in the Antebellum South," *Peabody Journal of Education* 11, no. 3 (1933), 117–21.
20. Charles C. Jones, *The Religious Instruction of the Negroes in the United States* (Savannah, GA: Thomas Purse, 1842), 6.
21. Bruner, "An Abstract of the Religious Instruction of the Slaves," 117.
22. Edmund S. Morgan, *American Slavery, American Freedom: The Ordeal of Colonial Virginia* (New York: W. W. Norton, 1975), 331.
23. Morgan, *American Slavery, American Freedom*, 331.

24. Frank Lambert, "'I Saw the Book Talk': Slave Readings of the First Great Awakening," *Journal of African American History* 87, no. 1 (2002), 15.
25. Cotton Mather, *The Negro Christianized: An Essay to Excite and Assist that Good Work, the Instruction of Negro-Servants in Christianity* (Boston: B. Green, 1706), 14.
26. Mather, *The Negro Christianized*, 16.
27. Bruner, "An Abstract of the Religious Instruction of the Slaves," 118.
28. Rice, "The First American Great Awakening," 104.
29. Rice, "The First American Great Awakening," 104.
30. Loveland, *Southern Evangelicals and the Social Order*, 227–31.
31. Bruner, "An Abstract of the Religious Instruction of the Slaves," 118.
32. Bruner, "An Abstract of the Religious Instruction of the Slaves," 118.
33. Bruner, "An Abstract of the Religious Instruction of the Slaves," 119.
34. Bruner, "An Abstract of the Religious Instruction of the Slaves," 119.
35. Douglas R. Egerton, "'Why They Did Not Preach Up This Thing': Denmark Vesey and Revolutionary Theology," *South Carolina Historical Magazine* 100, no. 4 (1999), 304.
36. Egerton, "'Why They Did Not Preach Up This Thing,'" 299.
37. Bruner, "An Abstract of the Religious Instruction of the Slaves," 119.
38. Loveland, *Southern Evangelicals and the Social Order*, 225.
39. Bruner, "An Abstract of the Religious Instruction of the Slaves," 120.
40. Bruner, "An Abstract of the Religious Instruction of the Slaves," 121.
41. Bruner, "An Abstract of the Religious Instruction of the Slaves," 121.
42. *Proceedings of the Meeting in Charleston, S.C., May 13–15, 1845, on the Religious Instruction of the Negroes, Together with the Report of the Committee, and the Address to the Public* (Charleston, SC: B. Jenkins, 1845), 9.
43. *Proceedings of the Meeting in Charleston, S.C.*, 9–10.
44. Bruner, "An Abstract of the Religious Instruction of the Slaves," 121.
45. *Thirteenth Annual Report of the Association for the Religious Instruction of the Negroes, in Liberty County, Georgia* (Savannah, GA: Edward J. Purse, 1848), 40, available at https://archive.org/details/12960556.4723.emory.edu (accessed March 3, 2020)
46. *Thirteenth Annual Report*, 60.
47. *The Catechism of the Protestant Episcopal Church in the Confederate States* (White Catechism) (Raleigh, NC: Office of "The Church Intelligencer," 1862).
48. *A Catechism, to Be Taught Orally to Those Who Cannot Read; Designed Especially for the Instruction of the Slaves, in the Prot. Episcopal Church in the Confederate States* (Slave Catechism) (Raleigh, NC: Office of "The Church Intelligencer," 1862).
49. James Conroy Jackson, "The Religious Education of the Negro in South Carolina Prior to 1850," *Historical Magazine of the Protestant Episcopal Church* 36, no. 1 (1967), 45.
50. Slave Catechism, 43.
51. White Catechism, 1.
52. Slave Catechism, 1.
53. James Orr, "Dust," in *International Standard Bible Encyclopedia* (Grand Rapids, MI: Wm. B. Eerdmans, 1939), available at https://www.internationalstandardbible.com/D/dust.html (accessed March 3, 2020).

54. Slave Catechism, 20.
55. White Catechism, 3.
56. Jackson, "The Religious Education of the Negro," 58.
57. Slave Catechism, 22–3.
58. White Catechism, 5.
59. Slave Catechism, 39.
60. Slave Catechism, 39–40.
61. White Catechism, 6.
62. White Catechism, 2.
63. Slave Catechism, 8, 11.
64. Slave Catechism, 11.
65. Slave Catechism, 25.

THIRTEEN / The Religions of Black Resistance and White Rage: Interpenetrative Religious Practice in the 1963 Civil Rights Struggle in Danville, Virginia

1. Dorothy Miller and Danny Lyon, "Danville, Virginia," Student Nonviolent Coordinating Committee, August 1963, available at https://www.crmvet.org/docs/danville63.pdf (accessed March 3, 2020).
2. Delores J. Page and Margaret P. Dillard v. Chief Eugene McCain et al. (4th Cir. 1963). Other accounts state forty-five or forty-seven hospitalized victims: Emma C. Edmunds, "Danville Civil Rights Demonstrations of 1963," *Encyclopedia Virginia*, December 7, 2016, http://www.encyclopediavirginia.org/Danville_Civil_Rights_Demonstrations_of_1963 (accessed March 3, 2020); Sally Belfrage, "Danville on Trial," *New Republic*, November 2, 1963, 12. I follow the figure included in the court brief submitted later on that year.
3. David J. Garrow, "Religious Resources and the Montgomery Bus Boycott," *Criterion*, no. 34 (1995); David L. Chappell, *A Stone of Hope: Prophetic Religion and the Death of Jim Crow* (Chapel Hill: University of North Carolina Press, 2004).
4. Robert Darden, *Nothing but Love in God's Water, Vol. 2: Black Sacred Music from the Sit-Ins to Resurrection City* (University Park: Pennsylvania State University Press, 2016); Aldon Morris, "The Black Church in the Civil Rights Movement," in Christian Smith (ed.), *Disruptive Religion: The Force of Faith in Social-Movement Activism* (New York: Routledge, 1996); Richard Lischer, *The Preacher King: Martin Luther King, Jr. and the Word That Moved America* (New York: Oxford University Press, 1995).
5. Carolyn Renée Dupont, *Mississippi Praying: Southern White Evangelicals and the Civil Rights Movement, 1945–1975* (New York: New York University Press, 2013); Stephen R. Haynes, *The Last Segregated Hour: The Memphis Kneel-ins and the Campaign for Southern Church Desegregation* (New York: Oxford University Press, 2012); Charles Marsh, *God's Long Summer: Stories of Faith and Civil Rights* (Princeton, NJ: Princeton University Press, 1997).
6. Paul Harvey, "'The Color of Skin Was Almost Forgotten,'" in Winfred B. Moore, Jr., Kyle S. Sinisi, and David H. White, Jr. (eds.), *Warm Ashes: Issues in Southern*

History at the Dawn of the Twenty-First Century (Columbia: University of South Carolina Press, 2003); David P. Cline, *From Reconciliation to Revolution: The Student Interracial Ministry, Liberal Christianity, and the Civil Rights Movement* (Chapel Hill: University of North Carolina Press, 2016); Tobin Miller Shearer, *Daily Demonstrators: The Civil Rights Movement in Mennonite Homes and Sanctuaries* (Baltimore: Johns Hopkins University Press, 2010); Allan W. Austin, *Quaker Brotherhood: Interracial Activism and the American Friends Service Committee, 1917–1950* (Urbana: University of Illinois Press, 2012).

7. Edward J. Blum, Tracy Fessenden, Prema Kurien, and Judith Weisenfeld, "Forum: American Religion and 'Whiteness,'" *Religion and American Culture* 19, no. 1 (2009), 4.
8. Charles H. Long, *Significations: Signs, Symbols, and Images in the Interpretation of Religion* (Philadelphia: Fortress Press, 1986), 7.
9. "Encyclopedia of Southern Jewish Communities—Danville, Virginia," Goldring/Woldenberg Institute of Southern Jewish Life website, http://www.isjl.org/virginia-danville-encyclopedia.html (accessed March 3, 2020).
10. "Kathleen Cleaver Oral History Interview Conducted by Joseph Mosnier in Atlanta, Georgia, 2011 September 16," Library of Congress, https://www.loc.gov/item/2015669150 (accessed March 3, 2020).
11. "A Guide to the 1963 Danville (Va.) Civil Rights Case Files, 1963–1973," Library of Virginia, September 1999, http://www.lva.virginia.gov/findaid/38099.htm (accessed March 3, 2020); Edmunds, "Danville Civil Rights Demonstrations of 1963."
12. "Virginia Clergymen Pray in Courtroom," *Afro-American*, February 3, 1962.
13. "A Guide to the 1963 Danville (Va.) Civil Rights Case Files."
14. "A Guide to the 1963 Danville (Va.) Civil Rights Case Files."
15. Edmunds, "Danville Civil Rights Demonstrations of 1963."
16. "A Guide to the 1963 Danville (Va.) Civil Rights Case Files."
17. For footage from WDBJ Television see "Danville Demonstrations, Court Steps," *Encyclopedia Virginia*, https://www.encyclopediavirginia.org/media_player?mets_filename=evm00002400mets.xml (accessed March 3, 2020).
18. Miller and Lyon, "Danville, Virginia"; Edmunds, "Danville Civil Rights Demonstrations of 1963."
19. "A Guide to the 1963 Danville (Va.) Civil Rights Case Files"; Miller and Lyon, "Danville, Virginia."
20. Edmunds, "Danville Civil Rights Demonstrations of 1963"; "A Guide to the 1963 Danville (Va.) Civil Rights Case Files."
21. Miller and Lyon, "Danville, Virginia."
22. Lawrence Campbell, "Sermon, Danville, VA, 1963," in *Voices of the Civil Rights Movement: Black American Freedom Songs, 1960–1966* (Washington, DC: Smithsonian Folkways Recordings, [1980] 1997).
23. Miller and Lyon, "Danville, Virginia."
24. Tobin Miller Shearer, "Invoking Crisis: Performative Christian Prayer and the Civil Rights Movement," *Journal of the American Academy of Religion* 83, no. 2 (2015), 490–512.

25. Miller and Lyon, "Danville, Virginia."
26. Belfrage, "Danville on Trial," 12.
27. Page and Dillard v. McCain et al.; Miller and Lyon, "Danville, Virginia."
28. "Fire Hoses Turned on Va. Demonstrators," *Chicago Daily Defender*, June 11, 1963.
29. Miller and Lyon, "Danville, Virginia."
30. "WSB-TV Newsfilm Clip of Mayor Julian R. Stinson Speaking to Reverend Lendell W. Chase after a Civil Rights Demonstration in Danville, Virginia, 1963 June 13," Civil Rights Digital Library, http://dlg.galileo.usg.edu/crdl/id:ugabma_wsbn_36357 (accessed March 3, 2020).
31. Miller and Lyon, "Danville, Virginia."
32. "A Guide to the 1963 Danville (Va.) Civil Rights Case Files"; James H. Hershman, Jr., "Archibald M. Aiken (1888–1971)," *Encyclopedia Virginia*, https://www.encyclopediavirginia.org/Aiken_Archibald_Murphey_1888-1971 (accessed March 4, 2020).
33. Miller and Lyon, "Danville, Virginia."
34. "Dixie Cops Break into Church to Nab Leaders," *Chicago Daily Defender*, June 24, 1963, 3.
35. Edmunds, "Danville Civil Rights Demonstrations of 1963."
36. "A Guide to the 1963 Danville (Va.) Civil Rights Case Files."
37. Harold A. Middlebrook, L. G. Campbell, and L. W. Chase, letter to A. Philip Randolph, August 22, 1963, ProQuest History Vault (henceforth PQHV), Black Freedom Struggle in the 20th Century: Organizational Records and Personal Papers, Part 1, Bayard Rustin Papers, Chronological Subject File—March on Washington—1963, folder 001581-009-0674; David H. Marlin, memo to Burke Marshall, September 17, 1963, PQHV, Civil Rights during the Kennedy Administration, 1961–1963, Part 2: The Papers of Burke Marshall, Assistant Attorney General for Civil Rights (henceforth Marshall Papers), folder 001351-026-0767, 2–4.
38. Louis M. Kauder, memo to Burke Marshall, August 28, 1963; David H. Marlin, memo to Burke Marshall, August 27, 1963; David H. Marlin, memo to Burke Marshall, August 23, 1963; David H. Marlin, memo to Burke Marshall, August 21, 1963, 5; Denis E. Dillon, memo to Burke Marshall, August 21, 1963; all from PQHV, Marshall Papers, folder 001351-026-0767.
39. For footage from WDBJ Television see "Danville Civil Rights Demonstration in 1963," *Encyclopedia Virginia*, https://www.encyclopediavirginia.org/media_player?mets_filename=evm00002399mets.xml (accessed March 4, 2020).
40. "250 Mourn Birmingham in Danville," news release, September 16, 1963, Samuel C. Shirah, Jr., Papers, 1961–1964, Wisconsin Historical Society, Madison, WI, Archives Main Stacks, Mss 540, Box 1, Folder 2, WIHVS2640-A.
41. Harold Middlebrook, memo to Wyatt T. Walker, September 19, 1963, PQHV, Series I, Records of Andrew Young, Program Director, 1961–1964, Subseries 3, Records of the Voter Education Project, 1962–1964, Subseries iii, Field Reports, [1962–1964] (henceforth Young Papers), folder 001569-006-0226.
42. David H. Marlin, memo to Burke Marshall, September 23, 1963, PQHV, Marshall Papers, folder 001351-026-0917.

43. David L. Chappell, *Inside Agitators: White Southerners in the Civil Rights Movement* (Baltimore: Johns Hopkins University Press, 1994), xv, xvi, xxi, xxiv, 212.
44. Heslip M. Lee, "Strictly Confidential," Department of Justice, Attorney General's Office, 1963, PQHV, Marshall Papers, folder 001351-026-0287, 1.
45. Benjamin Muse, "Confidential Memorandum, Danville, Va., September 28–October 4, 1963," PQHV, Marshall Papers, folder 001351-009-00213.
46. Muse, "Confidential Memorandum," 1.
47. Muse, "Confidential Memorandum," 3.
48. Muse, "Confidential Memorandum," 4.
49. Muse, "Confidential Memorandum," 2–4.
50. Muse, "Confidential Memorandum," 1–2.
51. Marlin memo to Marshall, September 17.
52. Dorothy O. Harris and Emma Edmunds, "Danville Civil Rights Demonstrations: 1963 Violence," in "Dorothy O. Harris, Teacher and Principal (b. 1930)," Virginia Center for Digital History, 2003, http://www.vcdh.virginia.edu/cslk/danville/bio_harris.html (accessed March 4, 2020).
53. Edmunds, "Danville Civil Rights Demonstrations of 1963"; "WSB-TV Newsfilm Clip of African Americans Being Arrested Following a Night-Time March for Civil Rights in Danville, Virginia, 1963, July 11," Civil Rights Digital Library, http://crdl.usg.edu/id:ugabma_wsbn_wsbn31815 (accessed March 4, 2020).
54. "WSB-TV Newsfilm Clip of African Americans Being Arrested."
55. "Danville Protests to Go On," *Chicago Daily Defender*, December 16, 1963, A17.
56. "Registration Drive Ends in Danville," news release, 1963, PQHV, Young Papers, folder 001569-006-0250.
57. Edmunds, "Danville Civil Rights Demonstrations of 1963"; Emma Edmunds, "Robert A. Williams, Attorney, Williams, Luck & Williams, Martinsville, Virginia (b. 1944)," Virginia Center for Digital History, 2011, http://www.vcdh.virginia.edu/cslk/danville/bio_williams.html (accessed March 4, 2020).
58. Ibid.; Dorothy O. Harris and Emma Edmunds, "First Black Mayor and Voting: Charles H. Harris," in "Dorothy O. Harris, Teacher and Principal."
59. Jennifer Ritterhouse, *Growing up Jim Crow: How Black and White Southern Children Learned Race* (Chapel Hill: University of North Carolina Press, 2006); Renee Christine Romano, *Race Mixing: Black-White Marriage in Postwar America* (Cambridge, MA: Harvard University Press, 2003); Lee Sigelman, Timothy Bledsoe, Susan Welch, and Michael W. Combs, "Making Contact? Black-White Social Interaction in an Urban Setting," *American Journal of Sociology* 101, no. 5 (1996), 1306–32.
60. Katharine L. Dvorak, *An African-American Exodus: The Segregation of the Southern Churches* (Brooklyn, NY: Carlson, 1991).
61. See, for example, Victor Anderson, *Beyond Ontological Blackness: An Essay on African American Religious and Cultural Criticism* (New York: Continuum, 1995); Emilie Maureen Townes (ed.), *Embracing the Spirit: Womanist Perspectives on Hope, Salvation, and Transformation* (Maryknoll, NY: Orbis, 1997); Kelly Brown Douglas, *The Black Christ* (Maryknoll, NY: Orbis, 1994).

62. James W. Perkinson, *White Theology: Outing Supremacy in Modernity* (New York: Palgrave Macmillan, 2004), 166.
63. J. Russell Hawkins and Phillip Luke Sinitiere (eds.), *Christians and the Color Line: Race and Religion after "Divided by Faith"* (New York: Oxford University Press, 2013); Dupont, *Mississippi Praying*; Michael O. Emerson and Christian Smith, *Divided by Faith: Evangelical Religion and the Problem of Race in America* (New York: Oxford University Press, 2001).

CONCLUSION / Race, Religion, and Labor Studies: The Way Forward

1. Originally entitled "The Defence of Fort McHenry" in 1814.
2. David R. Roediger, *The Wages of Whiteness: Race and the Making of the American Working Class*, 3rd edn. (London: Verso, 2007); Saidiya V. Hartman, *Scenes of Subjection: Terror, Slavery, and Self-Making in Nineteenth Century America* (New York: Oxford University Press, 1998); See the discussions of race and religion in modernity in this chapter and elsewhere in the volume.
3. Frank Wilderson, III, "Gramsci's Black Marx: Whither the Slave in Civil Society?" *Social Identities* 9, no. 2 (2003), 226–40.
4. Frank B. Wilderson, III, *Red, White, and Black: Cinema and the Structure of U.S. Antagonisms* (Durham, NC: Duke University Press, 2010).
5. Roediger, *The Wages of Whiteness*, 49.
6. Roediger, *The Wages of Whiteness*, 47–50.
7. Roediger, *The Wages of Whiteness*, 44–5.
8. Antonia Michelle Daymond, "Can These Bones Live?: Addressing the Necrotic in U.S. Theo-Politics," *CrossCurrents* 68, no. 1 (March 2019), 135–58, esp. 136–7, 143–4; cf. Stephen C. Finley and Biko Mandela Gray, "God *Is* a White Racist: Immanent Atheism as a Religious Response to Black Lives Matter and State-Sanctioned Anti-Black Violence," *Journal of Africana Religions* 3, no. 4 (2015), 443–53; Achille Mbembe, "Necropolitics," trans. Libby Meintjes, *Public Culture* 15, no. 1 (2003), 11–40; Lewis Gordon, "Race, Theodicy, and the Normative Emancipatory Challenges of Blackness," *South Atlantic Quarterly* 112, no. 4 (2013): 725–36.
9. Theodore Vial, *Modern Religion, Modern Race* (New York: Oxford University Press, 2016), 1–4.
10. Vial, *Modern Religion, Modern Race*, 1.
11. Vial, *Modern Religion, Modern Race*, 6–7.
12. Vial, *Modern Religion, Modern Race*, 12.
13. Michael D. Parsons, "Labor Studies in Decline," *Labor Studies Journal* 15 (1990), 66–81.
14. Parsons, "Labor Studies in Decline," 69.
15. Parsons, "Labor Studies in Decline," 69.
16. Edward Webster, "Recasting Labor Studies in the Twenty-First Century," *Labor Studies Journal* 33, no. 3 (2008), 249–54.

17. Parsons, "Labor Studies in Decline," 69.
18. Parsons, "Labor Studies in Decline," 175.
19. Parsons, "Labor Studies in Decline," 175.
20. W. Bradford Wilcox, Andrew J. Cherlin, Jeremy E. Uecherk, and Matthew Messel. "No Money, No Honey, No Church: The Deinstitutionalization of Religious Life among the White Working Class," *Research in the Sociology of Work* 23 (2012), 227–50.
21. Wilcox et al., "No Money, No Honey, No Church," 230.
22. Michèle Lamont, Bo Yun Park, and Elena Ayala-Hurtado, "Trump's Electoral Speeches and His Appeal to the American White Working Class," *British Journal of Sociology* 68, no. S1 (2017), S154–S180.
23. Lamont et al., "Trump's Electoral Speeches."
24. Lamont et al., "Trump's Electoral Speeches," S163.
25. Victor G. Devinatz, "Donald Trump, George Wallace, and the White Working Class," *Labor Studies Journal* 42, no. 3 (2017), 233–8.
26. Devinatz, "Donald Trump, George Wallace, and the White Working Class," 234.
27. Devinatz, "Donald Trump, George Wallace, and the White Working Class," 234.
28. Devinatz, "Donald Trump, George Wallace, and the White Working Class," 234.
29. Devinatz, "Donald Trump, George Wallace, and the White Working Class," 234.
30. Otis Duncan, "A Socioeconomic Index for All Occupations," in Albert J. Reiss (ed.), *Occupations and Social Status* (New York: Free Press, 1961), 108–34.
31. Melvin L. Oliver and Thomas M. Shapiro, *Black Wealth, White Wealth: A New Perspective on Racial Inequality*, 10th anniversary edn. (New York: Routledge, 2006).
32. Oliver and Shapiro, *Black Wealth, White Wealth*.
33. Lori Latrice Martin, Hayward Derrick Horton, and Teresa A. Booker, *Lessons from the Black Working Class: Foreshadowing America's Economic Health* (Santa Barbara, CA: Praeger, 2015), 133.
34. Venise Wagner, "Living in the Red: Black Steelworkers and the Wealth Gap," *Labor Studies Journal* 42, no. 1 (2017), 52–78.
35. W. E. B. Du Bois, "Politics and Industry," May 31, 1909, W. E. B. Du Bois Papers, Special Collections and University Archives, University of Massachusetts Amherst Libraries, MS 312 (hereafter Du Bois Papers).
36. Du Bois, "Politics and Industry," 3.
37. Du Bois, "Politics and Industry," 3.
38. Du Bois, "Politics and Industry," 3.
39. Du Bois, "Politics and Industry," 6.
40. W. E. B. Du Bois, letter to *Revolutionary Age*, September 23, 1931, Du Bois Papers, 1.
41. Du Bois, letter to *Revolutionary Age*, 1.
42. Heidi Gottfried, "New Directions, Old Approaches: Labor Studies at the Crossroads," *Labor Studies Journal* 27, no. 2 (2002), 1–6.
43. Parsons, "Labor Studies in Decline," 81.
44. Parsons, "Labor Studies in Decline," 69.
45. Parsons, "Labor Studies in Decline," 81.

46. Parsons, "Labor Studies in Decline," 81.
47. Gottfried, "New Directions, Old Approaches," 2.
48. Gottfried, "New Directions, Old Approaches," 1; Howard Kimeldorf, *Battling for American Labor: Wobblies, Craft Workers, and the Making of the Union Movement* (Berkeley: University of California Press, 1999), Ching Kwan Lee, *Gender and the South China Miracle: Two Worlds of Factory Women* (Berkeley: University of California Press, 1998).
49. Cedric de Leon, "Black from White: How the Rights of White and Black Workers Became 'Labor' and 'Civil' Rights after the U.S. Civil War," *Labor Studies Journal* 42, no. 1, 10–26.
50. Leon, "Black from White," 10.
51. Leon, "Black from White," 11.
52. Leon, "Black from White," 15.
53. Evelyn Brooks Higginbotham, *Righteous Discontent: The Women's Movement in the Black Baptist Church, 1880–1920* (Cambridge, MA: Harvard University Press, 1993).
54. Wagner, "Living in the Red," 69.
55. Wagner, "Living in the Red," 69.
56. Wagner, "Living in the Red," 69.
57. Wagner, "Living in the Red," 69.
58. Eric D. Larson, "Black Lives Matter and Bridge Building: Labor Education for a 'New Jim Crow' Era," *Labor Studies Journal* 41, no. 1 (2016), 36–66.
59. Larson, "Black Lives Matter and Bridge Building," 36.
60. Larson, "Black Lives Matter and Bridge Building," 36.
61. Larson, "Black Lives Matter and Bridge Building," 36.
62. Larson, "Black Lives Matter and Bridge Building," 47.

BIBLIOGRAPHY

"14 Words." ADL website. https://www.adl.org/education/references/hate-symbols/14-words

"250 Mourn Birmingham in Danville." News release, September 16, 1963. Samuel C. Shirah, Jr., Papers, 1961–1964, Wisconsin Historical Society, Madison, WI, Archives Main Stacks, Mss 540, Box 1, Folder 2, WIHVS2640-A.

Adeyinka, Tunji. "The Role of Patriotism in Sports Sponsorship." *Journal of Sponsorship* 4, no. 2 (2011): 155–62.

Ahmed, Sara. "Affective Economies." *Social Text* 22, no. 2 (79) (2004), 117–39.

Ahmed, Sara. *The Cultural Politics of Emotion.* New York: Routledge, 2004.

Ahmed, Sara. *The Cultural Politics of Emotion*, 2nd edn. New York: Routledge, 2014.

Ahmed, Sara. "A Phenomenology of Whiteness." *Feminist Theory* 8, no. 2 (2007), 149–68.

Ahmed, Sara. *The Promise of Happiness.* Durham, NC: Duke University Press, 2010.

Alexander, Jeffrey C. *The Meanings of Social Life: A Cultural Sociology.* Oxford: Oxford University Press, 2003.

Allport, Gordon W. and J. Michael Ross. "Personal Religious Orientation and Prejudice." *Journal of Personality and Social Psychology* 5, no. 4 (1967), 432–43.

Anderson, Benedict. *Imagined Communities: Reflections on the Origin and Spread of Nationalism*, rev. edn. New York: Verso, 2005.

Anderson, Carol. *White Rage: The Unspoken Truth of Our Racial Divide.* New York: Bloomsbury, 2016; paperback edn., 2017.

Anderson, Victor. *Beyond Ontological Blackness: An Essay on African American Religious and Cultural Criticism.* New York: Continuum, 1995.

Annual Report of the Missionary to the Negroes in Liberty County, Ga., 1833. Charleston, SC: Observer Office Press, 1834

Arendt, Hannah. *The Human Condition*, 2nd edn. Chicago: University of Chicago Press, 1998.

Armstrong, Karen. *Islam: A Short History.* New York: Modern Library, 2002.

Armstrong, Jennifer Keishin. "Why The Handmaid's Tale Is So Relevant Today." BBC Culture, April 25, 2018. http://www.bbc.com/culture/story/20180425-why-the-handmaids-tale-is-so-relevant-today

"Asks Webber Surrender Credentials." *Zion's Herald*, June 19, 1946.

Austin, Allan W. *Quaker Brotherhood: Interracial Activism and the American Friends Service Committee, 1917–1950*. Urbana: University of Illinois Press, 2012.

Bae, Bosco B. "Christianity and Implicit Racism in the U.S. Moral and Human Economy." *Open Theology* 2, no. 1 (2016), 1002–17.

Baker, John E. "Mourning and the Transformation of Object Relationships: Evidence for the Persistence of Internal Attachments." *Psychoanalytic Psychology* 18, no. 1 (2001), 55–73.

Bailer, Lloyd H. "The Automobile Unions and Negro Labor." *Political Science Quarterly* 59, no. 4 (1944), 548–77.

Bailer, Lloyd H. "The Negro Automobile Worker." *Journal of Political Economy* 51, no. 5 (1943): 415–28.

Bantum, Brian K. *The Death of Race: Building a New Christianity in a Racial World*. Minneapolis: Fortress Press, 2016.

Barkum, Michael. *Religion and the Racist Right: The Origins of the Christian Identity Movement*. Chapel Hill: University of North Carolina Press, 1994.

Bastide, Roger. "Color, Racism, and Christianity." *Dædalus* 96, no. 2 (1967), 312–27.

Bastién, Angelica Jade. "In Its First Season, *The Handmaid's Tale*'s Greatest Failing Is How It Handles Race." *Vulture*, June 14, 2017. https://www.vulture.com/2017/06/the-handmaids-tale-greatest-failing-is-how-it-handles-race.html

Bates, Beth Tompkins. *The Making of Black Detroit in the Age of Henry Ford*. Chapel Hill: University of North Carolina Press, 2012.

Beaumont, Peter and Amanda Holpuch. "How *The Handmaid's Tale* Dressed Protests across the World." *The Guardian*, August 3, 2018. https://www.theguardian.com/world/2018/aug/03/how-the-handmaids-tale-dressed-protests-across-the-world

Belfrage, Sally. "Danville on Trial." *New Republic*, November 2, 1963.

Bell, C. C. "Racism: A Symptom of Narcissistic Personality Disorder." *Journal of the National Medical Association* 72, no. 7 (1980), 661–5.

Bell, Catherine. *Ritual Theory, Ritual Practice*. New York: Oxford University Press, 1992.

Bella, Timothy. "Women 'Are the N-Word of the World,' Bette Midler Tweeted. She Apologized Hours Later." *Washington Post*, October 5, 2018. https://www.washingtonpost.com/news/morning-mix/wp/2018/10/05/women-are-the-n-word-of-the-world-bette-midler-tweeted-she-apologized-hours-later

Bellah, Robert N. *The Broken Covenant: American Civil Religion in Time of Trial*, 2nd edn. Chicago: University of Chicago Press, 1992.

Bellah, Robert. "Civil Religion in America." *Dædalus* 96, no. 1 (1967), 1–21.

Bennett, Larry. "The Legacy of Adolph Reed, Jr.'s 'Black Urban Regime.'" *Labor Studies Journal* 41, no. 3 (2016), 256–9.

Bergson, Henri. *The Two Sources of Morality and Religion*, trans. R. Ashley Audra and Cloudesley Brereton. Notre Dame, IN: University of Notre Dame Press, [1935] 1977.

Berr, Jonathan. "NFL's Tangled Ties with National Anthem Don't Run Deep." CBS News, May 28, 2018. https://www.cbsnews.com/news/the-nfls-tangled-ties-with-the-national-anthem-dont-run-deep

Berry, Damon T. *Blood and Faith: Christianity in American White Nationalism.* Syracuse, NY: Syracuse University Press, 2017.

Berry, Damon T. "Religious Strategies of White Nationalism at Charlottesville." *Religion and Culture Forum*, October 13, 2017. https://voices.uchicago.edu/religion-culture/2017/10/13/religious-strategies-of-white-nationalism-at-charlottesville

Black, Eric. *Our Constitution: The Myth That Binds Us.* Boulder, CO: Westview Press, 1988.

"Black Boys Viewed as Older, Less Innocent than Whites, Research Finds." American Psychological Association, March 6, 2014. https://www.apa.org/news/press/releases/2014/03/black-boys-older.aspx

Blackmore, Glenwood. "What's Wrong with FEPC?" *United Evangelical Action*, September 15, 1949.

"Blood & Faith: An Interview with Damon T. Berry." *606*, November 3, 2018. https://sixoh6.com/2018/02/15/blood-faith-an-interview-with-damon-t-berry

Blum, Edward J., Tracy Fessenden, Prema Kurien, and Judith Weisenfeld. "Forum: American Religion and 'Whiteness.'" *Religion and American Culture* 19, no. 1 (2009), 1–35.

Bohache, Thomas. "Embodiment as Incarnation: An Incipient Queer Christology." *Theology & Sexuality* 10, no. 1 (2003), 9–29.

Bonacich, Edna. "Advanced Capitalism and Black/White Race Relations in the United States: A Split Labor Market Interpretation" *American Sociological Review* 41, no. 1 (1976), 34–51.

Bonilla-Silva, Eduardo. *White Supremacy and Racism in the Post–Civil Rights Era.* Boulder, CO: Lynne Riener, 2001.

Borders, William Holmes. "The Spiritual and Economic Basis for Democracy in the South." *Christian Frontiers*, April 1947, 114–20.

Borjas, George J. "The Substitutability of Black, Hispanic, and White Labor." *Economic Inquiry* 21, no. 1 (1983), 93–106.

Bortolini, Matteo. "The Trap of Intellectual Success: Robert N. Bellah, the American Civil Religion Debate, and the Sociology of Knowledge." *Theory and Society* 41, no. 2 (2012), 187–210.

Bourdieu, Pierre. *Distinction: A Social Critique of the Judgement of Taste*, trans. Richard Nice. Cambridge, MA: Harvard University Press, 1984.

Bourdieu, Pierre. *The Logic of Practice*, trans. Richard Nice. Stanford, CA: Stanford University Press, 1990.

"Brett Kavanaugh's Opening Statement at Senate Hearing." CBS News/YouTube, September 27, 2018. https://youtu.be/eahnOcp883k

Brickman, Celia. *Aboriginal Populations in the Mind: Race and Primitivity in Psychoanalysis.* New York: Columbia University Press, 2003.

Bringhurst, Newell G. and Darron T. Smith (eds.). *Black and Mormon.* Urbana: University of Illinois Press, 2004.

Brinkley, Douglas. *Wheels for the World: Henry Ford, His Company, and a Century of Progress, 1903–2003.* New York: Viking, 2003.

Britt, Brian. "Taking a Knee as Critical Civil Religion." University of Chicago Divinity School, January 5, 2017. https://divinity.uchicago.edu/sightings/taking-knee-critical-civil-religion

Bronstein, Jamie L. *Two Nations, Indivisible: A History of Inequality in America.* Santa Barbara, CA: Praeger, 2016.

Brown, DeNeen L. "The Preacher Who Used Christianity to Revive the Klan." *Washington Post*, April 10, 2018. https://www.washingtonpost.com/news/retropolis/wp/2018/04/08/the-preacher-who-used-christianity-to-revive-the-ku-klux-klan

Brueggemann, John. "The Power and Collapse of Paternalism: The Ford Motor Company and Black Workers, 1937–1941. *Social Problems* 47, no. 2 (May 2000), 220–40.

Bruner, C. V. "An Abstract of the Religious Instruction of the Slaves in the Antebellum South." *Peabody Journal of Education* 11, no. 3 (1933), 117–21.

Bump, Philip. "The People Whom President Trump Has Called Stupid." *Washington Post*, August 6, 2018. https://www.washingtonpost.com/news/politics/wp/2018/08/06/the-people-trump-has-called-stupid

Burgess, David. "The Fellowship of Southern Churchmen: Its History and Promise." *Prophetic Religion*, Spring 1953, 3–11.

Bush, Carletta A. "Faith, Power, and Conflict: Miner Preachers and the United Mine Workers of America in the Harlan County Mine Wars, 1931–1939," PhD dissertation, West Virginia University, 2006.

Butler, Judith. *Bodies That Matter: On the Discursive Limits of "Sex."* Abingdon, England: Routledge, [1993] 2011.

Butterworth, Michael L. "Fox Sports, Super Bowl XLII, and the Affirmation of American Civil Religion." *Journal of Sport and Social Issues* 32, no. 3 (2008), 318–23.

Butterworth, Michael L. "Militarism and Memorializing at the Pro Football Hall of Fame." *Communication and Critical/Cultural Studies* 9, no. 3 (2012), 241–58.

Butterworth, Michael L. "The Passion of the Tebow: Sports Media and Heroic Language in the Tragic Frame." *Critical Studies in Media Communication* 30, no. 1 (2013), 17–33.

Butterworth, Michael L. "Race in 'The Race': Mark McGwire, Sammy Sosa, and Heroic Constructions of Whiteness." *Critical Studies in Media Communication* 24, no. 3 (2007), 228–44.

Butterworth, Michael L. "Ritual in the 'Church of Baseball': Suppressing the Discourse of Democracy after 9/11." *Communication and Critical/Cultural Studies* 2, no. 2 (2005), 107–29.

Butterworth, Michael L. "Saved at Home: Christian Branding and Faith Nights in the 'Church of Baseball.'" *Quarterly Journal of Speech* 97, no. 3 (2011), 309–33.

Butterworth, Michael L. and Stormi Moskal. "American Football, Flags, and 'Fun': The Bell Helicopter Armed Forces Bowl and the Rhetorical Production of Militarism." *Communication, Culture & Critique* 2, no. 4 (2009), 411–33.

Campbell, Lawrence. "Sermon, Danville, VA, 1963." In *Voices of the Civil Rights Movement: Black American Freedom Songs, 1960–1966*. Washington, DC: Smithsonian Folkways Recordings, [1980] 1997.

Capps, Walter H. *Religious Studies: The Making of a Discipline*. Minneapolis: Fortress Press, 1995.

Carpenter, Joel A. *Revive Us Again: The Reawakening of American Fundamentalism*. New York: Oxford University Press, 1997.

Carter, C. Sue. "Oxytocin Pathways and the Evolution of Human Behavior." *Annual Review of Psychology* 65 (2014), 17–39.

The Catechism of the Protestant Episcopal Church in the Confederate States. Raleigh, NC: Office of "The Church Intelligencer," 1862.

A Catechism, to Be Taught Orally to Those Who Cannot Read; Designed Especially for the Instruction of the Slaves, in the Prot. Episcopal Church in the Confederate States. Raleigh, NC: Office of "The Church Intelligencer," 1862.

Cavanaugh, William T. "The Myth of Religious Violence." In Andrew Murphy (ed.), *The Blackwell Companion to Religion and Violence*. Malden, MA and Oxford: Wiley-Blackwell, 2011, 23–33.

Chafe, William H. et al. (eds.). *Remembering Jim Crow: African Americans Tell about Life in the Segregated South*. New York: New Press, 2001.

"Chaplain to Labor Causes Dispute." *Zion's Herald*, September 3, 1947.

Chappell, David L. *A Stone of Hope: Prophetic Religion and the Death of Jim Crow*. Chapel Hill: University of North Carolina Press, 2004.

Cheng, Anne Anlin. *The Melancholy of Race: Psychoanalysis, Assimilation, and Hidden Grief*. New York: Oxford University Press, 2001.

Cheng, Patrick S. *From Sin to Amazing Grace: Discovering the Queer Christ*. New York: Seabury, 2012.

Cheng, Patrick S. *Radical Love: An Introduction to Queer Theology*. New York: Seabury, 2011.

Chothia, Farouk. "South Africa: The groups Playing on the Fears of a 'White Genocide.'" BBC News, September 1, 2018. https://www.bbc.com/news/world-africa-45336840

"Church Releases Statement Condemning White Supremacist Attitudes." Church of Jesus Christ of Latter-Day Saints website, August 15, 2017. https://www.churchofjesuschrist.org/church/news/church-releases-statement-condemning-white-supremacist-attitudes?lang=eng

Cline, David P. *From Reconciliation to Revolution: The Student Interracial Ministry, Liberal Christianity, and the Civil Rights Movement*. Chapel Hill: University of North Carolina Press, 2016.

Collier-Thomas, Bettye. *Jesus, Jobs, and Justice: African American Women and Religion*. New York: Alfred A. Knopf, 2010.

Collins, Patricia Hill. *Black Feminist Thought: Knowledge, Consciousness, and the Politics of Empowerment*. New York: Routledge, 2000.

Cone, James H. *A Black Theology of Liberation*. Philadelphia: Lippincott, 1970.

Convention on the Prevention and Punishment of the Crime of Genocide. UN Doc. A/810, adopted December 9, 1948, 78 UNTS 277.

Copeland, M. Shawn. *Enfleshing Freedom: Body, Race, and Being*. Minneapolis: Fortress Press, 2010.

Cox, Daniel, Rachel Lienesch, and Robert P. Jones. "Beyond Economics: Fears of Cultural Displacement Pushed the White Working Class to Trump." PRRI, May 9, 2017. https://www.prri.org/research/white-working-class-attitudes-economy-trade-immigration-election-donald-trump

"Creativity Movement." Southern Poverty Law Center. https://www.splcenter.org/fighting-hate/extremist-files/group/creativity-movement-0

Criss, Doug. "This Is the 30-Year Old Willie Horton Ad Everybody Is Talking About Today," CNN Politics, November 1, 2018. https://www.cnn.com/2018/11/01/politics/willie-horton-ad-1988-explainer-trnd/index.html

Cronin, Mary. "When the Chinese Came to Massachusetts: Representations of Race, Labor, Religion, and Citizenship in the 1870 Press." *Historical Journal of Massachusetts* 45, no. 2 (2018), 73–105.

Crystal, David. *Begat: The King James Bible and the English Language*. Oxford: Oxford University Press, 2010.

Curry, Tommy. *The Man-Not: Race, Class, Genre, and the Dilemmas of Black Manhood*. Philadelphia: Temple University Press, 2017.

Dailey, Jane. "Sex, Segregation, and the Sacred after Brown." *Journal of American History* 91, no. 1 (2004), 119–44.

Dailey, Jane. "The Theology of Unionism and Antiunionism." *Labor: Studies in Working-Class History* 14, no. 1 (2017), 83–7.

Danville Demonstrations, Court Steps." *Encyclopedia Virginia*. https://www.encyclopediavirginia.org/media_player?mets_filename=evm00002400mets.xml

"Danville Protests to Go On." *Chicago Daily Defender*, December 16, 1963, A17.

Darden, Robert. *Nothing but Love in God's Water, Vol. 2: Black Sacred Music from the Sit-Ins to Resurrection City*. University Park: Pennsylvania State University Press, 2016.

Davis, Angela Y. *Women, Race, & Class*. New York: Vintage, 1983.

Daymond, Antonia Michelle. "Can These Bones Live?: Addressing the Necrotic in U.S. Theo-Politics." *CrossCurrents* 68, no. 1 (March 2019), 135–58.

Delgado, Richard and Jean Stefancic. *Critical Race Theory: An Introduction*, 2nd edn. New York: New York Universty Press, 2012.

Delores J. Page and Margaret P. Dillard v. Chief Eugene McCain et al. (4th Cir. 1963).

"Demographics of Sports Fans in U.S." Demographic Partition, July 10, 2017. http://demographicpartitions.org/demographics-of-sports-fans-u-s

Department of Homeland Security Strategic Framework for Countering Terrorism and Targeted Violence. Embargoed Draft Text, September 19, 2019. Available at https://games-cdn.washingtonpost.com/notes/prod/default/documents/56c099f1-5905-42de-b542-69f790f02939/note/bebd1e86-e32a-40a2-892c-4a7dd4f84b25.pdf#page=1

Devinatz, Victor G. "Donald Trump, George Wallace, and the White Working Class." *Labor Studies Journal* 42, no. 3 (2017), 233–8.

DiAngelo, Robin. *White Fragility: Why It's So Hard for White People to Talk About Racism*. Boston: Beacon Press, 2018.

Dickerson, Sally S., Tara L. Gruenewald, and Margaret E. Kemeny. "When the Social Self Is Threatened: Shame, Physiology, and Health." *Journal of Personality* 72, no. 6 (2004), 1192–1216.

Dillard, Angela D. *Faith in the City: Preaching Radical Social Change in Detroit*. Ann Arbor: University of Michigan Press, 2007.

Dillon, Denis E. Memo to Burke Marshall, August 21, 1963, ProQuest History Vaults, Civil Rights during the Kennedy Administration, 1961–1963, Part 2: The Papers of Burke Marshall, Assistant Attorney General for Civil Rights, folder 001351-026-0767.

Dittmar, Helga, Emma Halliwell, and Suzanne Ive. "Does Barbie Make Girls Want to Be Thin? The Effect of Experimental Exposure to Images of Dolls on the Body Image of 5- to 8-Year-Old Girls." *Developmental Psychology* 42, no. 2 (2006), 283–92.

"Dixie Cops Break into Church to Nab Leaders." *Chicago Daily Defender*, June 24, 1963.

Dobratz, Betty A. "The Role of Religion in the Collective Identity of the White Racialist Movement." *Journal for the Scientific Study of Religion* 40, no. 2 (2001): 287–302.

Docherty, George. "Under God," sermon preached February 7, 1954. Transcript available at http://www.christianheritagemins.org/articles/UNDER%20GOD.pdf

Dochuk, Darren. *From Bible Belt to Sunbelt: Plain-Folk Religion, Grassroots Politics, and the Rise of Evangelical Conservatism*. New York: W. W. Norton, 2011.

Dockterman, Eliana. "The *Handmaid's Tale* Showrunner on Why He Made Some Major Changes from the Book." *Time*, April 25, 2017. http://time.com/4754200/the-handmaids-tale-showrunner-changes-from-book

Dodge, D. Witherspoon. *Southern Rebel in Reverse: The Autobiography of an Idol-Shaker*. New York: American Press, 1961.

Dorrien, Gary. *The New Abolition: W. E. B. Du Bois and the Black Social Gospel*. New Haven, CT: Yale University Press, 2015.

Driscoll, Christopher. *White Lies: Race and Uncertainty in the Twilight of American Religion*. New York: Routledge, 2016.

Douglas, Kelly Brown. *The Black Christ*. Maryknoll, NY: Orbis, 1994.

Douglas, Kelly Brown. *Stand Your Ground: Black Bodies and the Justice of God*. Maryknoll, NY: Orbis, 2015.

Douglas, Mary. *Purity and Danger*. New York: Routledge, [1966] 2002.

Du Bois, W. E. B. *Darkwater: Voices from within the Veil*. Mineola, NY: Dover, [1920] 1999.

Du Bois, W. E. B. "Letter to *Revolutionary Age*," September 23, 1931. W. E. B. Du Bois Papers, Special Collections and University Archives, University of Massachusetts Amherst Libraries, MS 312.

Du Bois, W. E. B. "Politics and Industry," May 31, 1909. W. E. B. Du Bois Papers, Special Collections and University Archives, University of Massachusetts Amherst Libraries, MS 312.
Du Bois, W. E. B. *The Souls of Black Folk*. Chicago: A. C. McClurg, 1903.
Dubofsky, Melvyn. *The State and Labor in Modern America*. Chapel Hill: University of North Carolina Press, 1994.
Dunbar, Anthony P. *Against the Grain: Southern Radicals and Prophets, 1929–1959*. Charlottesville: University Press of Virginia, 1981.
Duncan, Don. "Racism on Trial—A Brutal Portland Murder and the Southern Lawyer 'Who Broke the Klan': White Supremacy On Trial." *Seattle Times*, September 23, 1990. http://community.seattletimes.nwsource.com/archive/?date=19900923&slug=1094653
Duncan, Otis. "A Socioeconomic Index for All Occupations." In Albert J. Reiss (ed.), *Occupations and Social Status*. New York: Free Press, 1961.
Dupont, Carolyn Renée. *Mississippi Praying: Southern White Evangelicals and the Civil Rights Movement, 1945–1975*. New York: New York University Press, 2013.
Durkheim, Emile. *The Elementary Forms of Religious Life*, trans. Karen E. Fields. New York: Free Press, 1997.
Durkheim, Emile. *The Elementary Forms of Religious Life*, trans. Carol Cosman. Oxford: Oxford University Press, 2001.
Duster, Chandelis. "Gov. Andrew Cuomo Uses 'N-word' to Make Point about Derogatory Terms against Italians." CNN Politics, October 15, 2019. https://www.cnn.com/2019/10/15/politics/andrew-cuomo-racial-slur/index.html
Dvorak, Katharine L. *An African-American Exodus: The Segregation of the Southern Churches*. Brooklyn, NY: Carlson, 1991.
"Dwight D. Eisenhower and Susan B. Anthony's Dollar: Gasparo's Portfolio." National Museum of American History website. https://americanhistory.si.edu/collections/search/object/nmah_1396076
Edmunds, Emma C. "Danville Civil Rights Demonstrations of 1963." *Encyclopedia Virginia*, December 7, 2016. http://www.encyclopediavirginia.org/Danville_Civil_Rights_Demonstrations_of_1963
Edmunds, Emma. "Robert A. Williams, Attorney, Williams, Luck & Williams, Martinsville, Virginia (b. 1944)." Virginia Center for Digital History, 2011. http://www.vcdh.virginia.edu/cslk/danville/bio_williams.html
Edsall, Thomas B. "The Paranoid Style in American Politics is Back." *New York Times*, September 8, 2016. https://www.nytimes.com/2016/09/08/opinion/campaign-stops/the-paranoid-style-in-american-politics-is-back.html
Egerton, Douglas R. "'Why They Did Not Preach Up This Thing': Denmark Vesey and Revolutionary Theology." *South Carolina Historical Magazine* 100, no. 4 (1999): 298–318.
Egerton, John. *Speak Now against the Day: The Generation before the Civil Rights Movement in the South*. Chapel Hill: University of North Carolina Press, 1994.
Eliade, Mircea. *The Myth of Eternal Return, or Cosmos and History*, trans. Willard R. Trask. Princeton, NJ: Princeton University Press, 1954 and reprints.

Embry, Jessie L. "Oral History and Mormon Women Missionaries: The Stories Sound the Same." *Frontiers: A Journal of Women Studies* 19, no. 3 (1998), 171–88.

Emerson, Michael O. and Christian Smith. *Divided by Faith: Evangelical Religion and the Problem of Race in America*. New York: Oxford University Press, 2001.

"Encyclopedia of Southern Jewish Communities—Danville, Virginia." Goldring/Woldenberg Institute of Southern Jewish Life website. http://www.isjl.org/virginia-danville-encyclopedia.html

Equal Justice Initiative. *Lynching in America: Confronting the Legacy of Racial Terror*, 3rd edn. Montgomery, AL: Equal Justice Initiative, 2017. Available at https://eji.org/wp-content/uploads/2019/10/lynching-in-america-3d-ed-080219.pdf

Evangelicals Move Forward for Christ. Pamphlet published in Indianapolis. National Association of Evangelicals Records, Box 99, Billy Graham Center, Wheaton College, Wheaton, IL.

"Extreme Right/Radical Right/Far Right." ADL website. https://www.adl.org/resources/glossary-terms/extreme-right-radical-right-far-right

Fannin, Mark. *Labor's Promised Land: Radical Visions of Gender, Race, and Religion in the South*. Knoxville: University of Tennessee Press, 2003.

Fanon, Frantz. *Black Skin, White Masks*, trans. Charles Lam Markmann. New York: Grove Press, 1967.

Fanon, Frantz. *Black Skin, White Masks*, trans. Richard Philcox. New York: Grove Press, 2008.

Farzan, Antonia Noori. "BBQ Becky, Permit Patty and Cornerstore Caroline: Too 'Cutesy' for Those White Women Calling Police on Black People?" *Washington Post*, October 19, 2018. https://www.washingtonpost.com/news/morning-mix/wp/2018/10/19/bbq-becky-permit-patty-and-cornerstore-caroline-too-cutesy-for-those-white-women-calling-cops-on-blacks

Feagin, Joe. *Systemic Racism: A Theory of Oppression*. New York: Routledge, 2006.

Feimster, Crystal N. *Southern Horrors: Women and the Politics of Rape and Lynching*. Cambridge, MA: Harvard University Press, 2011.

Feurer, Rosemary. *Radical Unionism in the Midwest, 1900–1950*. Urbana: University of Illinois Press, 2006.

Fight White Genocide. "What is White Genocide?" FAQ's. Accessed November 21, 2018. http://www.fightwhitegenocide.com/faqs/.

Finley, Stephen C. "Signification and Subjectivity: Reflections on Racism, Colonialism, and (Re)Authentication in Religion and Religious Studies." *International Journal of Africana Studies* 19, no. 2 (2019), 15–35.

Finley, Stephen C. "The Supernatural in the African American Experience." In Jeffrey J. Kripal (ed.), *Religion: Super Religion*. Farmington Hills, MI: Macmillan Reference USA, 2017.

Finley, Stephen C. and Biko Mandela Gray. "God *Is* a White Racist: Immanent Atheism as a Religious Response to Black Lives Matter and State-Sanctioned Anti-Black Violence." *Journal of Africana Religions* 3, no. 4 (2015), 443–53.

Finley, Stephen C. and Lori L. Martin. "The Complexity of Color and the Religion of Whiteness." In Lori L. Martin, Hayward D. Horton, Cedric Herring, Verna M.

Keith, and Melvin Thomas (eds.), *Color Struck: How Race and Complexion Matter in the "Color-Blind" Era*. Rotterdam: Sense, 2017.
"Fire Hoses Turned on Va. Demonstrators." *Chicago Daily Defender*, June 11, 1963.
"Five Fundamental Beliefs." Creativity Alliance website. https://creativityalliance.com
Fletcher, Jeannine Hill. *The Sin of White Supremacy: Christianity, Racism, and Religious Diversity in America*. Maryknoll, NY: Orbis, 2017.
Flow, J. E. "The Federal Council and Race Segregation." *Southern Presbyterian Journal*, May 15, 1946.
Flynt, Wayne. *Alabama Baptists: Southern Baptists in the Heart of Dixie*. Tuscaloosa: University of Alabama Press, 1998.
Flynt, Wayne. "Religion for the Blues: Evangelicalism, Poor Whites, and the Great Depression." *Journal of Southern History* 71, no. 1 (2005), 3–38.
Frey, William H. "The US Will Become 'Minority White' in 2045, Census Projects Youthful Minorities Are the Engine of Future Growth." Brookings Institution website, March 14, 2018. https://www.brookings.edu/blog/the-avenue/2018/03/14/the-us-will-become-minority-white-in-2045-census-projects
Fones-Wolf, Elizabeth and Ken Fones-Wolf. "Sanctifying the Southern Organizing Campaign: Protestant Activists in the CIO's Operation Dixie." *Labor: Studies in Working Class History* 6, no. 1 (2009), 5–32.
Fones-Wolf, Elizabeth and Ken Fones-Wolf. *Struggle for the Soul of the Postwar South: White Evangelical Protestants and Operation Dixie*. Urbana: University of Illinois Press, 2015.
Fones-Wolf, Elizabeth and Ken Fones-Wolf. "'Termites in the Temple': Fundamentalism and Anti-Liberal Politics in the Post-World War II South." *Religion and American Culture* 28, no. 2 (2018), 167–205
Foote, Justin Gus, Michael L. Butterworth, and Jimmy Sanderson. "Adrian Peterson and the 'Wussification of America': Football and Myths of Masculinity." *Communication Quarterly* 65, no. 3 (2017), 268–84.
Forney, Craig A. *The Holy Trinity of American Sport: Civil Religion in Football, Baseball, and Basketball*. Macon, GA: Mercer University Press, 2007.
Frazier, E. Franklin. "The Pathology of Race Prejudice." *The Forum* 70 (1927), 856–62.
Freedman, Samuel G. "When White Sports Fans Turn on Black Athletes." *The Guardian*, October 5, 2017. https://www.theguardian.com/commentisfree/2017/oct/05/white-sports-fans-nfl-black-athletes-race-protest
Freud, Sigmund. *Civilization and Its Discontents*, trans. James Strachey. New York: W. W. Norton, 1961.
Freud, Sigmund. *Introductory Lectures on Psycho-Analysis*, trans. James Strachey. New York: W. W. Norton, 1966.
Freud, Sigmund. "Mourning and Melancholia." In *The Standard Edition of the Complete Psychological Works of Sigmund Freud, Volume XIV (1914–1916): On the History of the Psycho-Analytic Movement, Papers on Metapsychology and Other Works*, trans. James Strachey. London: Hogarth Press, [1957] 1964.
Freud, Sigmund. *Three Essays on a Theory of Sexuality*, trans. James Strachey. New York: Basic, [1962] 2000.

Fuller, Robert. *Naming the Antichrist: The History of an American Obsession.* New York: Oxford University Press, 1995.

Gans, Herbert J. "Race as Class." *Contexts* 4, no. 4 (2005), 17–21.

Garrison, Joey. "'Violent Terrorist': Who Is the White Supremacist Suspect in New Zealand Mosque Shootings?" *USA Today*, March 21, 2019. https://eu.usatoday.com/story/news/nation/2019/03/15/new-zealand-christchurch-mosque-shootings-who-brenton-tarrant/3172550002

Garrow, David J. "Religious Resources and the Montgomery Bus Boycott." *Criterion*, no. 34 (1995).

Gellman, Erik S. and Jarod Roll. *Gospel of the Working Class: Labor's Southern Prophets in New Deal America.* Urbana: University of Illinois Press, 2011.

Gilroy, Paul. "Scales and Eyes: 'Race' Making Difference." In Sue Golding (ed.), *The Eight Technologies of Otherness*. London: Routledge, 1997.

Gilsinan, Kathy. "Why Is Dylann Roof So Worried About Europe? Echoes of an International Conspiracy Theory in Charleston." *The Atlantic*, June 24, 2015. https://www.theatlantic.com/international/archive/2015/06/dylann-roof-world-white-supremacist/396557

Goetz, Rebecca Anne. *The Baptism of Early Virginia: How Christianity Created Race.* Baltimore: Johns Hopkins University Press, 2012.

Goff, P. A., M. C. Jackson, B. A. L. Di Leone, C. M. Culotta, and N. A. DiTomasso. "The Essence of Innocence: Consequences of Dehumanizing Black Children." *Journal of Personality and Social Psychology* 106, no. 4 (2014), 526–45.

Goldenberg, David M. *The Curse of Ham: Race and Slavery in Early Judaism, Christianity, and Islam.* Princeton, NJ: Princeton University Press, 2003.

Gordon, Lewis. *Bad Faith and Antiblack Racism.* Atlantic Highlands, NJ: Humanities Press, 1995.

Gordon, Lewis. "Race, Theodicy, and the Normative Emancipatory Challenges of Blackness." *South Atlantic Quarterly* 112, no. 4 (2013), 725–36.

Gordon, Linda. *The Second Coming of the KKK: The Ku Klux Klan of the 1920s and the American Political Tradition.* New York: Liveright, 2017.

Gottfried, Heidi. "New Directions, Old Approaches: Labor Studies at the Crossroads." *Labor Studies Journal* 27, no. 2 (2002), 1–6.

Gray, Biko M., Stephen C. Finley, and Lori L. Martin. "'High Tech Lynching': White Virtual Mobs and Administrators as Policing Agents in Higher Education." *Issues in Race & Society: An Interdisciplinary Global Journal* (2019).

"Great White Father." Merriam-Webster. https://www.merriam-webster.com/dictionary/Great%20White%20Father

Green, John C. "The American Religious Landscape and Political Attitudes: A Baseline for 2004." Available at https://assets.pewresearch.org/wp-content/uploads/sites/11/2007/10/green-full.pdf

Greene, Alison Collis. *No Depression in Heaven: The Great Depression, the New Deal, and the Transformation of Religion in the Delta.* New York: Oxford University Press, 2016.

Gregg, Melissa, and Gregory J. Seigworth (eds.) *The Affect Theory Reader.* Durham, NC: Duke University Press, 2010.

Griffith, David W. (dir.). *Birth of a Nation*. Thousand Oaks, CA: Epoch Producing Corporation, 1915.

Gruenewald, Tara L., Margaret E. Kemeny, Najib Aziz, and John L. Fahey. "Acute Threat to the Social Self: Shame, Social Self-Esteem, and Cortisol Activity." *Psychosomatic Medicine* 66, no. 6 (2004), 915–24.

"A Guide to the 1963 Danville (Va.) Civil Rights Case Files, 1963–1973." Library of Virginia, September 1999. http://www.lva.virginia.gov/findaid/38099.htm

Hall, Debra L., David C. Matz, and Wendy Wood. "Why Don't We Practice What We Preach? A Meta-Analytic Review of Religious Racism." *Personality and Social Psychology Review* 14, no. 1 (2009), 126–39.

Hall, Jacquelyn Dowd. *Revolt against Chivalry: Jessie Daniel Ames and the Women's Campaign against Lynching*. New York: Columbia University Press, 1979.

Halon, Yael. "Trump Has 'Deep Love and Support' for Police, Unlike Dems: Lahren on Police Union's 2020 Endorsement." Fox News, September 24, 2019. https://www.foxnews.com/media/lahren-on-police-union-2020-endorsement

Hammond, Phillip E., Amanda Porterfield, James G. Moseley, and Jonathan D. Sarna. "Forum: American Civil Religion Revisited." *Religion and American Culture: A Journal of Interpretation* 4, no. 1 (1994), 1–23.

Hangen, Tona J. *Redeeming the Dial: Radio, Religion, and Popular Culture in America*. Chapel Hill: University of North Carolina Press, 2002.

Hankins, Barry. *God's Rascal: J. Frank Norris and the Beginnings of Southern Fundamentalism*. Lexington: University Press of Kentucky.

Hare, Brian. "Survival of the Friendliest: *Homo Sapiens* Evolved via Selection for Prosociality." *Annual Review of Psychology* 68 (2017), 155–86.

Harris, Dorothy O. and Emma Edmunds. "Danville Civil Rights Demonstrations: 1963 Violence." In "Dorothy O. Harris, Teacher and Principal (b. 1930)," Virginia Center for Digital History, 2003, http://www.vcdh.virginia.edu/cslk/danville/bio_harris.html

Harris, Dorothy O. and Emma Edmunds. "First Black Mayor and Voting: Charles H. Harris." In "Dorothy O. Harris, Teacher and Principal (b. 1930)," Virginia Center for Digital History, 2003, http://www.vcdh.virginia.edu/cslk/danville/bio_harris.html

Harris-Perry, Melissa V. *Sister Citizen: Shame, Stereotypes, and Black Women in America*. New Haven, CT: Yale University Press, 2011.

Hartman, Saidiya. *Scenes of Subjection: Terror, Slavery, and Self-Making in Nineteenth Century America*. New York: Oxford University Press, 1998.

Harvey, Paul. "'The Color of Skin Was Almost Forgotten.'" In Winfred B. Moore, Jr., Kyle S. Sinisi, and David H. White, Jr. (eds.), *Warm Ashes: Issues in Southern History at the Dawn of the Twenty-First Century*. Columbia: University of South Carolina Press, 2003.

Harvey, Paul. *Freedom's Coming: Religious Culture and the Shaping of the South from the Civil War through the Civil Rights Era*. Chapel Hill: University of North Carolina Press, 2005.

Hauslohner, Abigail and Abby Ohlheiser. "Some Neo-Nazis Lament the Pittsburgh Massacre: It Derails Their Efforts to be Mainstream." *Washington*

Post, October 30, 2018. https://www.washingtonpost.com/national/some-neo-nazis-lament-the-pittsburgh-massacre-it-derails-their-efforts-to-be-mainstream/2018/10/30/3163fd9c-dc5f-11e8-85df-7a6b4d25cfbb_story.html

Hawkins, J. Russell and Phillip Luke Sinitiere (eds.), *Christians and the Color Line: Race and Religion after "Divided by Faith."* New York: Oxford University Press, 2013.

Hayes, John. *Hard, Hard Religion: Interracial Faith in the Poor South*. Chapel Hill: University of North Carolina Press, 2017.

Haynes, Stephen R. *The Last Segregated Hour: The Memphis Kneel-ins and the Campaign for Southern Church Desegregation*. New York: Oxford University Press, 2012.

Heer, Jeet. "Trump's Cult of Personality Takes Paranoia to the Next Level." *New Republic*, January 26, 2018. https://newrepublic.com/article/146786/trumps-cult-personality-takes-paranoia-next-level

Heideking, Jürgen. "The Federal Processions of 1788 and the Origins of 1788 and the Origins of American Civil Religion." *Soundings: An Interdisciplinary Journal* 77, no. 3/4 (1994), 367–87.

Hendrix, Steve and Michael E. Miller. "'Let's Get This Party Started': New Zealand Shooting Suspect Narrated His Chilling Rampage." *Washington Post*, March 15, 2019. https://www.washingtonpost.com/local/lets-get-this-party-started-new-zealand-gunman-narrated-his-chilling-rampage/2019/03/15/fb3db352-4748-11e9-90f0-0ccfeec87a61_story.html

Hershman, James H., Jr. "Archibald M. Aiken (1888–1971)." *Encyclopedia Virginia*. https://www.encyclopediavirginia.org/Aiken_Archibald_Murphey_1888-1971

Hewitt, Nancy A. "Taking the True Woman Hostage." *Journal of Women's History* 14, no. 1 (2002), 156–62.

Higginbotham, Evelyn Brooks. *Righteous Discontent: The Women's Movement in the Black Baptist Church, 1880–1920*. Cambridge, MA: Harvard University Press, 1993.

Highmore, Ben. "Bitter After Taste: Affect, Food and Social Aesthetics." In Melissa Gregg and Gregory J. Seigworth (eds.), *The Affect Theory Reader*. Durham, NC: Duke University Press, 2010.

Hill, Carla. "The Racist Obsession with South African 'White Genocide.'" ADL website, August 24, 2018. https://www.adl.org/blog/the-racist-obsession-with-south-african-white-genocide

Hochschild, Arlie Russell. *Strangers in Their Own Land: Anger and Mourning on the American Right*. New York: New Press, 2016.

Hofstadter, Richard. *The Paranoid Style in American Politics*. New York: Vintage, [1965] 2008.

Holland, Sharon Patricia. *The Erotic Life of Racism*. Durham, NC: Duke University Press, 2012.

Homans, Peter, *The Ability to Mourn: Disillusionment and the Social Origins of Psychoanalysis*. Chicago: University of Chicago Press, 1989.

Honey, Michael Keith. *Black Workers Remember: An Oral History of Segregation, Unionism, and the Freedom Struggle.* Berkeley: University of California Press, 1999.

Honey, Michael K. *Southern Labor and Black Civil Rights: Organizing Memphis Workers.* Urbana: University of Illinois Press, 1993.

Hood, Robert E. *Begrimed and Black: Christian Traditions on Blacks and Blackness.* Minneapolis: Augsburg Fortress, 1994.

Hopkins, Dwight N. "Slave Theology in the 'Invisible Institution.'" In Cornel West and Eddie S. Glaude, Jr. (eds.), *African American Religious Thought: An Anthology.* Louisville, KY: Westminster John Knox Press, 2003.

"How a Rising Star of White Nationalism Broke Free from the Movement." NPR, September 24, 2018. https://www.npr.org/templates/transcript/transcript.php?storyId=651052970

Hunter, Howard William. "All Are Alike unto God." Speech at Brigham Young University, Provo, UT, February 4, 1979.

Huntley, Horace and David Montgomery (eds.). *Black Workers' Struggle for Equality in Birmingham.* Urbana: University of Illinois Press, 2004.

Ingraham, Christopher. "Two New Studies Find Racial Anxiety Is the Biggest Driver of Support for Trump." *Washington Post,* June 6, 2016. https://www.washingtonpost.com/news/wonk/wp/2016/06/06/racial-anxiety-is-a-huge-driver-of-support-for-donald-trump-two-new-studies-find

Intravia, Jonathan, Alex Piquero, and Nicole Leeper Piquero. "The Racial Divide Surrounding United States of America National Anthem Protest in the National Football League." *Deviant Behavior* 39, no. 8 (2018): 1058–68.

Isenberg, Nancy. *White Trash: The 400-Year Untold History of Class in America.* New York: Penguin, 2017.

Jackson, James Conroy. "The Religious Education of the Negro in South Carolina Prior to 1850." *Historical Magazine of the Protestant Episcopal Church* 36, no. 1 (1967), 35–61.

Jacobson, Cardell K. and Darron T. Smith. "Emotion Work in Black and White: Transracial Adoption and the Process of Racial Socialization." In Patricia Neff Claster and Sampson Lee Blair (eds.), *Visions of the 21st Century Family: Transforming Structures and Identities.* Bingley, England: Emerald, 2013, 43–75.

James, Gilbert. "What's Right with FEPC?" *United Evangelical Action,* September 15, 1949.

Jennings, Willie James. *The Christian Imagination: Theology and the Origins of Race.* New Haven, CT: Yale University Press, 2010.

Johnson, Daryl. "Hate in God's Name: Religious Extremism and Its Relation to Violent Conflict." Southern Poverty Law Center, September 25, 2017. https://www.splcenter.org/20170925/hate-god's-name

Johnson, Micah E. "The Paradox of Black Patriotism: Double Consciousness." *Ethnic and Racial Studies* 41, no. 11 (2018): 1971–89.

Johnson, Sylvester A. *African American Religions, 1500–2000: Colonialism, Democracy, and Freedom.* New York: Cambridge University Press, 2015.

Johnson, Troy. "Native American Indian Spirituality." In Elizabeth M. Dowling and W. George Scarlett (eds.), *Encyclopedia of Religious and Spiritual Development*. Thousand Oaks, CA: Sage, 2006.

"Johnston, Parson Jack" file. Stetson Kennedy Papers, reel 2, New York Public Library.

Jones, Charles C. *The Religious Instruction of the Negroes in the United States*. Savannah, GA: Thomas Purse, 1842.

Jones, Jacqueline. *American Work: Four Centuries of Black and White Labor*. New York: W. W. Norton, 1998.

Jones, Robert P. *The End of White Christian America*. New York: Simon & Schuster, 2016.

Jones, Robert P. "White Evangelical Support for Donald Trump at All-Time High." PRRI, April 18, 2018. https://www.prri.org/spotlight/white-evangelical-support-for-donald-trump-at-all-time-high

Jones, William. *Is God a White Racist?: A Preamble to Black Theology*. Garden City, NY: Anchor Press, 1973; reprint Boston: Beacon Press, 1986.

Jones, William P. *The March on Washington: Jobs, Freedom, and the Forgotten History of Civil Rights*. New York: W. W. Norton, 2013.

Jordan, Winthrop D. *White over Black: American Attitudes toward the Negro, 1550–1812*. Chapel Hill: University of North Carolina Press, 1968.

Juergensmeyer, Mark. *Terror in the Mind of God: The Global Rise of Religious Violence*. Berkeley: University of California Press, 2001.

Kao, Grace Y. and Jerome E. Copulsky. "The Pledge of Allegiance and the Meanings and Limits of Civil Religion." *Journal of the American Academy of Religion* 75, no. 1 (2007), 121–49.

"Kathleen Cleaver Oral History Interview Conducted by Joseph Mosnier in Atlanta, Georgia, 2011 September 16." Library of Congress. https://www.loc.gov/item/2015669150

Kauder, Louis M. Memo to Burke Marshall, August 28, 1963, ProQuest History Vaults, Civil Rights during the Kennedy Administration, 1961–1963, Part 2: The Papers of Burke Marshall, Assistant Attorney General for Civil Rights, folder 001351-026-0767.

Kelsey, George D. *Racism and the Christian Understanding of Man*. New York: Charles Scribner's Sons, 1965.

Kendi, Ibram X. *Stamped from the Beginning: The Definitive History of Racist Ideas in America*. New York: Nation, 2016; Bodley Head, 2017.

Kennedy, Stetson. *Southern Exposure*. Garden City, NY: Doubleday, 1946.

Kersten, Andrew E. and Clarence Lang (eds.). *Reframing Randolph: Labor, Black Freedom, and the Legacies of A. Philip Randolph*. New York: New York University Press, 2014.

Khanna, Ranjana. *Dark Continents: Psychoanalysis and Colonialism*. Durham, NC: Duke University Press, 2003.

Kimeldorf, Howard. *Battling for American Labor: Wobblies, Craft Workers, and the Making of the Union Movement*. Berkeley: University of California Press, 1999.

Kimmel, Michael. *Angry White Men: American Masculinity at the End of an Era*. New York: Nation, 2013.
King, Martin Luther, Jr., *Where Do We Go from Here? Chaos or Community?* Boston: Beacon Press, 1968.
Kitch, John. "Football as American Civic Religion." *Law and Liberty*, February 2, 2018, http://www.libertylawsite.org/2018/02/02/football-as-american-civic-religion
Klassen, Ben. *Nature's Eternal Religion: Part One of the White Man's Bible*. Church of Creativity, [1973] 2015. Available at https://creativityalliance.com/eBook-BenKlassen-Nature%27sEternalReligion.pdf
Kohut, Heinz. "Forms and Transitions of Narcissism." *Journal of the American Psychoanalytic Association* 14, no. 2 (1996), 243–72.
Korstad, Robert Rodgers. *Civil Rights Unionism: Tobacco Workers and the Struggle for Democracy in the Mid-Twentieth-Century South*. Chapel Hill: University of North Carolina Press, 2003.
Kruse, Kevin M. *White Flight: Atlanta and the Making of Modern Conservatism*. Princeton, NJ: Princeton University Press, 2005
"Ku Klux Klan: The Invisible Empire." *CBS Reports*, September 21, 1965. Available at https://www.c-span.org/video/?433239-1/ku-klux-klan
"Labor Chaplain." *Zion's Herald*, July 24, 1946.
"Labor Studies." Society for the Study of Social Problems website, November 2019. https://www.sssp1.org/index.cfm/pageid/1235/m/464
Lacan, Jacques. *Ecrits: A Selection*, trans. Bruce Fink. New York: W. W. Norton, 2002.
Lahren, Tomi. "Tomi Lahren: I Support Law Enforcement, Not Because I'm White or Conservative but Because I'm an American." Fox News, March 12, 2019. https://www.foxnews.com/opinion/tomi-lahren-i-support-law-enforcement-not-because-im-white-or-conservative-but-because-im-an-american
Lambert, Frank. "'I Saw the Book Talk': Slave Readings of the First Great Awakening." *Journal of African American History* 87, no. 1 (2002): 12–25.
Lamont, Michèle, Bo Yun Park, and Elena Ayala-Hurtado. "Trump's Electoral Speeches and His Appeal to the American White Working Class." *The British Journal of Sociology* 68, no. S1 (2017), S154–S180.
Lane, Christopher (ed.). *The Psychoanalysis of Race*. New York: Columbia University Press, 1998.
Larson, Eric D. "Black Lives Matter and Bridge Building: Labor Education for a 'New Jim Crow' Era." *Labor Studies Journal* 41, no. 1 (2016), 36–66.
Lee, Ching Kwan. *Gender and the South China Miracle: Two Worlds of Factory Women*. Berkeley: University of California Press, 1998.
Lee, Heslip M. "Strictly Confidential," Department of Justice, Attorney General's Office, 1963. ProQuest History Vault, Civil Rights during the Kennedy Administration, 1961–1963, Part 2: The Papers of Burke Marshall, Assistant Attorney General for Civil Rights, folder 001351-026-0287.
Leon, Cedric de. "Black from White: How the Rights of White and Black Workers Became 'Labor' and 'Civil' Rights after the U.S. Civil War." *Labor Studies Journal* 42, no. 1 (2017), 10–26.

Lewis, Earl. *In Their Own Interests: Race, Class, and Power in Twentieth-Century Norfolk, Virginia*. Berkeley: University of California Press, 1991.

Lichtenstein, Nelson. *Labor's War at Home: The CIO in World War II*. New York: Cambridge University Press, 1982.

Lincoln, Bruce. *Holy Terrors: Thinking about Religion after September 11*, 2nd edn. Chicago: University of Chicago Press, 2006.

Lischer, Richard. *The Preacher King: Martin Luther King, Jr. and the Word That Moved America*. New York: Oxford University Press, 1995.

"LISTEN: 'BBQ Becky's' Viral 911 Call Made Public." KTVU/YouTube, August 31, 2018. https://www.youtu.be/LgaU1h0QiLo.

Lofton, Kathryn. *Consuming Religion*. Chicago: University of Chicago Press, 2017.

Lonergan, Bernard. *Insight: A Study of Human Understanding*. Toronto: University of Toronto Press, 1992.

Long, Charles H. *Significations: Signs, Symbols, and Images in the Interpretation of Religion*. Philadelphia: Fortress Press, 1986; reprints Aurora, CO: Davies Group, 1995, 1999.

López, Ian Haney. *White by Law: The Legal Construction of Race*, 2nd edn. New York: New York University Press, 2006.

Lorence, James J. *A Hard Journey: The Life of Don West*. Urbana: University of Illinois Press, 2007.

Lough, Adam Bhala (dir.). *Alt-Right: The Age of Rage*. Los Angeles: Alldayeveryday, 2018.

Loveland, Anne C. *Southern Evangelicals and the Social Order, 1800–1860*. Baton Rouge: Lousiana State University Press, 1980.

Lowe, Mary Elise. "Gay, Lesbian, and Queer Theologies: Origins, Contributions, and Challenges." *Dialog* 48, no. 1 (2009), 49–61.

Lynch, Gordon. *The Sacred in the Modern World: A Cultural Sociological Approach*. Oxford: Oxford University Press, 2012.

"Lynchings, Sept. 2, 1945 (V-J Day) thru September, 1946." Typescript memo, Southern Conference for Human Welfare Collection, Box 1, folder 10, Archives and Special Collections, Robert Woodruff Library, Atlanta University Center, Atlanta, GA.

MacGuill, Dan. "Did Donald Trump Encourage Violence at His Rallies?" *Snopes* (no date). https://www.snopes.com/fact-check/donald-trump-incitement-violence

MacWilliams, Matthew C. "Who Decides When the Party Doesn't? Authoritarian Voters and the Rise of Donald Trump." *PS: Political Science & Politics* 49, no. 4 (2016), 716–21.

Manis, Andrew M. "'City Mothers': Dorothy Tilly, Georgia Methodist Women, and Black Civil Rights." In Glenn Feldman (ed.), *Politics and Religion in the White South*. Lexington: University Press of Kentucky, 2005, 125–56.

Marlin, David H. Memos to Burke Marshall, August 21, August 23, August 27, and September 17, 1963. ProQuest History Vault, Civil Rights during the Kennedy Administration, 1961–1963, Part 2: The Papers of Burke Marshall, Assistant Attorney General for Civil Rights, folder 001351-026-0767.

Marlin, David H. Memo to Burke Marshall, September 23, 1963. ProQuest History Vault, Civil Rights during the Kennedy Administration, 1961–1963, Part 2:

The Papers of Burke Marshall, Assistant Attorney General for Civil Rights, folder 001351-026-0287.
Marsh, Charles. *God's Long Summer: Stories of Faith and Civil Rights*. Princeton, NJ: Princeton University Press, 1997.
Martelle, Scott. *Detroit, A Biography*. Chicago: Chicago Review Press, 2014.
Martin, Lori Latrice, Hayward Derrick Horton, Cedric Herring, Verna M. Keith, and Melvin Thomas (eds.). *Color Struck: How Race and Complexion Matter in the "Color-Blind" Era*. Rotterdam: Sense, 2017.
Martin, Lori Latrice, Hayward Derrick Horton, and Teresa A. Booker. *Lessons from the Black Working Class: Foreshadowing America's Economic Health*. Santa Barbara, CA: Praeger, 2015.
Martin, Robert F. *Howard Kester and the Struggle for Social Justice in the South, 1904–77*. Charlottesville: University Press of Virginia, 1991.
Martin, Steve and George F. McHendry, Jr. "Kaepernick's Stand: Patriotism, Protest, and Professional Sports." *Journal of Contemporary Rhetoric* 6, no. 3/4 (2016), 88–98.
Martínez, Jessica and Gregory A. Smith. "How the Faithful Voted: A Preliminary 2016 Analysis." Pew Research Center, November 9, 2016. https://www.pewresearch.org/fact-tank/2016/11/09/how-the-faithful-voted-a-preliminary-2016-analysis
Mason, Lucy Randolph. "The CIO and the Negro in the South." *Journal of Negro Education* 14, no. 4 (1945), 552–61.
Mason, Lucy Randolph. "Memo Memphis, April 25, 1941." Operation Dixie Records, reel 64, Rare Book, Manuscript, and Special Collections Library, Duke University, Durham, NC.
Massumi, Brian. "The Future Birth of the Affective Fact." In Melissa Gregg and Gregory J. Seigworth (eds.), *The Affect Theory Reader*. Durham, NC: Duke University Press, 2010.
Mather, Cotton. *The Negro Christianized An Essay to Incite and Assist That Good Work, the Instruction of Negro-Servants in Christianity*. Boston: B. Green, 1706.
Mathews, Donald G. "Charles Colcock Jones and the Southern Evangelical Crusade to Form a Biracial Community." *Journal of Southern History* 41, no. 3 (1975), 299–320.
Matias, Cheryl E. *Feeling White: Whiteness, Emotionality, and Education*. Rotterdam: Sense, 2016.
Matlon, Jordanna. "Racial Capitalism and the Crisis of Black Masculinity." *American Sociological Review* 81, no. 5 (2016), 1014–38.
Mbembe, Achille. *Critique of Black Reason*, trans. Laurent Dubois. Durham, NC: Duke University Press, 2017.
Mbembe, Achille. "Necropolitics," trans. Libby Meintjes. *Public Culture* 15, no. 1 (2003), 11–40.
Mbiti, John S. *Introduction to African Religion*, 2nd edn. Lone Grove, IL: Waveland Press, 1991.
McDaneld, Jen. "White Suffragist Dis/Entitlement: The Revolution and the Rhetoric of Racism." *Legacy* 30, no. 2 (2013): 243–64.

McDonald, Jermaine M. "A Fourth Time of Trial: Towards an Implicit and Inclusive American Civil Religion." *Implicit Religion* 16, no. 1 (2013), 47–64.

McGuire, Danielle L. *At the Dark End of the Street: Black Women, Rape, and Resistance—a New History of the Civil Rights Movement from Rosa Parks to the Rise of Black Power.* New York: Alfred A. Knopf, 2010.

McGuire, Meredith B. *Religion: The Social Context*, 5th edn. Belmont, CA: Wadsworth Thomson Learning, 2002.

McIntire, Carl. "The Modernist-Communist Threat to American Liberties." *Sword of the Lord*, September 14, 1945.

McIntire, Carl. "Private Enterprise in the Scriptures." *Sword of the Lord*, September 21, 1945.

McMichael, Jack R. "The New Social Climate in the South." *Social Questions Bulletin*, May 1945, 4–5.

McNeal, Laura Rene. "From Hoodies to Kneeling During the National Anthem: The Colin Kaepernick Effect and Its Implications for K-12 Sports." *Louisiana Law Review* 78, no. 1 (2017), 146–96.

Meier, August and Elliot M. Rudwick. *Black Detroit and the Rise of the UAW*. New York: Oxford University Press, 1979.

Memo about Klan public meeting, Knoxville, TN, May 18, 1946 (nine-page typescript). Stetson Kennedy Papers, reel 1, New York Public Library.

Merritt, Keri Leigh. *Masterless Men: Poor Whites and Slavery in the Antebellum South*. Cambridge, England: Cambridge University Press, 2017.

Mesa, José M. de. "Making Salvation Concrete and Jesus Real: Trends in Asian Christology." *Exchange* 30, no. 1 (2001), 1–17.

Metzl, Jonathan M. *Dying of Whiteness: How the Politics of Racial Resentment Is Killing America's Heartland*. New York: Basic, 2019.

Middlebrook, Harold. Memo to Wyatt T. Walker, September 19, 1963. ProQuest History Vault, Series I, Records of Andrew Young, Program Director, 1961–1964, Subseries 3, Records of the Voter Education Project, 1962–1964, Subseries iii, Field Reports [1962–1964], folder 001569-006-0226

Middlebrook, Harold A., L. G. Campbell, and L. W. Chase. Letter to A. Philip Randolph, August 22, 1963. ProQuest History Vault, Black Freedom Struggle in the 20th Century: Organizational Records and Personal Papers, Part 1, Bayard Rustin Papers, Chronological Subject File—March on Washington—1963, folder 001581-009-0674.

Millard, H. "True Religion, Meaning and Purpose are one with and Indissolubly Linked to Our White DNA Code." Western Spring website, April 19, 2016. http://www.westernspring.co.uk/true-religion-meaning-purpose-one-indissoslubly-linked-white-dna-code

Miller, Dorothy and Danny Lyon. "Danville, Virginia." Student Nonviolent Coordinating Committee, August 1963. Available at https://www.crmvet.org/docs/danville63.pdf

Minkenberg, Michael. "Religion and the Radical Right." In Jens Rydgren (ed.), *The Oxford Handbook of the Radical Right*. New York: Oxford University Press, 2018.

Moeggenberg, Zarah and Samantha L. Solomon. "Power, Consent, and the Body: #MeToo and The Handmaid's Tale." *Gender Forum*, no. 70 (2018), 4–25.
"The Monroe Incident." *Wesleyan Christian Advocate*, August 9, 1946.
Morgan, Edmund S. *American Slavery, American Freedom: The Ordeal of Colonial Virginia*. New York: W. W. Norton, 1975.
Morris, Aldon. "The Black Church in the Civil Rights Movement." In Christian Smith (ed.), *Disruptive Religion: The Force of Faith in Social-Movement Activism*. New York: Routledge, 1996.
Morse, Catherine. "The Handmaid's Tale Was Always about Race—So Is the Abortion Ban." *Medium*, May 18, 2019. https://medium.com/@morseca01/the-handmaids-tale-was-always-about-race-so-is-the-abortion-ban-c2cf2aa39025
Muse, Benjamin. "Confidential Memorandum, Danville, Va., September 28–October 4, 1963." ProQuest History Vaults, Civil Rights during the Kennedy Administration, 1961–1963, Part 2: The Papers of Burke Marshall, Assistant Attorney General for Civil Rights, folder 001351-009-00213.
"National Labor Relations Act." National Labor Relations Board website. https://www.nlrb.gov/how-we-work/national-labor-relations-act
Nelson, William Stuart. "The Christian Imperative and Race Relations." *AME Zion Quarterly Review* 54, no. 2 (1944).
Norris, Michele. "As America Changes, Some Anxious Whites Feel Left Behind." *National Geographic*, April 2018. https://www.nationalgeographic.com/magazine/2018/04/race-rising-anxiety-white-america
Nurser, John S. *For All Peoples and All Nations: The Ecumenical Church and Human Rights*. Washington, DC: Georgetown University Press, 2005.
O'Brien, Connor. "'I Don't Give Any Credibility' to New Zealand Shooter Citing Trump, Ambassador Says." *Politico*, March 17, 2019. https://www.politico.com/story/2019/03/17/new-zealand-shooter-trump-scott-brown-1224069
Oduyoye, Mercy Amba. *Introducing African Women's Theology*. Cleveland: Pilgrim Press, 2001.
Okafor, Chinyere G. "Global Encounters: 'Barbie' in Nigerian Agbogho-Mmuo Mask Context." *Journal of African Cultural Studies* 19, no. 1 (2007): 37–54.
Oliver, Melvin L. and Thomas M. Shapiro. *Black Wealth, White Wealth: A New Perspective on Racial Inequality*, 10th anniversary edn. New York: Routledge, 2006.
O'Meara, Michael. *Toward the White Republic*. San Francisco: Counter-Currents, 2010.
Omi, Michael and Howard Winant. *Racial Formation in the United States: From the 1960s to the 1990s*, 2nd edn. New York: Routledge, 1994.
Oral History Memoir of Acker C. Miller, August 5, 1971. Baylor University Institute of Oral History, Waco, Texas.
Orr, James. "Dust." In *International Standard Bible Encyclopedia*. Grand Rapids, MI: Wm. B. Eerdmans Publishing Co. (1939). Available at https://www.internationalstandardbible.com/D/dust.html
Otto, Rudolf. *The Idea of the Holy*, trans. John W. Harvey. London: Humphrey Milford, 1923; reprint New York: Oxford University Press, 1950.

"Out of the Best Books? Publications Continue to Promote Folklore." *Sunstone*, March 2003, 34–5.

Painter, Nell Irvin. *The History of White People*. New York: W. W. Norton, 2010.

Parker, Christopher Sebastian. "Race and Politics in the Age of Obama." *Annual Review of Sociology* 42 (2016), 217–30.

Parsons, Michael D. "Labor Studies in Decline." *Labor Studies Journal* 15 (1990), 66–81.

"Patricia Arquette Winning Best Supporting Actress." Oscars/YouTube, March 9, 2015. https://www.youtu.be/6wx-Qh4Vczc

Patterson, Vernon W. "Where Does the 'Social Gospel' Road End." *Sword of the Lord*, July 25, 1947.

Perkinson, James W. "The Ghost in the Global Machine: White Violence, Indigenous Resistance, and Race as Religiousness." *CrossCurrents* 64, no. 1(2014), 59–72.

Perkinson, James W. *White Theology: Outing Supremacy in Modernity*. New York: Palgrave Macmillan, 2004.

Perman, Michael. *Pursuit of Unity: A Political History of the American South*. Chapel Hill: University of North Carolina Press, 2009.

"Permit Patty Calls Police on 8-Year-Old for Selling Water without a Permit." Trish's World/YouTube, June 24, 2018. https://www.youtu.be/gbOkxqt_uiU

Peterson, Joyce Shaw. "Black Automobile Workers in Detroit, 1910–1930." *Journal of Negro History* 64, no. 3 (1979), 177–90.

Phan, Peter C. "Jesus the Christ with an Asian Face." *Theological Studies* 57, no. 3 (1996), 399–430.

Pierce, C., J. Carew, D. Pierce-Gonzalez, and D. Willis. "An Experiment in Racism: TV Commercials." In Chester M. Pierce (ed.), *Television and Education* (Beverly Hills, CA: Sage, 1978), 62–88.

Pinn, Anthony B. "Looking like Me?: Jesus Images, Christology, and the Limitations of Theological Blackness." In George Yancy (ed.), *Christology and Whiteness: What Would Jesus Do?* Abingdon, England: Routledge, 2012.

Pinn, Anthony B. *Terror and Triumph: The Nature of Black Religion*. Minneapolis: Fortress Press, 2003.

Porter, Rick. "The 100 Highest-Rated TV Programs of 2017: 60% Sports, 40% Everything Else." *TV by the Numbers*, December 28, 2017. https://tvbythenumbers.zap2it.com/more-tv-news/the-100-highest-rated-tv-programs-of-2017-60-sports-40-everything-else

Prasad, Monica, Andrew Perrin, Kieran Bezila, Steve G. Hoffman, Kate Kindleberger, Kim Manturuk, Ashleigh Smith Powers, and Andrew R. Payton. "The Undeserving Rich: 'Moral Values' and the White Working Class." *Sociological Forum* 24, no. 2 (2009), 225–53.

Proceedings of the Meeting in Charleston, S.C., May 13–15, 1845, on the Religious Instruction of the Negroes, Together with the Report of the Committee, and the Address to the Public. Charleston, SC: B. Jenkins, 1845.

"Proclamation: To the Great White Father and All His People." *Anthropology News* 11, no. 2 (1970), 2–12.

Proudfoot, Wayne. *Religious Experience*. Berkeley: University of California Press, 1987.
"A Rebirth of Constitutional Government." GOP website. https://www.gop.com/platform/we-the-people
"Registration Drive Ends in Danville." News release, 1963. ProQuest History Vault, Series I, Records of Andrew Young, Program Director, 1961–1964, Subseries 3, Records of the Voter Education Project, 1962–1964, Subseries iii, Field Reports [1962–1964], folder 001569-006-0250.
Rice, Cynthia A. "The First American Great Awakening: Lessons Learned and What Can Be Done to Foster a Habitat for the Next Great Awakening." *International Congregational Journal* 9, no. 2 (2010), 103–17.
Rice, Karlie, Ivanka Prichard, Marika Tiggemann, and Amy Slater. "Exposure to Barbie: Effects on Thin-Ideal Internalisation, Body Esteem, and Body Dissatisfaction among Young Girls." *Body Image* 19 (2016): 142–9.
Ritterhouse, Jennifer. *Growing up Jim Crow: How Black and White Southern Children Learned Race*. Chapel Hill: University of North Carolina, 2006.
Roediger, David R. *The Wages of Whiteness: Race and the Making of the American Working Class*, 3rd edn. London: Verso, 2007.
Roll, Jarod H. *Spirit of Rebellion: Labor and Religion in the New Cotton South*. Urbana: University of Illinois Press, 2010.
Romano, Renee Christine. *Race Mixing: Black-White Marriage in Postwar America*. Cambridge, MA: Harvard University Press, 2003.
Rubin, Jennifer. "Like His Lies, Trump's Racist Comments Don't Surprise, but They Should Be Counted." *Washington Post*, November 4, 2018. https://www.washingtonpost.com/news/opinions/wp/2018/11/04/like-his-lies-trumps-racist-comments-dont-surprise-but-they-should-be-counted
Russell, Jeffrey Burton. *Lucifer: The Devil in the Middle Ages*. Ithaca, NY: Cornell University Press, 1984.
"The Sapphire Caricature." Jim Crow Museum website, Ferris State University. https://www.ferris.edu/HTMLS/news/jimcrow/antiblack/sapphire.htm
Saslow, Eli. "The White Flight of Derek Black." *Washington Post*, October 15, 2016 https://www.washingtonpost.com/national/the-white-flight-of-derek-black/2016/10/15/ed5f906a-8f3b-11e6-a6a3-d50061aa9fae_story.html
Savage, Barbara Dianne. *Your Spirits Walk beside Us: The Politics of Black Religion*. Cambridge, MA: Belknap Press, 2008.
Schaefer, Donovan O. *Religious Affects: Animality, Evolution, and Power*. Durham, NC: Duke University Press, 2015.
Schleiermacher, Friedrich. *On Religion: Speeches to its Cultured Despisers*, trans. and ed. Richard Crouter, 2nd edn. Cambridge, England: Cambridge University Press, 1996.
Seigworth, Gregory J. and Melissa Gregg, "An Inventory of Shimmers." In Melissa Gregg and Gregory J. Seigworth (eds.), *The Affect Theory Reader*. Durham, NC: Duke University Press, 2010.
Sexton, Jared. "The Social Life of Social Death." *InTensions* 5 (2011).

Shattuck, John, Aaron Huang, and Elisabeth Thoreson-Green. "The War on Voting Rights." Carr Center for Human Rights Policy, February 2019. Available at https://carrcenter.hks.harvard.edu/files/cchr/files/ccdp_2019_003_war_on_voting_final.pdf

Shearer, Tobin Miller. *Daily Demonstrators: The Civil Rights Movement in Mennonite Homes and Sanctuaries*. Baltimore: Johns Hopkins University Press, 2010.

Shearer, Tobin Miller. "Invoking Crisis: Performative Christian Prayer and the Civil Rights Movement." *Journal of the American Academy of Religion* 83, no. 2 (2015), 490–512.

Sherman, Aurora M. and Eileen L. Zurbriggen. "'Boys Can Be Anything': Effect of Barbie Play on Girls' Career Cognitions." *Sex Roles* 70, no. 5–6 (2014): 195–208.

Sigelman, Lee, Timothy Bledsoe, Susan Welch, and Michael W. Combs. "Making Contact? Black-White Social Interaction in an Urban Setting." *American Journal of Sociology* 101, no. 5 (1996), 1306–32.

Simon, Bryant. *A Fabric of Defeat: The Politics of South Carolina Millhands, 1910–1948*. Chapel Hill: University of North Carolina Press, 1998.

"Sixteen Commandments." Creativity Alliance. https://creativityalliance.com/home/16commandments

Smith, Darron T. "Negotiating Black Self-Hate within the LDS Church." *Dialogue: A Journal of Mormon Thought* 51, no. 3 (2018), 29–44.

Smith, Darron T. *When Race, Religion, and Sport Collide: Black Athletes at BYU and Beyond*. Lanham, MD: Rowman & Littlefield, 2015.

Smith, William A. "Toward an Understanding of Misandric Microaggressions and Racial Battle Fatigue among African Americans in Historically White Institutions." In Eboni M. Zamani-Gallaher and Vernon C. Polite (eds.), *The State of the African American Male* (East Lansing: Michigan State University Press, 2010), 256–77.

Smith, William A., Man Hung, and Jeremy D. Franklin. "Between Hope and Racial Battle Fatigue: African American Men and Race-Related Stress." *Journal of Black Masculinity* 2, no. 1, 35–58.

Smith, William A., Jalil Bishop Mustaffa, Chantal M. Jones, Tommy J. Curry, and Walter R. Allen. "'You Make Me Wanna Holler and Throw Up Both My Hands!': Campus Culture, Black Misandric Microaggressions, and Racial Battle Fatigue." *International Journal of Qualitative Studies in Education* 29, no. 9 (2016), 1189–1209.

Soady, Viki. Review of Benjamin Valentine (ed.), *In Our Own Voices: Latino/a Renditions of Theology*. *Journal for Peace and Justice Studies* 25, no. 2 (2015), 193–5.

Sorek, Tamir and Robert G. White. "American Football and National Pride: Racial Differences." *Social Science Research* 58 (2016), 266–78.

"Southern Baptists Study Race Relations." *Religious Herald*, September 1, 1949.

Southern Poverty Law Center. "Creativity Movement." https://www.splcenter.org/fighting-hate/extremist-files/group/creativity-movement-0.

Sparrow, James T. *Warfare State: World War II Americans and the Age of Big Government*. New York: Oxford University Press, 2011.

Spillers, Hortense. "Mama's Baby, Papa's Maybe: An American Grammar Book." *Diacritics* 17, no. 2 (1987), 64–81.
Spillers, Hortense. "Martin Luther King, Jr. and America's Civil Religion." *Nanzan Review of American Studies* 29 (2007), 39–49.
"Stanford University Reacts to BBQ Becky Calling Cops on Black People." *News One*, May 16, 2018. https://newsone.com/3799344/stanford-university-allegedly-jennifer-schulte
Stanton, Elizabeth Cady. "This Is the Negro's House." Letter to the editor, *National Anti-Slavery Standard*, December 26, 1865.
Stein, Michael. "Cult and Sport: The Case of Big Red." *Mid-American Review of Sociology* 2, no. 2 (1977), 29–42.
Stevens, Maryanne (ed.). *Reconstructing the Christ Symbol: Essays in Feminist Christology*. Eugene, OR: Wipf & Stock, [1993] 2004.
Stewart, Carole Lynn. "Civil Religion, Civil Society, and the Performative Life and Work of W. E. B. Du Bois." *Journal of Religion* 88, no. 3 (2008), 307–30.
"STOP White Genocide, by Halting MASSIVE Third World Immigration and FORCED Assimilation in White Countries!" Obama White House Archives, December 3, 2012. https://petitions.obamawhitehouse.archives.gov/petition/stop-white-genocide-halting-massive-third-world-immigration-and-forced-assimilation-white
"The Story behind the Race Conflicts." *United Evangelical Action*, October 25, 1943.
Sturges, Fiona. "Cattleprods! Severed Tongues! Torture Porn! Why I've Stopped Watching the Handmaid's Tale." *The Guardian*, June 16, 2018. https://www.theguardian.com/tv-and-radio/2018/jun/16/handmaids-tale-season-2-elisabeth-moss-margaret-atwood
Sugrue, Thomas. *The Origins of the Urban Crisis: Race and Inequality in Postwar Detroit*. Princeton, NJ: Princeton University Press, [1996] 2014.
Sullivan, Sharon. *Revealing Whiteness: The Unconscious Habits of Racial Privilege*. Bloomington: Indiana University Press, 2006.
Sutton, Matthew Avery. *American Apocalypse: A History of Modern Evangelicalism*. Cambridge, MA: Belknap Press, 2014.
Sutton, Matthew Avery. "Was FDR the Antichrist? The Birth of Fundamentalist Antiliberalism in a Global Age." *Journal of American History* 98, no. 4 (2012), 1052–74.
Swain, Carol M. *The New White Nationalism in America: Its Challenge to Integration*. Cambridge, England: Cambridge University Press, 2002.
Swartz, David L. "Bridging the Study of Culture and Religion: Pierre Bourdieu's Political Economy of Symbolic Power." *Sociology of Religion* 57, no. 1 (1996), 71–85.
Tarantino, Quentin (dir.). *The Hateful Eight*. Los Angeles: Visiona Romantica, 2015.
Taylor, Jared. *If We Do Nothing: Essays and Reviews from 25 Years of White Advocacy*. Oakton, VA: New Century, 2017.
Terrill, Robert E. "The Post-Racial and Post-Ethical Discourse of Donald J. Trump." *Rhetoric and Public Affairs* 20, no. 3 (2017), 493–510.

Thirteenth Annual Report of the Association for the Religious Instruction of the Negroes, in Liberty County, Georgia. Savannah, GA: Edward J. Purse, 1848. Available at https://archive.org/details/12960556.4723.emory.edu

Thompson, Debra. "An Exoneration of Black Rage." *South Atlantic Quarterly* 116, no. 3 (2017), 457–81.

Thompson, Derek. "Which Sports Have the Whitest/Richest/Oldest Fans?" *The Atlantic*, February 10, 2014 https://www.theatlantic.com/business/archive/2014/02/which-sports-have-the-whitest-richest-oldest-fans/283726

Tillich, Paul. *Dynamics of Faith*. New York: Harper & Brothers, 1957; reprint New York: Perennial Classics, 2001.

Todd, Brian, Christina Maxouris, and Amir Vera. "The El Paso Shooting Suspect Showed No Remorse or Regret, Police Say." CNN, August 6, 2019. https://www.cnn.com/2019/08/05/us/el-paso-suspect-patrick-crusius/index.html

"Tomi Lahren's STUPID Response To Jesse Williams' BET Award Speech About Racism." Young Turks/YouTube, June 29, 2016. https://www.youtu.be/FlMoC9oz8Ac

Townes, Emilie Maureen (ed.). *Embracing the Spirit: Womanist Perspectives on Hope, Salvation, and Transformation*. Maryknoll, NY: Orbis, 1997.

Uenuma, Francine. "The Massacre of Black Sharecroppers That Led the Supreme Court to Curb the Racial Disparities in the Justice System." *Smithsonian Magazine*, August 2, 2018. https://www.smithsonianmag.com/history/death-hundreds-elaine-massacre-led-supreme-court take-major-step-toward-equal-justice-african-americans-180969863/.

Urban, Hugh. "Sacred Capital: Pierre Bourdieu and the Study of Religion." *Method & Theory in the Study of Religion* 15, no. 4 (2003), 354–89.

Valenti, Jessica. "The Handmaid's Tale Is Timely. But That's Not Why It's So Terrifying." *The Guardian*, April 27, 2017. https://www.theguardian.com/commentisfree/2017/apr/27/handmaids-tale-timely-terrifying-hulu-series-margaret-atwood

Valentine, Claire. "Women Show Up at Kavanaugh's Hearing Dressed as Handmaids." *Paper*, September 4, 2018. http://www.papermag.com/handmaids-tale-protestors-brett-kavanaugh-2601984117.html

Vance, J. D. *Hillbilly Elegy: A Memoir of a Family and Culture in Crisis*. New York: Harper, 2016.

Vargas, Alicia. "The Construction of Latina Christology: An Invitation to Dialogue." *Currents in Theology and Mission* 34, no. 4 (2007): 271.

Vial, Theodore. *Modern Religion, Modern Race*. New York: Oxford University Press, 2016.

Vice News. "Watch the 'Vice News Tonight' Episode 'Charlottesville: Race and Terror.'" *Vice*, August 14, 2017. https://www.vice.com/en_us/article/433vkq/watch-the-vice-news-tonight-episode-charlottesville-race-and-terror

"Virginia Clergymen Pray in Courtroom." *Afro-American*, February 3, 1962.

Wagner, Venise. "Living in the Red: Black Steelworkers and the Wealth Gap." *Labor Studies Journal* 42, no. 1 (2017), 52–78.

Wallace, Trevor. "God Changed His Mind about Black People: Race and Priesthood Authority in Mormonism." MA thesis, Uppsala University, 2016. Available at http://www.diva-portal.org/smash/get/diva2:1048951/FULLTEXT01.pdf

Wallis, Jim. *America's Original Sin: Racism, White Privilege, and the Bridge to a New America*. Grand Rapids, MI: Brazos Press, 2016.
Warren, Calvin L. *Ontological Terror: Blackness, Nihilism, and Emancipation*. Durham, NC: Duke University Press, 2018.
Warren, John T. and Kathy Hytten. "The Faces of Whiteness: Pitfalls and the Critical Democrat." *Communication Education* 53, no. 4 (2004), 321–39.
Watson, Veronica T. *The Souls of White Folk: African American Writers Theorize Whiteness*. Jackson: University Press of Mississippi, 2013.
Wayans, Keenan Ivory (dir.). *I'm Gonna Git You Sucka*. Los Angeles: Ivory Way Productions, 1988.
Webster, Edward. "Recasting Labor Studies in the Twenty-First Century." *Labor Studies Journal* 33, no. 3 (2008), 249–54.
Weed, Eric. *The Religion of White Supremacy in the United States*. Lanham, MD: Lexington, 2016.
Weisenfeld, Judith. *New World A-Coming: Black Religion and Racial Identity during the Great Migration*. New York: New York University Press, 2016.
"Welcome Labor Unions!" *Christian Frontiers*, November 1946, 277–8.
Weller, Dylan. "Godless Patriots: Towards a New American Civil Religion." *Polity* 45, no. 3 (2013): 372–92.
Welter, Barbara. "The Cult of True Womanhood: 1820–1860." *American Quarterly* 18, no. 2 (1966): 151–74.
Weyeneth, Robert R. "The Power of Apology and the Process of Historical Reconciliation." *Public Historian* 23, no. 3 (2001), 9–38.
"What is White Genocide?" "FAQ's" [sic], Fight White Genocide website. http://www.fightwhitegenocide.com/faqs
White, Kate (ed.). *Unmasking Race, Culture, and Attachment in the Psychoanalytic Space*. London and New York: Karnac, 2006.
"White Supremacists' Anti-Semitic and Anti-Immigrant Sentiments Often Intersect." ADL website, October 27, 2018. https://www.adl.org/blog/white-supremacists-anti-semitic-and-anti-immigrant-sentiments-often-intersect
Whitford, David. "A Calvinist Heritage to the 'Curse of Ham': Assessing the Accuracy of a Claim about Racial Subordination." *Church History and Religious Culture* 90, no. 1 (2010), 25–45.
Wilcox, W. Bradford, Andrew, J. Cherlin, Jeremy E. Uecherk, and Matthew Messel. "No Money, No Honey, No Church: The Deinstitutionalization of Religious Life among the White Working Class." *Research in the Sociology of Work* 23 (2012), 227–50.
Wilderson, Frank B., III. "Gramsci's Black Marx: Whither the Slave in Civil Society?" *Social Identities* 9, no. 2 (2003): 226–240.
Wilderson, Frank B., III. *Red, White & Black: Cinema and the Structure of U.S. Antagonisms*. Durham, NC: Duke University Press, 2010.
Wilkinson, Alissa. "Chris Cuomo Said 'Fredo' Is Like the 'N-Word' for Italians. It's . . . Not." *Vox*, August 13, 2019. https://www.vox.com/culture/2019/8/13/20804039/chris-cuomo-fredo-godfather

Williams, Dolores S. *Sisters in the Wilderness: The Challenge of Womanist God-Talk.* 20th Anniversary Edition. Maryknoll, NY: Orbis, 2013.

Williams, Scott. *Church Diversity: Sunday the Most Segregated Day of the Week.* Green Forest, AR: New Leaf, 2011.

Williams, Thomas Chatterton. "The French Origins of 'You Will Not Replace Us.'" *New Yorker*, December 4, 2017. https://www.newyorker.com/magazine/2017/12/04/the-french-origins-of-you-will-not-replace-us

Wilson, Jake B. "The Racialized Picket Line: White Workers and Racism in Southern California Supermarket Strike." *Critical Sociology* 34, no. 3 (2008), 349–67.

Wilson, Jason. "'Young White Guys Are Hopping Mad': Confidence Grows at Far-Right Gathering." *The Guardian*, July 31, 2017. https://www.theguardian.com/us-news/2017/jul/31/american-renaissance-conference-white-identity

Winnicott, D. W. *Playing and Reality.* London: Tavistock, 1971.

Winston, Kimberly. "'Blood and Faith': A New Book Links White Nationalists to Christianity." *Religion News Service*, August 23, 2017. https://religionnews.com/2017/08/23/blood-andfaith-a-new-book-links-white-nationalists-to-christianity

Wolcott, Victoria W. *Remaking Respectability: African American Women in Interwar Detroit.* Chapel Hill: University of North Carolina Press, 2001.

"Woman in 'Permit Patty' Video Speaks Out: I Feel Manipulated." CNN/YouTube, June 26, 2018. https://youtu.be/lyJOYzof9R4

Wondra, Ellen K. *Humanity Has Been a Holy Thing: Toward a Contemporary Feminist Christology.* Lanham, MD: University Press of America, 1994.

Woodrum, Eric and Arnold Bell. "Race, Politics, and Religion in Civil Religion among Blacks." *Sociological Analysis* 49, no. 4 (198), 353–67.

Wright, Bobby E. *The Psychopathic Racial Personality and Other Essays.* Chicago: Third World Press, 1984.

"WSB-TV Newsfilm Clip of African Americans Being Arrested Following a Night-Time March for Civil Rights in Danville, Virginia, 1963, July 11." Civil Rights Digital Library. http://crdl.usg.edu/id:ugabma_wsbn_wsbn31815

"WSB-TV Newsfilm Clip of Mayor Julian R. Stinson Speaking to Reverend Lendell W. Chase after a Civil Rights Demonstration in Danville, Virginia, 1963 June 13." Civil Rights Digital Library. http://dlg.galileo.usg.edu/crdl/id:ugabma_wsbn_36357

Wynn, Neil A. *The African American Experience During World War II.* Lanham, MD: Rowman & Littlefield, 2010.

Yancy, George (ed.). *Christology and Whiteness: What Would Jesus Do?* Abingdon, England: Routledge, 2012.

Yancy, George. *What White Looks Like: African American Philosophers on the Whiteness Question.* New York: Routledge, 2004.

"The Year in Hate: Trump Buoyed White Supremacists in 2017, Sparking Backlash among Black Nationalist Groups." Southern Poverty Law Center, February 21, 2018. https://www.splcenter.org/news/2018/02/21/year-hate-trump-buoyed-white-supremacists-2017-sparking-backlash-among-black-nationalist

Zhao, Christina. "Evangelicals Who Don't Support Trump May Be 'Immoral,' Jerry Falwell Jr. Says." *Newsweek*, January 1, 2019. https://www.newsweek.com/evangelicals-who-dont-support-trump-may-be-immoral-jerry-falwell-jr-says-1276488

Zieger, Robert H. *The CIO, 1935–1955*. Chapel Hill: University of North Carolina Press, 1995.

Zieger, Robert H. *For Jobs and Freedom: Race and Labor in America since 1865*. Lexington: University Press of Kentucky, 2007.

INDEX

abolitionist movements, 199, 200
affect
   affective exorcisms, 171, 178
   affective legitimation of whiteness, 6, 7
   affective performances of gender, 170, 174–8
   affective responses to black bodies, 34, 35
   anti-black affect, 169–70, 171–2, 175
   concept of, 15
   legitimation of white rage, 16–18
   relationship with religion, 177
   of threat, 171–4
African American churches
   Black Christ figure, 126–7, 131
   Christianity of, 147–8
   Henry Ford's ties with, 63, 65, 70
   rejection of communism, 93
   religious resources in the civil rights movement, 215, 217–18, 221, 224, 225–6
   as sites of black activism, 94–5, 99, 215–16
   skepticism over the New Deal, 90–1
   Social Gospel movement, 87–8, 91
   see also Danville, Virginia
Ahmed, Sara, 6–7, 12, 18, 166, 170, 173, 175, 181–2, 188, 190
American civil religion
   American identity and, 74–5, 78
   as co-constitutive with the state, 81
   the Constitution, 74, 140

   defined, 74–5, 78
   function of football in, 79–81
   the pledge of allegiance, 77–9
   rituals, beliefs and symbols, 74
   scholarship on, 77
   "The Star-Spangled Banner," 227, 228
   typology of racial consciousness and belief in, 81–4
   as whiteness, 75
American Federation of Labor (AFL), 86
American religion, 20, 214–15, 229–32, 232; *see also* religion of white rage
Anderson, Benedict, 153
Anderson, Carol, 18, 58, 61, 68
anger
   of Brett Kavanaugh, 1–2, 3, 8
   religiosity of white women's anger, 189, 190
   righteousness of, 2, 3
   silencing of black women's anger, 181–2
   use by Trump at his rallies, 3
   see also rage; white rage
Anthony, Susan B., 183
Arquette, Patricia, 183, 186, 189
Association for the Religious Instruction of the Negroes (ARIN), 200, 203, 204–5
Atwood, Margaret, 186–8

Barkun, Michael, 51, 52, 53
Bastién, Angelica Jade, 188

Bates, Beth Tompkins, 65
Bell, Catherine, 68
Bellah, Robert, 61, 74-5, 77
Bergson, Henri, 50-1, 52
Berry, Damon T., 51, 152, 153, 161, 163
Black, Derek, 154, 161-2
Black, Don, 154
black bodies
    black women as ungendered, 176
    destructuration and, 34, 35, 36
    as *imagos*, 35, 36
    lynching of, 157
    perceptions of threat of, 171-2, 173-4
    as phobogenic, 34-5, 37, 38, 50, 172, 174
    as problem bodies, 50
    profound misreadings of, 174-5
    replacement woes, 43
    as sites of redemption, 56
    sublimated homoerotic envy of, 36, 41
    as threats to white space and place, 46, 50, 55
black equality
    black churches as sites of black activism, 99
    Double V campaign, 97, 100
    postwar activism, 100
    religion of black resistance, 215-16, 217-18
    theology of brotherhood, post-WW II, 99-100
    wartime campaigns for, 97-9
    white supremacist opposition to, postwar, 101-3, 104-7
    see also civil rights movement
Black Lives Matter movement, 17, 237
black women
    black women as ungendered, 176
    labor issues and, 237
    silencing of their anger, 181-2
    union representation for, 96
black workers
    aspirational black labor, 59, 61, 77
    auto workers, 67-8
    black bodies as, 10
    Christianization of slaves, 196, 200, 203, 204, 205
    expectations from union representation, 94
    at the Ford Motor Company, 63-4, 66-7, 69-71
    labor issues and, 236-7
    labor organizations for, 86, 89, 91, 93, 94-7, 98
    lack of unionization of, 63, 66, 67, 70-1
    migrants to the North, 64
    under the New Deal, 89, 93
    1959 steelworkers' strike, 237
    relations with white workers, 11, 234
    religious beliefs and union membership, 89
blackness
    anti-blackness of Christianity, 193-4, 211
    binary taxonomies of, 33-4, 37-8, 42
    non-white identities, 14
    normativity of, 169-70
Bowers, Robert, 164
Brinkema, Eugenie, 173
Brown, Michael, 167, 172, 230
Brueggemann, John, 65, 66, 68
Bruner, C. V., 195, 198, 199, 200, 201-2
Burke, Tarauna, 4
Butler, Judith, 166, 170, 175, 176
Butterworth, Michael, 79

Carter, James, 183
Castile, Philando, 81
Cayton, Jr., Horace, 63, 65
Charlottesville rally, 16, 18, 19, 20, 43, 143
Cheng, Anne Anlin, 39
Christian Americans, 101, 106
Christian Identity movements, 51-2
Christianity
    of African American churches, 147-8
    anti-blackness of, 193-4, 211
    Christian principles of Trump followers, 134-5
    Christianity as a redemptive religion, 126, 130-1, 132
    the curse of Ham, 145, 193
    enslaved blacks conversion to, 194-205 211-212

Christianity (cont.)
  folk Christianity, 87
  forced conversions of indigenous peoples, 139
  the Great Awakening, 198–9
  The Negro Christianized (Mather), 196–8
  religious fervor for the Christianizing of slaves, 201–5
  Republican Party as synonymous with, 140–1
  slavery's early incompatibility with, 195–6
  white nationalism's relationship with, 153–4, 161
  white supremacy and, 62
Church of Creativity, 154, 158
Church of Jesus Christ of Latter-Day Saints (LDS Church) *see* Mormon Church
civil rights movement
  interracial religious practitioners during, 214, 225–6
  religion of black resistance in Hopewell, 217–18
  religious resources for, 215, 217–18
  white rage and black resistance, 215–16, 217, 219–21, 223, 224
  see also black equality; Danville, Virginia
Civil War
  American civil religion and, 75
  and the formation of the KKK, 126, 127
  mental illness following, 119
  subsequent threat to white labor, 147
class
  class insecurity in America, 133–4
  historical class insecurity, 127–8
  intra-white class consciousness, 49
  laborer, term, 21
  racial wealth inequalities, 233, 237
Cleaver, Kathleen, 216
Clinton, Hillary Rodham, 76, 233
colonialism
  black religion of the diaspora, 55
  deconstruction of by psychoanalysis, 34

  gendered work regimes from, 19
  as the originator of racism, 139
  white violence of, 10
  whiteness as imperialistic, 9–10
communism
  and fears of racial advancement, 85
  rejection of by black churches, 93
  in unions, 85, 103–4
Cone, James, 132
Congress of Industrial Organizations (CIO)
  premillennial evangelical opposition to, 85, 86–7, 104–5
  role of black members, 89, 91
  Southern Baptist Convention opposition to, 105–6
  Southern Organizing Campaign, 102–3
  unionization of the South, 86
  during WW II, 94, 96
the Constitution
  and American civil religion, 74, 108, 140
  as idealized parent imagos, 120–1
  for the protection of white bodies, 61, 108–9
  "we the people" of the Preamble, 108–9
  white being in, 109, 118–19
  white women, 110
Copeland, M. Shawn, 55–7
Copulsky, Jerome, 77, 79
Crutcher, Terrence, 167, 172
culture
  culture-religion relationship, 60
  fears over white cultural hegemony, 45–6, 47, 51, 54
Cyrus, Miley, 183

Danville, Virginia
  activists' protests, 218–19
  activists' use of legal options, 218
  African American voters, 223
  the civil rights movement in, 216–17
  cooperation strategy of the city council, 223
  prayer vigil, 213–14, 216–17, 219–20
  religious resources, 215, 217–18, 221, 224, 225–6

white and black religious practitioners during, 214, 225–6
the white community of, 221–2
white rage and black resistance in, 213–14, 215–16, 217, 219–21, 223, 224
Danville Christian Progressive Association (DCPA), 217, 218, 220, 223
Davis, Angela, 184
Daymond, Antonia Michelle, 229
de Leon, Cedric, 236
Detroit *see* Ford, Henry; Ford Motor Company
Devinatz, Victor, 233
DiAngelo, Robin, 38
Dobratz, Betty A, 155–6, 159
Docherty, George, 78–9
Douglas, Kelly Brown, 46, 50
Driscoll, Christopher, 5, 46
Du Bois, W. E. B., 1, 9–12, 32–3, 83, 234
Durkheim, Emile, 44, 52–3, 60

Elaine Massacre, 31
Eliade, Mircea, 9
emotions
  fear of blackness, 190
  responses to black bodies, 34
  as the surface of subjects and objects, 6–7, 181
  see also anger; rage; religion of white rage; white rage
Ettel, Alison, 168–9, 173, 175–6
evangelism
  anti-unionism, 85–7, 92–3, 101–3, 104–7
  evangelical Protestantism of the KKK, 131
  importance of the religious instruction of slaves, 201–3
  Knoxville radio code protest, 85
  National Association of Evangelicals (NAE), 102
  opposition to fair employment practices, 104–6
  postwar evangelicalism, 100–2
  premillennial dispensationalism, 86–7, 92, 101–2, 104, 106

as pro-Christianization of slaves, 201–3
response to the black equality movement, 99–100
support for Trump, 137

Fair Employment Practices Commission, 98–9, 104–5
Fanon, Frantz, 29, 34, 35, 36, 37, 40, 41, 172
Felton, Rebecca Latimer, 185
Finley, Stephen C, 146, 157, 177, 229
Fletcher, Jeannine Hill, 155
folk Christianity, 87
football
  black athlete's protests at black unnatural deaths, 80–1
  function of in American civil religion, 79–81
  white worker fan bases, 80
Ford, Dr. Christine, 1, 2, 4
Ford, Henry
  paternalism of, 59, 63, 65–6, 69, 71
  ties with black churches, 63, 65, 70
Ford Hunger March, 70, 71
Ford Motor Company
  Battle of the Overpass, 70, 71
  black labor at, 63–4, 66–7, 69–71
  five dollar day, 64, 68
  prosperity and bust cycle, 68
  ritualized expressions of white rage in, 69–71
  Sociological Department, 64–5
  strike (1941), 70, 71
  unionization in, 66, 68, 70–1
Frazer, E. Franklin, 11
Freud, Sigmund, 34, 38

Garner, Eric, 230
gender
  affective performances of gender, 170, 174–8
  black women as ungendered, 176
  gendered nature of white rage, 4
  gendered work regimes, 19
  normatively gendered subjects, 169–70, 176
  womanist religious thought, 56–7
  see also black women; white women

genocide, 160, 162–3, 164–5
Gilroy, Paul, 55
Gilsinan, Kathy, 164
Gordon, Lewis, 6, 177
Gordon, Linda, 131
Gordon, Louis, 229
Gore, Mary Elizabeth "Tipper," 183
Gottfried, Heidi, 236
Gray, Biko Mandela, 229
Gray, Freddie, 230
Great Migration, 59, 63, 64, 67–8, 69, 128–9
Gregg, Melissa, 15

Hale, Matt, 159
Hayes, John, 87
Heyer, Heather D., 143
Higginbotham, Evelyn Brooks, 237
Highmore, Ben, 15, 170
Hill, Rev. Charles, 70
Hofstadter, Richard, 45–6, 47, 48
Holland, Sharon Patricia, 166, 169
Hood, Robert E., 29, 33–4, 41
Hopkins, Dwight, 61–2, 65–6
Horton, "Willie," 37

identity
  of America through civil religion, 74–5, 78
  closed societies and, 50–1
  the humanum, 56
  national identity post-9/11, 75–6
  religio-racial organizations, 51–2
  religious identity, 52–3, 60
  role of football in American life, 79–80
  Trump as symbolic justification for white identity politics, 135–6, 137
  white identity formation, 44, 48–9, 50–1, 52, 56
Isenberg, Nancy, 49

Jean, Botham, 46
Jennings, Willie, 55
Jesus Christ/Christ figure
  African American Black Christ figure, 126–7, 131
  the Christ figure in Christianity, 126, 138
  the KKK Christ figure, 126, 131–3
  MAGA Christ, 83
  as a symbol of white male supremacy, 130
  White Christ figure, 130–1
Jones, Charles C., 195
Jones, William P., 94–5, 132, 177
Jones, William R, 6
Judaism, 153, 154

Kaepernick, Colin, 3, 80–1, 179, 190
Kao, Grace, 77, 79
Kavanaugh, Brett
  the Handmaid figure and, 188
  myth of the white worker, 238, 239
  white rage of, 1–2, 3–4, 8, 14, 16, 17, 18
Kelsey, George D., 1
Key, Francis Scott, 227, 228
Kimeldorf, Howard, 236
Kimmel, Michael, 48
King, Jr., Martin Luther, 30, 31, 41, 216–17, 218, 223
Klassen, Ben, 153–4, 159
Klein, Teresa, 169, 173, 174–5
Ku Klux Klan (KKK)
  anti-black sentiments, 126, 128
  the Christ figure of, 126, 131–3
  as a defence against social equality, 85
  Don Black, 154
  evangelical Protestant theology, 131
  historical and religious symbolism, 125–6
  history of, 125, 128–30, 133
  perceptions of black progress/white loss, 129–30
  religious groups' opposition to, 106
  resurgence, post-WW II, 101

labor organizations
  accusations of communism, 85, 103–4
  black women's membership of, 96
  for black workers, 86, 89, 91, 93, 94–7, 98
  Christian-infused activists in the South, 88–9

at the Ford Motor Company, 66, 68, 70–1
lack of unionization of black labor, 63, 66, 67, 70–1
religious beliefs and union membership of black workers, 89
during the 2016 presidential elections, 233
unionization of white workers, 67, 86, 94
white evangelical anti-unionism, 85–7, 92–3, 101–3, 104–7
see also Congress of Industrial Organizations (CIO)
labor studies
canonical texts of, 235
challenges facing, 230–1
definition of, 230–1
race, religion, and labor studies, 235–9
in relation to race and religion, 229, 230
white worker definition, 232–4
see also black workers; white workers
Lacan, Jacques, 35
Lahren, Tomi, 179–80, 187, 189–91
Larson, Eric, 237–8
law enforcement agencies
as an anti-black institution, 169
calling the police on black people, 30, 166–9, 173, 174–6, 190
use of lethal force, 73, 80–1, 167, 171–2, 230
war on cops concept, 189–90
Lee, Ching Kwan, 236
Legend, John, 190
Long, Charles H.
critique of American civil religion concept, 74
grounding narrative of religion, 61
modernity and race, 229
religion as orientation, 2, 7–8, 51, 52, 60, 69, 75, 146, 151–2, 157–8, 159, 163, 192–3, 214
religious center of white supremacy, 9
on the second creation, 36
theory of the religious, 51
on the Trump era, 76–7

Lynch, Gordon, 60
lynching
of black bodies, 157
the Elaine Massacre, 31
for perceived sexual threats against white women, 98, 175, 185
in the South, postwar, 100, 106
of W. C. Williams (1938), 5–7, 19

MacGuill, Dan, 3
March for Our Lives, 16, 18
Martin, Lori Latrice, 157
Martin, Trayvon, 46
Massumi, Brian, 15, 170, 171
Mather, Cotton, 195, 196–8
Matlon, Jordanna, 19
Mbembe, Achille, 172, 229
Mbiti, John, 194
McDonald, Jermaine, 75
#MeToo movement, 4–5, 186
Meier, August, 65
melancholia, 38–9
Merritt, Keri Leigh, 48–9
Metzger, Tom, 158
Metzl, Jonathan, 72
Midler, Bette, 186, 189
Millard, Martin H., 160–1, 163
Minkenberg, Michael, 149, 163
Morgan, Edmund, 195
Mormon Church
black members of, 143, 144, 145, 146, 148
curse against the Lamanites, 193–4
political conservatism of, 137–8
racist beliefs, rituals, and practices, 142–3, 148
reversal of its anti-black doctrine, 141
view of marriage, 142
white rage of, 142, 148
Muse, Benjamin, 222
myths
America's mythic narrative, 61–2
of the hardworking American male, 2, 3, 4–5, 141, 238–9
power of, 2–3

National Association for the Advancement of Colored People (NAACP), 65, 217, 221
National Association of Evangelicals (NAE), 102
National Football League, 73
#NeverAgain movement, 17
New Deal
  black labor under, 89, 93
  churches response to, 88–91
  white fundamentalist opposition to, 91–2
normativity
  of the American racial order, 14, 16–17, 35–6
  of blackness, 169–70
  normatively gendered subjects, 169–70, 176
  performativity and, 175
  of rage, 170
  of religion, 7–8
  of the religion of white rage, 20
  religious view of marriage, 142
  of white rage, 5–7, 16–18
  of whiteness, 5–6, 8, 12–14, 19

Obama, Barack, 44, 48, 76, 133
Oliver, Revilo Pendleton, 153–4
O'Meara, Michal, 152
Otto, Rudolph, 41–2

Painter, Nell, 62–3
Parsons, Michael, 231, 235
Perkinson, James W., 32, 33, 34, 41, 225
Pinn, Anthony, 127
police *see* law enforcement agencies
politics
  conservative politics/religious group links, 139–41
  paranoid style in, 45
  racial motivations of the electorate, 49
  Republican Party (GOP), 140–1, 142, 147
  right wing politics, 45–8
  status politics, 48
  see also Trump, Donald
power
  ritualization and power relationships, 68
  ritualized power-restoration of white supremacy, 69–71
psychoanalysis
  for the deconstruction of colonialism, 34
  Lacan's mirror period, 35
  melancholia, 38
  neurosis, 38
  see also Fanon, Frantz

race
  American racial schema, 14
  and modernity, 229–30
  non-white identities, 14
  race, religion, and labor studies, 235–9
  racial wealth inequalities, 233, 237
  in relation to religion and labor studies, 229, 230
  in relation to religion and the American state, 227–8, 229
  and the sexual justice movement, 4–5
  theodicy and, 6
racial battle fatigue (RBF), 144–5
racism
  birth of in America, 139
  of Christianity, 193–4, 211
  microaggressions, 144, 145, 146
radical right *see* white supremacy
rage
  excessive sensitivity, 173, 174
  expressions of, 172–3
  of Handmaids, 187
  legitimation of by threat, 173–4
  normativity of, 170
  silencing of black women's anger, 181–2
  see also anger; religion of white rage; white rage
religion
  affect's relationship with, 177
  America's mythic narrative, 61–2
  church support for social reform in the South, 89–90
  conservative politics/religious group links, 139–41
  exclusionary theologies, 55–6
  five components of, 194

hereditary heathenism notion, 194
Identity religious thought, 51–2
interracial faith ties during the Great Depression, 87–8
and modernity, 229–30
myths, symbols and rituals of, 60
notion of ultimate orientation, 2, 7–8, 51, 52, 60, 69, 75, 146, 151–2, 157–8, 159, 163, 192–3, 214
and the numinous, 41–2
as one's ultimate concern, 60, 69, 151–2, 157–8, 159, 163
Protestant Episcopal Catechisms, 205
race, religion, and labor studies, 229, 230, 235–9
race and religion in America, 227–8
racial identity formation and, 138–9
religious identity, 52–3
strength of belief/xenophobia correlations, 137
as *sui generis*, 41–2
term, 20–1
totemic religious ideology, 52–3
the White Catechism, 205, 206, 208–11
white workers-American religion relationship, 20
of whiteness, 7, 8–12, 32–3, 36–7, 40–1
World Council of Churches, 99–100
see also African American churches; Christianity; evangelism; Mormon Church
religion of white rage
affective exorcism as, 178
during the civil rights movement, 215–16, 217
concept of, 10–11, 20, 61, 150
normativity of, 20
perceptions of black progress, 18, 20, 58, 59, 68
as specifically American, 11, 33
white supremacy as the goal of, 5–7, 59–60, 62, 66, 68, 72, 140–1
the white worker and, 11–12, 20–1, 59, 62–3, 69–71
see also white rage
Republican Party (GOP), 140–1, 142, 147

Rice, Cynthia A, 198
Rice, Tamir, 167, 172
right wing politics, 45–8
ritual theory, 68
rituals
 in American civil religion, 74
 post 9/11, 75–6
 of religion, 60
 ritualized power-restoration of white supremacy, 69–71
Rudwick, Elliot, 65
Russell, Jeffrey Burton, 193

Schulte, Jennifer, 166–8, 173
Seigworth, Gregory, 15
sexual justice movement, 4–5, 186
Simmons, William Joseph, 125, 128, 133
slave rebellions, 199, 200, 210
slavery
 anti-slavery movements, 199, 200
 Association for the Religious Instruction of the Negroes (ARIN), 200, 203, 204–5
 the curse of Ham as justification, 193
 early incompatibility with Christianity, 195–6
 evangelism's support for religious instruction of slaves, 201–3
 The Negro Christianized (Mather), 196–8
 as the originator of racism, 139
 perceived link between slave insurrections and religious instruction, 199, 200, 210
 perceptions of slaves' intellectual capacities, 208
 religious conversion to Christianity, 194–205, 211–12
 religious experiences in slave narratives, 61–2
 the Slave Catechism, 205, 207, 208–11
 and the terminology of white labor, 228
 white religious fervor for the Christianization of slaves, 201–5

Smith, William A, 144–5
social exclusion, practices of, 143–4
Social Gospel movement, 87–8, 91
Southern Baptist Convention, 90, 105–6
Spillers, Hortense, 77, 170, 176
Stanton, Elizabeth Cady, 184, 185–6
Sterling, Alton, 80, 81, 167, 172
Swain, Carol M., 161
symbols
  of American civil religion, 74
  of American identity, 76, 83
  Confederate markers, 83
  of white priestly preservationists, 83

Taylor, Jared, 53–4
terrorism
  Robert Bowers' synagogue attack, 164
  by white supremacists, 133–4, 135
the Other
  black bodies as *imago*s, 35, 36
  as non-whiteness, 14, 35–6, 38
  the paranoid style in politics, 45
the sacred, defined, 60
theodicy, 6, 177
Thigpin, Sheriff Bryan, 5–7, 8, 19
Thompson, Debra, 16–17
Tillich, Paul, 60, 69, 151–2, 157–8, 159, 163
totemic theory of religion, 52–3
Trump, Donald
  "America First" ethos, 47
  challenge of Obama's birthplace, 76
  Christian principles of Trump followers, 134–5
  emergence as a paranoid spokesman, 46–8
  "Make America Great Again" slogan, 30, 39–40, 41, 76, 134
  Mormon support for, 137–8
  pro-white rage manipulation, 3
  racial politics of, 3, 12, 29–30, 37, 54, 76, 135, 136–7, 192, 233
  response to players' protests, 73
  response to the Charlottesville rally, 18
  as symbolic justification of white identity politics, 135–6, 137
  use of anger during his campaign rallies, 3
  white worker fan bases, 80, 232–3
Turner, Nat, 200, 210

United States of America (USA)
  birth of racism in, 138–9
  first census in 1790, 61, 62–3
  hypocrisy of, 11
  normativity of the racial order, 14, 16–17, 35–6
  the religion of white rage in, 11, 33
  as a religio-necropolis, 229
  white population numbers, 162
  see also American civil religion

Vesey, Denmark, 199, 210
Vial, Theodore, 229–30

Wagner, Venise, 237
Wallace, George, 233
Wallis, Jim, 61
Weed, Eric, 155
Weisenfeld, Judith, 51
Welter, Barbara, 182
white consolidation
  as a backlash, 30, 33
  the black object and, 33, 37–9, 41
  the Elaine Massacre, 31
  "Make America Great Again" slogan, 30, 39–40, 41
  methodology of, 31–2
  the mythical white worker and, 32
  in response to black progress, 30–1
  threat of the black man, 36–7
white fervor
  for the Christianizing of slaves, 201–5
  the Great Awakening, 198–9
  for the religious instruction of slaves, 194–5
  white religious shock and, 73
white loss
  feelings of in white nationalism, 44–5, 47–8, 51, 54
  and the Ku Klux Klan, 129–30
white nationalism
  the Charlottesville rally, 16, 18, 19, 20, 43, 143

as a closed white-race society, 51
conspiratorial paranoia, 46
defined, 44
exclusionary logics of, 55–6
fears for a white genocide, 160, 162–3, 164–5
fears for white cultural hegemony, 44, 45–6, 47, 54, 160
feelings of white loss, 44–5, 47–8, 51, 54
14 Words, 54, 160
global 'rebranding' of, 152–3
identity formation, 44, 48–9, 50–1, 52, 56
"my race as my religion," 150–1, 157–9, 162, 165
references to religion and genocide, 149–51, 157, 159–60, 164–5
relationship with Christianity, 153–4, 161
as a religious system, 44, 52–3, 160–1
replacement woes, 43, 45, 46, 47, 48, 51, 55, 133–4
terrorist activities, 133
Tiki-torchers, 43, 83, 133–4
white victimization discourse of, 154–5
white rage
aggressive white rage, 18, 19
Angry White Woman figure, 180–1, 185, 188, 190–1
at black advancement, 18, 20, 58, 59, 68
of Brett Kavanaugh, 1–2, 3–4, 14, 16, 17, 18
at civil rights activism, Danville, Virginia, 213–14, 215–16, 217, 219–21, 223, 224
during the civil rights movement, 215–16, 219–21
diffuse white rage, 18, 19
function of religious organizations, 142, 148
gendered nature of, 4
legitimation of, 16–18, 19
and the maintenance of white supremacy, 5–7, 140–1
of the Mormon Church, 142, 148

normativity of, 5–7, 16–18
religiosity of, 7–8, 59–63
ritualized expressions of in the car industry, 69–71
use by Trump at his rallies, 3
see also religion of white rage
white religious shock
in American civil religion, 73, 75
Barack Obama's presidency, 76
concept of, 75
the Great Recession, 76
white supremacy
and the Christ figure, 130
within Christianity, 62
as the goal of the religion of white rage, 5–7, 59–60, 62, 66, 68, 72, 140–1
postwar opposition to black equality, 101–3, 104–7
of the Republican Party, 139–41
ritualized power-restoration of, 69–71
through affective performance, 176–8
Tomi Lahren's political commentary, 179–80, 187, 189–91
white femininity/morality relationship, 180–1, 182–3, 185, 187–8, 189–90
women's suffrage and, 184–5
white violence, 10, 12, 13; *see also* lynching
white women
Angry White Woman figure, 180–1, 185, 188, 190–1
calling the police on black people, 30, 166–9, 170, 173, 174–6, 190
"Eleanor Clubs," 98, 99
enacting legitimated rage, 174–6
exclusion of black womanhood, 175–6
Handmaid figure, 186–8
religiosity of anger, 189, 190
within the religious view of marriage, 142
within the sexual justice movement, 4–5, 183, 186
suffrage under the Constitution, 110

white women (*cont.*)
  the Suffragette figure, 176, 183–6, 188
  support for Trump, 232
  True Woman figure, 182–3, 189
  as vulnerable to black sexual assault, 98, 175, 185
  white femininity/morality relationship, 180–1, 182–3, 185, 187–8, 189–90
  see also black women
white workers
  construct of, 21
  definitions of within labor studies, 232–4
  in football's fan base, 80
  forgotten-man theme, 49
  laborer, term, 21
  myth of the hardworking bootstrapper, 2–3, 4–5, 7, 141, 238–9
  as mythological site, 2–3, 4–5, 7, 9, 21, 32, 39, 232, 234, 238–9
  1959 steelworkers' strike, 237
  as products of colonialism, 19
  relations with black workers, 234
  and the religion of white rage, 11–12, 20–1, 59, 62–3, 69–71
  status political aspirations of, 48
  sublimated homoerotic envy of black bodies, 36, 41
  support for Trump, 80, 232–3
  terminology of, 228
  threat of aspirational black labor, 59, 61, 77
  unionization of, 67, 86, 94
  violence of during the Civil Rights movement, 213, 214
  wages and identity relationship, 19
  within white consolidation, 32
  white male capitalist patriarchy, 139–40
  white workers-American religion relationship, 20
  see also black workers

whiteness
  affective legitimation of, 6, 7
  affective theodicy of, 177
  in American civil religion, 75
  of American religious mythology, 4–5
  Brett Kavanaugh's enactment of, 1–2, 3–4, 8, 14
  critical whiteness studies, 8
  cultural and institutional death of, 45–6, 47, 51
  definition of, 8
  as group consciousness, 151
  as homoerotic, 36, 41
  as imperialistic, 9–10
  as industriousness, 156
  invisibleness of, 11, 12
  as melancholia, 38–9
  mythic center of, 9
  normative understandings of, 5–6, 8, 12–14, 19
  origin-of-whiteness approach, 155
  as pathological, 11, 34, 39
  phenomenology of, 12–13
  profile of, 32–3, 146–7
  as prophylaxis, 225
  in relation to blackness, 33–4, 37–8, 42
  as the religious, 7, 8–12, 32–3, 36–7, 40–1, 53, 147, 152, 155–8, 159, 161, 163, 165
  ritualized power-restoration of, 69
  role of True Womanhood, 182–3, 189
Whitford, David, 193
Wilcox, W. Bradford, 232
Williams, Thomas, 43
Williams, W. C, 5–7, 8, 19
women *see* black women; white women
World Council of Churches, 99–100
Wright, Bobby E., 11

Yancy, George, 8, 9, 12
Yockey, Francis Parker, 152

EU representative:
Easy Access System Europe
Mustamäe tee 50, 10621 Tallinn, Estonia
Gpsr.requests@easproject.com

www.ingramcontent.com/pod-product-compliance
Lightning Source LLC
Chambersburg PA
CBHW071828230426
43672CB00013B/2783